Buying a House in

Morocco

BUYING A HOUSE IN

MOROCCO

Abby Aron

Distributed in the USA by
The Globe Pequot Press, Guilford, Connecticut

Published by Vacation Work, 9 Park End Street, Oxford
www.vacationwork.co.uk

BUYING A HOUSE IN MOROCCO
by Abby Aron

First edition 2006

Copyright © 2006

ISBN 13: 978-1-85458-349-9
ISBN 10: 1-85458-349-2

Publicity: Charles Cutting

Cover design by mccdesign ltd

Typeset by Guy Hobbs

Cover photograph: kasbah walls, Ouarzazate

Printed and bound in Italy by Legoprint SpA, Trento

CONTENTS

PART I
MARHABA MOROCCO

LIVING IN MOROCCO

RESIDENCE & ENTRY

PART II
LOCATION, LOCATION

WHERE TO FIND YOUR IDEAL HOME

PART III
THE PURCHASING PROCESS

FINANCE

FINDING PROPERTY FOR SALE

WHAT TYPE OF PROPERTY TO BUY?

RENTING A HOME IN MOROCCO

FEES CONTRACTS AND COSTS

PART IV
WHAT HAPPENS NEXT?

SERVICES

MAKING THE MOVE

BUILDING OR RENOVATING

MAKING MONEY FROM YOUR PROPERTY

APPENDICES

MAPS

FOREWORD

Fourteen months ago when the research was started for this book, Morocco was just starting to catch the eye of British homebuyers. UK based international estate agents were making mutterings about Morocco and broadsheet property pages were enlightening readers on the pros and cons of restoring traditional homes in Marrakech but there was little in the way of surging interest. A year-and-a-bit on and Morocco is on the edge of a property boom not dissimilar to Spain and Portugal ten to fifteen years ago. There has been a steep rise in the number of Brits buying villas and apartments, particularly along the pristine Atlantic and Mediterranean coasts, UK based estate agents selling Moroccan property have multiplied from one to double figures and it is hard to pick up a newspaper or magazine without reading about the investment opportunities a house in Morocco will bring. This does not mean that the trend has come close to peaking it is only just, as the pages of this book will verify, beginning to perk up.

While most house buyers are initially drawn to Morocco for its cheap property prices and low cost of living, it does not take long for them to become enamoured by the country, which has since the Romans, charmed and fascinated those that land on its shores. In 1999, the new king, Mohammed VI came into power vowing to modernise Morocco, strengthen civil liberties and democratise the country. Foreigners are warmly welcome and there are no restrictions on foreign investment. This does not mean that investing in the country is necessarily easy. Morocco is a country bogged down in bureaucracy with a culture very different from home. Reading this book will help you weave your way through the administrative byways involved in buying and building property. It will also give you an insight into what is happening behind the solid wood front doors of Moroccan homes and ease the way for you to settling into your new house.

To live in Morocco, it helps if you love noise, colour, people, art, music and food. A sweet tooth for the copious glasses of mint tea you will be offered is useful while a tolerance for the hours it takes to complete the simplest of tasks, will make your life easier. If you learnt your French from watching re-runs of the sitcom 'Allo Allo', then you might consider a few lessons although having a smattering of colloquial Arabic will endear you to many more people. Islam is an all-encompassing feature of the Moroccan world and will therefore be an inescapable part of your life in Morocco whether you are Muslim or not.

Part of the king's modernisation plans involve improving the country's infrastructure, building new roads, electrifying the whole country and opening the skies to all European carriers including no-frills airlines. They also involve improving the quality of life for Morocco's poorest people and regenerating failing regions. In ten years time, Morocco will be a very different place to the Morocco we see today. Though the pace of life is blissfully slow, the changes taking place in the country are picking up speed. Whatever your reasons for buying property in Morocco whether it is to live in permanently, for holidays or to let out for an income, right now has never been a better time to buy.

Abby Aron
Morocco, March 2006

ACKNOWLEDGEMENTS

As this is the first book of its kind on Morocco, there are, unsurprisingly a number of people who need to be thanked for their assistance, their expertise and their time and patience. In Morocco, I am most indebted to Mouloud Wadoud for his fantastic knowledge of the south, Abdellatif Quortobi for his legal expertise, Adnane Draoui for his information on renovations, Greggy Ait Bella for his political insights, Kamar Tinfaty, Rob Knight, Laurent Paul Alteresco, Michel Welter, Hicham Hajjami and Miloudi Lamnaouar for their time, patience and speedy answers to my constant questions. The people I owe the biggest thanks to, however, are my family, without whom this book could never have been completed. Mum, Mims, Dad, PJ, I am eternally grateful to you all for looking after baby Hope and bigger baby Solo, Liam 'how does this sound' Plowman for always listening, Charli Aron for her lovely illustrations and most of all, for quite simply everything, Tim.

Part I

MARHABA MOROCCO

LIVING IN MOROCCO

RESIDENCE & ENTRY

LIVING IN MOROCCO

CHAPTER SUMMARY

- **Climate**. Morocco is a country of extremes where it is possible to ski in the mountains in the morning and swim in the sea in the afternoon.
- **Geography**. Though double the size of the UK, Morocco has just half the population so the Brits can enjoy a feeling of space.
- **History**. Berber tribes, Arab *sherfa* and European generals have all governed Morocco at one time or another giving it a fascinating past much of which is reflected in its striking architecture.
- **Getting There**. An open skies policy has opened up the opportunities for low cost and flagship airlines.
- **Culture Shock**. A whole new way of life learnt amongst tolerant, hospitable people whose favourite pastime is to chat.
- **Food and Drink**. Moroccans rarely eat out because home cooked food tastes so much better, washed down with a refreshing glass of sweet mint tea.
- **Women**. Morocco is one of the most liberal and tolerant of all Islamic countries where women, so long as they are respectful of the culture are respected in return.
- **Crime.** While there is virtually no crime in the countryside, towns and cities experience little more than pickpockets, burglaries and petty theft.
- **Schools.** Though more expensive, Morocco's American schools are the best option for English speakers, although there are a number of very good Moroccan private (French) schools. Moroccan state schools do not, on the whole, provide a high standard of education.
- **Language.** While the ability to speak French is very helpful, being able to speak the local Arabic dialect will make all the difference to your time in Morocco.
- **Telecommunications.** Morocco has a state of the art modernised telephone and internet system with a low number of subscribers.

GEOGRAPHY AND CLIMATE

Morocco reclines against the northern edge of Africa spread over 446,550 sq km, roughly the size of France or California, gazing up to southern Europe and down to the windswept plains of the Western Sahara. To its west lies the Atlantic, to its north, the Mediterranean and to its east, attached by desert and coast, Algeria. Morocco is a country of geographical extremes; agricultural valleys and lunar landscapes, mud packed plains and lush palmeraies, cedar forests and volcanic outcrops, sandy bays and sheer gorges, sand dunes and snowy pistes. Over 3500km of coastline runs around Morocco's four mountain chains, the Rif, Middle Atlas, High Atlas and Anti Atlas, which, like a backbone, sear through the country from the east to the west separating the lush, fertile north from the arid, desert south. The snow capped peaks, the tallest, Jbel Toubkal in the High Atlas, exceeding 4000 metres, drain the great rivers of Moulouya, Sebou and Oum er Rbia, whose tributaries feed into the fertile plains of Fes and Meknes and the date-rich oasis valleys of the south.

Ask about the weather at any time of the year in Morocco and one can pretty safely predict sunshine. Even if there is a chilly Atlantic wind or a desert sandstorm, you can be sure the sun will be around to observe it. Weather forecasters claim 350 days of sunshine a year and if you are unfortunate enough to be around during the 15 cloudy days, you might be pretty glad of the break. The hottest place to live is in the desert around Zagora and Merzouga where summer temperatures climb to an average of 42°C with year round averages of 30°C. The coolest place is along the North Western edge of the country where Atlantic winds keep conditions at a fair temperature of 28°C during the summer months and around 16°-21°C during the winter. Areas close to the coast are most prone to small amounts of rainfall which spread in from the Atlantic Ocean, while great swathes of the interior fall victim to crippling droughts every couple of years or so. Snow, which is common in the high altitudes of the mountains, making skiing a popular pastime, fell around Casablanca in 2004 but this is not a common event.

What is important to bear in mind are the great variations in temperature throughout the course of a day. Hot midday summer sun in the desert and along the coast, where it is impossible to imagine a goose bump, quickly plunges into cool, breezy evenings when a sweater and a warm fire are welcome additions. The Atlantic Ocean for swimming around Agadir and the south remains pretty hospitable from February to November and not too unpleasant in between.

Arguably the best time to be in Morocco for warm, but not boiling weather is from March to May, when the green parts of the country are at their greenest and the souks are bursting with fresh fruit, meats and vegetables. Again September

through to November is equally enjoyable, when the leaves in the Middle
Atlas are turning russet brown and the dates and olives are ripening. During
the summer months, many Moroccans escape the heat by heading west to
the temperate coast and camping on the sand.

AVERAGE TEMPERATURES°C(°F)						
	Jan	April	June	Aug	Oct	Dec
Agadir	21(69)	24(75)	26(79)	26(79)	26(79)	21(69)
Casablanca	18(64)	20(68)	24(75)	27(81)	25(77)	18(64)
Essaouira	18(64)	19(63)	22(72)	21(70)	19(66)	
Fes	16(61)	22(72)	31(88)	36(97)	28(81)	15(59)
Ifrane	9(48)	13(56)	22(72)	29(84)	18(65)	9(49)
Marrakech	19(66)	26(79)	33(91)	38(101)	27(80)	16(61)
Meknes	15(59)	21(70)	28(84)	34(93)	26(79)	16(61)
Ouarzazate	17(63)	27(80)	36(96)	38(100)	27(80)	17(62)
Oujda	16(61)	22(72)	28(84)	33(91)	25(77)	17(63)
Rabat	17(63)	21(70)	25(77)	28(82)	25(77)	18(64)
Sidi Ifni	18(64)	21(70)	27(81)	31(88)	24(75)	18(64)
Tangier	15(59)	19(66)	25(77)	28(82)	23(73)	16(61)
Zagora	21(69)	30(86)	39(102)	41(106)	30(86)	21(70)

HISTORY

Early Morocco

The history of Morocco dates back to between 15,000 and 10,000 BC with
evidence of early settlers, thought, due to their fair skin and high cheekbones, to be a mix of European and Asian origin. They became later known
as *Berber*, a name given to them by the Arabs that simply means, not of Arab
descent. The Berber were pastoral dwellers who inhabited the mountain and
deserts, working the inhospitable terrain and surviving on very little. Though
lumped together and known simply as Berber, there were a vast array of tribes
each fiercely independent and strictly loyal only to their kinsmen and family
clan.

When the wealthy Phoenicians travelling from their capital Tyre (modern
day Lebanon), first set foot on Morocco's shores in the 12th century BC,
their intent was simply to mount isolated trading posts along the coastline
to service and shelter their ships. With their power base already set up in
Carthage (present day Tunis), they had no intention of venturing into
what they considered to be hostile territory. As the Punic Empire grew, the
Carthaginians, more civilised than their Phoenician ancestors, however,
wanted more than simple trading posts, so expanded the ports into towns

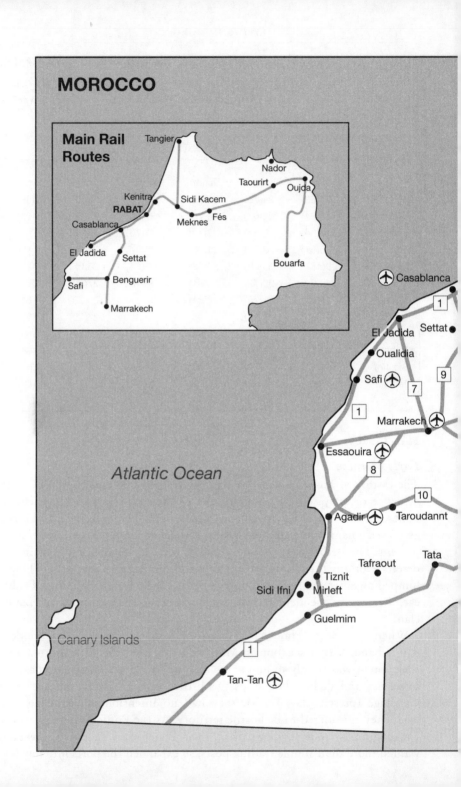

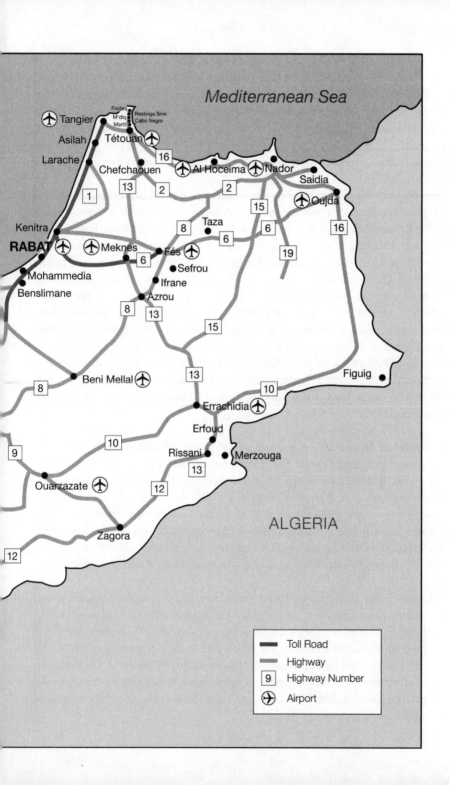

and cities, the most important of which were *Tingis* (Tangier), *Lixus* (near Larache) and *Chellah* (in Rabat). Fish salting was the prime industry but it was with the introduction of the vine and olive trees and the harvesting of wheat that relations with the more coastal dwelling Berber were first instigated. These Berber assimilated the Punic lifestyle adopting farming techniques and language and even blending Punic cults with their own folk religion. Inland, however, in the mountainous regions, where the majority of Berber were concentrated, there was no interaction.

After the sacking of Carthage by the Romans in 146 BC and the subsequent waning of Carthaginian power, the influence of Berber leaders grew. In 40 AD, the Romans sought direct control of Morocco's north making Tingis their capital and *Volubilis*, 250km south, the seat of the provincial governor. Many North Africans were assimilated into Roman society, but no attempts were made to penetrate the territories of or beyond the hostile Rif or Atlas ranges where the majority of the Berber tribes maintained their pastoral way of life whilst in addition, mounting endless campaigns to try and oust the Imperial rulers. Roman occupation continued in Morocco for the next 400 hundred years but as it was never of prime importance to Rome, it was one of the first parts of the Empire to fall into decline, with Rome, unable to maintain its defences against both the endless harassment from mountainous tribes and the Germanic Vandal warriors who came down from Southern Spain to seize control of the western Mediterranean.

The Arrival of Islam. After the death of the prophet Mohammed in 632 AD, Islam started spreading beyond the boundaries of Arabian soil and outwards in all directions. It arrived on North African shores in 669 in the form of the Syrian Commander Uqba ben Nafi who undertook a 5000 km march through every region of Morocco, spreading the word of Islam and violently defying anyone who dared rebel against him. Unsurprisingly such an approach did not go down well with the proud tribes who had quashed all previous attempts at domination. The Berber chieftain Qusayla defeated Uqba and expelled all Arabs from the entire region.

The next Syrian commander, thirty years later, Musa ben Nasir proved more successful in his attempts at conversion. He undertook a befriending policy towards the local Berber tribes. Uptake of Islam increased considerably but there was a wave of resentment towards the Arabs due to their treatment of Berber as lesser citizens and the implementation of steep taxes. By the mid 8th century, the Berber warriors fuelled by their new found faith, succeeded in expelling all leading Arabs from the Maghreb, making this the first and last time for Morocco to fall under the direct rule of Arabia.

Berber Dynasties

The Idrissids. Thirty years later an Arab named Moulay Idriss, arrived in Morocco fleeing persecution in Baghdad, which was dispelling all Shia Muslims as the great split between Shia and Sunni sects took place. He was a *Shereef* meaning a direct descendent of the prophet, Mohammed and therefore it was believed he possessed some of the prophet's spiritual powers. Due to such a lineage, when he arrived in the city of Volubilis he was immediately welcomed as the new spiritual and political leader by the recently converted Berber tribesmen and given the title of king by the presiding chief. Over the next three years before his death by poison, at the hands of the Sunni caliph in Baghdad, Idriss established Morocco's first state in the north of the country and is claimed to have founded Fes. He was buried in Moulay Idriss, a city next door to Volubilis, which was named in his honour. The site became and still is, one of Islam's holiest shrines.

Idriss II, the half Berber son of Idriss, started building up the city of Fes into the state's capital. He welcomed 8000 Arab refugees expelled by the Christians in Cordoba, Spain into the city and later, a further 2000 refugees from the holy site of Kairouan in Tunisia. Rapidly Fes and as a result the new state of Morocco had became the country's first Arab kingdom. Replicating his state on the more eastern forms of government, Idriss II furnished the northern half of Morocco with its own army, administration and currency. He was unable, however, to fulfil his one great dream, which was to rule the whole of the country.

When Idriss II died in 829, Morocco's leadership went into a state of decline. While Fes remained the spiritual Arab city, the rest of the state disbanded and tribal groups seized control.

The Almoravids. The next tribe to govern were the Almoravids who emerged from the ancient Sanhaja tribe of the Sahara. They were known as the veiled ones as they wrapped their faces in swathes of turban as protection from the sands. For one hundred years, the Almoravids had been converting the countries of central Africa to Islam, led by a sheikh who had made the pilgrimage to Mecca and decided that strict, religious reforms were necessary. The Almoravids became a strong military force, spreading their austere version of orthodoxy from ancient Ghana into Morocco by waging holy wars (*jihads*). As their power increased so did the need for a central site for the storage of their weapons and spoils of war so they established a new capital, Marrakech, in 1062, which was governed by Youssef ben Tachfine one of the country's great leaders.

The Almoravids then spread north conquering Fes and the northern state of Morocco before moving on to Spain and Algeria. When Youssef ben Tachine died, his son Ali took over. Though devoutly religious, he was not a military ruler and after 37 years of power his only claim to fame were Marrakech's original ramparts. By the time of his death both the 85-year reign of the Almoravids and the strict orthodox form of Islam, which had gripped the region was over and a new power was emerging.

The Almohades. The Almohades were vehemently religious and greatly angered by the lapsed state Islam had fallen into under the rule of the idle Ali and saw it as their mission to reform Berbers and Arabs alike to their new, strict doctrine, which was based on the foundation of complete unity with God. Led by Mohammed ben Tumart, who claimed to be a direct descendent of Ali, the prophet Mohammed's son-in-law, the tribe set up forces in the High Atlas overlooking Marrakech.

Together with his disciple, Abd el Mumene, Tumart travelled the country spreading his authoritarian doctrine and attacking anyone who dared deviate from his puritanical creed. While many audiences, disenchanted by the Almoravids, were ready to accept a new, clean form of faith, the resistance from the old dynasty was strong. When Tumart died suddenly, control fell to Abd el Mumene, who due to his military genius was able to tumble the old dynasty by displacing Fes and Marrakech. In 1147, he declared himself the new sultan. His rule and that of the next sultan, Yacoub El Mansour was to mark the Golden Age of the Maghreb as the Almohades, swept into defeat the Christians of Spain, regain Tunisia from the Normans and seize power in Tripoli. During this era, the whole of the western Muslim hemisphere was under the control of the Almohades.

As well as being a strong military leader, Yacoub also had a great respect for culture. During his reign, he was responsible for some of the biggest building projects including the founding of Rabat as the country's new capital, the great mosque of Seville, and the ornate minarets, some of which, to this day are dotted along Marrakech's skyline.

Such a spread of power could not last and after the death of Yacoub, weaker sultans led the dynasty to collapse. Spain was returned to the Christians and by the mid 13th century, control of Morocco had once again, fallen into the hands of disparate tribes.

The Merenids and Wattasides. Unlike the previous two dynasties, the Merenids, were not motivated by religion but by patriotism. Having sensed that the country was falling into disarray, they quietly took control of Fes and Marrakech, regained control of some territories in Spain and won the respect of the country, which was looking for a new, unified form of leadership. The most important sultan of the Merenid dynasty was Yousef Yahya, who in 1276 reclaimed Fes as the capital and founded Fes el Jdid, a new town, next to the original city of Fes, which had become overcrowded. Fes el Jdid, became the capital's administrative centre.

The Merenids were responsible for installing the mellah or Jewish enclave in all major towns to enable Jews to live in their own quarters, without harassment and also for building the ornate student lodgings and lecture rooms known as *merdersas* to prevent students having to walk great distances in order to study their faith. It was also during the Merenids rule, that the rules of hospitality and courtesy were implemented, which are still respected, to this day.

By the 14th century, the dynasty, not known for its success abroad, had weakened. The Spanish territories had been lost, Portugal was strengthening its sea power in the Atlantic and Mediterranean and the rest of the Maghreb was in the hands of the Turks.

The Wattasides who usurped the Merenids in 1465 are most renowned for having given away much of the Moroccan western coastline to the Portuguese, while in the interior, Berber tribes were desperately trying to reclaim the interior back from the hordes of Christians who had seeped into the region while the Merenids were stuck fast in Marrakech and Fes. This marked the end of Moroccan Berber rule. After this, governance of Morocco would remain into present day, the hands of sherfa Arab dynasties.

Arab Dynasties

Saadians. The Saadians were sherfa tribesmen originally from Arabia, who in the 12th century had settled in the south of Morocco. In the mid 16th century, led by Mohammed esh Sheikh, the Saadians started progressing north with the sole aim of bringing order to the divided country. They reclaimed the majority of the west coast from the Portuguese and on account of their religious status, were given rule of Fes by the residing Wattasides, with minimal resistance. They founded a new capital in Taroudannt, close to Agadir and for the next 150 years set to work embellishing Fes and Marrakech with prestigious royal palaces. So much wealth and energy was put into improving the aesthetics of the country that the needs of the people were neglected and civil war broke out. By 1655 the Saadian reign was over.

The Alawites. Like their predecessors, the Alawites were also sherfas who had travelled from Arabia in the 13th century and settled in the desert south. In 1666, the people of Fes invited them to come to the capital and take up the throne. Peace was restored but the reign of the first Alawite monarch was short lived as he died six years later. The next Alawite ruler was Moulay Ismael, cited as being one of the greatest tyrants Morocco had ever known. His reign began in 1672 and lasted 55 years during which time he made great inroads into creating stability and improving the country's international relations, which had soured over the last century. These achievements came at the cost, however, of a huge number of lives. As a celebration of his successes, he built 12 palaces in Meknes, close to Fes, which he named the Imperial City enclosed by mammoth imposing ramparts. The next Alawite sultan of note who emerged in 1757, thirty years after Ismael's death, was Mohammed ben Abdallah who founded Essaouira and the medina in Casablanca.

The Europeans. Over the next one hundred years, Europe started paying an increasingly interested role in North Africa. With Moroccan rule in a dishevelled state and Alawite decadence and corruption widespread, Morocco did not provide much of an obstacle. The first country to make a move on North Africa was France in 1830 by taking occupation of neighbouring Algeria. Britain permitted France to occupy Tunis in return for an agreement on its occupation of Cyprus. British intervention in Egypt went unheeded by the French and so Britain turned a blind eye towards France's activities in Morocco. In secret, France and Spain made plans to divide Morocco between them. When Germany became aware of French plans for occupation, they offered to protect the Moroccan sultan, but this pledge was short lived as France bought them off with the offer of a stake in the Congo.

The Protectorate. On 30th March 1912, the *Treaty of Fes* was signed by the then sultan, Moulay Hafid, placing Morocco under the control of a French protectorate. A treaty was also signed giving Spain a small zone in the north. The sultan then abdicated, horrified at what he had done, leaving the throne to his brother Moulay Youssef, who held no power, but remained spokesman for his people. Control of Morocco went to the resident general Lyautey, who was sensitive to the needs of the Moroccan people and respected their faith. Modern towns with wide boulevards and tree-lined streets were built outside the old towns in Marrakech,

Rabat, Fes and Meknes and a large port constructed in Casablanca. A modern education system was implemented, road and rail networks introduced, the legal system was modernised and agricultural methods reformed. French became the language of schools, commerce and power. Authority was exercised by the French in all aspects of Moroccan life with the exception of the Muslim faith.

While Spain's treatment of its territories was unobtrusive and tolerant of its Moroccan inhabitants, French colonisation was rapid. From a few thousand foreigners living in Morocco prior to 1912 the figure rose to 200,000 by the mid 1930's, three-quarters of who were French.

Waves of nationalism were apparent as early as the 1920's with Moroccans, spurred on by the rest of the Muslim world who saw colonisation as un-Islamic. Nationalist demonstrations lead to wide scale arrests, which served for a time to quell the fervour, but World War II reignited Morocco's desire for freedom. Attempts were made by the French to increase the tension between the Berber and Arabs so that the two groups would turn against each other and break up the nationalist unity, but the plan served only to tighten the bond.

French goods were boycotted, parades, demonstrations and terrorist attacks took place attempting to rid the nation of the colonists and officials. In the late 1940's, the protectorate firmed up their control by increasing troop strength. The new sultan, Mohammed V, was deposed of and exiled to Madagascar, for deeming to show sympathy to the nationalist movement. Such an action, however, only served to increase the tensions.

Independence. The return of the sultan in 1955 to a hero's welcome paved the way to independence. In 1956, France and Spain signed an agreement returning sovereignty to Morocco, although Spain maintained the enclaves of Ceuta, Melilla and Sidi Ifni. Moroccan officials gradually took over the administration and Arabic resumed as a first language. The sultan adopted the title of King and Prime Minister in recognition of his role as ruler, religious leader (based on his shereefa ancestry) and champion of the independence movement. In 1961, he died suddenly and was replaced by his son, Hassan II.

King Hassan's first reform was to present a new constitution to the people of Morocco, which declared the kingdom to be a social, democratic and constitutional monarchy, giving the king, as ruler, the right to appoint or dismiss ministers. In 1963, the first parliamentary elections were held and a coalition of pro-monarchy parties assembled in parliament. In 1965, riots broke out among disillusioned students and the unemployed in Casablanca, leading the king to invoke Article 35 of his constitution and declare a state of emergency during which, he assumed all legislative and executive power. A revised constitution in 1970 called for an even more powerful monarchy. This was approved and the state of emergency, called off. An abortive coup in 1971 lead to Morocco's third constitution, approved in 1972, which enabled the king to maintain his power but increased the number of directly elected parliamentary representatives.

Despite several assassination attempts, King Hassan ruled for the next four decades until his death in 1999. He made great strides in modernising the country, which he ran as a theocracy led by his position as Commander of the Faithful, keeping such a tight grasp on the nation's affairs, that when he died, many feared a political vacuum that would reopen many of the deep divisional wounds and rivalries.

Present Day. Transition from the old king to the new, however, ran smoothly. King Hassan's successor was Sidi Mohammed ben Hassan, his son, who on ascension to the throne changed his name to King Mohammed VI and took immediate control, showing the country that he was not going to live in the shadows of his predecessor. A young man in his mid thirties, married to a computer engineer and father to an heir, born in 2003, Mohammed VI has already in his short reign, made a great impact on a country in dire need of repair. His first activities were to visit the troubled north around the Rif, an area largely neglected by his father and to sack the highly unpopular interior minister, Driss Basri. He has introduced reforms to improve health and education and is taking great strides in decreasing poverty. New roads are being constructed, electricity installed country-wide and social housing projects undertaken on a large scale. Much like his father, he is playing a major role on the international stage, actively encouraging foreign investment and foreign participation in privatisation programmes. One of the king's most radical reforms has been in the sphere of women's rights. In 2004, he implemented landmark changes to the Family Law or *Moudawana*, giving equality to women and granting them protection and rights in marriage, divorce and custody of children.

With the new monarch, those Moroccans who can afford it are starting to open up and feel pride in their country. Money, once kept in offshore accounts is being spent back home, expat Moroccans are moving back, setting up companies and starting families in their old neighbourhoods. The mood is one of optimism.

Life is getting easier and the future of Morocco, though torn between western democracy and its eastern roots is gradually beginning to gain a momentum in line with the rest of the world.

THE DISPUTED WESTERN SAHARA

The Western Sahara is a desert territory bordering the Atlantic Ocean between Morocco and Mauritania. The northern portion was known as Saguia El Hamra, the southern two-thirds, Rio de Oro before becoming known as Western Sahara. From 1904 until 1975, the entire region was occupied by Spain. In 1969 a group called the Polisario Front representing the indigenous Saharawi people, formed to combat Spanish occupation and reclaim the territory as their own. Their attempts were marred, however, in 1975 when Morocco's King Hassan II, mobilised 350,000 unarmed civilians into the region in order to demonstrate Morocco's claim to the territory. The Green March, as it became known due to the green Islamic banners carried by the civilians, led to the agreement that an administrative authority should be formed shared between Morocco, Mauritania and Spain with no attempts made to decide on the sovereignty. After a short while, however, unable to contend with the two more local authorities, Spain relinquished its control and withdrew from the region. Hostilities between Morocco and Mauritania led to Mauritania also withdrawing in 1979. Morocco took over Mauritania's portion of the territory later claiming it as reintegrated into Morocco and built a fortified defence line around three quarters of the region. The next nine years saw constant clashes between the indigenous Polisario Front and Moroccan troops ending with a ceasefire in 1988 and agreement between the two groups for a UN initiated peace deal. No decision has yet been reached on the sovereignty of the region although there was a breakthrough in August 2005 when the Polisario Front released all of its Moroccan prisoners of war, many of whom had been held in captivity for over 20 years Over 600 million US dollars have been spent by the UN trying to broker an agreement.

POLITICAL STRUCTURE

Morocco has been a constitutional monarchy since 1972, with the king in the role of head of state and commander in chief of the armed forces and in charge of all military and civil appointments. He is also responsible for the appointment and dismissal of the government, which incorporates a coalition of parties, and in his role as Commander of the Faithful, the nation's spiritual leader. The national parliament is split into two chambers; the lower chamber of representatives (*majlis al-nuwab*) with 325 members and the upper chamber of counsellors (*majlis al-mustasharin*) with 279 members. Every five years elections are held for the lower chamber in which 2002 claimed to be the freest and fairest with 35 women elected thanks to a system of 'women only' lists. Unions, local communes and business organisations elect the upper chamber for nine year, non-consecutive terms. Parties receive state funding based on the number of votes received and their number of seats in parliament.

Following the 2002 elections, the king chose the son of a grocer from El Jadida, Driss Jettou, ex-Interior Minister, to be his prime minister. Jettou stands outside Morocco's traditional mesh of *makhzen* (elite), who have traditionally wielded the power. A technocrat himself, Jettou has replaced many politically minded ministers with technocrats, more focused on results than the processes involved in obtaining them.

29 parties make up the broad coalition in the Chamber of Representatives with the centre-left *Union Socialiste des Forces Populaires* (USFP) and the conservative *Istiqlal* the major parties followed by the mainstream *Islamic Justice and Development party* (PJD).

Parliament's role lies in budgetary matters, the approval and implementation of legislation, setting up commissions of enquiry and in more dramatic times, declaring war. The highest court is the Supreme Court with the judiciary reporting to the Minister of Justice. The legal system is based on Islamic, French and Spanish law.

Administration. Morocco is divided into 16 regions or *wilaya*, 67 provinces and prefectures and 1500 urban and rural communes. Overall responsibility for the regions falls under the remit of the *Ministre de l'Interior* and the *Ministre de l'Habitat et de l'Urbanisme*. Each region is governed by a *wali*, who is appointed by either the Interior Minister or the king. The wali is responsible for security and policing in the region. In every regional capital and some provinces, there is an Urban Agency, which oversees the zoning, planning and development of individual regions. The more development needed, the more Urban Agencies there are. Managing the regions at a provincial level are governors, who are responsible to the wali but have overall control of their own province.

Each province is divided into locally elected Communes (*Jema'a*). These can be either Urban Communes (*Jema'a El Hadaria*) or Rural Communes (*Jema'a Karawia*). Each individual district or quartier has access to a satellite commune. Local issues are initially referred to the *qaid* (local councillor) who works in the *Qaida*, otherwise known as the *Baladia*, and referred up the chain of command as and when necessary. In each city, there is a locally elected mayor (*mairie*).

Population

Though Morocco is double the size of the UK, it has half the population. There are 31.1 million people living in the kingdom of which 45% live in rural regions. Casablanca is the largest conurbation with 3.6 million people. Other urban areas are:

Agadir	680,000
Rabat	1,600,000

Tangier	670,000
Marrakech	823,000
Meknes	536,000
Fes	1,000,000
Oujda	410,000
Tetouan	321,000

MOROCCAN MENTALITY

Language in Morocco

Moroccans love to talk. Hours are spent every day conversing in cafés, on street corners, outside doorways, through windows, at shop counters, on telephones. There is no shortage of conversation and anyone and everyone is welcome to put their oar in. Modern Standard Arabic is the official language of Morocco found in newspapers and magazines, but it is not the every day Moroccan spoken on the street. Morocco has its own dialect called *d-darija*, which has different grammar and vocabulary from official Arabic. Intellectuals frown upon it as being an inferior language and consider it fine for everyday chat but not worthy of sophisticated discourse. It is, however, the most useful language to learn.

Three different dialects of native Berber or *Amazigh*, make up Morocco's unofficial second language, spoken mainly in rural areas by around a third of all Moroccans either exclusively or bilingually with d-darija. Berber has no alphabet of its own, but uses a mix of Roman and Arabic, there is no standard system for writing Berber and it is dissimilar to any other tongue. Despite Berbers being the indigenous people of Morocco, the language had no official status until 2003 when the government allowed it to be taught in schools alongside European languages. The king, being half Berber himself, has greatly aided the indigenous cause. He was instrumental in setting up a Royal Institute of Amizigh Culture, opened in an exclusive part of Rabat, which has done much to academise the language, but laws still exist, which inhibit the culture, such as the stipulation that all Moroccan children must be given Arabic first names

The average educated Moroccan also speaks fluent French. It is the language of business, refinement and sophistication in Morocco and some 'westernised' Moroccans in cosmopolitan cities such as Casablanca and Rabat choose to speak only French. It is the country's official second language, taught to children at primary school and written, along with Arabic, on most road signs and shop's façades. Foreigners are normally addressed in French and it is assumed that the majority will be able to reply.

Many Moroccans in the north of the country speak Spanish while English, though lagging behind, is gradually, thanks to the internet, films and music, becoming the preferred language of the educated youth with a recent government drive to promote it in schools and universities. Though English is far down the pecking order, it would be unusual to find yourself in a situation where someone close by did not speak a smattering of phrases. Most Moroccans are very keen to speak English and there are ample opportunities for providing English lessons or reciprocal arrangements such as teaching English in return for Arabic.

The mix of language and dialects as well as a keenness to converse, means the majority of Moroccans are skilled linguists who have the ability to switch between several languages in the course of a sentence. Intimidating as this might sound for non-Arabic or French speakers, one of Morocco's most charming features is that the focus is on what you say rather than how you say it. It is not uncommon for English people to admit that they would never dare let their 'Moroccan French' loose in France due to the risk of being quartered and strung up for grammatical blasphemy. In Morocco, no grammar - no problem, Moroccans will go out of their way to understand the gist of what you are saying. In addition, they are always delighted at any attempt you make to speak Arabic, particularly the religious pleasantries such as *Bismillah*, in the name of Allah, which is said before meals or *Allah Ihennik*. God leave you in peace, which usually means goodbye. These praises to God, form a large part of the language.

This easygoing attitude provides the perfect environment for learning a language. You will not be judged, only encouraged and once Moroccans hear that you are keen to learn Arabic, they will put time and effort into teaching you new words, test you on words you should already know and praise you, often undeservedly, well.

Meeting and Greeting

No amount of time will ever be enough to accommodate the minutes it takes greeting Moroccan friends and associates. There is no such thing as a brief hello and attempts at it are considered discourteous. Whether you are meeting an old friend, the taxi driver from three days ago or colleagues from work, saying hello, takes time.

All greetings begin with a handshake, followed by the touching of the heart with the right palm. This is a sign of affection. If there is more than one person present, the first handshake is with the person on the right. It then works its way anticlockwise around the group. If a woman does not extend her hand to a man, he will not offer his but will bow his head in her direction. Friends of the same sex and particularly men, will kiss both cheeks, sometimes twice, occasionally more and then remain affectionately close holding hands or hugging shoulders throughout the whole exchange. If you are a non tactile British man, you will need to become quickly accustomed to the feel of a stubbly upper lip rub against your cheek as, you too will often be party to such affections.

The pleasantries begin with each party asking the other, simultaneously, about their family, their work or their health in a continuous stream, where neither party waits for the response and indeed, is so busy asking the pleasantries that they never actually get around to replying to the questions. This interchange ends only when someone utters the greeting, *Al hamdu li'llah*, Thanks be to God, at which time there are more kisses and handshakes before everyone carries on their way.

It takes a while for non-Moroccans used to sincere small talk, to learn that such pleasantries are more ritualistic than born out of a real desire to know the state of your health. It is best, therefore, to keep all answers brief both for your own time keeping and so as to avoid an instant glazing over of the eyes.

THE INFLUENCE OF ISLAM

It is impossible to spend more than a couple of minutes in Morocco without experiencing firsthand, the overriding influence of Islam. The modest female dress, the muezzin's five times daily call to prayer, the insertion of Allah into virtually every conversation, the domes and minarets of Morocco's numerous mosques. Islam is present in all aspects of Moroccan life, as deep set in the roots of society as the *tagine*, Morocco's traditional dish and the indigenous Berber.

Almost 99% of Moroccans are Sunni Muslim, 1.1% are Christian and 0.2% Jewish. The Jewish population was much larger prior to the creation of Israel and most towns and cities have Jewish enclaves called mellahs. Friday is the Muslim holy day known as *salat juma*. Although it remains a typical working day, people are given an extended break to attend congregational prayers at the mosque. The traditional lunch on the holy day is couscous, which is believed to have strong spiritual and emotional significance based around its simplicity and sustenance. For Muslims, to live a fulfilled devout life, they are expected at the very least, to carry out a range of commands known as the five pillars of Islam.

FIVE PILLARS OF ISLAM

O **Shahada:** This is the profession of faith to be said by anybody who wishes to become a Muslim. It cites that 'there is no god but Allah and Mohammed is his prophet'. It simply needs to be recited in the presence of two male Muslim witnesses in order for a non Muslim to convert.

O **Zakat:** Giving alms to those in need, namely beggars on the street or more formally through various charities. This applies to all Muslims who live above subsistence level. The Koran states that if one has amassed some capital, 2.5% of one's income and 10% of one's crops should be given in alms.

O **Sala:** To pray five times a day between sunrise and sunset. The exact times depend on the location of the sun. Most Muslim men pray in a mosque, women are not allowed in mosques at the same time as men as they are thought to be a distraction, so a large number will commonly pray at home.

○ **Sawm:** For one month in every year, Muslims are expected to carry out the strict fast, *Ramadan*, which prevents them from eating, drinking, smoking or having sex between the hours of sunrise and sunset.

○ **Hajj:** the pilgrimage to holy places. Once a year, Muslims converge on the holy sites in and around Mecca namely Islam's holiest shrine, the Holy Ka'bah (House of Allah). This trip is the pinnacle of every devout Muslim's life and those who have made the journey are greatly revered by their contemporaries.

Although so many Moroccans claim to be Muslim, it does not mean that everyone is faithfully practicing. In fact, for lots of people, faith is something, which they can give or take. Some publicly adhere to fasting during Ramadan, but eat in private or speak in praise of Allah, but rarely visit the mosques. Despite this, such individuals do not believe themselves to be of any other belief but Muslim and will vehemently defend their faith at all times.

Even though Moroccans view Islam as the most perfect of all monotheistic religions and would never consider converting to any other faith (conversion and attempting to induce conversion from Islam to another faith is illegal in Islamic law) they will acknowledge Jews and Christians as being 'people of the book,' but on an inferior level. Catholic/Protestant churches and cathedrals can be found in a lot of towns and cities, built during the many periods of European colonisation and most mellah neighbourhoods in the medina have a number of synagogues. Morocco takes great pride in the harmony that exists between its minority religions and its Muslims. What most Moroccans fail to fathom, however, are people who have no religion at all. Atheism is not an option in Morocco and if you admit to being an atheist, you are likely to be pitied and attempts made to convert you to the 'perfect' faith.

For non-Muslims living in Morocco, the adherence of Muslims to an all-consuming faith has its frustrating moments. In Ramadan, jobs are left dangling as hungry workers leave the building on the dot of sunset to celebrate the break of fast, or fail to work at all due to excessive post sunset feasting; alternatively shops will close at unpredictable times as shopkeepers attend the mosques to pray. Most frustrating (or you might say refreshing), is the Islamic view of fatalism, the belief that all events, which occur in our lives, are pre-ordained. That the future is already mapped out and there is nothing anyone can do to change it means that there is seemingly no ambition or entrepreneurialism among Moroccans to improve their circumstances. The term *In sha' allah* is one of the most frequently used phrases in Arabic. It means 'If God wills,' and no Moroccan will commit to anything without adding an In sha' allah. 'I will see you there tomorrow morning In sha' allah (if god wills)'. The downside of this is that if God does not will, the rendez-vous will not take place. In Moroccan society things happen when they are fated to happen not at the time arranged.

Fundamentalism. Morocco is among the most liberal of all Islamic countries. It makes and exports its own beer and wine and alcohol can be bought in off-licenses and consumed in an increasing number of restaurants. There are no laws dictating how women should dress and as a result some, especially in cosmopolitan cities such as Casablanca, choose western style clothing; many schools and universities offer co-education and a large number of women are in professional positions such as doctors and lawyers. The king, Mohammed VI, though anti the war in Iraq, is a staunch ally of the United States and is pursuing a modernising path towards democracy. This is, as can be expected, a route that is fiercely opposed by some. There are a growing number of Islamic fundamentalists in Morocco, who view America, democracy and anyone who pursues democracy as sinful. In Morocco's 2002 elections, the fundamentalist Islamic Justice and Development Party (PJD) tripled its share of lower parliament seats from 14 to 42, making it the third largest party in government and the official opposition, despite attempts to prevent this by the ruling monarchy. The PJD agree with Sharia law and the creation of an Islamic republic. One of their first activities after gaining power was an attempt to ban the Miss Morocco contest claiming it to be pornographic. Hotels hosting the contest were threatened with bomb attacks and anyone taking part was deemed un-Islamic. The contest did go ahead, but was held at a private location.

The 2003 suicide bombings in Casablanca and the 2004 Madrid train attacks both targeted at westerners and undertaken by Moroccan citizens have placed Morocco more on a par with many of the better known fundamentalist states such as Pakistan and Saudi Arabia. Much of Morocco's fundamentalism, however, does not stem from a hate for the 'free world', but from a severely mismatched social class system, which acknowledges the rich and neglects the poor. The deprived areas around Fes, Tangier, Salé and Casablanca are breeding grounds for fundamentalism. The terrorists from the Casablanca bombings all came from one of the most disadvantaged shantytowns in Morocco with homes constructed out of cardboard boxes and planks of wood, no running water, sewers or electricity, hidden from the rest of society behind corrugated walls as if they do not exist. Most of these social outcasts, earn their living from petty theft and people trafficking, but a new wave are reportedly being spurred on by Algerian and Saudi Arabian organisations who are financing terrorist activities.

In an attempt to improve living conditions and halt the rise of fundamentalist supporters, the government, pressed by the king (who has earned himself the nickname 'the King of the Poor'), is investing 5.5 billion dh (£344 million) into projects, which will eradicate the shantytowns throughout Morocco, but with a particular focus on Casablanca where 30% of the country's slum dwellers reside. New housing units and relocation programmes are underway with the government releasing some of the land owned by the state agricultural companies to make way for such developments and incentives are being offered to property developers to undertake social housing projects.

AT HOME AND IN PUBLIC

The cornerstone of Moroccan life and the pride of any individual is the family. It is rated above work, friends, material objects and personal development. The family is the engine that drives society and shapes its citizens. This is why on meeting a Moroccan, you can guarantee one of the first questions you will be asked is, 'are you married' or 'do you have children?' Answer yes to either of these questions and Moroccans will instantly warm to you as someone they can relate to. Answer no, and you can expect a barrage of further questions around the subject of, why not? In most regions, there is still great stigma attached to unmarried (known insensitively in French as *celibataire)* women over the age of 27 who are usually considered unfortunate, although big cities such as Casablanca are beginning to accept the growing number of women, primarily the well educated and financially self sufficient, who are choosing to remain single.

Traditional Islamic marriage negotiations are still common especially in smaller towns and the countryside. They involve arranged marriages with partners being picked, based on their family history, class and dowry. For the less traditional, other more mutually beneficial factors are considered, namely educational backgrounds, degree of religious faith, career plans and at the bottom of the pecking order, love. The family still plays a pivotal role in the decision making process. The foreign man wishing to marry a Moroccan woman is expected to become Muslim and all future children will be born as Muslims.

The average size of a household is 5.9 people with 2.3 people per room. Most are made up of grandparent(s), parent(s), unmarried children, married son(s), their wife(s) and any children they might have. Moroccans do not value personal space or privacy in the same way as a westerner might and in fact, would rather be surrounded by others than spend any private time with themselves. This need for constant companionship can be a little overwhelming for the foreigner used to space and time alone, yet for the Moroccan the idea of anyone actually choosing to spend time by him/herself, is abhorrent. Moroccans deep-rooted respect for the family means that jobs and careers are not held in the same esteem as in the west. A person is judged by their parentage or marriage status not by the position they hold in a job. Few Moroccans ask the standard, 'what do you do for a living?' question and those who do are likely to be asking it more to assess your level of income and any back scratching you can do on their behalf, than as a way of understanding what makes you tick. For most Moroccans, a job is something you do simply to support your family and most stick to jobs best suited to the class they were born into. Personal ambition and success are not goals people seek. The purpose of a job is to do what is expected of you and nothing more. Any sign of 'thinking out of the box' is considered risky and could result in the loss of a job, which in a developing country where unemployment is rife would be detrimental.

Despite their sociability and enjoyment of company, Moroccans, behind the walls of their home, are very private people. The way they behave outside the house is very different to the way they behave at home. They are often referred to as having two personas; the public and the private. The public persona is the one you see when you are out and about: men in the cafés drinking tea or beckoning to passers by, women covering their heads and walking in the shadows. As the street belongs to no one, there is no need to behave hospitably or respectfully. It is each man for himself as anyone who has ever bought a bus ticket or paid an electricity bill will verify. In such situations, swarms of people will storm the desk clerk thrusting dirham under his/her nose, elbowing one another out of the way and shouting louder than the next person to be heard. This is acceptable public behaviour just as a stranger approaching you in the street or a grumpy shopkeeper is acceptable behaviour. As the street is public property, there are no expectations about how one is meant to behave.

The private persona is totally different. The private Moroccan is the Moroccan at home with the door shut and the world outside as the Berber proverb cites, 'home is a tomb this side of heaven'. It is the woman's domain. Here she can remove her headscarf, talk freely, relax and be in charge. Home is where a man can most proudly show off his family and his heritage. Visitors dropping in unannounced will shatter the peace and privacy of the home and are unlikely to be let in beyond the entrance hall. For those invited, however, 'the guest is king' and reams of hospitality abound.

CULTURE SHOCK

Foreigners generally get an easy time of it in Morocco. The social contexts in which the majority of men and women are expected to fit tend not to apply. While it helps to be married and have a few children, the more traditional Moroccans will not class you in the same unfortunate light as their own, if you do not. Instead, they will just blame it on the 'loose' way of living in the west. Foreign women by themselves in Morocco are likely, just by the very nature of the country, to spend a lot more time in the company of men than women, particularly at the beginning as it is men who they will meet out and about. Such social proximity to women is not something Moroccan men are inherently used to and platonic relationships between the opposite sexes rarely exist. If women wish for nothing more than friendship, it is important they make clear their intent from the outset. It is also a good idea to ask for an introduction to any female family members as a way of opening up and, in the eyes of a Moroccan, 'normalising' the social circle.

All foreigners are perceived by Moroccans to be wealthy and, compared to the majority of Moroccans, most are. The average annual wage of a Moroccan is $16,500 dh (£1035) with a fifth of the population surviving on just 8 dh (54p) a day. This is with the exception of the king, who much to the outrage of his subjects spends 58 million dh (£3.6 million) on staff wages each month (as well as £53,000 on animal feed!).

Foreigners are able to come to Morocco and live in relative luxury, hiring staff, eating well and entering and leaving the country as they please, something many Moroccans are unable to do. In return for this, foreigners will be charged more for products and work done than their local counterparts, particularly if their face is new to the area, and no matter how much bargaining you do and how many, 'I am making no profit on this' laments you hear, you can be sure you will be paying above the odds. The best way to handle this is simply to ask yourself before undertaking any transaction, 'how much would I feel comfortable paying for this?' This secures your negotiating position and makes you feel like you have got a personal bargain even if the Moroccan you just paid is clapping his hands with glee. After a while, most resident foreigners learn local prices and fall into the relationship culture by befriending particular shopkeepers they know they can trust to give them quality products for a reasonable price.

The activity of finding people you can trust is at the heart of ensuring a happy, stress-free time in Morocco and most foreigners will make it their mission to build up a community of tried and tested friends. For Moroccans, friendship and trust is greatly valued whereby levels of friendship are measured by the amount you are prepared to put your neck out for your friend and vice versa. Doing favours for one another form a large part of such friendship and for the foreigner, it is often the case that they can do a lot more for their Moroccan friend than their Moroccan friend can do for them. For westerners not used to such alliances, it is easy to feel quite pressured, especially if you have been reliant on your Moroccan friend to show you around and introduce you to Moroccan life. The thing to bear in mind is that most Moroccans are more interested in how you handle the requests they have placed upon you than whether you actually undertake them, therefore, the best way to deal with this is to not commit to anything. While a straightforward 'no' will compromise the friendship, a lack of commitment will mean you are prepared to make some effort on their behalf and leave the rest up to fate, something Moroccans will be able to relate to. Having said this, generosity is a quality greatly respected in Moroccan society especially when you as a foreigner are deemed to be a lot richer than your Moroccan counterpart, so in situations, which you can control, the act of giving will go a long way in securing future friendships.

GETTING THERE

By Plane from the UK. While it is imminently about to happen with Easy Jet soon to start flying to Marrakech, Morocco is yet to be hit by the revolution of low cost airlines, which have transformed travel around Europe. In 2004, an open skies policy was implemented to fully liberate air transport to the country increasing the opportunities for low cost and flagship airlines flying to Marrakech, Agadir, Ouarzazate, Fes, Oujda and Tangier. For the time being, however, the national carrier Royal Air Maroc (RAM) and British Airways (BA) remain the two carriers into Morocco from the UK and as a result, both are expensive. One very welcome addition has been the introduction of Atlas Blue, a subsidiary of Royal Air Maroc, which flies from Gatwick and provides lower cost flights. While it rarely offers seats for less than £100 return (including a meal) and flies only to Marrakech, it is usually cheaper than the other two airlines.

Royal Air Maroc. Mohammed V International Airport, Casablanca (30km south east of Casablanca) is the hub for Royal Air Maroc and accounts for around 60% of all flights into and out of the country with the majority of internal flights routed via Casablanca, which can be infuriating if you are simply wishing to hop the short distance from, for example, Ouarzazate to Er Rachidia. Unlike cities elsewhere, Casablanca is going to remain protected from the open skies policy in order to maintain the strength of the flag carrier, Royal Air Maroc.

Royal Air Maroc flies from Heathrow directly to Tangier and Casablanca. Flights to Marrakech, Fes, Agadir, Oujda and Ouarzazate are connected the same day, via Casablanca. If you wish to fly direct from the USA to Morocco, Royal Air Maroc and Delta fly from New York to Casablanca (around $800-1000 return) although if you are coming this distance, it might be worth stopping off in Paris or Amsterdam, where it is possible to get cheap direct flights to a wider range of airports in Morocco. Having said this, it is sometimes worth weighing up the cost of a couple of nights in a European hotel versus a more expensive direct flight to Morocco.

British Airways. British Airways flies daily to Casablanca and Marrakech from both Heathrow and Gatwick. From October to the end of April, it flies directly to Agadir and from September to the end of June, it flies directly to Fes. Direct flights to Tangier are only during the summer months of July and August. There are also three flights a week from Manchester to Marrakech from the end of October to end of April.

Internal flights around Morocco are not cheap. Around 2000 dh (£125) return flight Casablanca-Marrakech/Ouarzazate, 2300 dh (£145) return flights Casablanca-Oujda. The two main internal carriers are Royal Air Maroc and Regional Airlines, who between them cover each of Morocco's 28 airports.

Useful Information

As flight schedules are subject to change, you are advised to stay up to date with the airlines.

Royal Air Maroc, 205 Regent Street, London, W1R 7DE; ☎ 0207 307 5800; www.royalairmaroc.com/ENG.

Royal Air Maroc, 666 Fifth Avenue at 52nd Street, New York, NY10103; ☎ 059 74 38 50/51/52/53; www.royalairmaroc.com.

British Airways, ☎ 0870 850 9850; www.britishairways.com.

Atlas Blue, www.atlas-blue.com.

Charter Flights. Charter flights are excellent if you are very flexible about when you want to go to Morocco as most of the best deals are from/to specific dates and last for a set amount of days, usually 7-14. If you need to go and return at a set time, they are less effective.

Most charter companies offer 'flight only' deals as well as all-inclusive packages. The best way to get cheap deals is to book last minute, although you are not guaranteed you will get a seat. Marrakech and Agadir are the most popular charter destinations although some routes only run during the winter months. The package holiday market is slowly starting to pick up again to Tangier after a bad couple of years when the general state of hotels was so poor that tour operators dropped it from their itineraries. For Tangier, though, it is worth doing a price comparison between charter flights direct and a low cost carrier to either Malaga in southern Spain or Gibraltar from where you can travel by bus/taxi to Algeciras and hop on to one of the regularly departing ferries to Tangier.

The best way to find charter flights is via the internet where a Google search will throw up loads of deals or by looking in the back pages of the travel sections in weekend papers.

Panorama Holidays, ☎ 0870 238 7744; www.panoramaholidays.co.uk.

First Choice, ☎ 0870 850 3999; www.firstchoice.co.uk.

Directline Holidays, www.directline-holidays.co.uk.

Cheaper Holidays, ☎ 0870 0541303; www.cheaperholidays.com.

Thomsonfly.com

By Car/Ferry

If you need to drive and are in a hurry to arrive, it is possible to travel from the UK to Tangier in just two days so long as you do not come up against any unforeseen weather conditions, which might affect your ferry crossings. The far more satisfying way is to take up to four or five days and enjoy the journey. You have the option of travelling from Sete in the south of France to Tangier on *The Marrakech.* This is a thirty-nine hour crossing that leaves every other day. As you will need to have accommodation on the ferry, you must pre-book. This can be done from the UK with Southern Ferries on 0870 499 1305. The more preferable option, however, is to travel down to Algeciras or Almeria in southern Spain where the crossing is short. From Algeciras there are around ten ferries a day to Tangier taking either 2 hours 30 minutes or 1 hour for the fast ferry. It is possible to buy an open ticket for these giving you the option of any ferry at any time. From Almeria, there are several crossings a day to Nador and Melilla (Spanish enclave 13km from Nador) all year round and some crossings to Al Hoceima (June-September only) but you must book the actual ferry and time you wish to travel. Easter and summer periods (July, August), are the very busy months so you are advised to pre-book all your journeys prior to departure. Again, all bookings from southern Spain can be made via Southern Ferries (see above) or you could log on to www. ferrimaroc.com.

Driving in Morocco. For information on the necessary documentation for bringing a car into Morocco, see *Moving to Morocco*.

It is compulsory to wear a seatbelt when driving in Morocco and being caught speaking on a mobile phone when driving will now incur a fine of 100 dh (£6) (see Traffic Violations below). Petrol, both super and unleaded, are available in most areas and marginally cheaper than in the UK. Most large bookshops such as Waterstones and Borders sell Moroccan road maps or you could buy one online via www.amazon.co.uk.

PETROL PRICES	
Super (leaded)	10.35 dh/l (65p)
Premium/Ordinaire (leaded)	9.95 dh/l(62p)
Sans plomb (unleaded)	10.35 dh/l (65p) available in larger petrol stations
Diesel (gasoil)	6.96 dh/l (43p)

There are three types of intercity roads. The main arteries are called *Autoroute Nationale* (motorways) and are indicated by an N, followed by a single or double digit. The second category is the *Route Regionale*, indicated by an R followed by three digits. The third category is the *Route Provinciale*, indicated by a P followed by 4 digits. The speed limit in city centres is 40km/h, main roads in built up areas, 60km/h, main roads in non-built up areas, 100km/h. The Gendarmerie patrol intercity roads with gusto and cars should slow down when approaching roadblocks, which are a common occurrence and so licences/ID should be carried at all times.

Moroccan roads are among the most dangerous in the world. Around 11 people die on Moroccan roads each day and a further 200 are injured. Most of the problem does not stem from the roads but the drivers. Highway laws are rarely adhered to, traffic lights ignored and overtaking often a hair-raising experience for any passenger. Driving licences are more often than not bought rather than obtained through proficiency and 'lesser' vehicles such as motor/push bikes, donkeys and horse and carts, not to mention pedestrians, often travel in the dark without lights or much road sense.

ROAD TRAFFIC VIOLATIONS

Using a mobile phone when driving	100dh (£6)
Not wearing a seatbelt	100dh
Excessive use of car horn in towns and city centres	300dh
(although the horn is used so often, you would be forgiven	
for thinking there is a penalty for not using it!)	
Children under 10 years in front seat	100dh
Standing still on highways/on bridges and in tunnels	3000dh (£187)
Illegal car racing	7000dh (£430)
Not stopping for Stop signs	7000dh
Not stopping for red lights	7000dh
Crossing a continuous white line	7000dh
Double parking	1500 dh (£95)
Failure to show driver's licence, registration and insurance	600 dh (£37)
Driving 0-9km over speed limit	600dh
Driving 10 km over speed limit	600dh
Driving 20km over speed limit	1500dh
Driving 30km over speed limit	3000dh
Driving 40km over speed limit	7000 dh

Trains

Most Moroccans travel around the country by train and Morocco has an excellent train system to accommodate them. ONCF *(Office National des Chemins de Fer)* runs the train network with fares amongst the cheapest in the world. The main routes are:

- Marrakech-Casablanca-Rabat-Meknes-Fes-Oujda
- Marrakech-Casablanca-Meknes-Fes
- Casablanca-Rabat-Tangier.

There is no train network in the south of the country below Marrakech. This includes Ouarzazate, Essaouira and Agadir
For fares, routes and times see www.oncf.ma

COMMUNICATIONS

Internet.

Around 1 million people, 3.2% of the population use the internet in Morocco. It took a while to catch on mainly because subscriber costs were high and the telecoms structure inadequate to support it. The introduction of Asymmetric Digital Subscriber Line (ADSL) and a reduction in user costs has led to a recent surge in private usage from 2700 in 2003 to 28,000 in 2004 for a 128 Kbs connection although since then the speed has increased fivefold and the price dropped considerably (see box). The largest internet service provider (ISP) is Menara owned by Maroc Telecom, followed by Wanadoo. There is also www. mtds.com, which is an English language ISP. There are two systems on offer for accessing the internet, dial up using a standard modem and ADSL.

According to many young Moroccans, one of the best features of the internet is the internet cafés, which have popped up in all towns and cities providing internet access to the many who are unable to afford a household computer. In place of bars and pubs, the internet café is often the place to be when dusk falls. Men and women meet for dates, groups of youths pass the time of day and for young women, it is often one of their only opportunities to escape from the house. High illiteracy rates means, however, that internet usage, will not be of any interest to large swathes of the population for the foreseeable future.

ISP's

- ○ *www.menara.ma*
- ○ *www.wanadoo.ma*
- ○ *www.mtds.com*
- ○ *www.jawebs.com/en/index.htm*
- ○ *www.maghrebnet.net.ma/*

GUIDE TO INTERNET TARIFFS	
Dial up subscriber	79dh/month
Dial up non-subscriber	around 1.6dh/minute (10p)
ADSL 128kbs	199dh/month
ADSL 256kbs	299dh/month
ADSL 512kbs	419dh/month
ADSL 1024kbs	555dh/month
Please note that these tariffs are subject to frequent changes.	

Moroccan internet terminology is written in French and as in English contains much jargon. The main words you will need to know are:

attach	*annexe*
@ symbol	*arobase*
Bookmark	*le signet*
byte	*octet*
to click	*cliquer*
directory	*le catalogue, le répertoire*
download	*télécharger*
to drag	*glisser, déplacer*
homepage	*la page d'accueil*
hyperlink; to link	*le lien; relier*
keyboard	*clavier*
keyword	*le mot cle*
kilobyte	*kilo-octet*
log on; to log on	*démarrer*
online	*en ligne, en mode connecte*
password	*le mot de passe*
to search	*chercher, rechercher*
search engine	*le moteur de recherche,*
to surf	*naviguer, surfer*
Web address; UR	*l'adresse Internet*
Web browser	*le navigateur, le fureteur*
Web site	*le site du Web, le site W3*
World Wide Web	*le World Wide Web, le Web, le W3*

Telephoning

Morocco's telephone system is very modern. The country's entire backbone is fibre optic based and fully digital. Maroc Telecom are the monopoly providers of fixed lines, of which there are only 1.3 million subscribers versus the 8 million mobile phone subscribers. Fixed lines are expensive for most Moroccans and density is low with only 5.2 lines per 100 people. The competition between the two mobile phone providers Maroc Telecom and Meditel has meant that it is cheaper to use a mobile phone than a fixed line. This situation is likely to change very soon as two new fixed line licences have been sold to Meditel and Maroc Connect who are going to invest large sums in the sector. In response, Maroc Telecom has already started decreasing their tariffs so the number of users should begin to rise.

The telephone system has recently undergone a major overhaul. All former five figure numbers have been replaced by six figure numbers and the country has been divided into eight code districts:

Casablanca	022
Settat	023
Marrakech	044

Fes and Meknes	055
Rabat and Salé	037
Tangier and Tetouan	039
Agadir and the south	048
Oujda	056

Newspapers

Moroccan newspapers are not big on the gossip, quips and jibes we have come to expect from the UK national press, preferring instead the dry, serious tone more common in French newspapers. Journalists practice self-censorship due to the risk of a prison sentence should they write anything that is construed to be attacking Islam, sensitive political issues such as the Western Sahara or the monarchy. Readership levels are limited due to both the high rates of illiteracy and the Moroccan preference for listening to the radio or TV to stay abreast of current events.

It is possible to purchase English language newspapers in the more touristy regions of Agadir, Marrakech and Tangier such as the Guardian Weekly, Independent, Newsweek magazine and sometimes the tabloids but these tend to be a couple of days out of date and expensive to buy. The majority of Moroccan newspapers are written in French. The most liberal one is *Al Ahdath*, which has a readership of around 70,000, *Al Alam* (French version L'Opinion) is linked to the opposition party Istiqlal with a circulation of some 80,000. *Al Itchiraki*, the paper of the socialist party, has the widest circulation with around 120,000 readers. French newspapers such as *Le Monde* and *Figaro* are usually easy to a get a hold of and are cheaper than the English language papers.

The Morocco Times (*www.moroccotimes.com*) is an English language news website and an excellent way of keeping up with Moroccan events as is the Friends of Morocco website (*www.friendsofmorocco.org*), which is the informative website of the US Peace Corps, which has weekly news updates plus reviews and events listings.

Television.

Morocco has just two TV stations, the state run *Radio-Television Morocaine (RTM)* and the partly state owned TV 2M. Both broadcast in Arabic and French and carry advertising. Programming is highly eclectic ranging from documentaries, Egyptian love movies/soaps (which Moroccans love, the soppier-the better), Hollywood blockbusters, music, religious texts and news. There is talk of another national channel in the pipeline along with two regional channels, but these will take a while to emerge.

For variety (and sanity) many households have satellite dishes, which can pick up a wide selection of European, North American and Middle Eastern channels.

The Moroccan Government has recently launched a public satellite channel called Al Maghribia, which is dedicated to the 2.6 million or so expatriate Moroccans living around the world as a way of keeping them in touch with Moroccan life and hopefully luring some of them back home.

Satellite Dishes. Satellite dishes are sold pretty much everywhere from hypermarkets such as Marjane through to sole traders in the new town and the medina. Receivers with a decoder, cost between 400-2500 dh (£25-150) and dishes between 800-2000 dh (£50-£125). Installation takes around a morning and costs in the region of 400 dh (£25). Available satellites include Intelsat, Hellas, Eutelsat, Eurobird and Astra (the main satellite for UK channels – requires a 2 metre satellite dish). For more information on satellite TV in Morocco, the magazine *TELE Satellite*, available from any magazine shop, is a good source of information.

Cinema

Over the last few years, Morocco has experienced a surge of popularity (not to mention millions of dollars) from worldwide film makers, who are clambering over the sand dunes to get a feel, touch and taste of the authentic injected into their movies. Praised by directors Oliver Stone and Ridley Scott and actor, Sean Connery as the perfect backdrop for making films, Hollywood's A List such as Brad Pitt and Martin Scorsese are frequent visitors as are the 1000 or so French, Italian and German production companies who film in Morocco each year. The most sought after location for filming is in and around the dusty city of Ouarzazate sitting amongst rolling deserts. Here, the Moroccan government, keen to boost the region's international appeal with film makers, has reduced plane fares and rerouted flights to ease access. It is also from the new film school in Ouarzazate that most of Morocco's film crews are trained. Close to Ouarzazate is the very popular location of Aï Benhaddou where Atlas Film Studios have been built (see Sous Massa Draa in *Where to Find Your Ideal Home*). Morocco's diverse landscape always works as a stand in for other parts of the world such as Somalia in Ridley Scott's *Black Hawk Down* and Tibet in Martin Scorcese's *Kundun*.

The increasingly famous 3-day Marrakech Film Festival, marketed as the Cannes of Africa and running since 2001, is attracting big names, which is all helping to kick start Morocco's own underdeveloped film industry. Until recently this was confined to low budget, state funded films, limited by traditions and taboos. Private investors are starting to feel brave enough to invest in Moroccan filmmakers and there is emboldened talk of Morocco attempting to take on the mammoth Egyptian film industry, which has always dominated the Arabic speaking world.

MOVIES FILMED IN MOROCCO

Year	Title	Director	Location
1949	Othello	Orson Welles	Essaouira
1955	The Man Who Knew Too Much	Alfred Hitchcock	Marrakech.
1962	Lawrence of Arabia	David Lean	Aït Benhaddou.
1985	The Jewel Of The Nile	Lewis Teague	Aït Benhaddou.
1988	The Last Temptation of Christ	Martin Scorsese	Aït Benhaddou.
1990	The Sheltering Sky	Bernardo Bertolucci	Tangier.
1999	The Mummy	Stephen Sommers	Er Rachidia.
2000	Gladiator	Ridley Scott	Ouarzazate.
2001	Spy Game	Tony Scott	Ouarzazate.
2001	Black Hawk Down	Ridley Scott	Salé.
2004	Hidalgo	Joe Johnston	Ouarzazate.
2004	Alexander	Oliver Stone	Essaouira.
2005	Kingdom of Heaven	Ridley Scott	Essaouira.

FOOD AND DRINK

Though western inventions such as pressure cookers, instant couscous (the name for both the separated grain of the wheat plant and a traditional cooked dish) and convenience meals have seeped into some urban kitchens, traditional cuisine remains the mainstay for most Moroccans. Many view it as an art form, born over the centuries, which does more than satisfy the belly. As cooking remains strictly a woman's craft in a society dominated by males, it has become a form of self-expression through which individuality, mood and creativity can be conveyed to onlookers who, in turn and indirectly, can judge, discuss and admire without stepping over social barriers.

Culinary wisdom is passed down the generations, from mother to daughter. Girls are shown how to cook through the use of taste, feel and smell as opposed to the more cerebral methods of weighing scales, egg timers and cookbooks. Culinary expertise indicates a sound upbringing and counts as an important, albeit subtle, selling point, when it comes to attractiveness for marriage. This is especially true in Fes, where women are considered to be the most skilled cooks and a man is said to be lucky if he marries a Fassi woman.

Home Cooking

Moroccans love home cooked food. It is rare to see families eating out in restaurants. After all, why pay a stranger to cook for you, when you can eat a far tastier meal within the private seclusion of your own home? This is true. While there are many high-class eateries serving traditional fare, mainly to suit the needs of foreigners, nothing beats a home cooked Moroccan meal when it comes to flavour, succulence and hospitality.

Moroccan cuisine is blissfully free from chemicals, preservatives or pesticides. Fruits and vegetables come straight from the land without the excessive packaging, which inflicts most products in the west. Animals are slaughtered just hours before they are eaten or in the case of poultry, they are still living until you request them in the souk, at which time they are slaughtered, plucked on the spot and given to you in a plastic bag, still warm.

As part of the desire to share their enjoyment of home life with others, Moroccans are very quick off the mark to invite new friends into the family fold and, most importantly, to feed them. No matter how poor the host, if he has invited guests, they must be given the very best and their every need must be met. In turn the guest must eat as much as they can feasibly squeeze in or at least make the pretence of doing so in order to avoid hurting the feelings of the host who will assume you are not eating because you do not like the taste of the food

Most foreigners new to the at-home dining experience in Morocco are overwhelmed by the endless stream of dishes that keep appearing at the table. A standard number is 5-6 courses, although at formal events, it can be up to 50. There are often several starters, served in unison, mainly cooked vegetable salads (asparagus and artichoke hearts, beetroot and cinnamon, eggplant stuffed with herbs, okra dipped in tomato sauce), olives pickled in lemon juice and salt and large quantities of warm bread. These are followed by several meat dishes, primarily lamb or fish usually cooked with vegetables in tagines (the tagine refers to both the stew and the conical lidded pot in which it is prepared), *mechoui*, roasted lamb marinated with paprika and cumin spice or Morocco's flagship dish, *bastila,* usually prepared for festive occasions. This is a sweet and savoury chicken and or pigeon pie with multilayered leaves of pastry covered in almonds, icing sugar and cinnamon. Most meals are rounded off with a huge, colourful dish of couscous mixed with meats, vegetables and/or dried fruit and nuts.

The best advice is to pace yourself, although this is easier said than done, as the host is likely to keep piling the best portions of food on to your plate and insisting that you eat up. When you sit down at the table, it is hard to predict quite how many dishes are to come. One indication will be the number of bowls piled on top of small plates, on top of larger plates, although this is not always reliable as sometimes all the plates are replaced with new ones half way through the meal. If you are the main guest, Moroccans will take their cue from you. When you start eating, they will start and when you stop, they will do the same even if they have only just got going.

A FEW EATING RULES

○ Never help yourself to bread. Leave it up to the host to give you more bread when you need some. More than one person handling the bread is believed to instigate quarrelling in the home.

○ If possible, always remember to eat with your right hand. The left is considered unclean.

○ Always take food with your thumb and first two fingers, anymore is considered greedy.

○ Keep the conversation at the table light and easy going. Moroccans do not like to talk business over food. It is also best to avoid issues relating to religion and politics altogether as differences of opinion can very quickly sour the mood.

○ Do not feel the need to scrape every plate clean. Finishing up all the food on the communal plates indicates to the host that there was not enough provided and it will be assumed that the guests left unsatisfied, which breaks all the rules of hospitality.

○ Praise the chef. If you are the only guest dining with the host and his family, you will find you are the sole one praising the food. In fact those around you might even be going so far as to criticise it. This is simply a ruse to ward off the evil eye, which does not bide self-applause. Undeterred by the evil eye, your role is to express your pleasure.

Returning the Hospitality

Sooner or later, the time will come when you have to reciprocate on the hospitality front. This can be an unnerving prospect. How can you ever be as focused on your guest's every need as they are on yours? How can you cook as good a meal for them as they have for you? The simple answer is, you most probably can't, so don't worry about it.

The food Moroccans eat in their own homes is, as far as they are concerned perfection - nothing comes close to the mark. So do not even attempt it. Instead, prepare the meal you enjoy eating and hope that the pleasure you put into making it and the anticipation you have for eating it, will rub off on your guests.

Remember that Muslims are not allowed to eat pig meat, on religious grounds, so avoid serving up pork or ham (which can be found in French-style delicatessens and hypermarkets). Moroccans will not take offence if you offer them alcoholic beverages, but you will find that most will turn them down in favour of soft drinks.

Moroccan Dishes

Herbs and Spices. Moroccan cuisine is rich in herbs and spices, the most commonly used being cinnamon, coriander, saffron, ground ginger, mint and paprika. Saffron, cumin, chilli powder and coriander are grown on Moroccan soil, ginger and cinnamon, are imported from the Middle East. *Ras el Hanout*, which translates as 'head of the shop', is a mix of 10-100 spices, sold in newspaper pouches and mixed on the spot. Its ingredients vary depending on whether you are adding the spices to a fish/meat or chicken tagine. Each vendor has his own secret Ras el Hanout recipe and no two mixtures are the same. *Harissa*, is a garlic, chilli, olive oil and salt paste added to meat dishes to give them a bit of a kick. Preserved lemons are a Moroccan staple found in tagines and salads

Sweet and Savoury. Moroccans love to blend sweet with savoury and many meat dishes are enhanced with dried fruits such as figs, prunes and apricots. Dried fruits are a sign of prosperity and happiness in Morocco, eaten at weddings and births. In the desert regions, newlyweds are showered with dates and the date festival in Erfoud is a much-celebrated event. Almond trees grow in abundance in the Anti Atlas regions. The nuts are made into a paste, for filling fruits and pastries or are toasted and sprinkled on dishes as a garnish.

Street Snacks. Morocco has some of the most abundant and varied street foods in the world. Selling their wares on upturned cardboard boxes, carts, stalls or grilling on braziers, Morocco's street vendors do a roaring trade especially after the sun has set when most Moroccans stroll and shop. Some of the more popular street foods include *brochettes de kefta* (minced lamb kebabs, mixed with parsley, paprika and coriander*)*, spicy snails, marinated olives, steaming lentils or chickpeas served in conical shaped paper wraps, warm bread drizzled with honey, popcorn, fritters in sugary syrup. Street snacks are generally safe to eat as most are cooked on the spot and should be served piping hot. If you are in any way doubtful, however, it is best not to risk it.

Fast Food. American style fast food outlets are soaring in popularity. *McDonalds, Pizza Hut* and *Domino's* are all features of the larger cities often positioned in pride of place close to ancient landmarks.

MOROCCAN SPECIALITIES	
Baghir	Pancakes made from flour and semolina eaten for breakfast
Bastila	A traditional sweet and savoury chicken/pigeon pie wrapped in paper thin warqa pastry
Brik	Deep fried triangular pastries stuffed with eggs, fish or meat
Brochettes	Skewered meats or kebabs
Chorba	A beef and vegetable soup from Fes
Couscous	Traditional Moroccan dish of semolina, eaten mainly on Fridays with meat and vegetables
Couscousiere	The cooking pot for boiling couscous

Harira	The national soup of lentils, chickpeas and meat, eaten at sunset during the 30 days of Ramadan, to break the fast
Harissa	Fiery spice and chilli paste
Ka'b ghzal	Moroccan pastry shaped like the ankle of a gazelle
Kahwa nos u noss	A half coffee, half hot milk beverage
Kefta	Herby meatballs
Mechoui	Lamb roasted on a spit; a Berber speciality
Smen	Preserved, melted and salted butter used in cooking
Tagine	A slowly simmered Moroccan stew, cooked in a conical earthenware pot also called a tagine
Thé a la menthe	Mint tea
Warqa	Thin pastry similar to filo
Zit	Oil
Zit argan	Argan oil, from the nuts of the argan tree used in salads.

Mint Tea

Mint tea or some might say mint sugar with a hint of tea is the main drink in Morocco. Spend more than a few minutes in the company of a Moroccan and you will be joined by a metal teapot, a flourish of rich green mint, a set of gold-patterned glasses, gunpowder or green tea and a box of highly refined sugar all laid out on a low metal tray with legs. The making of mint tea involves an elaborate ceremony that includes the blending of ingredients, the test run and the final deliverance of tea into the glasses from a teapot hovering half a metre above the receptacle, so that the honey coloured liquid elegantly sloshes in, cooling down to a drinkable temperature en-route.

Mint tea is more than a refreshment it is an icebreaker, a time passer, a 'let me tell you why my rug is better than any other rug in Rabat' convincer. Moroccans will find any opportunity for a mint tea and it is amazing the number of glasses a small teapot can accommodate. Moroccans love their mint tea sickly sweet, so that it leaves a furry layer of residue round the gums, which is manageable after a couple of cups, but anymore and you feel like you have a small furry animal nesting on your tongue. From every teapot's worth of tea, it is customary to drink around three glasses although this is by no means necessary. The times it is best to turn down the offer of a tea is when you are in a shop, toying with the idea of a purchase. The shopkeeper will try to lull you into a sense of loyalty by offering you a mint tea. Accepting the tea is equivalent to you making up your mind that you will purchase the product.

Alcohol

Though the drinking of alcohol is prohibited in Islamic law, many Moroccans drink in bars, restaurants and nightclubs with alcohol widely available in most French supermarkets. Locally produced beer such as *Flag Speciale* and *Stork* is the most popular beverage accounting for 72% of all alcohol consumed. Its appeal lies in the fact that it is far cheaper than wine and spirits and as it has a lower alcohol content, is considered to be less harmful than wine and spirits and therefore, more in keeping with Islamic law. Moroccan wines come a close second in popularity, ranging in price, from 22-50 dirham (£1.70-£3) with price being the greatest dictator of quality. Most wines are produced in the Middle Atlas region around Meknes, which is referred to as the Versailles of Morocco. Wines are improving although it is unlikely, despite the 600,000 hectares of vines, that they will ever gain wide international acclaim due to reluctance on behalf of the Muslim government to really encourage it. Red or gris, a sweet, light form of red is generally preferred to white wine as the climate tends to produce weak tasting white grapes. The drinking of spirits tend to be confined to foreigners and the urban elite as they are imported, highly taxed and in many drinking dens, charged at five times their retail price, well out of the price range of the average Moroccan.

POPULATION AND ECONOMY

As you drive through the tree-lined boulevards of Morocco's bustling *villes nouvelles*, you might be lulled into thinking that Morocco is on the edge of a boom. Cafés and restaurants are always full, upmarket boutiques are bursting with merchandise and swanky 4x4's clog up the highways. To all intents and purposes, things are on the up. The economy, headed up by the business minded prime minister Driss Jettou, which until recently lacked any clear stewardship has been kick started with a series of positive reforms including major privatisations and increased foreign investments, which have set the path towards stimulated growth. Inflation is stable at around 2% on a level with industrial countries, foreign exchange reserves are strong and the payments of the external debt (3.2% of GDP) are being met. Change is underway with attempts being made to reduce the immense economic disparities that exist between great sections of the population.

Having said this, there is still a long way to go. Beneath the sweet smelling bougainvillea is a country dogged by social and developmental problems that place it on a par with some of the poorest regions in the world. 53% of men, 66% of women are illiterate and many rural villages are still without schools or running water. Over the last fifty years, population figures have soared from 8 million in 1952 to the 30 million of today (including 51,000 foreigners) with 50% of the population under the age of 20 and a quarter of this age group, primarily those with university degrees, unemployed. National unemployment currently sits at around 12%. There are not enough jobs to satisfy the population and many of the jobs that do exist tend to be very poorly paid. Most people, particularly in the rural regions, leave school young, with little hope for the future, while those who can afford it, head to Europe either legally, if they have contacts, or illegally and often at great risk.

In terms of workforce, agriculture (citrus fruit, olives, livestock, cereals) is the biggest sector, employing 50% of the working population but accounting for just 13-20% of GDP. Droughts are very common tending to occur every three or so years, destroying crops and forcing desperate farmers out of the countryside into the urban shantytowns where 20% of the population already reside. Recent attempts have been made to stabilise the agricultural supply such as investment into irrigation, water use programmes and rural development projects but many problems still remain. 96,000 families in the mountainous Rif region of northern Morocco make a living from cannabis (*kif*) cultivation, the majority of which is exported, with 134,000 hectares dedicated to its production. Until recently, the government turned a blind eye to the industry, which generates approximately £7 billion a year and provides an excellent income for farmers. Under pressure from drug control organisations, however, attempts are being made to curb production with a combination of pesticides and re-education programmes for farmers but quite how successful this will be particularly when Morocco supplies 80% of the hashish consumed in Europe, is questionable.

Things are more promising along the Atlantic coast where Morocco has some of the richest fishing opportunities in the world with over 240 species of fish. 60% of the catch is made up of sardines, which are tinned and exported to the EU. New ports are being built such as the Tangier Med port just outside Tangier and old ones expanded on the northern coast such as Nador and Al Hoceima, as Morocco continues to boost its levels of production.

Diversifying the economy away from an over-dependence on agriculture into something more economically stable is a major government aim, with all eyes turning to the tourism industry as one possible and equally labour intensive solution. Morocco with its rich landscape and year round sun is a major contender on the tourist trail. Being more liberal than most Islamic countries means that it is classed as 'safe to travel to' and in terms of foreign visitors, was relatively unscathed after either 9/11 or the terrorist attacks in Casablanca. A $4 billion government plan is underway to increase tourism numbers from the current 4 million to 10 million by 2010. Financial incentives have been offered to encourage hotel building and resort development.

One of Morocco's greatest assets is its domination of the world's reserves in phosphates where it is in a higher league than Russia, China and the US. While only employing 2% of the population, it is the country's most successful industry followed by oil refining and cement. The textiles industry, which had enjoyed a gradual growth thanks to competitive labour costs and free access to EU markets is now under threat from Chinese competition with job cuts of 90,000 threatened in Morocco's factories.

Funds sent home by Moroccans working abroad is one of the key sources of foreign currency. 2004 figures claim this to be around 10 billion dh (£625 million), although this only accounts for around 30% of income as actual figures are hard to come by. Moroccan real estate is the main investment for 65-70% of all emigrants.

In 2004, Morocco signed a Free Trade Agreement with the US with the intention of strengthening bilateral ties, boosting trade and investment flows and proving Morocco's position as a moderate Arab state. Prior to the signing, US exports to Morocco, faced tariffs of 20% versus a 4% tariff for Moroccan exports into the US with US trade accounting for only about 5% of Morocco's total trade. The FTA now means that 95% of bilateral trade in consumer and industrial products are duty free with all other tariffs due to be eliminated over the next 8 years. In addition, Morocco has also already signed up to a European-Mediterranean free zone, which will incorporate 27 countries and is expected to come into operation in 2010. This will include both vertical free trade with Europe, as well as horizontal free trade with Morocco's Arab partners.

Foreign Relations
Morocco is a friend to both the east and the west. It has a good relationship with Europe and the US, is a member of the UN, the Arab League, and Arab Maghreb Union (along with Algeria, Libya, Tunisia and Mauritania) and is heavily involved in African diplomacy. Seeing itself as a force for stability in the region, the government plays an important role in the Middle East peace process and is involved in many UN peacekeeping missions. Morocco's biggest bugbear is Algeria with whom there is continuing disagreement over the sovereignty of Western Sahara. (Algeria contests Morocco's claim to the territory and supports the Western Sahara independence movement, the Polisario Front. The border between Morocco and Algeria has been closed since 1994.

Diplomatic relations between Britain and Morocco extend back 800 years with trade between the two countries flourishing in the 17th century, when Britain with its penchant for all things sweet, sent its first Consul to Morocco to oversee the maritime trade of among other products, almonds, dates and sugar, which it exchanged for English cloth. The two countries became allied against Spain in the 18th century with Morocco requesting British help to defend it against its neighbour's increasing dominance. In return, Morocco stationed a garrison in Gibraltar to protect Britain's new colony. In the 19th century, the UK was Morocco's main trading partner, until the arrival of the French protectorate in 1912.

UK trade with Morocco has trebled over the last ten years with 20% of all tourists visiting Morocco hailing from the UK. Major British companies working in Morocco include British Airways, GlaxoSmithKline, Shell, Unilever and Marks and Spencers.

CRIME

Overall, Morocco is an incredibly safe country. Crime is virtually non-existent in the countryside while in towns and cities, petty theft; pickpockets, purse-snatchers, burglaries, the falsifying of credit card vouchers and muggings are the offences most frequently reported although it should be said, they are no worse than in many other big cities around the world. Travelling into the Rif Mountains has its risks and is not recommended as people can fall victim to the drug lords and become embroiled in dangerous schemes, which involve the illegal activity of purchasing/trafficking hashish.

LAWS
O Even though the cultivation and exportation of marijuana is a $billion industry, smoking it or being in the company of someone in possession of it (even if you are unaware that you are), is illegal and can lead to a harsh prison sentence of up to ten years in a Moroccan jail with no remission for good behaviour.
O Homosexual activity is against Islamic law and can result in between 6 months and three years imprisonment.
O Sexual relations outside of marriage are against the law.
O It is illegal to remove children born to Moroccan fathers from the country without the father's consent as any child born to a Moroccan father is considered to be a Moroccan citizen. In line with this, it is also illegal for foreigners to adopt orphans and take them out of the country.
O Converting from Islam or attempting to induce conversion is punishable with imprisonment as is eating during Ramadan and any public criticism of the royal family.
O Taking photographs of anything that can be perceived as military or security-related such as government buildings, embassies or airports can lead to problems with the authority. If you feel the need to photograph such sites, it is best to seek permission first. Be warned, however, getting approval through Morocco's laborious bureaucracy will be a long drawn out process.

PUBLIC HOLIDAYS

Morocco has sixteen official public holidays during which all banks, post offices and most shops are shut. Many of the days and dates are based on the Islamic lunar calendar so change annually according to local sightings of various phases of the moon. Public holidays tend to be spent with all the family en masse and primarily consist of eating and during particularly holy events, praying. During the month of Ramadan fasting during the day and feasting during the night, means that many days during this period will become unofficial holidays. Celebrations for *Aïd al-Adha* (feast of the sacrifice) and *Aïd al-Ftor* (end of Ramadan) can last for anything between 2 to 10 days depending on which region you are in.

PUBLIC HOLIDAYS	
January 1st	New Years Day
January 11th	Manifesto of Independence
February/March	The Haj and Aïd al-Kebir
	Feast of the Sacrifice
February/March	Faith Mouharram
	Muslim New Year
May 1st	Labour Day
May/June	Aïd al Mawlid
	Prophet's Birthday
July	Feast of the Throne
July	Young People's Day
August 14th	Oued Eddahab
	Allegiance Day
August 20th	Revolution du Roi et du Peuple
	The King and the People's Revolution Day
August 21st	King Mohammed's Birthday
Oct/Nov	Ramadan
November 6th	Marche Verte
	Anniversary of the Green March
Nov/Dec	Aïd el F'tor
	End of Ramadan
November 18th	Fete de l'Independence
	Independence Day

EDUCATION

In Morocco, the rich send their children to school in Europe, primarily France, the middle class study at private schools in which the main instruction is in French, while the poor and lower middle classes send their children to the free Moroccan state schools. Whether or not you find a school good enough to educate your children will be a deciding factor both for making the decision to move to Morocco and, if you have the choice, in deciding what area to move to.

International Schools

If you choose to educate your children in an English speaking school, the decision making process will be greatly eased by the fact that there are only seven soon to be eight, such schools to choose from. These are located in Casablanca, Tangier, Rabat, Marrakech, Ifrane (near Fes), Fes and soon to be, Agadir (opening end 2006). These are American schools working with the American curriculum, although some of the schools offer the International Baccalaureate diploma programme (Casablanca, Rabat, Marrakech and Tangier). Each of these schools is independent, offering education from kindergarten (3 years) up to 12th Grade (18 years old) with the exception of the Amicitia International Academy of Fes, which is for 3-12 years olds.

Although, based on the American schooling system, these schools will be largely international attended by a broad range of nationalities, offering French and Arabic as important parts of the curriculum. The advantage of such a school is that your child will be mixing with a wide spectrum of cultures, obtaining a high level of education and surrounded by excellent facilities. Annual school fees for the American Schools are around 118,500 dh – 145,000 (£7400 – £9000).

There is also one English speaking university in Morocco. This is the highly prestigious Al Akhawayn University in Ifrane, 70km from Fes. Set up in 1995 with Moroccan, Saudi Arabian and American funding and teaching a mix of Moroccan and international students.

Casablanca American School, Route de la Mecque; ☎ 022 214 115; fax 022 212 488; e-mail cas@cas.ac.ma; www.cas.ac.ma.

George Washington Academy, Rue de Tah, Casablanca, 20200; ☎ 022 98 38 00; fax 022 98 39 45; e-mail; info@gwa.ac.ma; www.gwa.ac.ma.

Rabat American School, B.P 120, Rabat, ☎ 037 671 476; fax 037 670 963; e-mail eskiredj@ras.ma; www.ras.edu.ac.ma.

Tangier American School, Rue Christophe Colomb, Tangier; ☎ 039 939 827 fax 039 947 535; e-mail ast@mtds.com; www.as-t.org.

Marrakech American School, Rue d'Ouarzazate km10, Marrakech; ☎ 044 32 98 61/62.

The Amicitia International Academy of Fes, 152 Rue Changuit, Mont Fleuri II, Fes; ☎ 055 61 46 40; fax 055 61 46 39; e-mail info@amicitiainternational. com; www.amicitiainternational.com.

Al Akhawayn - Ifrane School, (American school from pre-kindergarten to 12th grade), BP 104, Marrakech 53000; ☎ 55 56 74 07.

Al Akhawayn University, BP 104, Avenue Hassan II, 53000 Ifrane; ☎ 055 86 20 00; fax 055 56 71 50; e-mail;admissions@aui.ma; www.aui.ma.

French Schools

Private schools can be found in every Moroccan city and a large number of towns. These are called French schools as all the teaching is in French and they follow the French system, although predominantly Moroccans attend. Much like in the UK, the French system incorporates a primary school system (*école primaire*), which is from 6-11 where pupils receive a basic education. They then go to the secondary school (*école secondaire*) until aged 14 at which point they take an exam called the *Brevet des Colleges*, which enables them to go on to the high school (*lycée*) level, which they attend until 18 years old. It is compulsory for all French schools in Morocco to teach Arabic and Moroccan culture as a key part of the curriculum. Many French schools also teach English.

For a list of French schools in Morocco, contact:

The British Council, 36 Rue de Tanger, Rabat; ☎ 037 76 08 36; fax 037 76 08 50; e-mail bc@britishcouncil.org.ma; www.britishcouncil.org/morocco.

French Embassy, 3 rue Sahnoun, Agdal, Rabat; ☎ 037 68 97 00; fax 037 68 97 01; www.ambafrance-ma.org.

Moroccan Schools

Schooling in Moroccan schools is free (5% of GDP) and compulsory for all Moroccans from 6-14 years of age. While the primary school uptake is high (87% girls, 95% boys), only around 39% of Moroccans go on to secondary education. Modern Standard Arabic is the main language of instruction and French is taught in secondary schools.

While it might be an excellent experience for your child to study at a Moroccan school for a year or so in order to learn Arabic, it would not be wise to do this over the long term unless you have every intention of remaining in Morocco for the full extent of their education and beyond. Though modelled on France, the Moroccan schooling system is inferior to Europe and resources are often greatly lacking, outdated and do not effectively prepare students for the job market. Much like France, education revolves around memorizing facts as opposed to encouraging independent thinking. One of the biggest problems is the language of instruction. In the 1980's, education stopped being instructed in French as it had been during the protectorate in favour of modern standard Arabic. This is, however, difficult for the many Berber Moroccans who speak their own dialect. All that has happened, in effect, is one unfamiliar language has been replaced with another. Attempts are being made to improve the system with new educational reforms such as the opening of over 2000 schools in rural areas and an $800 million (£460 million) contract with US Agency for International Development (USAID) to furnish every school with computers and IT training for teachers. What is also needed, however, is a change in the mindset of many Moroccans, particularly in rural areas, who do not value education and would rather their children worked from a young age, to boost the household income. Moroccan schools can be found in every town and city in Morocco.

Learning Arabic

The best way to get by in Morocco is to learn Arabic, ideally colloquial Moroccan Arabic, *d-darija*, although if you have a good grounding in Modern Standard Arabic, it will ease the process for learning the Moroccan dialect. Very few Moroccans expect foreigners to speak their language and most will be highly flattered and proud that you have taken the time to learn. It will also improve your quality of life as you will be able to converse with a far greater number of people and have a much wider network of friends and acquaintances. Most courses offer the option of both Modern Standard and colloquial Moroccan Arabic although it is recommended that you learn Modern Standard first as this is the Arabic used widely through the Arab-speaking world. The two most highly recommended places for learning Arabic in Morocco are:

Arabic Language Institute in Fes (ALIF) B.P 2136 Fes; ☎ 055 62 48 50; fax 055 93 16 08; e-mail alifez@iam.net.ma; www.ali-fes.com. Courses in either Modern Standard Arabic or colloquial Moroccan Arabic (d-darija) last 6 weeks and are taught in small classes of 8. Instruction is in Arabic except for the most elementary levels where English is kept to a minimum. 6 week courses cost 8900 dh (£555).

Al Akhawayn University, BP 104, Avenue Hassan II, 53000 Ifrane; ☎ 055 86 20 00; fax 055 56 71 50; e-mail admissions@aui.ma; www.aui.ma. A summer programme of intensive Modern Standard Arabic classes are taught here, which claim to be able to teach a year's Arabic in 8 weeks. Beginner, intermediate and advanced courses are offered with colloquial Moroccan Arabic taught to intermediate and advanced levels. This is an excellent place to learn, but courses do not come cheap; 40,500 dh (£2500) for an 8 week course, 61,240 dh (£3800) to include accommodation and food.

HEALTH AND HEALTH INSURANCE

The Moroccan healthcare system does little to inspire confidence in people used to healthcare in the west. Just 4.5% of GDP is spent on health in comparison to 7% in the UK and 16% in the US with only 15% of the population benefiting from any social security cover, although new government measures are underway to increase this to 34%. Even in emergencies, priority is given to those who can pay and underhand payments in return for bed space are a common occurrence. The Ministry of Health is responsible for the public health sector and healthcare and controls the conditions in which the private health sector can get involved. Away from the big cities, namely Casablanca and Rabat, hospitals are scarce, particularly in rural regions where just 22 hospitals offer a total capacity of 2000 beds. Childbirth mortality is twice that of other Arab countries with three-four women between the ages of 18 and 35 dying everyday during childbirth. This makes it less surprising that indigenous health practices prevail in many villages where traditional healers armed with exorcising therapies and herbal remedies, are the first port of call for the sick.

Of the 69 provinces, 43 have hospitals creating a total of 10,000 beds with a further 14 hospitals catering to specialist needs such as psychiatry while the cities of Agadir, Meknes, Fes, Rabat, Casablanca and Marrakech each have one of their own (or more) hospitals. On a nationwide level the patient to hospital bed ratio is 1:1062.

Many foreigners in Morocco are fortunate enough to be able to afford private healthcare and it is in this sector that 57% of all doctors practice, a fair proportion of whom are either Europeans or foreign trained. Having said this, it would be wise to look into the possibility of obtaining some form of health insurance just to feel that you are safely covered in the event of any accidents or illness. International health insurance is not cheap as you generally have to take out worldwide cover, so it is worth doing cost comparisons between what you are likely to pay for treatment in Morocco, versus monthly payments to an international insurance company. If you do have international health insurance, you will be issued with a credit card sized document giving you information on the name of the insurance company to contact in the case of an emergency, which you should carry at all times as many private hospitals will refuse to give any treatment until you have proved that you have the means to pay them, either in cash or through the insurance company. Do note, however, that just because you have proof of medical cover, this might not always be accepted by hospitals especially if it is a lesser-known insurance company or a smaller hospital. In these circumstances, you will need to rely on cash or credit cards and reclaim, post-event.

There are local insurance companies who provide medical insurance, the best being AXA Assurance who are a global company with offices located throughout most large towns and cities in Morocco with the headquarters in Casablanca. Local medical insurance will be cheaper to obtain, as it is more on a par with the cost of treatment in Moroccan hospitals. The best way of obtaining this insurance is to do it face to face with a representative from the company who will be able to get you immediate cover as well as give you an in depth description of the services provided.

In the case of all medical insurance, you will need to confirm that it includes emergency aeromedical treatment to a city hospital, which will be necessary if you are far away from a city. Neither country roads nor ambulance services can be relied upon.

Of the 200 private units, half are concentrated in Casablanca and the rest spread out between Rabat and the other main cities. Most private hospitals are actually clinics with a capacity of around 30 beds per clinic and limited resources. The private sector is, however, in crisis due to competition stemming from an over concentration in big cities and lack of purchasing power from the majority of the population. In most private hospitals, patients are requested to buy their own drugs from nearby pharmacies, as the hospitals tend not to hold much in stock.

Doctors and Dentists. Over 65% of all doctors in both the public and private sectors work in the regions of Casablanca and Rabat. For the population as a whole there is 1 doctor for every 3000 inhabitants. The best way to find a doctor is to get a recommendation from a trusted friend and ideally ensure they speak more English than 'a little'. If you have a particular medical condition, it would be wise to get the name and a general spiel about it, translated into both French and Arabic and written down, so that you can be sure whoever you are communicating with fully understands your needs. Dentists are even harder to come by with around 1 dentist for every 15, 000 inhabitants and their reputation is mired in urban myths relating to tooth extraction as the answer to every dental need. Having said this, many Moroccans will claim that they have the best dentists in the world, if you can find them. The best advice is, again, to find a recommended private dentist or maintain your dentist in the UK and pay a visit on trips home.

Pharmacies. Where there might be a dearth of trained medical staff and hospitals in Morocco, there is an overkill of pharmacies. These can be found literally everywhere even in remote villages. Pharmacies identify themselves with a green cross or crescent and sell a broad range of health and hygiene related products as well as pharmaceuticals. Moroccans are prescribed drugs for just about every ailment and in some cases, several types for one particular condition. Like the French, Moroccans do not feel satisfied with their healthcare unless they have been prescribed a long list of drugs and, also like the French, most drugs administered are in the suppository form as opposed to the capsule. Control on prescription drugs is generally relaxed and in many cases, if you know the generic name of a particular drug, it is likely you can buy it over the counter.

Vaccinations. It is important to be aware that Morocco is still a developing country with a number of diseases and health risks no longer present in many richer parts of the world. You are advised to have the following vaccinations before arriving:

- Hepatitis A (2 weeks before departure)
- Hepatitis B (particularly if you are likely to be staying for over 6 months) (2 months before departure)
- Typhoid (10 days before departure)
- Diphtheria (3 months before departure)
- Tuberculosis (3 months before departure)
- Rabies (1 month before departure)
- Meningococcal meningitis and yellow fever are not required

There is a low risk of benign malaria in the north of the country particularly prevalent from May to October, around the province of Chefchaouen. If you are in this area you would be advised to carry mosquito repellent/net and wear long sleeves. Anti malarial drugs are not necessary. Bilharziosis (also known as schistosomiasis), an infection of the blood caused by parasitic flatworm is prevalent in lakes, ponds, rivers and streams throughout the country but particularly on the slopes of the Anti and High Atlas. You are at risk of bacterial, parasitical and viral infections if you eat/drink infected foods/water, the most serious of which are the parasitic diseases giardiasis, amebiasis, or cryptosporidiosis. Greatest risk is in tourist areas during the fasting month of Ramadan when food tends to be less fresh. There is a relatively high prevalence of hepatitis B in Morocco with around 6% of the population known carriers and around 1500 people suffer from HIV/Aids, 38% of whom are women. There are sporadic cases of rabies, usually from rabid dogs in northern urban and rural areas. Tuberculosis is a major health problem and toxoplasmosis, caused by undercooked meat or infected animals has infection levels of around 52%. There is a high incidence of the parasitic skin disease, leishmaniasis in semi-arid rural areas of Morocco, particularly between June and September with Er Rachidia, Ouarzazate and Tata province most at risk. In 2000, 52 people became infected with typhoid around Tetouan in the north of the country, through polluted water. Cases for both typhoid and diphtheria are rare, but happen sporadically.

SHOPPING

Inevitably, the cost of living in Morocco is considerably cheaper than in Europe. Price comparisons between food /alcohol/cigarettes generally brings Morocco in around 30% cheaper than the UK.

Hypermarkets. The hypermarket trend has caught on dramatically working its absolute hardest to alter the traditional shopping habits of upper income urban Moroccans. Aggressive marketing campaigns, particularly from European retail outlets, offering cheap prices and discounts in addition to quality and hygiene are doing much to lure modern-minded shoppers. All the major cities can now lay claim to one, if not two outlets of the French owned superstore, Marjane with smaller supermarkets opening every other month throughout the country. Hypermarkets and many supermarkets largely specialise in imported produce (with preference for US products following the signing of the Free Trade Agreement) as well as white goods, garden furniture, clothes etc, while the souks sell locally produced fresh food to a majority of lower income families. With the dearth of amusements, leisure parks and nightlife, Moroccans shop invariably till they drop or get hungry, and the brightly coloured shopping malls that spring up around the hyper/supermarkets invariably stocking much loved European and US fast food franchises provide ample entertainment.

Thankfully, it is unlikely that the hyper/large supermarkets will ever replace traditional-style food shopping. For a start 45% of Moroccan citizens live in rural areas both far away from large retail outlets and on low incomes, which makes the majority of the stocked items inaccessible. For those who do live in the city, the stores, being located several kilometres outside, means that a car is necessary to get there, which is again, a luxury many Moroccans cannot afford. More importantly, the souks are the main outlet for the majority of Morocco's fresh produce so their eradication would be tantamount to a dagger through the heart of the agricultural industry.

HYPERMARKETS

Marjane Mainly imported produce.
51% French and 49% Moroccan
Locations: Casablanca, Rabat, Marrakech, Agadir, Meknes, Tangier, Fes, Mohammedia and Tetouan

Metro Wholesale Cash and Carry, a Dutch company. Mainly locally imported produce.
Locations: Casablanca, Rabat, Marrakech, Agadir and Fes

Aswak Assalam is 100% Moroccan.
Mainly locally imported produce
Locations: Rabat, Marrakech, Khenitra

Souks. Souks are outdoor markets, which can be found in every medina throughout Morocco and in rural towns and villages on certain set days of the week. Souks sell pretty much everything one needs to get by on a day to day basis; fruit, vegetables, meats, fish, dairy, (usually unpasteurised), herbs, spices, grains saucepans, plugs, crockery plus many things one simply might want; jewellery, rugs, doors, lanterns. They are the main outlet for farmers, fishermen and artisans to sell their wares. The souks are at their busiest first thing in the morning when the women do the shopping for the midday meal and in the evening, when the sun has set and families take a leisurely stroll. Souks open around 6am and close at around 10pm, although times are not set in stone.

The price of food is generally not up for negotiation. Most fruit, vegetable and spice stalls will have a hand written tag stating a price per gram or kilogram, occasionally you can strike up a deal when buying meat/fish but this depends on the quantity, time of day (the later the better) and your relationship with the shopkeeper. Unless it has a price tag (and even if it has a price tag in some cases), everything else for sale in the souks can and must be bartered for.

For more information on shopping, see *Building or Renovating*.

BARTERING

If you accept the first price you are given (usually sky high), you will be considered not only highly naïve or ridiculously rich by the shopkeeper but also a spoilsport. Shopping is a social activity. You need to dedicate time to it and to have the patience to undertake it. Simply choosing something, paying for it and walking away is unsatisfactory. It is the equivalent of walking into a pub, ordering a pint, drinking it with your back to everybody and leaving – job done but where was the pleasure in that? Moroccans are playful people who love to laugh, gossip and pass the time doing very little except working their vocal cords. The best deals come to people who play back and treat the shopping experience as an exercise in light heartedness.

The general rule of thumb is that whatever price the shopkeeper gives you, you reduce it to one third. He will tell you that the price you offer is not only so low, it barely covers the price of the glue, it is also deeply insulting of you to assume such a low price for such a unique piece of workmanship. You tell him you saw the same unique piece three stores away. He asks, 'Where? Here, in the medina? No, not possible. This table/ornament/door is Berber, very old. There is only one other quite like it and that is in the museum in Marrakech'. Such a dialogue is likely to go back and forth until one of you, (no doubt you, generally fatigued by the whole affair)) either walk away (to be no doubt chased back) or offers a reasonable figure, at which time you shake hands, he calls you his friend and reminds you that you have got a very unique object for a very special price, and you carry on your way. No matter what kind of sob story he gives you about 'making no profit' feeding his family, etc, you can be sure that the shopkeeper has not lost out.

If you really know you do not want to buy something from a particular shop, then do not enter it, whatever the enticement. To leave without buying anything could create bad feelings and/or give offence.

Bear in mind that the best time of day to shop is first thing in the morning as shopkeepers consider it bad luck if their first customer of the day, leaves empty handed or late in the evening when everybody just wants to go home.

FESTIVALS

Moussems are traditionally, annual pilgrimages to visit the tombs of saints, but the word is now used to describe festivals in general, specifically those with religious roots. There always seems to be a moussem going on in one town or village with dancing, music, and feasting the main form of celebration. Quite when the moussems occur depends on lunar cycles, harvest festivals, the whim of the regional governor or Morocco's Tourism Office, which has spent many dirhams on the promotion of cultural festivals. The following is a list of some of the more accessible festivals and events happening around the country:

FESTIVALS AND EVENTS IN MOROCCO

Month	Festival	Location
January	*Marrakech Marathon*. 5000 runners on a beautiful route in 20-25°C temperatures	Marrakech
February	*Almond Tree Blossom Festival*. Dancers, musicians and storytellers in the Almond capital of Morocco	Tafraoute
April	*The Marathon des Sables*. A 240km gruelling course lasting seven days	Ouarzazate
	Wax Lantern Procession. Huge wax lanterns held on poles to honour the town's patron, Sidi Abdullah ben Hassoun	Salé
June	*Fes Sacred Music Festival*. World music in a variety of spiritual styles	Fes
	Cherry Harvest Festival. 3 day harvest festival with music, dance and a colourful souk	Sefrou
	Essaouira Gnaoua and World Music Festival. Gnaoua (descendants of slaves from central Africa) trance music and dancing with traditional musical instruments	Essaouira
July	*Marrakech Popular Arts Festival*. Performers from all over Berber Morocco fill Marrakech's most scenic sites	Marrakech
	Camel Festival. A parade of camels and ancient dance rituals	Goulimine
August	*Imilchil Marriage Festival*. When brides and fiancées meet, dowries are discussed and the town dances and sings	Imilchil
October	*Date Feast*. Traditional music, folk dance and singing plus the chance to sample around 30 different types of date	Erfoud
	Horse Festival. A competition between a wide range of horse breeds	Tissa near Fes
November	*Marrakech Film Festival*. The place to see and be seen, attracts an increasing number of A list style stars	Marrakech
December	*National Film Festival*. A chance to watch some of Morocco's best feature and short films	Tangier

RESIDENCE AND ENTRY

CHAPTER SUMMARY

○ **Visas.** No visa is needed for British, American, Australian or Canadian visitors to Morocco.
○ **Residency.** If you are planning on becoming a Moroccan resident, you must declare your intention at a local police station within 15 days of your arrival.
  ○ Residence Permit. The residence permit is called a *carte de sejour*. Once received, this is valid for 10 years.
  ○ Documentation needed to obtain the carte de sejour varies from region to region. Check exactly what you need before you go and always carry extra passport photos.
○ Work Permits. These are obtained by the employer on behalf of the employee from the Ministry of Employment.

RESIDENCE PERMITS

The only entry requirement for British citizens to Morocco is a passport valid for six months from the date of entry and a return ticket. Visitors are allowed to stay for a period of three months, although this can be lengthened by applying for an extension from the foreign registration department (*Service des Etrangers*) of the local police station. The same also applies to American, Australian and Canadian visitors. Due to Morocco's strict laws on adoption, any child travelling on the passport of a parent or guardian must carry their own photograph on the passport.

If you intend to become a resident, you must declare this at the local police station in the town or city you are staying within 15 days of your arrival date or you must leave Morocco within the three months permitted on arrival.

If you wish to become a resident in Morocco, you must apply for a residence permit (*carte de sejour*) in the area in which you plan to reside. This can be obtained from the Foreign Registration Department (*Service des Etrangers*) of the central police station (*Surête National*) if you are in a town or city and the Gendarmerie if you are in the countryside. Exactly what documentation is needed to support the permit, changes often and varies between regions so you are best advised to firstly, visit the police station to find out exactly what is needed and then return a second time with the required documents. Even then the amount of passport photos required can vary depending on which clerk you are dealing with at the time, so it is most probably wise to take more than you possibly think you might need. The whole process is long and drawn out and can be all the more complicated if you do not speak French.

The actual receiving of the carte de sejour takes time to chug its way around the different levels of bureaucracy so if you wish to receive it before two to three months, it is best to keep the pressure on. Until you actually receive the carte, your passport and the receipt given to you on application count as your identity, so do not forget to request a receipt when applying for the permit. Once received, the card is valid for 10 years. The main benefits of having a carte de sejour is that you can obtain free healthcare and education, but chances are, you will prefer to pay for both of these privately.

Documentation

The following documentation and procedures are required before you can obtain the carte de sejour:

- A valid passport
- Six recent passport sized photographs
- Three complete application forms, available from the Moroccan Immigration office
- A fee of 50 dirham (£3)
- Evidence of your means of livelihood or source of income such as pension, bank statements, savings, annuities
- If you are moving to Morocco for employment, you must provide a contract signed by your employer, which needs to be approved by the Ministry of Employment in Rabat.
- Proof of residence such as rent receipts or if you have already bought a house in Morocco, the notary can supply documentation indicating proof of residency.
- An HIV test is compulsory for anyone between the ages of 15-60 years, which must be carried out at a facility approved by the Moroccan Ministry of Health. Positive carriers will not be granted entrance.

To avoid the bureaucracy, many non-Moroccans prefer to simply remain constant tourists leaving the country every three months and getting issued with a new tourist stamp on return. While this is effective if you live close to Tangier and can pop across to Spain, it becomes more of an effort and expense if you are living further south.

Work Permits

Work permits are obtained by the employer on behalf of the employee direct from the Ministry of Employment in Rabat. Legislation has recently been tightened up regarding foreigners working in Morocco with the general principle being that non-Moroccans can only be brought into work if it is a job that nationals are unable to do themselves. The process of obtaining the permit is lengthy– a couple of weeks is the average time, although this depends on the individual case.

Moroccan Embassies and Consulates

Moroccan Embassy, London, 49 Queens Gate Gardens, London SW7 5NE; ☎ 020-7581 5001/4; fax 0207 225 3862.

Moroccan Consulate, London, Diamond House, 97-99 Praed Street, London W2 INT; ☎ 020-7724 0624.

Consulate General of the Kingdom of Morocco, 10 East 40th Street, New York, NY 10016; ☎ 0212 758 2625.

British Embassies and Consulates in Morocco

British Embassy Rabat, 17 Boulevard de la Tour Hassan, Rabat; ☎ 037 23 86 00; fax 037 70 45 31; e-mail british@mtds.com.

British Consulate General, Casablanca, 36 rue de la Loire-Polo, Casablanca; ☎ 022 85 74 00; fax 022 83 46 25.

British Consulate Tangier, Trafalgar House, 9 Rue Amerique du Sud, Tangier; ☎ 039 93 69 39; fax 039 93 69 14.

Embassy of the United States of America, Morocco, 2 Avenue de Mohammed el Fassi, Rabat; ☎ 037 76 22 65; fax 037 76 56 61; www.rabat.usembassy.gov.

Consulate General of the United States of America, Casablanca, Morocco, 8 Boulevard Moulay Youssef; ☎ 022 26 45 50; fax 022 20 41 27.

Part II

LOCATION, LOCATION...

WHERE TO FIND YOUR IDEAL HOME

GOLF IN MOROCCO

Name	Telephone	Holes	Length (km)	Par	Average Green Fees (dh)	Club House	Restaurant	Hire Shop	Practise Range	Putting Green	Buggy Hire
Agadir											
Agadir Royal Golf Club	048 24 85 51	18	3.6	36	200/9						
The Dunes Club Med	048 83 46 90	27	3-3-3	36-36-36	560/18	✓	✓	✓	✓	✓	✓
Soleil Golf Course	048 33 73 29	27	3-3-3	36-36-36	500/18	✓	✓	✓	✓	✓	✓
Ben Slimane											
Royal Golf Club	03 32 87 93	9	3.1	36							
Casablanca											
Anfa Royal Golf Club	022 36 53 55	9	2.7	35	250 pd	✓		✓			
Mohammedia Royal Golf	023 31 48 02	18	5.4	31	300pd		✓				✓
Bouznika Bay Golf Course	037 74 33 72	9	3	35	230pd						
Settat											
University Royal Golf Club	023 40 07 55	9	3.2	37							
El Jadida											
El Jadida Royal Golf Club	023 35 22 51	18	6.8	72	250/9	✓	✓	✓		✓	✓
Fes											
Fes Royal Gold Club	055 66 52 10	18	3.1	37	300						
Meknes											
Meknes Royal Golf Club	055 53 07 53	9	2.6-2.2	36	200pd	✓	✓	✓		✓	✓
Marrakech											
Marrakech Royal Golf Club	044 40 98 28	18	6.2	72	300/18	✓	✓	✓	✓	✓	✓
La Palmeraie Golf Club	044 36 87 66	18	6.2	72	500/18	✓	✓	✓	✓	✓	✓
Amelkis Golf Club	044 40 44 14	18	6.6	72	450pd	✓	✓	✓	✓	✓	✓
Ouarzazate											
Ouarzazate Royal Golf Club	044 88 22 18	18	3.1	36	200/18	✓	✓				
Rabat											
Dar es Salam Royal Golf	037 75 58 64	45	6.7-6-2	73-72-32	400pd	✓	✓	✓	✓	✓	✓
Tangier											
Royal Country Golf Club	039 93 89 25	18	5.5	70	400pd	✓	✓	✓	✓	✓	✓
Tetouan											
Cabo Negro Golf Club	039 97 83 03	18	6.3	36	400pd	✓	✓	✓	✓	✓	✓

WHERE TO FIND YOUR IDEAL HOME

CHAPTER SUMMARY

○ **Regions.** Morocco is divided into 16 regions, each one headed up by a regional governor or wali, appointed by the king.

○ **Plan Azur.** There are six new coastal areas being developed in Morocco. Five of these are along the Atlantic coast and one on the Mediterranean. As well as hotels, conference centres and leisure facilities, there are a number of new villas being built for sale.

○ **Bargains.** While property prices in Casablanca and Marrakech are more on a par with prices in Europe, in the smaller towns, villages and countryside, there is much that can be found for less than £20,000.

○ **Golf.** This is a very popular sport in Morocco and the conditions for playing are excellent. As well as the already existing 14 golf courses, several new ones are being built. Green fees cost around £19 and caddies in the region of £6.

○ **Upcoming Areas.** Morocco's upcoming areas include Fes el Bali, Tetouan (Cabo Negro, Mdiq, Restinga Smir), Saidia/ Oujda, Sidi Ifni, coastal areas around Asilah, desert areas around Ouarzazate and Er Rachidia.

○ **Cuisine.** The cuisine varies between the regions of Morocco. It is at its very best in the gastronomic capitals of Fes, Marrakech and Tetouan.

○ **History.** Morocco has a fascinating and varied history depending on where you are in the country. Having a good understanding of the history of each region will enable you to better communicate with the local population.

○ **Buying for the Future.** Much of Morocco is still undeveloped. When buying property, it helps if you look beyond the here and now, ten years into the future when infrastructure, should be greatly improved.

ADMINISTRATIVE ORGANISATION

There are 16 regions (*wilay'at*) in Morocco including two in the disputed Western Sahara, which are further divided into provinces and prefectures that are then divided into urban and rural communes. At the head of each region is a regional governor or a *wali*, appointed by the king with powers over regional development, healthcare, education, public services and the maintenance and extension of roads. Each province then has its own governor, also appointed by the king, but answerable to the wali, whose role it is to oversee the development of the individual province. At a local level, there is the locally elected qaid to whom all local issues; rubbish collections, noisy neighbours, billing disputes etc are referred.

Postcodes in Morocco are five digits long with the first 2 digits referring to the province or prefecture. House numbers, sometimes handwritten onto the door, like Arabic writing run from the right to the left

In the north of Morocco, there are two Spanish enclaves Melilla and Sebta (Ceuta Spanish spelling), measuring a total of 32sq km, which despite endless attempts by Morocco for reintegration are firmly in Spanish hands and have been for the last 500 years. So keen is Spain to maintain its territory and keep Morocco and Moroccans out, that a seven-kilometre steel, razor wire fence curbs entry to Melilla, the more common migratory route.

UPCOMING REGIONS IN MOROCCO

In line with the Plan Azur, which is part of the government's strategy for attracting 10 million tourists by 2010, six new top end coastal resorts are being built, five on the Atlantic coast and one on the Mediterranean. The purpose of these is to regenerate the economy in areas where there is very little other industry. The resorts will guarantee high levels of employment and do much to boost the development of the regions. Each resort will have hotels, golf courses, private villas and apartments and some will have much needed conference centres to attract a business market.

- **Plage Blanche** is a very attractive beach close to Guelmim in southern Morocco. This will be marketed as 'an oasis by the sea', and is expected to appeal to an ecotourist market with its rare birds, fossils and archaeological sites (see *Guelmim-Es Semara* region)
- **Taghazout** just north of Agadir will be marketed as a resort for sport and leisure activities, currently very popular with surfers (see *Souss Massa Draa* region).
- **Mogador** is located a couple of kilometres from the UNESCO World Heritage site medina of Essaouira. Essaouira is already an established tourist destination and much of the infrastructure is already in place (see

Marrakech-Tensift-Al Haouz region).

○ **El Haouzia** is located between Azemmour and El Jadida. This resort will largely focus on the business tourist market with conference centre and sports facilities (see *Doukkala-Abda* region).

○ **Khemis Sahel** is located close to the northern area of Larache near Tangier and the ancient Roman ruins of Lixus (see *Tangier-Tetouan* region).

○ **Saidia** is located on the Mediterranean coast, close to the city of Oujda, ferries to Spain and the border with Algeria, which is currently closed (see *The Oriental* region).

The resorts most close to completion (2006/7) are Saidia, Mogador, El Haouzia and Khemis Sahel. Developers are still being sought for the Plage Blanche and Taghazout developments.

MOROCCO'S UNESCO WORLD HERITAGE SITES

○ The Medina of Fes (1981)
○ The Medina of Marrakesh (1985)
○ Ksar Aït-Ben-Haddou, Ouarzazate (1987)
○ The Historic City of Meknes, centre of Morocco near Fes (1996)
○ The Archaeological Site of Volubilis, NW Morocco, near Rabat (1997)
○ The Medina of Tetouan, N Morocco on Mediterranean Coast (1997)
○ The Medina of Essouira (2001)
○ The Old Portuguese City (Magazan) El Jadida (2004).

WHAT YOUR MONEY WILL BUY

Price	Property	Location
£3000	small kasbah house unrenovated	Villages surrounding Er Rachidia
£12,000	1000sq m of land	close to Aïi Ben-Haddou, Ouarzazate
£12,500	Small fisherman's house, unrenovated, next to the sea	Sidi Ifni
£18,000	2 bedroom apartment	Meknes ville nouvelle centre
£20,000	3 bedroom traditional house, unrenovated	El Jadida medina
£21,000	4 bedroom, unrenovated riad	Meknes medina
£25,000	2 bedroom apartment	Fes centre ville nouvelle
£28,000	Large farmhouse, unrenovated with sea views	20km south of Essaouira

£30,000	2 bedroom unrenovated riad	Fes el Bali
£37,000	3 bedroom renovated house, 15 minutes from sea	Agadir
£37,000	4 bedroom 3 storey renovated farmhouse	countryside, Chefchaouen
£40,000	2 bedroom renovated apartment	Essaouira medina
£45,000	2 bedroom apartment with seaviews	Mohammedia
£45,000	French colonial chalet style house unrenovated	Ifrane
£45,000	Traditional house (45sq m), unrenovated	Tangier medina
£60,000	4 bedroom, unrenovated houses close to sea	Aglou, south Morocco
£65,000	2 bedroom apartment, downtown	Casablanca
£70,000	2 bedroom apartment	Marrakech centre ville nouvelle
£110,000	Five bedroom villa with private pool	Tangier suburbs
£170,000	3 bedroom, luxury new villas next to the sea	Aglou Plage
£187,000	4 bedroom villa, swimming pool,	Anfa suburb Casablanca. lawned garden, terraces, maid quarters
£188,000	4 bedroom duplex, communal	La Palmeraie, Marrakech swimming pool
£200,000	4 bedroom, 4 bathroom, 2 salon riad,	Bab Doukkala, Marrakech small swimming pool medina
£200,000	5 bedroom, 5 bathroom riad with	Essaouira medina sea views
£280,000	6 bedroom, 5 salon villa	ville nouvelle, Marrakech
£375,000	Hotel with 19 bedrooms in riad style	Essaouira medina
£400,000	4 bedroom villa with swimming pool	countryside, Essaouira and 15,000sq m of land
£700,000	4 bedroom, 4 salon villa with swimming	Ain Diab, Casablanca pool
£750,000	3 bedroom, 4 salon villa	Agdal, Rabat

THE REGIONS OF MOROCCO

CASABLANCA

Population: 3.6 million
Area: 1,615sq km
Regional capital: Casablanca
Main areas: Casablanca and Mohammedia

The region of Greater Casablanca basically begins and ends with Casablanca or Casa as it is known, and as far as the 3.6 million inhabitants are concerned, it is the only city in Morocco worthy of a mention. It is a modern, architecturally confused, vibrant, all-absorbing city, which could, if it were not for the soaring 200-metre minaret attached to the Great Mosque of Hassan II, be mistaken for any European city, in terms of style of dress, array of restaurants and glass fronted office blocks.

Surrounding Casablanca is the Chaouia Plain, which stretches north up to Rabat. This is not a particularly picturesque area especially now that there are two main highways and a railway line running through it, but from the train it is possible to spot waterfalls amidst the swathes of dense forest.

Casablanca is positioned on the west coast of Morocco bordering the Atlantic Ocean, 70 kilometres south of Morocco's capital Rabat. It is the country's economic powerhouse, responsible for 60% of all GDP and 55% of all international trade via both its port and the port of neighbouring Mohammedia, 25 kilometres north. The city consumes 30% of all the country's electricity, employs 46% of the working population and is the headquarters for all the major Moroccan banks.

Like most of the Atlantic coastal regions, it enjoys a temperate climate. At its hottest, during the summer months, it rarely gets above 24°C and at its coolest it drops to a mild 12 or 13 °C. Having said this, in the winter of 2004, it experienced icy cold conditions and snow, much to the shock of its inhabitants, many of who had to take to their beds with colds and flu!

Casablanca's Mohammed V airport, 30 kilometres outside the city, is Morocco's busiest airport. The majority of flights from Western Europe, North America, West Africa and the Middle East fly to Casablanca and it is the hub for all Royal Air Maroc's domestic flights. It also has two main train stations, which cover most destinations throughout Morocco.

Casablanca's nearest beach is a short way out of the city centre in the suburb of Aïn Diab, along the Boulevard de la Corniche. This is where Morocco's trendy strut their stuff hanging out in cafés, restaurants, the multiplex cinema and nightclubs and bars with names like Tahiti and Miami. Some of the beach here is private, attached to clubs, which charge a fee, often a preferable option as you can guarantee some space. Unlike elsewhere along the coast, the ocean around Casablanca is rough and generally not considered safe to swim in. Mohammedia, further north, offers much better swimming conditions.

Casablanca's roots lie in the bourgeois, boutique lined avenues of Anfa a northwest suburb where the earliest inhabitants, a Berber tribe called the Bargawhata were already well established by the time the Arabs arrived in the 7th century. In 1188, the Almohads seized the settlement, followed by the Merenids a hundred years later. As their dynasty began to decline, the Berber reclaimed their territory and took to piracy, plundering heavily laden Spanish and Portuguese ships. By the mid 15th century, they had become such a threat to Portuguese seafarers, that Lisbon launched an attack on Anfa and its inhabitants, leaving it in a state of ruin. It took 60 years, however, for the Portuguese to successfully quash the Berber tribes and claim the territory as their own, naming it Casa Branca, meaning White House.

The Lisbon earthquake and tsunami in 1755, which destroyed much of Portugal, Spain and Morocco, greatly diminished the Portuguese empire causing them to abandon their Atlantic colony. It was the Alawite sultan, Sidi Mohammed ben Abdullah who succeeded the Portuguese and rebuilt much of the town, following the earthquake including the construction of most of the houses and mosques in the medina, many of which are in a similar architectural style to Essaouira, also built by the sultan. He renamed the town Dar el Beida meaning White House in Arabic. It was shortly after in the mid 1800's that the town took the name Casablanca from Spanish merchants who were trading with the wool-growing region of Chaouia, in the hinterlands of the town. Casablanca at this time was little more than a backwater with a population of around 800. It was with the arrival of the French that it started to take on a form more familiar to what we see today. The first French resident general Lyautey decided that Casablanca should be to Morocco, what New York was to the United States much like Rabat should be Morocco's version of Washington DC. He transformed it into a modern metropolis, expanding the port and implementing large-scale infrastructure. The educated elite from Fes made a beeline for the city, seeing it as a place to prosper and benefit from the property boom.

Rapid industrialisation did not come without side effects namely, poverty, overcrowding and disgruntlement. In the 1930's, in an attempt to overcome the housing shortage brought about by the influx of rurals seeking work in the new factories, the French built a new medina called the *Quartier des Habous* (district of Holy Men), which much like the grid formation of Essaouira's medina, is orderly

REGIONS

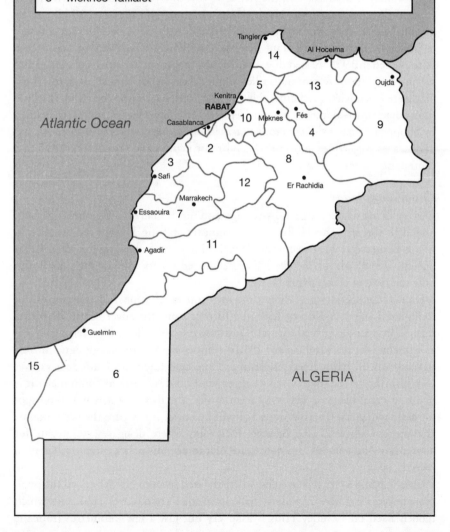

1	Casablanca	9	The Oriental
2	Chaouia-Ouardigha	10	Rabat-Sale-Zemmour-Zaer
3	Doukkala-Abda	11	Souss Massa Draa
4	Fes-Boulemane	12	Tadla-Azilal
5	Gharb-Chrarda-Bni Hsen	13	Taza-Taounate-Al Hoceima
6	Guelmim Es-Semara	14	Tangier-Tetouan
7	Marrakech-Tensift-Al Haouz	15	Western Sahara
8	Meknes-Tafilalet		

Tangier

Al Hoceima

14

5

13

Oujda

Kenitra

RABAT

Casablanca

10   Meknes   Fés

9

Atlantic Ocean

2

4

3

8

Safi

12

Er Rachidia

Marrakech

Essaouira   7

11

Agadir

Guelmim

15

6

ALGERIA

and uncomplicated with green spaces, wide passageways and a French-Moroccan (*Mauresque*) style architecture. This did little to quell the rise of poverty or narrow the distended gap between rich and poor. Squalid shantytowns (*bidonvilles*) engulfed the outskirts of the city, while palm-lined boulevards and state of the art office blocks furnished the centre.

Cuisine

Being a French built city, located on Morocco's Atlantic seafront makes it no surprise that French-style eateries and fish tend to dominate the food scene in Casablanca. The majority of the restaurants are French owned, serving French food, usually fish related and the city is known to have some of the best French chefs in the country. Most notable restaurants are *A Ma Bretagne*, 10 kilometres out of the city along Boulevard de la Corniche, with views over the sea and said to be the best French restaurant in Africa and *Taverne du Dauphin* close to the port opened in 1958, passed down the French family to the current grandson and serving fresh *fruits de mer* and grilled Dublin prawns for almost 50 years. Tuna, mackerel, anchovies, pilchards, shellfish and sardines can be found in the little cafés adjacent to Marché Central, deep-fried in a light batter and accompanied by chopped tomatoes and onions. *Tagine Busroque* is a regional dish consisting of potatoes, vegetables and mussels and most tagines and couscous use fish as a central ingredient.

Casablanca Today

Despite being released over 60 years ago and not actually having one single shot filmed in the city, the Hollywood blockbuster starring Humphrey Bogart and Ingrid Bergman is what many people still think of when hearing the word 'Casablanca'- a romantic, exotic city where bejewelled expats wile the night away sipping martinis in lavish piano bars.

Unless you spend your whole time in 5 star hotel salons, the Casablanca of today (and then) could not really be further from the silver screen depiction (filmed in a studio in California). Downtown is a medley of modern, concrete apartment blocks, sumptuous, 1930's edifices of Mauresque design, mirror-fronted offices, palm lined boulevards, four lane highways crammed, as ever with panting traffic, banks, travel agents and hordes of suited commuters. It is not a peaceful place to 'get away from it all', which is why it is not a top spot for holidaymakers. Casablanca is a city of business. It is where the accountants, lawyers, stockbrokers and bankers hang out, where delegates congregate for conventions and hotels promote state of the art business centres rather than relaxing spas.

Casablanca is a city of extremes, where the rich seem to get richer and the poor, more poverty stricken. The luxury villa lined streets of quartier Californie, which models itself on Beverley Hills is a far cry but just a few kilometres from the scrubby shantytowns lacking in water, electricity and effective sewage systems. It was from *Sidi Moumen*, Casablanca's roughest shantytown that the young suicide bombers, all under 24 years of age, emerged in 2003, killing 41 people and devastating Morocco's most liberal-minded city. Since the attacks, the king has announced a massive nationwide plan to eradicate all shantytowns, the majority of which are located in Casablanca and several million US dollars are being injected into social housing projects as replacement accommodation for the country's poorest.

Casablanca is not a complicated city to navigate around. There are quite a few landmarks such as minarets, hotels and squares, which provide a good indication of location, not to mention the smell of the sea to the west of the city. At the present time, it is not recommended to rely on street names. A period of Arabisation means that these keep altering and only the most up to date map is likely to be abreast of the changes. Despite being Morocco's largest city, it is a long way down the tourist's pecking order of 'things to see and do' in Morocco. Many bemoan the fact that despite being in a country of culture it has no museums or theatres. In 2004, the city took an 11% share of all the country's tourism, but besides business tourists, this tended simply to be holidaymakers going via the city's train stations or car hire outlets, to get elsewhere. There are great plans afoot to change the tourist status of the city and, in line with the nationwide plan of 10 million visitors by 2010, Casablanca aims to up the number of visitors to the city to one million within the same time frame. The current main tourist attractions include the old medina, which is located next door to one of the two main city squares, *Place Nations Unies*. Though being referred to as old, it is actually relatively new, having been rebuilt in 1770 by sultan Sidi Mohammed ben Abdullah after being destroyed by the Lisbon earthquake in 1755. Only around 1000 people live in the medina, which is not a sprawling labyrinth like many of Morocco's old towns, but a well ordered, uncomplicated selection of passageways interspersed with little squares Despite being a tourist attraction, the old medina caters primarily to the Moroccan market with barbers, grocers and butchers, as opposed to the increasingly more tourist-focused selection of arts, crafts and furnishings made by local artisans.

The 'new medina' Quartier des Habous, a couple of kilometres to the south east of the centre, also interests tourists. It was built by the French in 1930 and is not so much described as a medina but as a western 'garden city' radiating out from a central green into tidy, neat arcades and arched streets. It is here that most of the crafts from around Morocco can be found, along with fresh produce and French-style patisseries.

The third big tourist attraction, besides the beaches around Aïn Diab is the great mosque Hassan II, built in 1993, the old monarch's greatest legacy. Bigger than St Peter's Basilica in Rome with the capacity to house St Paul's Cathedral in its entrance hall, the mosque cost in the region of 800 million US dollars (£450 million) to build, fully funded by public subscription – Christians and Jews as well as Muslims. It sits on the seafront with its 656 foot minaret visible 20 miles out to sea. 20,000 people can fit in the building and it is the only working mosque in Morocco that is also accessible to non-Muslims.

Part of the big tourist plan for the city, is to develop the area around the great mosque into a tourist zone complete with sea facing hotels, restaurants, cafés and a world class conference and exhibition centre. There is also talk of a 10 station light railway running along the Corniche just west of the mosque. 40-50 new hotels are planned for the city as a whole, adding a further 10,000 beds. There are also funds being injected into restoring the old medina and the public parks as well as some of the more striking art deco buildings.

For expatriates living and working in Casablanca, golf and tennis dominate the leisure scene. Royal Golf d'Anfa, located in the swish western suburb of Anfa, has an 18 and a 9 hole course and plans are underway to build a new golf course in the city. There are tennis courts in the 5 star hotels, the beach clubs along the Corniche and in Parc de la Ligue Arabe, to the south of the centre. There are two large hypermarkets Marjane and a wholesale Macro as well as a large Marché Central just off Boulevard Mohammed V, which sells a wide selection of fresh produce including Atlantic caught fish with several greasy spoon type fish cafés adjacent. Along Boulevard d'Anfa, there are many French style boutiques with stores such as Carré Blanc and for children, Sergent Major. Over a third of Casablanca's population is under 15 years of age, as the endless stream of pushchairs parading up and down Boulevard de la Corniche will testify. There are child-friendly elements to the city, such as children's play areas in the Parc de la Ligue Arabe, and swimming pools and playgrounds along the beachfront in Ain Diab. There are two American-style English speaking schools; the American School in the Quartier Californie and the George Washington Academy, both taking children from nursery age up to twelfth grade.

Properties

The majority of foreigners buying properties in Casablanca are individuals or families, who have relocated to the city for work. It is not an obvious choice for second homebuyers looking for a holiday home or upcoming pensioners seeking a peaceful spot to retire to. There is a market for buy-to-let style properties, due to the high number of foreigners looking to rent for the duration of their business contracts and it is still possible to find apartments in downtown Casablanca for around 600,000 dh (£37,000), which would suit single people or couples. As some of the regional government's tourism plans come to fruition, there are expected to be a greater number of tourists staying in the city as opposed to simply passing through. Whether this will increase the demand for holiday-let style properties, however, is questionable especially with the large number of new hotels being built along the beachfront and in the city centre. Would your holiday property be able to compete with the hotels? Would it have something unusual/special much like the riads/dars in tourist towns of Essaouira and Marrakech, that would make it a more interesting/attractive place to stay than one of the many hotels?

Five years ago, property prices in Casablanca were higher than in any other part of Morocco. They have now dropped into third place after Marrakech and Essaouira. The choice of properties, tend to range from upmarket family style villas in the leafy suburbs to apartments and duplexes closer to the city centre. Art deco style buildings generate the most interest while there is little demand for properties in the Quartier des Habous or new medina. The buying of land is not a common option in Casablanca as there is not much left to buy within the urban perimeter. Outside the perimeter, (which takes about 1.5 hours to cross in a car), much of the land is agricultural, so a VNA is required (see *What Type of Property to Buy?*). The majority of properties within the urban perimeter have titles, so purchasing is generally straightforward.

The most exclusive areas to live are within the golden triangle, which incorporates the quartier of Racine, Boulevard Al Massira and Boulevard d'Anfa. This is just west of the city centre and the location of many of the city's most upmarket boutiques. Apartments and more recently, duplexes are the main properties in this area. Prices tend to range from 1.2 million dh (£75,000) for a two bedroom apartment up to 6 million dh (£370,000) for a 4-5 bedroom duplex.

An upcoming area is Roche Noire, close to the port en route to Mohammedia. Here it is still possible to find properties costing around 4000-5000 dh (£250-300) per sq m.

The villa region tends to be around the suburbs of Quartier Californie, Aïn Diab, Anfa, Bouskoura en route to Marrakech and Route d'Azemmour in the direction of El Jadida. Villas in these areas are large - 250sq m and upwards - with several bedrooms, terraces, garden, servant's quarters and swimming pool. Prices tend to range from 3 million dh (£187,000) to 11 million dh (£600,000).

The Boulevard de la Corniche has recently become a more popular place to live due to an increased number of businesses moving to the area. This is also likely to become even more sought after with the upcoming tourist developments along the coastline, as will the area around the great mosque Hassan II.

MOHAMMEDIA

Mohammedia, which until 1960 was known as Fedala, lies 25 kilometres north of Casablanca and doubles up as both a large port specialising in petroleum and oil and a summer coastal resort, with what many say is the best beach in Morocco. Inhabitants of Casablanca escape the big city at weekends, for the 3 kilometres of sandy beach, tree lined avenues, the Ibn Batouta yacht marina, 18 hole Mohammedia Royal Golf Club, casino and race course. Sailing and fishing conditions are excellent – and there are a number of 5 star hotels to accommodate a highly affluent clientele. The resort is accessible either by the coastal road or the motorway from Casablanca and Rabat and has its own train station with frequent trains to/from Casablanca.

Mohammedia's port has been active since the 14th century, frequented by ships from the Mediterranean coast. In 1773, Sidi ben Mohammed built the kasbah, which is still inhabited today. In the 1920's only around 2500 people lived in Fedala exclusively inside the kasbah. It was not until 1960 when the town was renamed Mohammedia by Mohammed V, that it revved up into an industrial town/playground for the rich with several European oil companies kick starting a period of investment and growth. The town currently has a population of around 200,000, which increases dramatically during the summer months.

Properties

Until recently, most people wishing to own property in Mohammedia have bought land and built their own villas. There is, however, not much land now left to buy, so the buying of modern villas /apartments is becoming the trend. As the town is small, any of the boulevards leading away from the kasbah and down to the beach are considered popular places to buy with 'downtown' being anywhere between the train station to the east of the town and the port to the west. Villas and apartments tend to be low rise and white with either flat roofs or terracotta pitched roofs and there are clusters of forest and palm trees interspersed throughout. 2 bedroom apartments close to the beach tend to sell for around 750,000 dh (£45,000), villas with swimming pool, gardens, 3+ bedrooms and proximity to the sea range in price from 2 million (£125,000) to 6 million dh (£375,000). The stretch of coast between Mohammedia and Rabat is currently being developed and there are some good opportunities for investment, some refer to this area as an embryonic Costa del Sol, There are some very good beaches such as Skhirate (site of the king's summer palace), Essanoubar and Mansouria. Bouznika Bay is a purpose built resort with a 9 soon to be 18 hole golf course, a large lake, vineyards and soon a marina. Compared to Mohammedia, property here is expensive (add an extra million dirham or £62,000, to property prices) as it has been built specifically with luxury and affluence in mind.

Estate Agents

TB Immobilier, 22 Résidence Nakhil, Avenue des F.A.R, 20800 Mohammedia; ☎ 023 32 27 34/061 13 44 65; fax 023 32 27 35; e-mail tbimmobilier@yahoo.fr. Specialises in property in Mohammedia and Casablanca.

Vernet Immobilier, 158 Blvd d'Anfa, Casablanca; ☎ 022 36 88 66; fax 022 36 90 89; www.vernetis.com. A French run estate agency (limited English) with properties in Casablanca, Mohammedia and Bouznika.

CHAOUIA-OUARDIGHA

Population: 1.5 million
*Area:*16,760sq km
Regional capital: Settat
Main areas: Benslimane

The region of Chaouia-Ouardigha lies in the centre-east of Morocco, 120km east of Casablanca, bordering the region of Rabat-Salé to its northwest and the agricultural hinterlands of Marrakech and Beni Mellal to its east. It is the country's largest producer of phosphates and the heartland of the ancient Rehamna tribe of nomadic Arabs who ruled the plains for almost 400 years fighting off sultans and allying themselves with the French in the 20th century.

There is little demand for the Chaouia-Ouardigha plains nowadays, in fact more people are trying to get out of the region than enter it with the land in between the three main cities of Benslimane, Settat and Khouribga referred to as the 'triangle of death'. In 1999, 10 people from one village in the Chaouia-Ouardigha region drowned whilst attempting to illegally emigrate from Morocco. This was followed by a further 37 people in 2003 from the same village and 60 more in 2004, again from the same place. Despite these tragedies, the region still has the highest number of migrants in Morocco with the remaining population largely consisting of women and children. The main problem is that, besides the phosphates industry, which does not employ a large workforce, there is very little other industry in the region and unemployment levels are high.

The only area of any note among the flat, arid plains largely dominated by spoil heaps from the millions of tonnes of phosphate-rich rock extracted each year, is Benslimane, which lays claim to its own 9 hole golf course set among flowers, eucalyptus trees and tamarisk, and a 12,000 hectare cork oak forest.

DOUKKALA ABDA

Population: 1.93 million
Area: 13,285sq km
Regional capital: Azemmour
Main areas: Safi, Oualidia, El Jadida, Azemmour

The region of Doukkala Abda lies on the fertile Doukkala and Abda plains, bordered to its west and northwest, by 300km of Atlantic Ocean with sandy, white beachfronts, interspersed with woodlands, dunes and lagoons. To the south it runs against the edge of Essaouira province and eastwards as far as the neighbouring industrial lands of Settat. It is not a large region but being sandwiched between the Atlantic and the phosphate-rich territory of Khouribga, Youssoufia and Ben Guerir and in close proximity to Agadir, Marrakech and Casablanca, gives it an important industrial role to play. The two main cities in the region are Safi and El Jadida, both have large ports responsible for 30% of Morocco's exports. Fishing is the main industry in addition to a number of chemical, pharmaceutical and energy plants. Pottery is also a key industry in Safi. The coastline along the region is known as Al Jorfal Asfar, which means 'yellow coast'. This is because the soil is made up of yellow clay, which has turned Safi into one of the three main ceramic centres of Morocco (along with the Bou Rgreg River region in Rabat and Fes). In Safi, potters still use the identical techniques that their ancestors used including the same ancient kilns. It is from here that the green tiles in evidence on so many of Morocco's mosques and eminent buildings, originate.

The nearest international airports are Casablanca (100km from El Jadida), Marrakech (160km from Safi) and, in theory Essaouira (150km from Safi) but flights here are still very erratic.

Despite having some of Morocco's most lovely beaches and an interesting history, the region of Doukkala-Abda is not a major tourist destination. Many foreigners claim to living in Morocco for several years before discovering such paradise hotspots as Oualidia with its white sand lagoon. Reasons for this are most probably because much of the old and interesting is masked by the smoke emanating from factory chimneys and heavy goods trucks filled with phosphates. It could also be because this stretch of coast away from the lagoons, can be a tad nippy/windy for dipping not to mention overshadowed by the more publicised bathing resorts of Essaouira and Agadir.

That said, the stretch of coast between Azemmour and El Jadida will, by the end of 2007, have undergone a major transformation, being one of the sites chosen by the government to develop into a coastal resort as part of the Plan Azur. International property developers, Kerzner with Societé Maroc Emirates Arabs Unis de Developpement and Caisse de Dépôt et de Gestion are transforming 3km of the currently empty beachfront into a 5.3 billion dh (£3.3 million) resort with an 18 hole golf course, 600 bed hotel, restaurants, casinos and private residences.

The climate of the Doukkala-Abda region is semi arid kept at bay from the soaring temperatures of the interior by cool Atlantic breezes and the chain of Atlas Mountains. Rainfall is at its heaviest during the winter months (Nov-March) with around 180mm on average per month. Summer temperatures tend to hover around the 28°C mark with refreshing winds while in winter these drop to around 12°C.

Cuisine

Sardines, sardines and more sardines are a frequent visitor to the dinner plates of many of the region's inhabitants. Sardines are in abundance in the region. Shared between Essaouira, Agadir and Safi, over 350,000 tons of sardines are caught a year with the majority canned and exported from Safi. Most commonly, sardines are grilled on street side barbecues and served with chips or cooked in tagines with potatoes. Shrimp and red lobster are also common as are spicy mussels and fish couscous. Meat and chicken tagines with preserved lemon, the Moroccan staple, play a big role in the region's cooking, but instead of simply salting the lemons, the local way is to preserve them with cinnamon sticks, coriander seeds and cloves adding more depth to the flavour. Oysters are a year round delicacy in the lagoon resort of Oualidia, the oyster capital of Morocco. Over 200 tonnes are caught here each year and are readily available, always fresh and cheap to buy.

SAFI

Safi suffers from something of an image problem. The first glimpse most people get of the city is the huge chemical plant that hogs the skyline followed by the overpowering smell of sardines from the fish packing factories as you head in from the south.

While this is something of a nose/eyesore, it is not in anyway indicative of the modern, architecturally alluring city that lies beyond. Being off the main tourist trail, Safi is a peaceful, hassle-free city to wander around blending the ancient walls of the medina in the lower part of town, with the tree-lined, wide boulevards of the new town up the hills to the east.

The history of Safi dates back to the Phoenician and Roman days when it was an important port town, known as Asfi. With the arrival of the Arabs and Islam, Safi was one of the first places in Morocco to embrace the new doctrine and the Almohads in the twelfth century, turned the town into a spiritual centre. In 1508, Safi was seized by the Portuguese coming up from Essaouira, who built a citadel and renovated the old Almohad kasbah. In 1541, their rule ended abruptly under the Saadian onslaught and they left, demolishing what they could of the city. The Saadians built the Grand Mosque, which still stands today and turned Safi into a major port, trading, primarily in copper and sugar.

The rebuilding of Essaouira in the early 18th century marked the end of a prosperous period for Safi as all external trade became concentrated around the new port further south. The city was not again revived until the 20th century when the huge phosphate processing plant and the sardine packing factory were built, employing a large number of people and turning Safi into an important industrial zone.

Safi Today

The governor of Safi, Mr Sabbari Hassani has great plans for the city and is keen to transform Safi into a happening place much like its close neighbour, Essaouira. While the potential is there in terms of beaches, historic monuments and perks like outdoor fish restaurants and good (read ferocious) waves for surfing, the superstructure is currently lacking. There are 5 classified hotels and 16 unclassified, the majority 3 star providing a total of just 1000 beds. With the exception of a number of pottery shops that fill the streets of the medina with plates, vases and urns sold for fair/fixed prices, there is a dearth of other tourist-style outlets stocked with the Moroccan furnishings, that foreign visitors love to buy. The city beach suffers from pollution, being a general drop off point for much of the industrial waste, not to mention the trawlers returning with net loads of sardines. The governor has implemented beach cleaning into his tourist strategy, so things here are improving, but it is unlikely Safi beach will ever hold the same appeal as the beaches a little to the north of the city such as Lalla Fatna (15km from Safi) and Cap Bedouzza (23km from Safi), which remain blissfully clean, undeveloped and in the case of Lalla Fatna, protected from winds by steep cliffs.

What sets Safi apart from other destinations is the *Colline des Potiers* (Potter's Hill), filled with artisans working their clay and the ancient wood fired kilns. Safi is undoubtedly the best place in Morocco to buy ceramics. It takes the industry very seriously being the first place in Africa to have a school devoted to the traditional teaching of ceramics (*Centre de Qualification Professionnelle des Arts Traditionnels de Céramique de Safi*) and has won numerous international gold medals for its ceramic works.

Unlike Essaouira, Safi benefits from being on the train network, easily connected to Marrakech (3 hours) and Casablanca (4hr45mins). It has been chosen along with Agadir, Casablanca and Tangier, to be a cruise destination, with 200,000 cruise tourists expected by 2015. This will do little to boost the hotel/holiday-let industry or to reduce the pollution levels around the port, but it will add to the local artisan/restaurant economy.

Properties

Safi's medina is small and roughly triangular in shape with the Kechla (citadel) at the eastern end, a monstrous, heavily fortified structure with small windows. Until 1990, this was a prison, but now it houses ceramic exhibitions. The main street running through the medina is Rue du Souq, where all the shops are located particularly for a local market. Sea views are to the west of the medina. There is a higher level of crime in the run-down medina reducing its attractiveness and causing many people to move to the ville nouvelle. Most properties are in dire need of restoration but can be bought for very low prices, around 150,000 dh (£9,000) and as the government is seeking investment there are few rules or regulations regarding the building works that can be done on such properties. In the ville nouvelle, prices are still incredibly reasonable. The city has not succumbed to the mad growth of apartment blocks in place of older houses, so there are few apartments available and lots of two storey, square houses running alongside the palm lined streets. A 100sq m plot of land in the ville nouvelle costs around 120,000-140,000 dh (£7500-8750). Large 600sq m villas close to the sea cost around 2.2 million dh (£135,000). Land close to the beaches around Safi, is also well priced. In Lalla Fatna, it is possible to buy land for around 200 dh (£12) per sq m increasing to around 600 dh/sq m (£37) as you near Oualidia.

OUALIDIA

It is to Oualidia (60km north of Safi), the oyster and clam capital, that families from Marrakech and Casablanca head for weekends to stay in bourgeois villas, local hotels or campsites as the lagoon beach is safe, warm and utterly pollution free to swim/sail/windsurf in, making it ideal for children. Shaped like a crescent, the golden sandy beach is hidden from the small town of Oualidia (population 4000) by a wooded hill interspersed with villas. It is an idyllic resort with turquoise waters frequented by dolphin and migrating pink flamingoes, black-winged stilts and spoonbills. In the town itself, there is what is left of the 17th century crumbling kasbah built by the Saadian Sultan El Oualid, who used the lagoon as his only safe access into the sea and a deserted, neglected but still closely guarded summer palace overlooking one of the sea entrances into the lagoon that belonged to King Mohammed V (the present king's grandfather).

Surprisingly, the resort is not greatly frequented by foreigners even though it is heaving with Moroccans between June-September who dine on seafood delicacies, fish brochettes and traditional tagines in the local hotels and restaurants.

Delightful as it is, the town is in dire need of some infrastructural tlc. With a year round population of just 4000 but descended upon by 30,000 holidaymakers for weekends and extended periods over the summer months, the drains are old and worn, prone to overflowing and at risk of spreading disease. In addition, the road network and local roads are inadequate, little more than tracks in places. Government funding is being sought by local residents to improve conditions especially as Oualidia is a popular tourist resort but for the time being, in amongst the luxurious villas and paradise views there can be unpleasant sites and smells, which need to be addressed quite crucially.

Properties

The most sought after locations are those overlooking the lagoon where there are already a number of luxury villas, many of which are rented out as holiday lets for an average of 4000 dh-6000 dh (£250-375) per week for 4 person occupancy. Villas, though privately built by individuals are typically affluent Moroccan in style, whitewashed two storey buildings, with large terraces, balconies, dome shaped windows surrounded by high walls with grand entrance ways and small gardens. Land next to the sea costs in the region of 2000 dh/sq m (£125), 4-6 bedroom villas overlooking the lagoon typically sell for around 2.5 million dh (£150,000) and 2 bedroom apartments with swimming pools and terraces with views out to sea around 740,000 dh (£46,000).

EL JADIDA

El Jadida springs into life for half the year, during the spring and summer months but for the rest of the year becomes a little forlorn, bereft of the crowds, music, honking horns and relaxed, leisurely pace that gives it a holiday-resort style feel. The Portuguese founded El Jadida in the early 16th century starting out with a fort and then expanding into the current sized town, which they named Magazan. They built what is now one of El Jadida's most celebrated sites, the Portuguese Cistern, which sits in the centre of the old Portuguese citadel.

El Jadida was one of the few sites along the Atlantic coast that did not fall into the hands of the Saadians despite furious battles, but it was relinquished in the mid 18th century to Sultan Sidi Mohammed ben Abdullah. A Muslim quarter was built to the west of the Portuguese old town away from the sea. The Portuguese old town was deserted for the next 100 years until Sultan Rahman transferred many of the Jews from Azemmour into the empty streets and homes and renamed the town El Jadida (meaning New One). During the French protectorate, the town was revived as an administrative centre and seaside resort.

El Jadida Today

El Jadida nowadays is an attractive prosperous city, thriving on its agricultural hinterlands and a healthy textile industry. In 2006 the much-awaited 100km Casablanca-El Jadida stretch of motorway opened incorporating the city into the highway network linking it to Tangier, Agadir, Marrakech and Casablanca. This will bring more cargo to El Jadida's port, removing some of the pressure from Casablanca's overstretched facility. There is a train station in the ville nouvelle with regular trains to/from Casablanca (1hr 20). The city's population almost doubles to 350,000 during the summer months when city dwellers from Casa-blanca and Marrakech head to the 16km of sandy coast that lines the eastern edge of the city. Many own holiday chalets close to the sea, others rent houses/apartments and others camp on the beach. A wide, red paved boulevard dotted with cafés, runs along next to the beach lined with palm trees, ending in sand dunes and a forested nature reserve. It is along here that most of the evening strolls take place where people go to watch and to be watched. El Jadida has an incredibly relaxed feel. Moroccan men (uncharacteristically) wander around in shorts and flip-flops, bars (uncharacteristically) are filled till the early hours and people of both sexes (uncharacteristically) hang out together in groups.

The reason most foreign tourists visit El Jadida (and there are not a great deal) is for the old Portuguese city with its churches, ramparts and bastions. It was recently given World Heritage status by UNESCO. Though devoid of many inhabitants and crumbling in parts (but gradually being restored), it is one of the best-preserved examples of ancient Portuguese architecture in Morocco.

The ville nouvelle is modern and white with buildings rarely exceeding three stories high. There is a scattering of attractive, ornate art deco buildings in dire need of a nip and tuck but much work has gone into improving the city. Grassy squares with benches and sandy pathways, give the city a feeling of space along with wide, very tall palm lined streets.

With the arrival of the new highway and the large new coastal development being built a couple of kilometers north of the city, El Jadida has great plans to become a tourist destination for international visitors. While the city beach suffers rather from pollution from time to time, the beaches to the north and south are highly recommended, particularly Sidi Bouzid around 5km north west of the city. Lined with bungalows and smart villas, the sandy, clean bay, which curves around in a semi circle plays host to a couple of restaurants serving excellent seafood and large numbers of Moroccan campers. It is, however, a lot less crowded than the city beach.

7km north of the city is the El Jadida Royal Golf Club, an 18 hole course designed by Cabell B Robinson with lakes, beaches and dunes for views.

Properties

Properties in the old Portuguese city (medina) offer the most interesting range of styles and are likely to appreciate more over the years as the medina is restored into a better condition. Now is most probably the best time for bargains as the medina will soon start attracting both more tourists with those coming for day trips from the new Plan Azur coastal development just north of El Jadida and for those on UNESCO 'World Heritage' tours and more foreign buyers as this stretch of coast becomes more developed. From a holiday-let point of view, you have the advantage of being close to the Citerne Portuguese (Portuguese Cistern), which is fascinating in its own right and in near proximity to the sea. Properties in the medina are currently selling for around 335,000 dh (£20,000) for a small, unrenovated traditional house with views over the ramparts, 520,000 dh (£32,500) for a renovated apartment opposite the Citerne Portuguese and 750,000 dh (£47,000) for a large (200sq m) renovated property close to the Grand Mosque.

In the ville nouvelle, new, whitewashed 3 bedroom apartments of 95sq m with views over the sea are selling for around 540,000 dh (£33,000) and 100sq m 2 bedroom apartments with views over the park in front of the sea are costing 740,000 dh (£46,000). 3 bedroom villas in the centre of the ville nouvelle with swimming pool, 5 minutes from the beach are selling for 800,000 dh (£50,000). New 2 bedroom apartments next to Sidi Bouzid beach north west of El Jadida with communal pool and private garden are selling for 71,000 dh (£44,000) while land to the north of El Jadida next to the sea and close to the golf course, costs in the region of 800-1000 dh/sq m (£50-62).

AZEMMOUR

Flanked to the north and south by the mighty cities of Casablanca and El Jadida and sitting on the great Oum er Rbia River, the pretty, old town of Azemmour (15km north of El Jadida) with its 38,000 inhabitants and speciality in embroidery, used to get forgotten altogether with some claiming there to be fewer tourists visiting Azemmour than any other Moroccan coastal town. This is all likely to change very soon with the new 5.3 billion dh Plan Azur coastal development happening virtually on its doorstep. Already the town is starting to spruce itself up in preparation, not that its appeal lies in its being too ship-shape. Dating back over 500 years, the red walls of the medina were built by the Portuguese who ruled the town for only 28 years before being summoned to concentrate their efforts at El Jadida. The town then fell into decline until the 19th century when it regained importance as a fishing port and centre for rope-makers, shoe-makers, blacksmiths, tanners, potters and carpenters (as well as jewels from the Jewish community). As Casablanca and El Jadida enlarged, Azemmour became unable to compete and sunk into the backwaters where it has pretty much remained since.

The most notable features of the town are the red ramparts, which sit on the banks of the river interspersed with European-style gates and the blue and white low roofed houses of the medina, positioned on narrow concrete alleyways. There is a particularly fascinating Jewish quarter (mellah), which has been largely deserted since the departure of the Jews in the 1950's with many of the old houses and artisan workshops crying out for restoration. Azemmour medina is different from many because it has its souks located outside the walls making the old city purely residential.

Properties

The property market in Azemmour's medina is starting to pick up as the completion date for the Plan Azur development (2007) looms. Currently there is only one maison d'hôtes in action, the very lovely L'Oum Errebia located on the edge of the medina overlooking the river but several more are in the throes of renovation led by a large French majority. Being so close to El Jadida, the El Jadida Royal Golf club and the new golf club being built for the Plan Azur development, surfing beaches and eucalyptus forests in addition to having Casablanca with its hub airport and boutiques just 80km north makes this is a very promising place to buy. It is highly likely you should get some excellent bargains especially as so much of the medina is in a crumbling state. Property prices for traditional houses are currently being quoted between 240,000 dh (£15,000) and 450,000 dh (£28,000). Bear in mind most properties will be unrenovated so for budgeting purposes, it is worth doubling the asking price for a more accurate idea of how much the property and works will cost.

Estate Agents

Jadida Locations, no 9, Rue 8 Cité Portugaise 24000, El Jadida; ☎ (in France) 04 94 87 43 35; www.jadidalocations.com/sommaire.htm. Properties in El Jadida, Oualidia and coastal surrounds.

Les Jardins de la Lagune, Oualidia, ☎ 022 23 14 14; fax 022 99 37 83. Marketing a new property development in Oualidia.

marocreservation.com; If you click on Real Estate, you will find properties for sale in Safi and its surrounds.

Moroccan Properties, Immueble El Khalil, Avenue Hassan II, Marrakech 40000; ☎ 44 43 04 65; fax 044 43 04 30; www.moroccanproperties.com. Works mainly in Marrakech and Tangier but will soon be listing properties in Oualidia.

FES-BOULEMANE

Population: 1 million
Area: 20,000sq km
Regional capital: Fes
Main areas: Fes el Bali, Fes el Jdid, Sefrou

Bordering the Middle Atlas, the region of Fes-Boulemane is in the northern centre of Morocco comprising part of the green rolling countryside of the Sais plain, Morocco's most fertile and cultivated reach of land. 18% of the leafy, lush region is agricultural with the olive tree playing a key role in the local economy. 39% is forested with great swathes of the Middle Atlas covered by a blanket of oak and cedar trees, one of the last suitable habitats for the Barbary macaque. While the countryside features lakes, gorges, waterfalls, sulphur springs at Moulay Yakoub, apple orchards and mountains, it is not a 'must-see' on the itineraries of most visitors to the region who tend to get sucked inside the city walls of Fes without venturing out. It also rarely features on the itineraries of the outward-bound who are drawn by tour operators to trek, quad bike, paraglide etc in the High Atlas peaks and/or the desert. As a result the arguably more gentle countryside of the Middle Atlas is yet to be explored. As with much of Morocco, however, there is a feeling of anticipation in the region for greater things to come. A joint development programme between central and regional government was announced in July 2005 for the promotion of Fes Boulemane to international tourists using Fes as the principal draw but aiming to attract visitors to the wider region.

The climate is seasonal with cool (15°C), bright but short winters and hot, dry summers, (40°C), which tend to last for around nine months of the year.

Cuisine

Fes is the culinary capital of Morocco, it is purported to be the birthplace of the national dish bastila (pronounced pasteeya) (see *Living in Morocco*) and is home to the majority of the highly skilled warqa pastry chefs crucial to the preparation of a good bastila. Fassi cooking dates back to the 12th and 13th century and is admired throughout Morocco with Fassi women considered the best cooks and a Fassi wife, the best prize any man can hope for. Its culinary expertise is largely due to the luscious surrounding landscape, which grows olives, beans, cereals, oranges, lemons and grapes in abundance and farms sheep, goats and cattle delivering produce into the old city by donkey cart. It is also due to the richer, highly educated population, who over the centuries have been able to travel, gathering spices and culinary knowledge from Andalucia, France and Turkey. In addition, many Fassi families also had large numbers of black African slaves and rural Berber women from the mountains, working for them, who would throw their own influence into the cooking.

Fes is renowned for its sweetened dishes and elaborate recipes. Harira soup is sweetened with dates, the traditional Friday dish of couscous will be crowned with caramelized onions and lamb, marinated in a ginger base, while the delicate flavours of the Fes tagine is considered the most delicious as it is the one region where ingredients are not fried before cooking, so the flavour is best conserved.

FES

Two thirds of the Fes Boulemane population and 96% of industry is located in and around the city of Fes, the region's capital and prior to the French protectorate, the capital of Morocco. Fes is divided into Fes el Bali - old Fes, Fes El Jdid - new Fes (actually, not new at all, almost as ancient as old Fes) and the tree-lined leafy boulevards of the ville nouvelle. Where Marrakech has its roots firmly in Africa, Fes is embedded in the Arab world. It was Morocco's first Islamic city and is still regarded as the country's religious and cultural capital.

The oldest site, Fes el Bali, was built by Moulay Idriss II, direct descendant of the prophet, Mohammed, in memory of his father whose last wish was to create a capital for the kingdom he had devoted his life to. In 818, early on in the development of the city, 800 Arab refugees expelled from neighbouring Spain by the Christians were invited by Idriss to make the city their home on the right bank of the River Fes, an area still known as the Andalucian Quarter. Seven years later, 2000 persecuted Arab families arrived from the sacred Islamic city of Kairouan in Tunisia. They were invited to settle on the left bank of the river. A thousand years on, the cultural split between the Arab and Spanish settlers is still apparent in the layout and design of the old medina. The families brought with them superior craftsmanship, intellectualism and trading expertise that led to the rise of Fes as the Moroccan capital and a centre of industrial and commercial growth.

In the 13th century, during the reign of the second sultan of the Merenid Dynasty, Abou Yusuf Yacqub, the newer city of Fes el Jdid was built next door to the old as a garrison town to house troops loyal to the sultan, it was also home to a Royal Palace and high ranking Merendid officials. A mellah was also constructed, protected by high walls, still visible today, to accommodate the increasing number of Jewish settlers then arriving in the city.

It was in Fes that the treaty was signed between Morocco, France and Spain leading to the installation of the French in 1912 much to the anger of the local population. French rule did have the decency, however, to acknowledge the historical significance of Fes. The French general, Lyautey, implemented policies to protect the ancient medina from Moroccan plans to demolish and modernise it thereby preserving it in its original form. The French built their ville nouvelle outside the city based around two main streets known today as Avenue Hassan II and Boulevard Mohammed V. The ville nouvelle, though nowadays sprawling far into the suburbs was designed with the wide, tree lined boulevards and art deco buildings typical of the villes nouvelles throughout Morocco. All administrative proceedings were transferred from old Fes into the ville nouvelle rendering the old medina redundant.

People from Fes are known as *Fassi*. They are regarded as the intellectual and economic bourgeoisie of Morocco, heading up most government ministries and esteemed by their fellow countrymen for their enhanced knowledge of art, cuisine and etiquette. In Fes, the craftsmen are the virtuosos, the most skilled in their trade, having passed down their expertise through the generations. Like the Parisians, Fassis believe themselves to be largely superior to their countrymen, who they see in comparison as rustic and unrefined, even beggars will occasionally return charitable donations if they are considered below the going beggarly rate. Once revered as a place of high learning, rich Arabs from around the world would send their sons to Fes to ensure they received a sound education.

Fes Today

During the French protectorate, Fes was demoted from its position as country's capital leading to the desertion of many Fassis from their home city to the new capital, Rabat and the commercial centre of Casablanca.

This led to a brain drain in the region and an influx of rural migrants into the medina, feeding off the low property prices. The changed demographics in the old town from rich merchants and educated elite to country folk too poor to improve the city led to the crumbling, collapse and deterioration of many of the buildings, which remains a major problem today.

In 1981 Fes obtained UNESO World Heritage status, which as well as giving much needed funding, put the city back in the public eye and inspired international and local organisations to restore the old medina back to its former glory. Satellite towns and industrial parks were built on the outskirts of the ville nouvelle to ease the overcrowding by luring inhabitants out of the medina to the bright lights of the all mod con apartment, many cherished monuments have been restored and rich Fassi families are gradually returning to transform their homes into much needed guesthouses or small hotels. Fes el Bali and Fes el Jdid are now in business primarily for the tourist trade as well as for the 200,000 residents still living inside the ancient walls.

Traditional industries such as flour and textile mills, oil processing, soap factories, tanneries and crafts, remain, as they have done for centuries, central to the economy, although unemployment in line with the rest of the country, sits at around 19%.

Compared to other parts of Morocco, Fes remains a relatively unexplored area for the British. Some say this is because the conservative city lacks the cosmopolitan hospitality of its southern counterparts. While this is true, the most likely reason is quite simply that until recently, few people knew about Fes. Compared to the tourist regions of Marrakech and Agadir and the commercial capital of Casablanca, it receives very little publicity. Until Nov 2004, there were no direct flights to the city from the UK and even now, flights only run for some of the year. There are only 80 registered hotels/guesthouses in the medina, which considering its size is very few.

For those people who do know Fes, opinions are divided between those who love it, its rich culture, ancient ways and ramshackle opulence and those who hate it for its smell, its arrogance and its 'foreignness'.

Fes el Bali

Fes el Bali is the oldest and largest medieval city in the world. The whitewashed medina was built in a valley by the banks of the River Fes and is surrounded by green hills. It spans 300 hectares of which there are around 550 inhabitants per hectare. Unlike other medinas, such as in Essaouira, which have been logically built in a grid-like layout, Fes el-Bali has simply evolved over the centuries as new houses have been built up and down the surrounding hills and passageways added. This means that there is no rhyme or reason to its design. Alleyways lead off main thoroughfares, some ending in doorways, others in brick walls, For first (and second) time visitors, the medina is almost impossible to navigate without the help of a guide. There is no point hunting around for a map as no such thing exists. One of the more reliable ways of telling your location is to see whether or not you are heading up or down hill as much of the medina is on a steep gradient. The old city is split on either side of the River Fes. On one side is the ancient Andalucian Quarter and on the other, joined by just two bridges, the more recently built, more touristically interesting and more exclusive, Karaouyine Quarter.

If Fes el Bali is your first port of call in Morocco, you could find it intimidating with its crowded, cobbled streets, dawdling mules and overpowering stench of pigeon dung and fermented chaff used to treat the animal hides, that wafts across from the ancient but fully functioning leather tanneries. Note: there is talk of a filtration system being installed in the old medina to reduce the smell, which is a shame as it is an alluring feature of Fes. Many of the streets are no wider than 6 feet, with six storey high buildings and all street signs written in Arabic. This is where its appeal lies, along with its spectacular properties hidden behind towering doorways, its elaborately decorated mosques including the Karaouyine Mosque, second biggest in North Africa and able to accommodate 20,000 people, Koranic schools (merdersas) with courtyards paved in marble and the covered market (Kissaria) with its vast array of little stores and workshops. Hours can be spent simply watching craftsmen at work; carpenters, goldsmiths, embroiderers, engravers, weavers, blacksmiths often squeezed into spaces little bigger than an elevator. The streets are alive with the sounds and smells of a city unchanged in centuries. Goat's feet, quinces and fresh cheese sell on shabby wooden boxes and barrows overflow with avocadoes, artichokes and mint. Altogether there are 10,539 little shops in the old medina selling anything and everything from pig's trotters, offal and spices to tambourines, jewellery and doors.

The best way to learn your way around is by getting to know your own neighbourhood (quartier). The medina is made up of 187 quartiers, each one required, by law, to have a mosque, a Koranic school, a communal oven where families can bake their own bread, a public bath (hammam) and a water fountain - both the water fountains and the hammams are served by a 70km traditional water supply network, running throughout the medina. There are 4000 water fountains in the old medina. A large number of households obtain their water from these fountains, as private water supply into the home is expensive.

Fes el Bali has won accolades for being the world's largest contiguous car and bike free zone based on population size with just one road penetrating the city walls that does not enter into the heart of the medina and offers only minimal parking opportunities.

Fes el Jdid

Fes el Jdid is the 'newer' medina built in the 13th century, 10 minutes walk to the west of Fes el Bali. It was originally built as a military town to house troops loyal to the Merenid sultan, so its architecture is much more plain and functional than that of Fes el Bali. Half of Fes el Jdid, over 80 hectares, is taken up with the Royal Palace, accessed via Place des Alouites, which includes within its walls, a mosque, a merdersa, pavilions, squares and gardens. Compared to Fes el Bali, there is little of historic or cultural interest in Fes el Jdid and most tourists only pay the white-washed city a morning or afternoon's lip service before returning to the sights next door. Perhaps of most interest is the mellah, the Jewish compound, thought to be the largest in Morocco. The mellah was constructed by the Merenids to accommodate the Jews who they moved away from the outskirts of the Karaouyine mosque in order to create more space for the building of merdersas. It became a highly illustrious neighbourhood filled with jeweller's shops, synagogues and specific architecture (wooden balconies, high walls and windows with wrought iron grills), which to this day, even after the majority of Jews have left and the neighbourhood replaced by rural migrants, sets it apart from the rest of the medina.

Properties

The popularity of Fes as a place to buy and restore houses has only started to catch on over the last couple of years largely as a result of property prices in Marrakech having risen out of many would-be house buyers reach. The range of properties available to buy for the highly affordable prices makes it an exciting place to be. In fact, people are being actively encouraged to buy and restore properties here by the Agency for the Dedensification and Rehabilitation of Fes (ADER), which is largely responsible for improving the medina. Grant programmes sometimes come available to anyone involved in restoring riads, which you can obtain information about by visiting the ADER-Fes office, situated by Bab Al Makina.

When it comes to architectural style, Fes is where the intricate, opulent, elaborate and grand come together under one roof. Mosaic wall and floor tiles (*zelliges*), sculpted plasterwork above and below the windows and around the doorways, cedar wood doors and ceiling beams, decorative pillars, stained glass windows and wrought iron balconies. Traditional Fes colours are white with bottle green trimmings. The more prosperous the homeowner, the more elaborate the décor and in Fes, with its rich, affluent lineage, there is a vast array of houses palatial in their size and design.

The houses are traditionally riads and dars (see *What Type of Property to Buy?*) with walls made out of sand, bricks and lime with lime being used to enable the walls to breathe making the houses cooler in the summer and warmer in the winter. Riads tend to be much larger than similar style properties in other medinas. Ceilings are high, rooms are airy, archways and pillars are sculpted in plaster or swathed in mosaics. Some riads come with huge gardens in addition to spacious courtyards, which are enclosed within tall walls and often stuffed with orange/lemon trees and luscious grass.

In Fes, the older properties are in the centre of the medina, spiralling outwards, so that the most modern houses are on the outer edges. Which part of the medina you choose to buy in will dictate the age, style, size and amount of restoration needed. Despite being more residential and spacious than the Karaouiyine quarter, the Andalucian quarter is a less popular place to buy because properties are older and there is a greater amount of restoration needed. It is for this reason, however, that houses here are cheaper, so you get a lot more property for your money, 320,000-480,000 dh (£20,000-£30,000) for 3 bedroom/3 salons. Batha and Ziat on the outer rims of the medina are the 'Beverley Hills' quarters of Fes. Here, houses are more modern (20th century), large, close to parking and double the price of other areas, 1.5 million dh (£94,000). They do not however need much work done to them, which could even out the price a little more. Many house buyers choose properties in areas around 5-10 minutes walk inside the medina such as Wad Rchacha and Zak Al Bghal. These properties tend to be 17th-18th century, in need of some work but not too expensive to buy. Currently there are around 15 properties in this area, which have recently been restored by both foreigners and Moroccans.

Other popular areas are on the side streets off the two main thoroughfares of Talaa Kibera and Talaa Sghira, which have a range of old properties. These areas are not far from Bab Bou Jelood, the main entrance into the medina, so convenient for access to parking. Also, close by Aïn AzLitine, is an increasingly chic part of the medina where a large number of guesthouses are located. Please note that it is highly likely that properties you buy in the medina will be untitled (see *Fees, Contracts and Costs*)

Ville Nouvelle. Apartment blocks are a la mode in the ville nouvelle. Old houses are disappearing at a rapid pace and apartment blocks being thrown up in their place. The most sought after area is around the main streets of Blvd Mohammed V and Hassan II where 2 bedroom apartments are selling for between 400,000-600,000 dh (£25,000-37,000). Further out of town are the detached swanky villas, many newly built, similar in décor to the palace riads with floor to ceiling mosaics, decorative pillars and *bejmat* (half brick terracotta) floors. Many have large gardens and terraces and most are in neighbourhoods complete with pharmacy, small shop (*hanut*) and a private clinic. Around Champ de Course and Saada, these are selling for around 1.6million dh (£100,000) and upwards. The road out to Ifrane offers some of the most exclusive properties and there is talk of land in this area being turned into the Palmeraie of Fes, much like the highly elite Palmeraie of Marrakech. Currently land is selling for starting figures of around 1500 dh per sq m (£94) There is an 18-hole golf course along this route, Fes Royal Golf 17km out of town.

Sefrou. The ancient Jewish/Berber town of Sefrou, 30km south east of Fes and with a population of 45,000, is a possible location for keen walkers as it is nestled in the foothills of the Middle Atlas, close to waterfalls, hot springs and spectacular views. Few tourists currently visit Sefrou or its attractive woody surrounds, which means that prices, people and lifestyle are much more moderate. It actually existed as a city prior to Fes but never became one of the Imperial Cities. This does not mean that Sefrou is without charms that are often overlooked by its high quantity of street-side rubbish and its close proximity to the more exciting Fes, one key charm being that it is a lot cooler in the summer due to being high in the mountains. Until the 1950's, the town was one-third Jewish and much of the medina is taken up by the mellah, which has distinctively tall walled houses, wooden balconies and streets like rabbit warrens. A market runs every Thursday where Berber from the surrounding mountains come and sell their wares, artisans produce ironwork, carpentry and embroidery from little green booths lining the thoroughfares and every June, the streets come alive for the Cherry Harvest Festival which involves folk dancing, parades and music.

> While Sefrou will always live in the shadow of Fes, it should not be overlooked as a place to invest. The history of the town means that it has traditional houses of architectural interest around half the price of Fes 160,000-240,000 dh (£10-15,000), it enjoys the benefits (international airport, railway station, shops and restaurants) of a large city on its doorstep and has a pretty, whitewashed medina. As more investment is put into improving tourism to the Fes Boulemane region, Sefrou with its history and proximity to the mountains and wildlife will be a key beneficiary.

Estate Agents

Carre d'Azur, 16 Avenue Lalla Aicha, Champ de Courses, Fes, ☎ 055 93 02 92; www.carredazur.com. An English speaking French/Moroccan estate agency.

fesproperties.com; an American run estate agency specialising in properties in Fes medina and ville nouvelle.

houseinfez.com for information about buying a restoring property in Fes.

Fes Medina Consulting; e-mail medina@insidefesmedina.com; www.insidefes-medina.com. Property consultancy service helping foreigners buy houses in Fes.

Moroccan Homes, 43 Station Road, Thorpe on Hill, Lincoln LN6 9BS; ☎ 01522 535 052 or Calle Daire 46, Sedella Malaga, Spain; ☎ 95 25 08 961; e-mail info@Moroccan-homes.com; www.Moroccan-homes.com. English speaking agency with properties for sale in Fes.

GHARB-CHRARDA-BNI HSEN

Population: 1.6 million
Area: 8940sq km
Regional capital: Kenitra
Main areas: Kenitra

Gharb-Chrarda-Bni Hsen is one of the smallest regions in Morocco (around 1.2% of the surface area of the country) incorporating predominantly agricultural terrain (7900sq km) with around 68% of the population involved in farming. Running parallel to the Atlantic Ocean positioned between Larache in the north and the nation's capital, Rabat, the region incorporates a lake, a couple of beaches and 1250sq km of forest. To its east, it borders the region of Fes and Meknes, in close proximity to the ancient sites of Volubilis and Moulay Idriss. The principal city is Kenitra, which lies on the Sebou River and the main beach is Plage Mehdiya, 7km west. Positioned as it is in between the major cities of Casablanca, Tangier, Fes and Rabat means that the region benefits from an excellent road and railway network with a number of motorways and train connections to most parts of the country.

Despite being well connected, the region is not a popular one with holidaymakers, international homebuyers or foreign visitors, that is, with the exception of avid bird watchers who come to be awed by the plethora of migrant birdlife (over 200 species) that stop off to refuel at the fresh water Lac de Sidi Bourhaba whilst winging their way between Europe and sub–Saharan Africa. The 200 hectare lake runs alongside the Sebou estuary and is one of Morocco's few protected areas being almost the last place left in the world where it is possible to see marbled ducks.

The history of the region dates back to the Romans as is still apparent from the ancient sites of Thamusida and Banasa, close to Kenitra on the banks of the Sebou River, which were both towns that prospered into the third century AD. Still just about visible within the ancient walls are public baths and a temple. More recently, the history of the region revolves around Kenitra, which was built by the French resident general Lyautey in 1912 as a replacement port to Larache, which had been absorbed into the Spanish zone. Known as Port Lyautey, its aim was to channel trade from Meknes and Fes. It never really got going, however, having to compete with the port and industry in Casablanca. Port Lyautey was used by the US as a military base during World War II and expanded into a naval air station in 1951. The base was shared with the Royal Air Force of Morocco until the Gulf War, when the US personnel left and Morocco reduced the scale of its operations.

The agriculture-rich terrain of the region depends largely on rainfall, which fortunately falls in abundance. October to April is the rainy season, when crops can expect around 785mm of rain. May to September is drier and warmer, although being on the Atlantic coast and therefore tempered by cool winds, temperatures rarely soar much higher than 24°C in summer. The winters are mild with temperatures of around 14°C.

Cuisine

While Gharb-Chrarda-Bni Hsen is not known for its culinary expertise, it is rich in produce. Rice, artichokes, pears, honey, olives, apples, peaches, prunes and strawberries are grown in abundance in the region's green hinterlands. Shad (*alose*) is found in the Sebou river, which is often eaten stuffed with dates, which themselves are stuffed with almonds and cinnamon.

KENITRA

A large proportion of Kenitra's population (around one-third of the region) works in the paper mill factories and the fish cannery, which in addition to overspills from the industrial hubs of Casablanca and Rabat, constitute the main industry in the city. It is not the most stimulating of places. Historians and culture vultures will be hard pushed to find much of any great interest. Most of the city's character disappeared along with the US military who left in their wake a small taste of America in the form of pizza joints, nightclubs and bars, which seem a little out of place in one of Morocco's less cosmopolitan cities. It is not an unattractive place, there is a handful of elegant art-deco buildings scattered across the city, lining the wide boulevards, many now dressed with rusting satellite dishes that are frequent additions to most of Morocco's roof tops. What is refreshing about Kenitra, however, is that it is simply a Moroccan city getting on with Moroccan life without trying to attract or involve a tourist market. The downside of this, though, is that there is nothing particularly here for tourists to do. Plage Mehdiya is the closest beach, several kilometers long and one of the safer places along the Atlantic coast for swimming. It is not one of Morocco's most attractive beaches, but it does have good sand and only tends to get crowded in the middle stretch, leaving lots of space on either side for more private bathing. Plage Mehdiya draws a primarily Moroccan crowd with most foreigners preferring the more resort-style beaches such as Plage des Nations, closer to Rabat.

Properties

Properties in Kenitra are largely modern, the oldest ones having been built during the years of the French but the majority in downtown Kenitra are new, white, square apartment blocks around the standard six storeys high, some with narrow, ornate balconies and tinted glass. There are a number of white, square houses lining the beachfront in a higgledy-piggledy fashion at Mehdiya, most quite basic inside and not particularly inspiring to look at but in fantastically close proximity to the sea. As it is flat land running up to the beach, however, only those in the front row, so to speak, have sea views, those behind have views only of other houses. If this beachfront particularly appeals, you could consider purchasing one of the existing houses and rebuilding.

Kenitra is not an obvious place for property hunters wishing to buy a house in Morocco. For investment buyers, second homebuyers looking for a holiday home or a property to let to holidaymakers, there is not very much here likely to attract a tourist crowd especially when Rabat with its ancient monuments and chic cafés/restaurants is only 40km away. While this means that property prices are generally lower in comparison to the other industrial cities of Casablanca and Rabat, there is unlikely to be much of a return on investment as it is not a sought after location.

Estate Agent
Ramses Consulting, 31 Avenue Tarik Ibn Ziad, Hassan, Rabat; ☎ 068 65 79
79/065 12 11 88; e-mail ramses_consulting@yahoo.fr. Specialises in property
in Rabat, Kenitra and the surrounding coastline.

GUELMIM ES-SEMARA

Population: 386,075
Surface area: 32,114sq km
Regional capital: Guelmim
Main areas: Guelmim, Tata, Tan Tan

Guelmim-Es Semara is in terms of sq km, Morocco's largest region. Located beneath the Anti Atlas, with its eastern edge rubbing shoulders with the deserts of
the Western Sahara, its western edge running alongside 200km of Atlantic coast
and its interior incorporating lush palmeraies, curative thermal springs and vast
stretches of flat, stony nothingness interspersed with kasbahs and dried up riverbeds. The region traditionally marks the 'Gateway to the Sahara', although there is
very little of the romance one equates with desert life in the region's rocky, inhospitable landscape. There are none of the picturesque soaring, white sand dunes of
Merzouga, for example, to the east of the country. For kilometres of golden sand,
the places to be are the very beautiful beaches, which start with Plage Blanche,
60km southwest of Gulemim and continue south through Tan Tan Plage.

The region's nearest international airport is Agadir, 185km north of Guelmim
with scheduled and charter flights from the UK and the rest of Europe. There
is no train network and buses and shared taxis are the main form of public
transport.

Plage Blanche has been earmarked by the Ministry of Tourism as one of 6
coastal sites to be developed as part of the Plan Azur. 1200 hotel beds are envisaged
for the resort, which it is stated will focus on ecotourism, taking advantage of
the diverse and abundant wildlife in the area including pink flamingoes. At the
time of writing, however, the site is still without a developer. This is not that
surprising. Even though Plage Blanche is a beautiful beach, it is incredibly basic
and there is very little in the local vicinity, in terms of infrastructure (roads,
airports, electricity, healthcare) and towns/cities, to attract large investment.

The region has always been an important trade route. In the 8th century, salt
mined in the Sahara was traded for West African gold using Guelmim as its
centre and during the rule of the Almoravids in the 11th century, the region was
an important link in an empire that stretched from Spain through to Ghana. It
is in Guelmin-Es Semara, that the legendary 'Blue Men' can be found. The Blue
Men refer to the tribes of Western and Central Sahara who kit themselves out in

loose, flowing robes and turbans (tagilmust), coloured indigo. As water is scarce in the desert, the indigo is not boiled but pounded into the cloth. When the wearer sweats, the dye runs on to the skin, leaving a bluish tint, hence the name, 'Blue Men'. Being a Blue Man is something of an attraction among tourists who are coached down from Agadir to Guelmim each week to gaze at the tribesmen and their camels at the weekly camel market (which, nowadays is more of a goat market than a camel market, in fact, you will be lucky to see anything even closely resembling a camel, unless it is marinated in a thick stew and served with potatoes. In addition, most of the Blue Men hanging around the camel market, are not really Blue Men, but normal coloured men, dressing up as Blue Men in order to earn an extra bob or two from gullible tourists). It is also from here, that the *Guedra*, an ancient tribal desert dance can be observed. Guedra is performed by women perched on their knees, in order to be seen from inside nomadic tents, and moving only the upper part of their body in erotic displays to a repetitive, trance-like music. The dance is often 'put on' for tourists but does not really have the same affect on them as it does on nomadic tribesmen.

The region has a pretty harsh, unforgiving climate. During the day, temperatures can soar to 45°C only to drop to around 0°C at nightfall. Rain is a scarcity with little more than 125mm a year. This lack of moisture leaves the skin and eyes feeling dry and gritty, compounded in the springtime by powerful sandstorms.

Cuisine

Camel meat is the main protein for the desert region, followed by gazelle, foxes, hedgehogs, jackals and any other creature of the sand. Eaten with couscous or served in tagines, meat is often quite scarce in regional dishes in comparison to a wide and varied number of vegetables. Almonds, figs and dates are found in abundance, sardines are popular around Tan Tan, grilled and eaten fresh.

GUELMIM (GOULMIME)

Guelmim is the main town in the region, 60km south of Sidi Ifni, with a population of 150,000. It is a largely modern place with little of architectural interest to woo visiting tourists with the exception of the attractive ruins of an old red pisé kasbah, which is unfortunately marred by the smell of urine. The centre of the town is Place Bir Anzarane, a roundabout surrounded by café's and the post office. It is also from here that buses come and go to Tiznit (north) and Tan Tan (south).

Properties

Guelmim is not likely to ever be a popular place to buy property despite the generally attractive red stone, one-two story houses with blue shutters. It is located around 60km from the sea and so will not attract a beach market, most of the tourists who visit are either day trippers from Agadir who come to the souk, watch the traditional dances and head back to Agadir or overnight tourists who stay in one of the characterless hotels before heading on to the deep south. As a result of this properties are cheap to buy, 90,000 dh (£5000) for 100sq m parcel of land.

Around Guelmim
Aïn Abainou, Aït Bekkou and Plage Blanche. Where there is marginally more of a property market is in the pretty oasis villages around Guelmim such as Aïn Abainou, 14km north of Guelmim, which has thermal (38°C) springs, known to treat dermatological conditions and Aït Bekkou, 17km southeast of Guelmim, which is the largest oasis palm grove in the area. Both these places and their surrounds have electricity and water and are popular with the handful of foreigners buying here, the majority of whom build guesthouses and touristique ventures as opposed to private homes. Many people buy the old red mud houses and either restore them but more often, demolish them and rebuild newer 'old-style' properties of 1-2 stories within keeping to the local surrounds. Such properties cost around 90,000 dh (£5000) and usually come with land. The government in its efforts to boost investment in the region is selling off much of the land to Moroccans and foreigners alike for around 200 dh per sq m (£12).

Currently the only houses around Plage Blanche are the fishermen's cabins. These are not officially for sale. If the Plage Blanche resort development does go ahead, the price of land in this area is likely rise as is happening around Saidia, the Mediterranean coastal resort in the north east of Morocco, being developed by Fedesa, although at the moment there is very little in the way of water, electricity or roads, which detracts many from considering it as a viable place to buy.

TAN TAN

Tan Tan is a sparsely populated province, 125km southwest of Guelmim inhabited predominantly with pastoral nomads and fishermen. Its main claim to fame is that it was the starting point for the 1975 Green March into Western Sahara led by the late king Hassan II. The town itself is uninspiring. Several attempts have been made on a number of occasions, however, to turn Tan Tan Plage (Tan Tan beach) 25km away into a resort for package tourists, but these have largely failed, as the sad looking derelict hotel on the beach will testify. There is a fishing port at Tan Tan Plage, which is responsible for a large chunk of Morocco's sardine industry but besides this, there is currently nothing else here to attract holidaymakers.

The government is, however, once again, keen to have as many investors here as possible and so is offering cheap land packages, but there is little uptake at this present time. There are very few houses or dwellings in the area of Tan Tan Plage, which makes it feel decidedly remote and cut off from other parts of Morocco. It is worth keeping an eye on this area, however, if the deep south of Morocco appeals as Tan Tan Plage and its surrounds do have some potential even if it is just a case of buying a very cheap piece of land aided by the government and building a large villa. The beach could do with being cleaned up as it is strewn with litter and the waters around the port, polluted, but if the Plage Blanche resort goes ahead, it could have a knock on effect on its southern neighbour. The town is less likely to draw many property buyers, particularly at the present time when it is shared with an anti social number of army and police bods due to its proximity to the Western Sahara.

Tata. Tata is located 300km west of Guelmim, close to the Algerian border and lays claim to the most important palmeraie in southern Morocco with over 1 million (largely unkempt) palms. It is a simple desert town visited by tourists on the Taroudannt-Tata-Tiznit loop. The town is pastel red contrasting prettily with green palm trees, overlooked by a military fort. Watered by three streams from the Anti Atlas, Tata's very green central square is known as Place March Verte, which also serves as the bus station. Mud houses characterise the desert countryside around Tata. Low, thick walls and solid wood front doors serving as protection from a searing sun. Close to Tata are the villages of Akka and Foum Zguid, both with attractive palmeraies, which serve as the main attraction. Life here is tough, hot and windy, but the government is attempting to lure investors with the promise of cheap land. People who do come and live here, primarily expatriate Moroccans living in Europe as opposed to foreigners, take advantage of the cheap 200 dh per sq m (£12) land and tend to build large touristique ventures for passing tourists, which is pretty much the main industry in the area. Unlike places along the Atlantic coast, Tata will never be a majorly popular location as it is tricky to travel to and with the exception of nature and solitude, there is not very much to do or see.

MARRAKECH-TENSIFT-AL HAOUZ

Population: 3 million
Area: 31,000sq km
Regional capital: Marrakech
Main areas: Marrakech, Essaouira

The region of Marrakech-Tensift-Al Haouz incorporates the central south west of Morocco. To the south it borders the High Atlas, to the west, the Atlantic Ocean and to its north and east the inland industrial/farming regions of Chaouia

Ouardiga and Tadla Azilal. Nearly 3 million people live in the region, one third of this population are urbanites, primarily living in Marrakech. While by no means the largest region, Marrakech-Tensift-Al-Haouz lays claim to two of the most important areas in Morocco in terms of tourism and property, Marrakech and Essaouira.

Climate varies greatly depending on where you are. Inland from the Atlantic coast, the weather is reliably hot for 8 months of the year with temperatures soaring up to between 33-40°C from May to August a dry heat, with intense sunshine. The temperature drops during the winter months of November to February to around 18-21°C. Along the coast of Essaouira, there is much more of a temperate climate, generally milder and more stable with average temperatures of 24°C year round, blue skies and sunshine. Ironically, Essaouira feels at its chilliest during the summer months, when Marrakech just 2 hours away is at its hottest. This is because of the strong northeast trade winds created by the humid Atlantic anticyclones, which beat down on the town at speeds of 40knots (46 mph), giving Essaouira the name 'Windy City Afrika'. Just a short way inland, 10km or so and the temperatures climb till they are more on a par with Marrakech.

Cuisine

Along with the Arabic cuisine of Fes and Andalucian Tetouan, the Berber capital of Marrakech, home of the pomegranate, is the third gastronomic capital of Morocco with some of the country's best restaurants, food stalls, cookery schools (see www.rhodeschoolofcuisine.com) and patisseries. All types, variations and flavours of food can be found in Marrakech from the 100 mini street stalls of Djemaa el Fna selling anything from fried fish, grilled meat and sheep heads to cinnamon tea, tubs of couscous and snails to the banquet style haut cuisine of restaurants such as Dar Marjana and Dar Moha. Italian, French and Japanese restaurants, fast food joints, an uncountable plethora of cafés serving delights such as *shwarma* (spit grilled meat sandwiches) fried fish and lemon chicken and plenty of highly stylish cocktail bars crowd the streets, many hidden away in darkened cul de sacs, up flights of stairs or on roof terraces. Traditional Marrakchi fare is *tanzhiyya*, a lamb dish, slow cooked in a communal oven (10-12 hours) with vegetables, water and spices. Peppery foods are preferred to the sweet of Rabat and Fes, dishes with a bit of a kick such as spicy tagine with camel meat or *tagine kebab meghdor*, grilled lamb marinated in a spicy butter sauce. Olive oil, processed just outside the city, is used generously, smothering dishes such as *tangia*, a lamb dish made with garlic and cumin.

Relative to its size, Essaouira also has something of a gastronomic reputation, stemming from its previously large Jewish community who added their own variations to the coastal cuisine. Fish balls, *breewaht* (triangular warqa pastry) stuffed with fish and *dafina* or *Sabbath stew*; chickpeas, onions, garlic, eggs, beef and cow's feet mixed together with spices such as cumin, turmeric and saffron, slow cooked (24 hours) on the embers of a dying fire. Fish from the fish souk is very cheap to buy and highly delicious, *tegree*, dried and spiced mussels is also a speciality, the fish grills by the port and fish cafés in the souk are popular places to eat and the fish tagines are renowned throughout Morocco. Street stalls in Essaouira sell popcorn, chickpeas, snails and brochettes (barbecued meat), the regional speciality of argan oil is drizzled over hot bread for breakfast (see *cuisine Sous Massa Draa*), cafés line the streets of the main square Place Moulay Hassan and a slowly increasing number of restaurants (seafood, Italian and traditional Moroccan) are opening around the medina.

MARRAKECH

Mention Morocco to most people and the first place that will pop into their head is Marrakech. It is, for many, the beginning, middle and end of Morocco, an all-absorbing city, easily accessible from the UK, Europe and North America and lying north of the Atlas mountains, easy to get to from the country's northern regions. It is both poverty stricken and chic, funky and traditional, serene and frenetic. It is also the most written about city in North Africa. Marrakech lies on the semi arid Haouz plain, south of the seasonal Wadi (river) Tensift. It is a low-lying city, set against the backdrop of the snowy Atlas, built with the same red hues as the earth so that from the air, it is barely visible as it blends into its surrounds.

Marrakech is Berber in origin and more African than Arab. It has been the country's capital on two occasions. Firstly when it was founded in the 11th century by Berber Muslim tribesmen, the Almoravids and again, in the 16th century, during the Saadians dynasty. The city was built by the Almoravid leader, Youssef ben Tachfine,who chose it as a place to pitch camp based on its location on a warm plain protected from the Saharan winds by the mountains. He immediately constructed a kasbah and a mosque and to overcome the water shortage, planted pipes (*khettara*) made out of baked mud in the ground, to carry water into the city, from the High Atlas, still in evidence around the Palmeraie just outside the city. When Youssef died, his son, Ali succeeded him and built the city's original ramparts. In 1147, after many battles, Marrakech eventually fell to the vehemently religious, Almohads who became the next dynasty. After demolishing many of the Almoravids main monuments, the Almohads rebuilt Marrakech adding such relics as the Koutoubia mosque, which had to be rebuilt 50 years later as the previous one was not completely in line with Mecca, the El Mansour mosque and Bab Agnaou, the gateway to the kasbah, all of which are still very much in existence today.

When the Merenids succeeded the Almohads, they moved the country's capital to Fes, taking little interest in Marrakech. As a result the city fell into decline only to be resurrected 300 years later by the Saadians, who transferred the capital back from Fes to Marrakech and spared no expense in its revival. Palaces, hammams, mosques and hospitals were built, only a few of which survive today. In the 17th and 18th century, the capital once again left Marrakech and was moved to Meknes, followed by Fes. Despite attempts by Sultan Moulay Ismael, to maintain the city, it fell back into decline.

In the late 19th century, the wildly corrupt, tribe-berating Thami el Glaoui was appointed the role of Pasha of Marrakech by Sultan Moulay Hassan, When the French came to rule in 1912, Glaoui was their main ally, used by them to control the warring Atlas tribes. The French also built a ville nouvelle named Gueliz (taken from the French word église, which was the Catholic Church of St Anne just north of the medina), to the west of the medina and furnished it with roads, hotels, schools, hospitals, pylons and a railroad. They also restored the crumbling, neglected medina to its current state, so that the Moroccans could maintain their traditional way of life.

Marrakech Today

The Marrakech of today is basking in the glory of yet another heyday. Home to some of the world's most beautiful gardens, hotels, houses and monuments, resided in by some of the world's most famous designers, writers, artists and entrepreneurs, host to the glamorous International Film Festival and recipient of over one-third of all visitors to the country, a figure set to rise in line with Vision 2010. It is a city of noise, entertainment and colour that thrives on attention and appears to blossom the busier it gets. From the snake charmers, storytellers and acrobats of Djemaa el Fna (see below) to the hustling, playful chitchat in the souks, the honking horns on Avenue Mohammed V, the dashing bursts of bougainvillea and the art galleries, exhibitions and boutiques. It is a city where the old and new seamlessly join and you feel as comfortable on the back of a braying mule as you do in the front of a polished 4X4.

It is also a city where in amongst the opulence and affluence, there is severe poverty. Migrants from the rural Atlas looking for work to feed their families, beggars and street children rifling through dustbins, hustling tourists and conning the naïve in order to get a bite to eat or a scattering of loose change. Once recommended by Winston Churchill as having the air to cure bronchitis, it is now one of Morocco's most polluted cities where every road is a traffic jam and the smell of fumes, overpowering.

Despite this, investment in Marrakech is soaring. The combination of a young, forward thinking monarch and a highly effective regional governor Mohammed Hassad, has done much to improve the quality of life in the city. Social housing projects are underway to get the city's poorest out of the shantytowns, the bureaucracy, notorious for impeding investment and entrepreneurialism has been hacked down to manageable sized chunks and touts who harass foreigners are at risk of arrest by heavy-handed tourist police.

The main investors are the French many of whom still feel they have something of a hold over the city and, expatriate Moroccans looking for a project they can sink their hard earned foreign currency into. The last five years, though, have seen a sharp growth in the number of British people buying property in Marrakech either as second homes, guesthouses or holiday lets.

What most appeals about Marrakech is that it is a place where the most creative can really express themselves and show off their talents. Cheap labour, skilled artisans and idyllic settings, makes Marrakech an artist's dream. Here, more than any other part of Morocco, homes are designed as if for exhibiting with every curve, fabric, stone and tile, crucial to the whole look and feel of the house. It is a city where the most chic can kit themselves out in tailor made kaftans, do lunch in stylish bistros, promote Berber jewellery as a fashion accessory, peruse flea markets and decorate designer riads - if they get into the pages of *Elle Decoration*, then all the better. Marrakech is a city for pushing the boundaries, where upcoming chefs, designers and painters can make a name for themselves as everyone is looking for the next best thing.

On a more down to earth level (and there is also a very earthy element), the St Tropez of the Maghreb appeals because it has pretty much everything one would expect from a European city in terms of restaurants, cafés, cinemas, an opera house, a hypermarket, hospitals, private clinics, international schools (including an American school), a wide selection of shops, markets and ancient monuments but it also has perks that certainly many Brits can only dream of. Three luxury golf courses, ski slopes 80km south into the High Atlas, cultural attractions that are affordable, mountains for trekking and climbing and, less appealing but for a touch of the exotic; sandstorms that sweep across the city.

Medina. Marrakech's rose red medina is enclosed within 10km of ancient ramparts, 9 metres high, built in the twelfth century. There are 20 gateways into the old town from all different sides of the city and it is very, very easy to get lost if you lose your gate. Just outside the ramparts are flowerbeds rich in roses, hibiscus and jasmine following a recent planting scheme aimed at re-greening the city.

The heart of the medina is the famous square called Djemma el Fna, which translates as the Place of the Dead as it was once the site of public hangings. It is now one of Morocco's most lively spots filled day and night with spectacles and extravaganzas. It is quite simply nothing more than a square covered in tarmac and surrounded by cafés that the municipality of the 1980's attempted to turn into a car park. Thankfully tireless campaigning prevented this and it is now a UNESCO World Heritage site. During the day, the square is filled with barrows selling nuts and freshly squeezed orange juice, mopeds whizzing through the strolling crowds, children playing ball, random performers; acrobats, colourfully clad water sellers, story tellers and snake charmers entertaining a circle of tourists.

It is, however, when the sun sets that the square really takes off. Out come the tables, benches, chairs, gas lamps, barbecues and fairy lights as the whole site transforms into the world's largest kitchen and food hall, selling anything and everything from pigs trotters to sheep eyes, barbecued fish, lamb on a spit, salads, rice, shwarma sandwiches, false teeth, second hand shoes. All around, drums beat, people dance in a trance, the sky fills with smoke. It is like a food hall, circus, carnival and theatre all packed into 50sq m.

An equally big medina landmark three hundred metres to the east of Djemma el Fna, is the Koutoubia mosque built in 1158, whose minaret towers 70m above the ground. It is the tallest point in flat Marrakech and can be seen from miles around.

Koutoubia mosque is the starting point from which the urban perimeter of Marrakech is measured. Recently in line with the growth of the city, the perimeter was extended by an extra 5km to incorporate suburbs, which were once just countryside. This has affected surrounding areas as will be explained in the Properties section below.

The souks start at the northern edge of Djmaa el Fna down a road called Rue Souk Smarine, which splits into two smaller streets, Souk el Attarin and Souk el Kabir and covered markets (*kissarias*) at the top. This is where the majority of souks are clustered, grouped together into specialisms but joined via alleyways. All manner of everything is sold in the Marrakech souks and for the best bargains, it is wise to head out early in the morning before it gets too hot.

Ville Nouvelle. The main thoroughfare running through the ville nouvelle, connecting the Koutoubia mosque with **Gueliz**, is Avenue Mohammed V, a 3km stretch of very busy road upon which many hotels, restaurants, cafés, banks and apartment blocks can be found. There is also a large market, Marché Central, where it is possible to buy everything you might need (wines, pates, breads, nuts, cheeses, salamis, olives and wicker baskets) for a picnic in one of the cities luxuriant gardens; Menara, Marjorelle, Agdal, Mamounia.

Running a couple of roads away from Mohammed V, but parallel, is Avenue Mohammed VI (called, until 2004, Avenue de France). Recently this road has been extended from 4 kilometres to 8 kilometres. The new extension has done much to improve access to the city for roads such as the Route d'Ourika and the Route d'Amiziz, It is now a matter of one road straight to the centre (and for many, the highly regarded French school) as opposed to the winding, trafficky routes of before.

A short way to the south of Gueliz is the upmarket, very quiet and largely French area of Hivernage, a small neighbourhood with exclusive 5 star hotels, low, expensive apartment blocks and hibiscus-lined roads. It is a different feeling city altogether from the noise and fumes of Gueliz.

Properties

The housing market in Marrakech is, along with Essaouira, one of the most developed in Morocco and as a result of this, prices have stabilised. The buying of land outside the urban perimeter ie agricultural land, however, is still in its early stages and prices are unstable and vary dramatically depending on who you are and whom you are buying from. There are no issues relating to foreigners buying land within the urban perimeter but there are strict zoning regulations which change depending on where you choose to buy land. These relate to how many stories you are permitted to build, the size of the house in relation to the size of the land. It is not permitted for buyers to purchase over 3 hectares within the urban perimeter, for private use. Such large amounts of land can only be bought for touristique projects such as guesthouses or hotels. In addition, new properties are not allowed to be higher than 9 metres and all must adhere to the red colour of the city.

The buying of land and building tailor made villas is particularly popular with foreigners who already own, for example, riads in the medina. After a while many crave the gardens, views, pools and parking areas that a villa provides, so rent out their medina properties, normally as holiday lets and live in their new villas.

Medina Properties. Traditionally the biggest lure for first time foreigners looking to buy properties in Marrakech has been the ancient medina. Around one riad/dar is sold every week with foreigners now owning around 30% of the 12,000 or so properties. Marrakech has a very high number of riads in comparison to dars, which is unusual compared to other medinas. This is because space has never been a problem and plots of land have traditionally been sold larger than elsewhere. While dars tend to be located in the more densely populated areas such as in the centre of the medina, riads are generally situated on paved alleyways that are wide enough to fit, in current circumstances, cars. They have large gardens, often with a small basin-like pool (swimming pools are not permitted as there is a water shortage), which also irrigates the rich foliage; lemon, orange, pomegranate trees, jasmine bushes etc, some have gazebos or in more extreme cases, a pavilion to give shade from the sun. Until the 20th century, many of the large riads were single storey, now many spread on to two floors.

Unlike the ornate, flourishing décor of Fes, Marrakech, being a 'city of the earth' built by country Berber, is simple, unaffected and minimalist. Lime is a major constituent used to strengthen floors and protect outer walls from the extreme heat. Tadelakt, the polished wall covering of different coloured pigments, which has recently had a revival in Marrakech, is largely the finish of choice in the salons, bathrooms, kitchens and hammams and sometimes, floors. Prestigious properties tend to have rounded green, enamel tiled roofs, which add a colourful contrast to the exterior red clay walls. Unlike other regions where zelliges are used to cover large stretches of wall, in Marrakech, they tend only to be seen on fountains or around washbasins. While carved plaster is sometimes present above doors and windows, its design is simple.

The most popular and expensive neighbourhoods in the medina are those close or adjacent to Djemma el Fna. This is where there are the majority of guesthouses and hotels. Kssour and Mouassine, north of Djemma el Fna, are the most sought after due, also to their proximity to the ville nouvelle. Of the 15,000 tourists who visit Marrakech each day, many will enter these neighbourhoods en route to the surrounding souks, they are therefore very busy and touristy. The old Pasha residence, Dar el Glaoui, frequented by the king, is in Kssour, while this is private property, large renovated riads surrounding the palace can be found for around 5 million dh (£300,000), which benefit from the lush greenery of the palace grounds and the tight security. It is also possible to find smaller, fully renovated riads in the area for around 9 million dh (£56,000), which are medium sized (160sq m) with three bedrooms.

Also popular for property buyers is the neighbourhood of Zitoun. Zitoun el Kdim (old area) and Zitoun el Jdid (new area), south of Djemma el Fna, leading down to the mellah and close to the El Badia palace, a popular tourist site. Compared to the north of Djemma el Fna, this area is generally less touristy and more rundown. There are two car parks in the neighbourhood, patrolled 24 hours a day. It is possible to find large (220sq m) unrenovated riads for around 1.1 million dh (£69,000). Similarly priced properties can be found around Bab Doukkala, which straddles the medina and the ville nouvelle. Here, 100sq m 4 bedroom renovated riads are selling for around 700,000 dh (£43,000) and unrenovated riads of 180sq m with seven bedrooms selling for around 820,000 dh (£50,000).

South of the medina is the kasbah quarter, which houses the Royal Palace and the Saadian tombs. This part of the medina is on the right side of town for the airport with good views over the Atlas and the grounds of the palace. Roads are wide, so can accommodate cars. Large, properties overlooking the palace tend to sell for around 4.5 million dh (£280,000).

On the east side of the medina, in the right direction for Marrakech's golf clubs, is Bab Aylen. This is one of the more modern parts of the medina and generally cheaper than the west side. Roads are wide, so accessible to cars and it has the advantage/disadvantage of being off the main tourist routes. Nearby, the area of Sidi Ayoub is an upcoming neighbourhood, uncharacteristically attracting a Moroccan crowd, mainly from Casablanca and Rabat. The neighbourhood has recently benefited from having a facelift with zellige and street lighting giving a much needed, oomph to the local square.

The most residential areas are in the middle of the medina. Neighbourhoods like Kinnaria, Derb Dabachi and Ben Salah. The roads around here are very narrow so do not permit cars, with the nearest parking being around Djemma el

Fna 10 minutes walk away. Properties here tend to be smaller riads or dars selling for cheaper prices between 500,000 dh (£30,000) and 900,000 dh (£55,000).

Ville Nouvelle Properties. Most of the old properties in prime locations around Gueliz, have been demolished and new apartment/duplex blocks built. Until recently buildings of no higher than 2 stories were allowed in the ville nouvelle but this has now changed to 5 stories although no building is allowed to overhang the tallest palm tree. Most tend to adhere to the red colour code of the city. In downtown Gueliz - around Mohammed V, Hassan II, Avenue des Nations Unis - the pied a terre, studio or 1 bedroom apartment market, is highly sought after by affluent Moroccans from Casablanca and Rabat, who visit Marrakech for weekend shopping sprees. With the arrival of low cost carrier, Atlas Blue, this pastime is also appealing to an increasing number of Europeans who can both enjoy the property and have it as a sound investment. Many Europeans who own riads in the medina will buy apartments in Gueliz and rent out their riads. It is also the property of choice for singles/couples living and working in Marrakech. 1-3 bedroom apartments tend to sell for between 700,000 dh (£44,000) to 1.8 million dh (£110,000).

Another popular, exclusive place to live in Gueliz is around the more residential neighbourhood of Semlalia, a little north of downtown. The benefits of this area are the views over the picturesque Marjorelle Gardens. Properties here tend to be more luxurious than in the centre of Gueliz and are largely Moroccan owned. 3 bedroom properties with views over the gardens cost in the region of 1.8 million dh (£110,000).

In the exclusive area of Hivernage, south of Gueliz, the market again is mainly apartment blocks. This area tends to appeal to older Europeans who have lived or owned property in Marrakech for several years and prefer to be away from the pollution and frenetic activity of Gueliz. Apartment properties tend to be larger than in Gueliz, ranging in price from 1.5 million dh (£94,000) for a 2 bedroom property to 2.5 million dh (£150,000) for three bedrooms.

Marrakech Suburbs

Palmeraie. The Palmeraie, 10km north of Marrakech between the Route de Casablanca and the Route de Fes, is Marrakech's version of Millionaire's Row. 180,000 palm trees line over 6000 hectares of dry, dusty sand. This is where Morocco's richest live in luxury, red villas with bright green lawns, turrets and private pools, hidden behind high walls with, depending on the status of the resident (ambassador, minister, celebrity), very tight security. Water is supplied via a number of reservoirs and artesian wells although it is still possible in this area, to view the original khettara pipe system devised by the Almoravids in the twelfth century. There are strict zoning regulations for anyone planning to buy land. These tend to revolve around the treasured palms. Anyone who cuts down or damages a tree, risks three years in prison. Although it is unlikely to ever come to this, all adhere to the regulations, some taking them to the furthest extreme by literally building around the palms so that they become a feature inside the property, much like an ornament on a mantelpiece. It is not possible to buy less than one hectare of land to build on.

The Palmeraie is divided into four areas. The first (146 hectares) is for villas of at least 200sq m. The next (3300 hectares) is for villas between 2000-10,000sq m. The third (17 hectares) is dedicated to communal estates (apartments and duplexes) and the fourth (2300 hectares) is solely for the reforestation of a further 100,000 palm trees and is not for building on.

To the north of the Palmeraie, there is a new Club Med village and on the outskirts, the Palmeraie Golf Palace, which as well as an 18 hole par 72 golf course designed by Robert Trent Jones includes an American style clubhouse, squash and tennis courts, stables and swimming pools.

The price of luxury villas in the Palmeraie tend to start at around 10 million dh (£600,000), 4 bedroom duplexes with communal pool sell for around 3 million dh (£188,000) and 2 bedroom apartments cost around 1.4 million dh (£88,000). All facilities such as roads, telephones, mains electricity, water and sewage exist. These need to be paid for in addition to the price of the land and cost in the region of 20,000 dh (£1250).

Targa. Targa is a relatively new residential area to the west of Marrakech, only 2km from the *Victor Hugo Lyceé Français*, and the French Institute. Here, the land has been organised into plots selling for around 3000 dh (£180) per sq m including service connections and ranging in size from 400 to 1200sq m. This area is popular both with Moroccans who tend to build villas and sell them on and foreigners, particularly the French for its proximity to the Lyçee, who tend to build villas and live in them. As zoning regulations enable properties to take up 80% of the land, most are built to maximise this space, which means small gardens and houses generally packed in close together. Fully built villas tend to range in price from 1.5-5 million dh (£95,000-310,000).

Zone Touristique de L'Agdal. A few minutes drive from Hivernage, to the south of Marrakech, Zone Touristique de L'Agdal is an area in the process of being developed into one of the most luxurious residential and tourist spots in Marrakech with gardens, swimming pools, club house, hammams and restaurants. With investment from the third richest Saudi prince, the development is located within the grounds of the Four Seasons Hotel, which is due to open around the beginning of 2008. Twenty 2-3 bedroom riads and twenty 3-4 bedroom villas with prices ranging from 6.7 –12 million dh (£450,000-750,000) are on offer. There are also 2/3/4 bedroom apartments for sale with a starting price of 1.5 million dh (£94,000). See Hampton International www.hamptons-int.com.

Route de l'Ourika. The Route de l'Ourika is one of the most popular places to buy land. Ourika is a pretty little red mud valley in the mountains, 40 kilometres from Marrakech. With views over the snowy Atlas, the road leading to it is very picturesque surrounded by countryside and lined with all of Marrakech's lush garden nurseries. It is not possible to buy land within the first 10km of Route de l'Ourika, from the city centre as this houses the Royal Palace. The urban perimeter has recently been extended by 3 kilometres in the direction of Ourika. The result of this is that land, which was once 10 kilometres out of the city, is now only 7 kilometres so commands a higher price. Route de l'Ourika has benefited, however, from the new extended Avenue Mohammed VI as it makes it much more convenient to get to the centre of the city. Titled land around 10km out of town with access to electricity, water and wells, costs in the region of 1 million dh (£62,000) per hectare and decreases in price the further out of the city you head.

Route de l'Ourika is also popular place for developers. Many luxury villa complexes have been built over the last couple of years with Moorish architecture being the favoured look in addition to private pools, balconies, gardens and views over the Atlas. These tend to be gated residences guarded by security and highly sought after as second homes. Such villas are proving very popular with Brits and are normally sold through international property agents based in the UK.

Route d'Amizmiz. This route has become a popular place to live since the extension of Avenue Mohammed VI, which has greatly facilitated access to the city centre. As Amizmiz is a small Berber settlement, 50km out of Marrakech on a mountainous road it does not have a great deal of traffic heading towards it unlike the bigger Routes de Fes and Casablanca, which are inundated with endless streams of lorries and cars. Another appealing feature is that this road leads to the beautiful man-made Lake Takerkoust, which is the only oasis in the Marrakech area and the main water supply for the city.

The first 6 kilometres skirt around the new, luxury tourist resort of Agdal (see below) the Royal Horseriding club and the new aquapark. Just 7 kilometres out of the city you are already into countryside and there is much water along the route and access to electricity within 500m-2km. There are also plans to build an 18 hole golf course 14 kilometres out of the city. The urban perimeter has been extended by 5 kilometres in this direction, which puts a lot more land into the city limits but also ups the price, although it is considerably cheaper to buy land here than along the more developed Route de l'Ourika. Plots tend to be set back one kilometre from the road with titled land selling for around 700,000 dh (£44,000) per hectare.

Route de Fes. Like Route d'Ouarzazate, this road is also to the east of the city, which means there is no direct route into Marrakech. It is a busy road with trucks heading to and from the city of Fes but the countryside is attractive with palms, olive groves and lush vegetation. While large villas and grounds along this route tend to sell for around 4 –5 million dh (£250,000-310,000), titled land 10km out of Marrakech, with proximity to electricity and water tends to sell for around 300,000 dh (£19,000) per hectare.

Route de Ouarzazate. This is a cheaper alternative to the Routes de l'Ourika and Amizmiz as it is a generally a blander road and busier with traffic heading to the city of Ouarzazate. It is also located to the east of the city, which means that there is no direct route into the city centre, which adds time on to the journey. There are, however, some appealing features most notably for English speakers, the American School of Marrakech, which was opened in 1995 and accommodates 330 students. There are also two 18 hole par 72 golf clubs, the Royal Golf Club 2 kilometres out of the city and the Amelkis at 12 kilometres attached to the luxurious 5 star Amanjena hotel, the first Aman resort in Africa. Titled land with access to electricity and water is around 300,000 dh (£19,000) per hectare.

ESSAOUIRA

Essaouira is arguably Morocco's most loved town. Its 10 kilometres of sandy, white beach, dunes and sea dotted with windsurfs, the whitewashed UNESCO protected medina enclosed within pink sandstone ramparts, the lively, bustling fishing port and colourful wooden boats, fish grills, souks, artisan workshops, art galleries and white paved piazzas have long appealed to artists, musicians and cosmopolitan crowds of visitors. Jimi Hendrix, Orson Welles and Hollywood directors Ridley Scott and Oliver Stone have all lived or worked in the medina, located on the south west coast of Morocco in between Agadir (2 hours south) and Casablanca (4 hours north).

In the early 16th century, King Manuel of Portugal seized the town, then known as Mogador, in his attempt to dominate the whole Atlantic coast, and built fortifications around the harbour. The Saadians recaptured it, but favouring the port in Agadir, from where they built up a highly lucrative trading post, they let it fall into a state of neglect. The succeeding Alawites shifted all trade from Agadir to the town they named Essaouira, as revenge to the inhabitants of Agadir who were becoming increasingly rebellious to their rule. The Alawite leader, Sidi Mohammed ben Abdallah commissioned architect, Theodore Cornut, his French captive to design the street layout, walls and bastions of the medina. By the 19th century, Essaouira had become the busiest port in Morocco exporting almonds, ebony, ivory and ostrich feathers and importing tea and cottons from the UK. Muslims, Christians and Jews, invited in from Agadir, lived harmoniously together inside the town walls, in addition to an endless stream of merchants from around the world. During the French protectorate, the town was renamed Mogador but much trade was lost in favour of the big new city ports of Casablanca and Tangier. In 1956, with independence, the Moroccans renamed the town Essaouira.

Essaouira Today

For many, what most appeals about Essaouira is that everywhere is reachable on foot. There is very little need for a car in the town as the medina is compact and fully pedestrianised, walkable from end to end in 20 minutes (not taking into account the endless stops en route to chat and pass the time of day). The sea smacks against the medina walls and the beach is opposite the southern gate, Bab es Sebaa. The ville nouvelle is outside Bab Doukalla, to the north of the medina with streets as bustling as inside the walls. The fact that the layout of the medina was specifically designed as opposed to simply evolved like many of Morocco's more sprawling cities, means that it is easy to navigate. Cornut who preferred organised medinas as opposed to confusing labyrinths, designed it on a grid like system much like a noughts and crosses board where all roads lead to or cross over the two central streets, Avenue de l'Istiqlal and Avenue Sidi Mohammed ben Abdullah.

In July 2005, Essaouira was awarded the international Blue Flag ecolabel meaning that its beaches meet all the criteria for water quality, environmental management, safety and services. In terms of the strong currents that prevent swimming in many of the other bays along the coast, Essaouira is a safe place to swim. Being 'Windy City Afrika' due to its strong northeasterly winds makes Essaouira one of the world's top spots for windsurfing. There are a few windsurfing outlets along the beach where it is possible to rent equipment, have lessons and hire kitesurfs. The beach is only now starting to get more developed. The 5 star Sofitel hotel a little way down the beach has constructed an upmarket bar/café on the sand, besides this there are just two or three other cafés/bars, catering to the high numbers of summertime holidaymakers, a large number of whom have come to the coast, from Marrakech to escape the intolerable heat.

Another very appealing feature for foreigners in Essaouira is that it feels like a holiday town. Despite the busy port and crowded souks, few people actually appear to be working. The cafés are always full, shopkeepers lounge around on rugs, sipping mint tea or strong coffee, there is a constant game of football being played on the beach. The only people who wear suits and tie are the notaire and bank clerks and they stand out like crows in a sky full of seagulls. It is a great place simply to hang out and much time is wiled away doing just this. The downside of all this free time, however, is high unemployment, 19% of the population, primarily under 24, is without work, factories have closed, the fishing port cannot support large numbers and many children leave school at 14 because they see little point in carrying on their education. Tourism and construction have become the new masters, and provide employment for some

Souiris, but this tends to be low skilled and low earning.

Much like Marrakech, Essaouira attracts a wide range of property buyers from all over the world, but primarily France, Belgium and an increasing number of British. It is a cosmopolitan town that is used to westerners sporting minimalist beach gear even if it does not approve. The laid back, friendliness of the town lures people here as well as the chance to be close to the sea and surrounded by culture. It is worth bearing in mind, however, that Essaouira is a small town with a small town feel to it. Everyone knows who you are and what your business is. This provides a community spirit and makes it very easy to get to know people, but if you are used to living anonymously, it can be a touch claustrophobic.

There is an international airport in Essaouira around 12 kilometres out of the town. It is however, very small with a short runway and tends only to have one or two international flights coming from Paris, which are normally overbooked. There are two internal flights a week from Casablanca (returning twice a week on different days), operated by Regional Airlines, but these are not always reliable and the days of travel often change. For the time being, most people travel to Essaouira via Marrakech or Agadir.

Plans for Essaouira

The town has been chosen as one of the six sites to be developed with a luxury coastal resort, in line with the government's Plan Azur. The Belgian Luxembourgeois group, *Thomas & Piron/TPR L'Atelier* is responsible for Station Balnéaire de Mogador, the 356 hectare site 4 kilometres south of Essaouira, which is currently under construction, due to be completed around 2008. There will be 525 luxury villas, 32 hotels and guesthouses, two golf courses, spas, a beach club, cafés, parks and gardens. Quite what the impact of this will be on properties in the medina is not yet clear. Essaouira has always prided itself on being a town that attracts independent travellers as opposed to large package tour groups. Such a development will bring a different clientele to the town, it might also decrease business for guesthouses and holiday lets inside the medina as more people stay in the luxury resort visiting the medina only for day trips. On a positive note, it is expected to give a boost to both the local economy and employment rates in the area, although the lack of educational institutes in Essaouira means that highly skilled personnel are traditionally, sourced from the big cities such as Casablanca, leaving the lowlier, unskilled positions to the locals.

Properties

Medina. Properties in Essaouira's medina adhere to a blue and white colour code. Whitewashed walls and sky blue shutters, much like the Atlantic coastal town of Asilah in the north of Morocco. White is a predominant colour for internal walls, usually painted on to plaster although many recently restored properties have opted for tadelakt as a smooth, satiny finish in bathrooms and sometimes salons.

Unique to Essaouira is the abundance of thuya wood from the hard, knotty, thuya tree that grows in the flat, sandy countryside around Essaouira. This fragrant wood, used prolifically by Essaouira's artisans to create trinkets and furnishings, is sometimes used to clad ceilings, as it does not rot in the Essaouira damp. Rustic yellow sandstone, from Salé north of Rabat or pink sandstone from Essaouira, is used for pillars and around fireplaces and zelliges often dark blue within keeping to the colours of Essaouira, are used in kitchens and hallways. Ironwork is a popular feature of many homes, ornate designs used as windows grills around fireplaces or on balustrades. Until the 19th century, iron was used only for farming implements and considered a poor man's material, the large number of ironwork artisans now operating in Essaouira, proves that this is no longer the case, despite the fact that the damp air makes it quickly rust. Rugs and fireplaces are a welcome feature of coastal homes, as the evenings can get chilly especially when the wind howls.

Of the 16,000 properties in Essaouira's medina, roughly 1000 have been bought and restored by foreigners and, as more new apartment blocks are built in the ville nouvelle, there are a greater number of Moroccans keen to move out of the medina into modern properties.

In terms of price, the general view is that houses and renovations in Essaouira's medina are marginally more expensive than in Marrakech as the town is smaller so there is more demand than supply, there are few artisans and builders to choose from and it is next to the sea, which invariably bumps up the price.

The medina is so small that in terms of location, there is not really any such thing as a good/bad part of town to live in. The most sought after place is around the kasbah, designed by Cornut as the quarter for the many Christians living in Essaouira with more European inspired designs and large, granderstyle properties with proximity to sea, sea and port views and the main cluster of cafés and restaurants. The main problem with this neighbourhood, however is that due to being next to the sea, it suffers from humidity and salt erosion, which causes paint to peel off walls and household objects to rust very quickly. Also, due to the high number of foreign-owned properties, there is not much community spirit as many of the houses are left empty or rented out to transient tourists, for much of the year, often making it feel like a ghost town as opposed to busy bustling Essaouira.

The mellah in the northern edge of the medina is the most run down part of town and often has the cheapest properties. It also suffers badly from the damp and a lot of rubbish. Properties in the mellah are taller and darker inside, with narrower streets.

Many people are finding that the previous poorer, more residential areas of neighbourhoods such as Chbanat and Bouakhar, to the west of the medina, close to Bab Marrakech, are a better location to live, as they are drier than elsewhere. This means there is much less maintenance needed on properties and being a less sought after area, house prices around Rue Ibn Khaldoun, Rue Baghdad and Rue Derb el Ghrissi are a lot cheaper. Like the mellah, such neighbourhoods, also benefit from having a dense Moroccan population, which keeps them lively and lived in. The downside of this, however is that they are also much noisier, which is something to consider if you are planning on renting the property out to holidaymakers favouring their lie-ins.

Properties in Essaouira medina tend to range in price from 700,000-1.5 million dh (£43-93,000) for unrenovated and around 1.5 - 3 million dh (£93-180,000) for a fully restored property of up to 5 bedrooms with a terrace and 2 salons. Two bedroom medina apartments often spread over one floor of a two/three floor property sell for around 500-800,000 dh (£31-50,000). Bear in mind that if you are planning on buying a property close to the sea, you will need to dry line all the walls to protect you from the damp. It is also worth painting them with a sealent to prevent the paintwork peeling off and protecting all external wood with a varnish to stop it becoming weathered from the wind.

A British run consultancy, Moroccan Property Services has recently opened in Essaouira, which gives advice and assistance to English speakers looking to buy/restore property in the town. Contact is via Jane Loveless, ☎ 078 64 8048; www.moroccanpropertyservices.com.

Outside Essaouira

As much of the land around Essaouira is agricultural, it is highly probable you will need to obtain a VNA before purchasing (see *What Type of Property to Buy?*)

Sidi Kaouki. The beach of Sidi Kaouki is one of Morocco's top surfing and wind-surfing spots, located 27 kilometres south of Essaouira. There are just a handful of properties, which have been built along the beach. This is mainly because the winds here can be even more ferocious than in Essaouira. It is, however, very picturesque with a row of shack-like cafés selling delicious tagines and salads drizzled with argan oil. The price of land here has increased recently as the area has become more of a tourist spot with a hectare of land costing in the region of 320,000 dh (£20,000).

Around Sidi Kaouki en route to Agadir, an old stone farmhouse in much need of restoration set amongst half a hectare of land and close to water and electricity costs around 450,000 dh (£28,000). A few kilometres further south, also en-route to Agadir, a simply renovated four bedroom farmhouse with a garden of 500sq m, costs 420,000 dh (£26,000).

Ounara. Ounara is a small town, 23 kilometres outside Essaouira en-route to Marrakech that is gaining in popularity as a place to buy primarily for foreigners who already own properties in the medina, but are looking for somewhere in the countryside with gardens and tranquillity. Currently it is very much a frontier town the highlight of which is a striking, red auberge with something of a salacious reputation. An old pot holed road runs south of the town with little traffic besides a man on a horse and cart ferrying people up and down, but this is set to change as a new, paved road is being built connecting Ounara with Agadir. Land and old farmhouses in dire need of modernisation are the main options to buy, in the price range of 500,000 dh (£30,000) for a hectare.

Route de Safi. The coast road linking Essaouira with Safi is only a couple of years old, so remains in good nick and smooth to drive on. Along this stretch of countryside there is an abundance of gnarled, knotted, thuya trees and in the spring time, meadows that fill with marigolds and agave flowers soaring up to 3 metres tall. The beaches are deserted except for the surf that batters the yellow sand. Land either on its own or with a rustic, square, stone farmhouse, 20-30 kilometres out of Essaouira, costs around 180,000 dh (£110,000) for a hectare.

Route d'Agadir. The route from Essaouira to Agadir is very scenic. Running for much of the way along winding coastal roads with lovely views over the ocean. Twenty kilometres out of Essaouira, it is possible to buy ancient stone farmhouses, in much need of work (often rebuilding completely), for around 450,000 dh (£28,000) plus half a hectare of land.

Route de Marrakech. As pretty much everone who has made the journey from Marrakech to Essaouira will testify, this is not a particularly attractive route. The road is long, straight and dull. A few kilometres off the road, however, the landscape perks up, gets a little greener and is decidedly pretty. Old farmhouses are plentiful in the area many in need of much work but there are some excellent bargains to be had especially for unrenovated property. A renovated 3-4 bedroom farmhouse 25km out of Essaouira costs in the region of 900,000 dh (£56,000) to include around 1000sq m of land.

Estate Agents

Most Agents based in Marrakech will also work in Essaouira and Ouarzazate

Agence Immobiliere Mogador (Mohammed Rkhaoui), 12 Rue Skala-Sous, B.P. 616 Essaouira 44000; ☎ 0061 33 88 54; e-mail fouad.soleil3@caramail.com.

Atlas Immobilier, 245 Ave Mohammed V, Imm Watanya Gueliz, Marrakech; ☎ 044 42 26 72; e-mail contact@atlasimmobilier.com; www.atlasimmobilier.com.

Cabinet Charles El Fassy, Residence Excelsior, Rue Tarik Ibn Ziad, Marrakech; ☎ 044 44 63 23/061 13 45 04; e-mail charles,elfassy@iam.net.ma; www.celfassy.com.

Le Comptoir de l'Immobilier, 94 Rue de Tensift, Quartier Semlalia, 40000 Marrakech; ☎ 044 43 32 17; e-mail contact@Marrakech-immobilier.net; www. marrakech-immobilier.net.

Francophiles, Barker Chambers, Barker Road, Maidstone, Kent, ME16 8SF; ☎ 01622 688 165; fax 01622 671 840; e-mail sales@francophiles.co.uk; www. francophiles.co.uk..

Jemaa el Fna Immobilier, Rd point du Jet d'eau, Ave Mohammed V, Appt no 2, Imm Berdai, 40000 Marrakech; ☎ 044 44 63 89; e-mail cr@villafrance.com; www.immobilier-pro-maroc.com.

Kantakari, 40 Rue des Banques, Kenneria, Marrakech Medina; ☎ 044 44 60 29/061 67 56 48; e-mail kantakari@menara.ma; www.kantakari.com.

Karimo (Marrakech), 171 Blvd Mohammed V, Gueliz, Marrakech; ☎ 044 42 01 03; e-mail info@karimo.net; www.karimo.net.

Karimo, (Essaouira), Place Moulay Hassan, 44100 Essaouira; ☎ 044 47 45 00; e-mail info@karimo.net; www.karimo.net.

Marrakech Riads, 8 Derb Cherfa Lakbir, Mouassine, 40000 Marrakech; ☎ 044 39 16 09/044 42 64 63/061 16 36 30; e-mail immobilier@marrakech-riads. net; www.Marrakech-riads.net.

Mauresque Immobilier, 5 Derb Kettara; Zaouia, Marrakech Medina, 40000; ☎ 060 00 66 66/060 00 55 55; e-mail contact@mauresque-immobilier.com; www.mauresque-immobilier.com.

Moroccan Homes, 43 Station Road, Thorpe on Hill, Lincoln LN6 9BS; ☎ 01522 535 052 or Calle Daire 46, Sedella Malaga, Spain; ☎ 95 25 08 961; e-mail info@Moroccan-homes.com; www.Moroccan-homes.com.

Moroccan Properties, Immueble El Khalil, Avenue Hassan II, Marrakech 40000; ☎ 44 43 04 65; fax 044 43 04 30; www.moroccanproperties.com.

One Source Home Search, 3 at 1 Munroe Terrace, London, SW10 ODL; ☎/fax 0207 376 7689; e-mail enquiries@onesourcehomesearch.com.

Vernet Immobilier, 28 Rue Tarik Ibn Ziad, Gueliz, Marrakech; ☎ 044 42 14 23; e-mail info@vernetis.com; www.vernetis.com.

MEKNES-TAFILALET

Population: 2 million
Area: 70,000sq km
Regional capital: Meknes
Main areas: Meknes, Ifrane, Azrou, Er Rachidia, Erfoud, Merzouga, Rissani

Meknes-Tafilalet is geographically one of Morocco's largest regions stretching from the rich, agricultural lowlands of Meknes, south over the forested plateaux of the Middle Atlas and the snowy eastern peaks of the High Atlas to the southern oasis valleys, sandy deserts and Berber villages bordering Algeria. En-route it takes in great swathes of forest covered with cedar trees, ski slopes, the Swiss style chalets of Ifrane, sand dunes, kasbahs, dramatic gorges, palmeraies and the Roman ruins of Volubilis.

Despite such striking diversity, Meknes-Tafilalet is one of the least visited regions in Morocco. There are only 41 classified hotels and these are mainly in the city of Meknes. There are no international airports and only one domestic airport in Er Rachidia. To get to the region, international tourists have to travel via either Fes or Ouarzazate or via Casablanca to transfer to Er Rachidia. As a result, the southern half and much of the northern part of the region tend to get overlooked by all except the most intrepid/time-friendly tourists. In addition, besides the Imperial city of Meknes (which plays second fiddle to all-absorbing Fes, 50 kilometres east), the Roman remains of Volubilis and Moulay Idriss (see below), there is very little of historical or cultural interest. Based on the fact that 76% of the region is rural with over 600,000 hectares dedicated to agriculture, much of the future tourism plan for the region is centred on ecotourism; Gites/B&B's run by Berber farmers, serving home grown foods, hiking, trekking and cycling.

As the region is so large, the climate varies greatly between the north and the south. The weather in Meknes is seasonal. From November to February, temperatures are around 14°C, during the spring and autumn they rise to an average of 24°C and in the summer months (June-September), they tend to soar to 36°C and above. March and December are the wettest months. In the Middle Atlas, the climate is more temperate, with large amounts of snow, up to one metre at a time, between November and February. Summers are hot, but never soar to the same temperatures as the foothills. To the south, the climate is arid, rainfall minimal and the temperatures high (between 24°C and 38°C) throughout the year.

Cuisine

While neighbouring Fes seems to win all the accolades for gastronomy, Meknes really comes into its own with its natural ingredients. Being located in the heart of a rich, fertile plain, it produces the best olives, grapes, cereals, vegetables, goats cheese and citrus in the country. It is also the leading producer of wine, responsible for 60% of all production blending Cabernet Sauvignon, Syrah, Merlot and Chardonnay with a vast array of homegrown vines. Berber cuisine tends to dominate the Middle Atlas, for example; barley couscous, which uses barley grains in place of couscous mixed with chicken, saffron, turnips, courgettes, milk and parsley, *therfist*, which is unleavened bread prepared in sheets and spread with aromatic *fenugreek* and water and *mechoui*, a Berber-style roasted lamb, marinated with paprika and cumin and slow cooked for several hours. Around Ifrane and Azrou, the rivers are filled with trout, which is a local favourite as are strawberries and wild asparagus. In the desert south of the region, dates appear pretty much everywhere. In the oasis of Erfoud, there are thirty different varieties to choose from as well as an annual date festival. Deep inside the remote sand dunes of

Merzouga, *poisons de sables,* which resemble tiny guinea pigs are eaten and sold in souks, by the locals as is gazelle.

MEKNES

Meknes is the principal city for the northern half of the region, lying in the centre of the country on the rich, fertile Saiss plain, which it shares with Fes. It is also one of Morocco's four Imperial Cities along with Fes, Marrakech and Rabat, having once been the nation's capital. 700,000 people live in Meknes, which is divided into an old medina, a ville nouvelle and a largely uninhabited Imperial City, enclosed within an immense 25 kilometres of mammoth walls.

Meknes originated as a hill top kasbah, winning acclaim for being one of the main bases of the Khajarite Berbers who overthrew the first Arab occupiers in 740AD. In the 12th century, during the Almohad dynasty, the medina was built with a neat layout revolving around the central mosque. It was not until the 17th century, however, that the city really came into its own when the ruling Alawite sultan appointed his younger brother, Moulay Ismael, the role of governor. When the Alawite sultan died suddenly, his twenty-five year old brother succeeded him to the throne and reigned for the next 55 years. Moulay Ismael was a paranoid sultan, sensing rebellion in Marrakech and Fes, he decided to relocate the nation's capital to Meknes, which he knew to be loyal. Employing 50,000 workers he built an Imperial City, just south of the medina ramparts, with enough palaces, ponds, gardens and pavilions to accommodate his 4 wives, 300 concubines, 800 children and 12,000 horses. He planned this city to be a mighty fortress, which would protect him as opposed to building a fortified city, which would protect his subjects. While it is generally agreed that Moulay Ismael did great things for Morocco in terms of unifying the nation, taming the unruly tribes and driving the British and Spanish out of northern regions, he was also a violent, cruel megalomaniac claimed to have said 'my subjects are like rats in a basket, unless I shake the basket, the rats will gnaw their way out'. Moulay Ismael's death in 1727 also signalled the beginning of the end for Meknes. The 1755 Lisbon earthquake that destroyed much of Morocco, hit Meknes hard and little attempt was made to restore it. Fes and Marrakech resumed their superior roles sidelining Meknes completely. The French colonisers in 1912 were the first to make any attempts to revive the city by making it their military headquarters. French farmers moved into the fertile hinterlands only to be removed by the Moroccan government, post independence and the land leased to local farmers.

Meknes Today

Meknes today remains overwhelmed by its past glory. Few inhabitants know how to deal with the great spaces and aspirant grandeur left behind by the overzealous builder and many of the more palatial areas remain uninhabited. Meknes is often accused of being a city with no soul. This could be because its historical opulence does not sit well with its Berber population who originate from the mountains and rural hinterlands. It could also be because of the sanitising/removal of many of the more 'characterful' aspects of the city, such as the water sellers and crafts-men who used to inhabit the lively Place el Hedim in between the medina and Imperial City.

In 1996, Meknes was awarded World Heritage status by UNESCO, for its 17th century Islamic and European design and harmonious layout. Besides the Imperial City, there is little in Meknes, which cannot be seen in other parts of Morocco. Unlike Fes el Bali (old medina in Fes), which gets more interesting once you know it better, there is little more than a few days worth of interest to occupy the average visitor, the majority of which revolves around impressive palaces such as the one belonging to Sultan Moulay Ismael, known as Dar Kebira (The Big), dungeons, which once housed over 40,000 prisoners, most of whom were European Christians, and gateways (babs) such as the famous Bab el Mansour, arguably Morocco's most beautiful gate, which, reproduced on postcards and in books, has come to symbolise the city. In between the medina and the Imperial City is the 9 hole par 36, Meknes Royal Golf Club surrounded by apricot, orange, olive and plum trees.

Meknes is the perfect base from which to visit some of the country's most impressive ancient relics such as the Roman ruins at Volubilis, 30 kilometres north and Moulay Idriss, 4 kilometres from Volubilis, the tomb of Morocco's most venerated saint, Moulay Idriss, direct descendant of the prophet Mohammed. It is also a good point from which to explore the Middle Atlas, which compared to the High Atlas do not receive much footfall from tourists.

Medina and Imperial City. The heart of Meknes lies at Place el Hedim, which sits in between the medina, accessed via Bab el Mansour, to its north, the old mel-lah, once home to 3000 Jews, to its west and the palace of Moulay Ismael, Dar Kebira, to its south. The souks and covered markets lie to the west and centre of the medina and are separated into wood, metals, carpets, textiles, food and spices. It is not a complicated medina to navigate, although most of the street signs are small and eroded, so it is best to work via landmarks such as the Grand Mosque in the centre.

Every May/June Meknes plays host to Morocco's largest Moussem (festival to honour a Saint) when visitors from all over the country visit the Mausoleum of Sidi ben Aissa, just outside the medina walls, and perform bizarre rituals such as glass eating along with more run of the mill dancing, singing and cavalry charges.

The main reason most people come to Meknes, however, is to see the Imperial City enclosed within 25 kilometres of walls. Built in just 55 years and filled with marble, plundered from Volubilis. It houses the huge Mausoleum of Moulay

Ismael, granaries, pavilions, the Royal Golf Course and the Aguedal Tank, a 4 hectare lake originally built to supply water for the palace gardens but now mainly supplying water for the golf course and attracting picnickers.

Ville Nouvelle. Twenty minutes walk from the medina, separated from the old towns by a deep gorge that runs into the Oued (river) Boufekrane is the ville nouvelle, which was built by the French as a military town. It is the location for most of the hotels as well as the train station, which connects to Fes, Marrakech, Casablanca, Oujda, Tangier and Rabat. It is a whitewashed prosperous town, which lives off its agricultural surrounds. The town benefits from a couple of cinemas, a Marjane hypermarket and more cafés per square mile than any other Moroccan city. Most nightlife is centred on the ville nouvelle where all the cafés are filled from dusk till late with, mainly, groups of men drinking mint tea. The few nightclubs are located in hotels and tend to be rather seedy affairs.

Properties

The medina is painted a cheerful orange, pink and sandy yellow interspersed with the Islamic green shiny tiles of the city's many minarets. The ground is cobbled; has many potholes and is in need of new paving and many of the walls on either side of the narrow passageways are starting to crumble. Small exterior windows are covered in elegant wrought iron and many of the houses have intricately carved cedar wood crowning their doorways. On an architectural par with Fes, intricately patterned zelliges, stucco walls, fountains and cedar clad ceilings are the main decorative features of properties, which tend to be tall with high ceilings. Most of the restored properties are around Place el Hedim and Bab el Mansour heading up towards the souks on the west side of the medina.

Compared to Fes, which has only within the last few years started a period of riad restoration, there are very few restored riads in Meknes and most of those, which have been restored are now restaurants and/or guesthouses owned and run by Moroccans. There are only two estate agents in the city and neither is English speaking, catering solely to a Moroccan market with the demand for properties from foreign owners currently very low.

While it is unlikely Meknes will ever warrant the same level of popularity as Fes, it should not be overlooked completely. The medina is much smaller, more laid back and hassle free than neighbouring Fes, while the size and style of many properties are not dissimilar. Proximity to the golf course in the centre of the old town, as well as to the Middle Atlas and ancient sites means that there is the possibility of a holiday letting/ second home market especially as it is possible to find highly affordable properties, currently much cheaper than in Fes (which itself is comparatively cheap) such as a 2 bedroom apartment in the ville nouvelle for 300,000 dh (£18,000), 4 bedroom unrenovated riad in the medina 350,000 dh (£21,000). Unlike the other Imperial Cities, however, which are becoming increasingly cosmopolitan, Meknes is likely to always remain a Moroccan city for Moroccans. Its proximity to the tomb of Moulay Idriss, one of the most important sites in the Muslim world and its vast number of mosques, means that it will always have an orthodox edge, which might or might not appeal to non Muslims living in the city. Most of the real estate focus in the area is currently on Fes and this is unlikely to change for a few years. If Fes becomes saturated with second home buyers/restored riad guesthouses, more eyes are likely to turn to Meknes as the next (relatively) big thing, but this is unlikely to be for a long time or with the same intensity as elsewhere.

IFRANE

If you arrived in Morocco in the dark and were driven straight to Ifrane, you would be forgiven for thinking that the plane had taken a wrong turn and landed in the midst of the Swiss Alps. This is how bizarre this French built hill town is, 50 kilometres south of Meknes in the heart of North Africa, with its white Swiss style chalets, red-pitched roofs, matching shutters and white picket fences. There are immaculately clean, tree-lined streets with ornate street lamps, wide pavements, red and white striped curbs and grassy islands in the road. The air is brisk and clean and the sky clear and blue. It is only after looking more closely that you realise this is Morocco after all; washing hanging out of windows, mint tea being poured in cafés and the 'M' dropped off the Mobil petrol station sign.

It is in Ifrane that the Moroccan bourgeoisie from Casablanca, Rabat, Meknes and Fes, own their second homes, visiting in spring for fly fishing and picnics by the lakes and winter, to ski in close by Mischliffen, which is the best time to come. The town was built in 1929 as a hill station for French colonial officials. It is in a picturesque location, surrounded on all sides by oak, cedar and pine forests at an elevation of 1655 metres above sea level. The population is small, around 14,000 inhabitants but this swells considerably when the king and his entourage holiday at the Royal Palace, to the east of the town, a gothic-style castle with a green roof and sandy coloured walls.

In 1995, Al Akhawayn University, (meaning 'brothers' in Arabic), opened on a 50 hectare site, to the north of the town, as a partnership between the previous Moroccan king, Hassan II and the late King Fahd of Saudi Arabia with additional funding from the United States. Modelled on the American system, with much of the teaching conducted in English and taught by American staff, it attracts students from around the world and, much to the chagrin of many, elite Moroccans, who are the only ones able to afford the high fees. It is, however, an excellent place to learn Arabic running an intensive summer course, which professes to be able to teach a year's Arabic in 8 weeks (see *www.aui.ma*).

Properties

Chalet style French colonial villas with the red pitched roofs are found in the area of Hay Riyadh (Villa Zone), in the centre of Ifrane in the quadrant between the Azrou road and the Fes road. These were predominantly built between 1929 and 1956. These properties, some of them empty and in much need of restoration cost in the region of 720,000 dh (£45,000) for unrenovated and between 1-1.6 million dh (£62-100,000) for renovated. All the villas built to the west of the town are modern (built in the 1990's and onwards) and lack the charm of the older style properties. As these villas were built with the intention of being second homes for wealthy Moroccans to live in during the summer months, they lack insulation and so are, essentially, freezing during the winter. This is also true of the new apartment blocks, which are being built on the site of many older style homes, from Rue de la Poste to Rue des Capuchins. It is a shame that so many of the old colonial houses are being knocked down in favour of these modern, whitewashed, featureless apartment blocks. The more old houses bought up to prevent this happening, the better.

AZROU

Azrou is a small Berber town in the Middle Atlas, 65 kilometres south of Meknes, 80 kilometres south of Fes, 20 kilometres south of Ifrane, with a population of 50,000. It is named after the large volcanic outcrop of rock (azrou means rock in Berber), which is attached to the main square, next to the new yellow and green grand mosque, Annour. The town has a few claims to fame. The first is its Tuesday souk, which is arguably the best in the Middle Atlas where Berber salesmen come from far and wide to sell their Berber carpets – not normally to a tourist market, so prices are fair. The second is the *Cedre Gouraud*, a huge cedar tree, ten metres in circumference and named after a French general and the third are the cedar wood carvings, typical of the area, sold in the *Centre d'Artisanat* on the route de Khenifra. There is also Morocco's prestigious Berber college, *Tarik Ibn Ziyad*, which was built by the French in order to create a French speaking Berber elite, who would pacify the region's fiercely loyal nationalists, who were rebelling against the occupation. Such attempts failed, but the college is still in use today. Barbary apes are a feature of the very exquisite and highly remote cedar forests in the Middle Atlas region, south of Azrou, although with so much of the forest being stripped for firewood and furnishings, more and more apes are going hungry and having to rely on human tidbits for their survival.

Properties

Azrou has an old kasbah, built in 1684 by the Sultan Moulay Ismael, the remains of which are still standing. The mountain slopes are covered with traditional beaten earth houses with flat, white roofs and sometimes waist-high stonewalls enclosing the surrounding plot of land. The modern town radiating from the main square is made up of traditional narrow steep streets with steps on to different levels and potholed passageways. Houses are a messy array of white, peach and brick, many with lime green or yellow shutters, all different shapes and heights. Like many less touristy Moroccan towns, it suffers from an excess of rubbish strewn across the streets, which greatly detracts from what is actually a very pretty place.

There is not much of a tourist market yet in Azrou with tour operators reluctant to bring tourists due to the general lack of facilities. With the exception of a few notables such as Gite Ras el Ma, in between Azrou and Ifrane, accommodation/hotels are few and far between. It is also not yet discovered by foreigners wishing to purchase second homes/ guesthouses in the area. It does, however, have a lot of potential being only 80 kilometres from the nearest international airport (Fes) and in the midst of beautiful countryside ideal for walkers and trekkers, shared with the Berber town of Aïn Leuh, 30 kilometres south (see below) with wildlife such as woodpeckers, booted eagles, butterflies, grasshoppers, cherry trees, lakes, caves, pink peonies, orchids, thyme, sage, juniper and the waterfall of Oum er Rbia, the source of Morocco's largest river.

It is good to bear in mind that roads in the Middle Atlas, though being improved, are subject to becoming both flooded and blocked by snow, making much of the area inaccessible during the winter months.

Properties in Azrou range in price from 110,000 dh (£7000) to 250,000 dh (£16,000)

Aïn Leuh. The Berber town of Aïn Leuh is 30 kilometres south of Azrou off the scenic route to the market town of Khenifra. It started out as a Berber market town, before being taken over as an administrative town by the Sultan Moulay Ismael, who built a kasbah here, in the 18th century. During the occupation, it was adopted by the French who constructed a number of Ifrane-style steep roofed chalets in the hills, which they share with semi-nomadic herdsmen, who spend the summers sleeping in tents next to their flocks. In the town itself, next to the market, houses are flat roofed and brown with terrace gardens.

Khenifra. Khenifra is a market town, 80 kilometres south of Azrou, with a popu-lation of around 90,000, and a weekly livestock market selling sheep, mules, cows and goats. Sitting on the banks of the Oum er Rbia, it is where the Zaiane Berbers emerge from, well known for their excellent horsemanship. It has a small, lively medina and a pretty kasbah with properties a striking red to match the red soil of the region. Few tourists visit Khenifra and those that do, tend to be passing through along the scenic route to the high plateaux of Imilchil, a small mountain village, well known for its traditional marriage fair. This happens every Septem-ber among the Aït Haddidou Berber tribe and involves girls with faces dabbed in henna and men with silver daggers meeting and dancing while in the wings, intricate arrangements are made by family elders regarding dowries.

ER RACHIDIA

While Er Rachidia itself is not the most inspiring of towns having been built as a military outpost for the French Foreign Legion and made up of little more than one main street, it benefits from having a wonderful location. Lying in the heart of the Ziz Valleys with its rusty golden hills and thick vegetation, 280 kilometres south of Azrou, close to the dramatic Ziz Gorge and north of the Tafilalet Oasis and sand dunes, it is at a crossroads between the north/south and the east/west of Morocco. It is also easy to travel to, having its own airport, with twice weekly flights from Casablanca. Just north of Er Rachidia is the Hassan Addakhil dam, which collects water from the Ziz, to irrigate the palm trees of the Tafilalet plain and the southern regions.

Some of the interesting local attractions include the little tourist village of Meski, twenty kilometres south of Er Rachidia, which lures visitors because it is the site of the Source Bleue. This is a spring of clear, blue water that gushes into a large concrete tank built by the French as a clean water pool to swim in. The Ziz Gorges, north of Er Rachidia are also dramatic attractions, created by the River Ziz, which has sheered a corridor through the Atlas.

Properties in/around Er Rachidia

Buildings in Er Rachidia are typically red and square, with flat roofs, brown shutters and rarely more than 2 stories high. Having been built by the French, there are no interesting/historical buildings. There is still a strong military presence in Er Rachidia and much of the town is dedicated to compounds inhabited by military personnel. The number of foreigners who have bought in the desert areas around Er Rachidia can be counted on the fingers of both hands and in all circumstances it is to build touristique projects such as guesthouses and hotels. The second home/holiday let market is still a way off but it is highly probable that it will come to the area, especially if the number of flights per week are increased, as it is too beautiful/unusual a part of Morocco, to ignore. As expected for an undeveloped property market, land/house prices are pretty much whatever you/the seller, wish them to be. kasbah homes in some of the villages around Er Rachidia, (which mainly house animals with the owners living in newer properties elsewhere), belong to Berber tribesmen and can be bought for as little as 50,000 dh (£3000) making the prospect of buying whole neighbourhoods, quite tempting. It is worth remembering, however, that the buying/renovation process for kasbahs can be highly complicated (see *What Type of Property to Buy?*).

ERFOUD, MERZOUGA AND RISSANI

If you keep heading south from Er Rachidia, you come to the three towns of Erfoud, Rissani and finally, Merzouga in the Tafilalet oasis. Erfoud, physically, is not that different from Er Rachidia, having also been a French-built military outpost, with a number of low, flat roofed, red, square buildings interspersed with palm and eucalyptus trees. It is now possible to reach Erfoud via a new road connecting it to the desert town of Zagora via Tazzarine, which lies to the west, this has opened up the southern stretch of desert from Ouarzazate to Zagora and on to Erfoud. Erfoud's main claim to fame, as well as being the last part of rebellious Morocco to be 'tamed' by the French, is its marble manufacturing industry, where it produces a high quality, black marble, the polished version of which can be found on every hotel reception desk and mantlepiece.

Rissani lies 22 kilometres to the south of Erfoud along endless oases of rich, flourishing crops. It was from here that the current monarchy first emerged in the mid 17th century, firstly conquering the southern regions and then seizing Marrakech and Fes from the Saadians. Around 25% of the Rissani population inhabit the maze-like, dark streets of a large 17th century ksar accessed via impressive gates. The modern town is the administrative centre for the southern regions.

The reason most people make the intrepid journey down to Merzouga, is for the spectacular Erg (meaning sand dune in Arabic) Chebbi, the first real touch and feel of the very striking Sahara desert, with its monstrously high sand dunes, becoming increasingly popular with sand skiers. Located 25 kilometres south east of Erfoud, the landscape is frequented by film crews and many of the locals will woo you with insider stories of Hollywood stars. The Paris-Dakar rally also passes through, as do several Land Rover loads of tourists. It is possible to drive a standard car down to Merzouga as there is a good tarmac road running from Rissani, although 4x4's are a common sight and can be useful in the event of sandstorms when the road quickly resembles a beach.

There is something of a very basic property market in the area, mainly in the form of touristique guesthouses, to catch the regular flow of tourist traffic. On the edge of the dunes, there is the elegant auberge, Kasbah Derkaoua aka Chez Michel, built and run by a French man and Riad Maria owned by an Italian couple plus a handful of other simple hotels. Most properties follow the kasbah style, built with pisé mud walls, turrets and towers. Buying land/property in this part of Morocco will have to be more out of love for the desert than as a money-spinning venture. If you plan to set up a touristique venture, you will be competing with a number of other tourist properties both at the site of the dunes and in Merzouga on the southern tip. Many visitors (with the exception of film crews) stay an average of one night only, awarding themselves with a 'been there, done that' tick, so there is little money to be made from tourism. Properties tend to be high maintenance due to the excessive dust and heat, so much time will need to be spent ensuring they are kept in an hospitable condition. Travel to the sand dunes from Er Rachidia airport, is only around 100 kilometres, so you are not desperately remote, although daytime temperatures can be intense especially during July and August with minimal shade.

THE ORIENTAL

Population: 2 million
Area: 83,000sq km
Regional capital: Oujda
Main areas: Oujda, Saidia, Berkane, Nador, Figuig

The exotically named Oriental region takes in the whole eastern edge of Morocco, running vertically parallel with the Algerian border (currently closed) down through desert to the isolated date palm oasis town of Figuig, from where pilgrims used to leave for Mecca, west through the Beni Snassen mountains and the mining area of Jerada up to the modern business town of Nador, which borders the Spanish enclave Mellila. From here it runs east along the sandy beachfront over the Moulouya estuary to Saidia and south across flat green plains to the region's capital and university city of Oujda. Around 2 million people inhabit the eastern region with around a quarter living in Oujda.

The Oriental region benefits from some of Morocco's most diverse and attractive landscapes such as the beaches in Saidia (one of the six coastal sites chosen for the Plan Azur), the forests and lakes in Jerada, rivers and fauna in Berkane and the desert oasis of Figuig, but it is largely unvisited by tourists.

Traditionally suffering from under investment by the government, the area has come to rely on the large number of expatriates who leave from the region to live and work in Europe. Current estimates state that 30% of expatriate Moroccans come from the Oriental sending money back both to their families and to invest in real estate. The main industries are agriculture, fishing and minerals. Proximity to Algeria and the Spanish enclave of Melilla also means that the region suffers from an active informal sector fuelled by smuggled goods from Algeria and Melilla (electronics, alcohol and tobacco, which are expensive in Morocco due to extremely high import duties) and the smuggling of hashish and illegal migrants into Europe.

Spain plays a big role in the life of the Oriental region, particularly around the port town of Nador. A large number of the population speak and understand Spanish and the most watched television channels are those broadcast in Spanish.

In 2003, the king visited Oujda vowing to start several investment projects such as the 320km Fes-Oujda motorway, which will run via the mountain town of Taza and be complete in 2010 and the EU funded building of a coastal road running along the whole Mediterranean front from Tangier, via Nador to Saidia. The king's aim is to improve the whole north coastal stretch, transforming it into a prime tourist resort on a par with southern Spain.

The Oriental shares a Mediterranean coastal climate of hot dry summers, tempered by southwest trade winds and wet winters with a searing arid climate in the desert and cold evenings particularly in the winter months of December and January. Many claim Figuig to be the hottest place in the country. Located in between sea and desert, next to the Rif mountains means the climate can swing from one extreme to the other. The agricultural plains around Oujda, for example, are prone to crippling droughts, while along the coast in Saidia, snow was reported on January 27th 2005.

Cuisine

The cuisine of the coastal areas is both Spanish influenced much like in Tangier and seafood based. Oysters, shrimp and scallops from the fish farm in Nador make their way into some of the town's restaurants attracting a large Spanish clientele as do the Mediterranean dishes of paella, grilled sardines and tortilla. Olives are Oujda's main speciality especially after the September harvest, when they fill the souks by the barrel. The slopes of Beni Snassen mountains are filled with vineyards, planted by the French, making the famous Vins des Beni Snassen one of Oujda's key economic activities, along with oranges in the province of Berkane, lemons, wheat and barley. Turkish desserts have also seeped into the Oriental region from Oujda's brief flirt with the Ottoman Empire, such as *cadaif,* known in Morocco as *ktaif,* a honey-walnut fried pastry, sickly sweet just as the Arabs like them. In the south of the region around the desert plains of Figuig, dates are the mainstay delivered by the 200,000 date palms that fill the oasis.

OUJDA

Oujda is Morocco's easternmost city located 17km from Algeria and 60km from the Mediterranean coast. It is the only city in Morocco where you can, without too much legwork, do the sea, the mountains and desert all in one day. It has a population of around 400,000 inhabitants including a number of students attending the large university, Mohammed I. The city sits on the plain of Angad, bordered by one of Morocco's most beautiful mountain ranges, the Beni Snassen, in the foothills of the Rif, with oaks, evergreens, vineyards, mountain springs and scattered Berber villages. To its north is the Mediterranean coast and to its south, the desert. It is the main border town for Algeria to its east and is waiting with bated breath for the border between the two countries to reopen, so that it can resume trade as before.

Oujda was founded by the Berber nomad, Ziri ben Attia in 994 as a citadel from which he could rule his eastern territory. In the mid 11th century, it fell under the rule of the Almoravids before being seized by the Almohads in 1206, who built its ramparts, which are still in place today, wrapped around the medina. In the 13th century, the Merenids furnished the town with mosques, fountains and merdersas. Most of the buildings still remaining today, however, were built

View of Medina from port, Essaouira

Ville Nouvelle, Fes

Apartments Marina Smir, near Tangier

Riad in Fes

Renovated riad

Traditional house, Tangier Medina

Goats in trees

Chefchaouen Medina

Bab (gateway), Essaouira

Plate and spice souk

Moroccan door

Old style estate agents

Camel on beach

Villa salon

Tetouan Ville Nouvelle

Apartments, Tangier City

Ironwork in renovated riad

Swiss style Ilfrane High Street

by the Alawite sultan tyrant, Moulay Ismael in the 17th-18th century. After Ismael's death, the city was fought over and conquered on so many occasions that it earned itself the name 'Oujda' which means 'City of Fear. One of the most notable battles was with the Turks, who had a short spell of rule making the region the only part of Morocco to come into the Ottoman Empire. In 1907, working their way up from Algeria, the French colonized Oujda, 5 years before the rest of Morocco, building their first ville nouvelle outside the medina walls. Throughout the 1900's, border wars were fought between Algerian and Moroccan tribes, the last one being in 1960.

Between 1989 and 1995, the border between the neighbouring countries was open and a lively tourist industry was born with Algerians visiting Morocco for shopping sprees and short holidays. This came to an abrupt end, however as a result of the ongoing dispute with Algeria over the Western Sahara, which caused the border to close again, making many of the businesses such as hotels, that were thriving on Algerian trade, redundant.

Oujda Today

Oujda today is a modern prosperous city surviving on agriculture, mining and handouts from relatives living in Europe. There is a small, 30 hectare medina in the heart of the city with 1000 year old ramparts but a modern interior rebuilt by the French in the 20th century and quite out of keeping with most medinas with wide streets and ease of navigation. 432 shops and 1250 people live in the medina, which has recently had a 20 million dirham injection from the government to renew the sewage works, repave the roads, restore many of the old houses, open new streets and rebuild parts of the ancient walls. Bab el Ouahab (meaning 'gate of heads' as it is the site where decapitated criminals used to be hoisted up on poles) is the best preserved and most attractive gateway into the medina, it is also the heart of the city, where cafés and restaurants spring into life at dusk and audiences are entertained by the street musicians and joke tellers.

Just outside the medina along the southern ramparts is Parc Lala Meriem, a peaceful, pretty, flower filled park and a little further along is the French cathedral Saint Louis, an attractive old building but in need of much work and attended by a weekly congregation of around fourteen.

The main street in the ville nouvelle is Mohammed V along which banks, cafés, restaurants and administrative offices can be found. The airport, with flights daily from/to Casablanca is 15km north of the city and the train station 5 minutes walk west from the medina.

Every year, Oujda plays host to a festival for filmmakers from the Maghreb region to exhibit their movies, discuss scripts and develop cinema in North Africa. Oujda was chosen as the site because it is traditionally a base for Maghreban resistance against colonisers.

Properties

Despite its long history, properties in Oujda are relatively modern and most are in a relatively good state of repair, simply needing some updating. Due to their age, many lack the old features, which lure most people to buy traditional style properties, such as low archways and old doors. The medina is split into nine districts or quartiers plus a market quartier and a kasbah, which used to house the *makhzen* (government elite).

There is currently next to no demand from Europeans looking to live in Oujda, but this is unlikely to be the situation for long as the city is close (60km) to the huge, new coastal development in Saidia (see *Saidia* below), which is housing predominantly Europeans, with a large number of Brits. This development will greatly increase tourist traffic through Oujda as many people will fly into its airport or take trains from the train station to visit other parts of Morocco. The government is injecting money into the city to make it look 'respectable' to the upcoming influx of foreigners and it is likely that it will start attracting property hunters in its own right due to its proximity to a number of diverse and highly attractive landscapes.

If you are considering buying property in Oujda to let out to visiting tourists, you will need to be aware that this market is currently very limited and unlikely to yield much income for the immediate future. It could, however, be a wise investment as Oujda is on the path to becoming a tourist destination, once the eastern regions become more established and the airport starts accepting European low cost airlines as has been mooted. While property prices will have risen slightly as a result of the recent interest in the Mediterranean coast, they are still incredibly cheap compared to elsewhere, around 200,000 – 400,000 dh (£12-24,000) for traditional style homes.

The medina is small and therefore does not take long to traverse, If you live in the northwest corner, you will be close to Place du 16 Aout, a lively square bordering the medina and the ville nouvelle. On the eastern edge you can be close to the bustling Bab Oudahab (although not so close that it is noisy), the grand mosque (again, not so close that the muezzin disturbs you) and kissaria (covered market) or in the south eastern corner in the large asbah properties, near to Bab Sidi Aissa, you will be next to the more tranquil Parc Lala Mereiem.

Berkane. Berkane is a provincial town of 250,000 lying between Oujda and Saidia on the edge of the Beni Snassen mountains. For Moroccans, the town holds two claims to fame, it is the orange capital of Eastern Morocco, filled with grove after grove of orange trees and it is the birthplace of one of Morocco's most loved sporting heroes; Hicham el Guerrouj, the first man in 80 years to win the 1500 and the 5000 metres in the 2004 Olympic games.

Berkane is a modern agricultural town, French and more recently Moroccan built with white washed square constructions. It is a prosperous town, due to its wine, almond and vegetable production in addition to citrus fruit. Being large and modern and lacking in any kind of historical monuments/pretty architecture or nightlife, the town itself does not have much to hold the attention of either tourists or potential house buyers but what it does benefit from, besides its succulent citrus fruit is its location both in close proximity to the Beni Snassen mountains, which can be reached and enjoyed in a day and, the very spectacular, Zegzel Gorge (or series of gorges), around 5km north of Berkane, which were created by the Oued (river) Zegzel, shearing through the limestone mountains.

SAIDIA

Saidia's 20km sandy beachfront and perfect bathing conditions make it the most attractive coastline along the northern rim of Morocco, accessed via a eucalyptus forest. It lies just east of the Moulouya estuary inhabited with 180 species of bird, a one-street town and a still occupied 19th century kasbah. It used to be a seasonal resort, deadly quiet in winter, heaving in summer with Moroccan and Algerian daytrippers and hardly a western face in sight. This has now all changed. Saidia was one of the six coastal sites chosen by the king to develop as part of the Plan Azur. Spanish property developers Fadesa, were chosen to undertake the large building project, which has put the eastern resort on to the map of virtually every international property agent, with a lean towards the Mediterranean. The resort will be complete in 2008 with the government investing 3.2 billion dirham (£200 million) into surrounding infrastructure and new tourist amenities. Every August, there is a folk festival in the town held in the Palais du Festival de Saidia, which attracts large numbers of Moroccans.

Properties

Fadesa's Mediterrania-Saidia development has been built along 6km of beachfront and incorporates 3000 apartments and villas. Property prices on the development start from 660,000 dh (£41,000) for one bed apartments. Three 18 hole golf courses (taking treated water from the sea), 8 hotels, an 840 berth marina, shops, bars, restaurants and a medical centre now exist on the site that is expected to generate 8000 direct jobs.

While all eyes are on the new development, it might be wise to look further afield around Saidia for properties/land outside the resort especially if you like the idea of an older style farmhouse or land on which you can build somewhere unique. You can currently expect to pay around 1000-1600 dh per sq m (£62-100) for plots of land close to the sea.

Nador. The reason most people will have heard of Nador is because of its position

13km south of the Spanish enclave of Melilla and, therefore, the first Moroccan port of call for many people arriving into Morocco by ferry from Almeria, Spain (although most people take the more frequent Algeciras-Tangier crossing). Highly relaxed with a strong Spanish influence, Nador has traditionally suffered at the hands of government, which has never quite known what to do with it. Post independence, they decided to make it a port town in its own right, independent of Spanish control for the export of minerals from the Rif. Unfortunately, the Rif was not as mineral rich as had been assumed, so the port became confined to the export of low grade ion ore, coal from Oujda and agricultural produce. There were also plans to turn the town into an urban centre encouraging industry to the north. Being delinked from the national economy, in close proximity to the dissident inhabitants of the Rif and suffering from poor infrastructure, however, has pretty much left the town out on a limb to fend for itself.

This 'fending for itself' has caused the residents of Nador to turn away from their own country to the Spanish enclave of Melilla, where the ties between the two towns, though unacknowledged by either Rabat or Madrid, are incredibly strong. For the citizens of Nador, Melilla has become the focal point of opportunity for commerce and employment with nearly 30,000 Nador residents entering and leaving the enclave on an almost daily basis to do business and to receive the services they lack in their own town. There are also a large number of entrepreneurs doing business on both sides of the border with Nador businesses working more closely with Malaga and Madrid than Casablanca and Rabat.

The Moroccan government's recent plans to revive the northern coastline does incorporate Nador, which will benefit from the new Tangier-Saidia coast road and the 2.25 billion dirham Nador-Taourirt rail link, which will attach Nador to the already existing Taourirt-Fes railway line and open up great swathes of the country to the northern town.

Nador is, however, a business town with a fish farm specialising in oysters and shrimp, a sugar refinery and a cement factory. There is little attraction for holidaymakers or potential house buyers. The main problem is that the town is facing the wrong way with its back to the sea. So the beachfront, which could be very pretty is just filled with the backside of grey/whitewashed, square, uninspiring buildings that fill up the town and you can never get the sun and the sea in front of you at the same time, which is a bit of an occupational hazard for a town that is hoping to hone in on tourism. Historically and culturally there is not much of interest, although the fish is good and plentiful and the palm-lined streets remind you that you are somewhere hot.

Figuig. While Figuig, known locally as Figi, is not a probable place for potential house buyers due quite simply to the fact that it is in the middle of nowhere with only 200,000 date palms, a water shortage (128mm of rainfall a year) and a few old ksours (desert-style walled towns) to keep it company, it is still worthy of a mention because it is the kind of place that just might appeal to someone who can think of nothing more joyous than almost complete isolation. Positioned in between Oujda (385km) and Er Rachidia (400km), just 2 km from the Algerian border (and therefore with a strong military presence), Figuig is made up of seven ksours each around 100 metres apart, constructed out of pisé (mud and straw) and each with their own palmery and crumbling turreted fortifications constructed to keep the inhabitants of the other ksours out. It obtains its water from three artesian wells, the shortage of which historically caused endless feuds, but which are now shared, on the whole, harmoniously. The population is around 15,000, made up of the Zenata Berber, the same group that inhabits the Rif Mountains. Surrounding Figuig is scrubby desert and the odd Berber village but very little else.

Of the seven ksour, the four main ones are; Zenaga, El-Oudarhir, El-Hammam and El Maiz-Ouled-Slimane. All are made up of winding, warren like alleyways, shaded from the light with thick walls. El Hammam has hot (50°C) water springs and subterranean passageways that lead down 100 steps to pools of warm water suitable for immersing oneself in. Zenaga is the prettiest of the ksours as it lies at the bottom of the oasis depression so has been least affected by the lowering of the water table as a result, it is filled with gardens hidden behind high, mud walls where almonds, pomegranate and vegetables grow in abundance.

Only the most intrepid tourists visit Figuig as it is a long car journey (with no petrol stations), from the nearest city, even though the roads are generally flat. For as long as the border with Algeria is closed, Figuig is at the end of the line as far as routes through Morocco are concerned there is therefore very little traffic and only one road heading to, in or around it. There is no tourist infrastructure and it is not within the government's sights to do much to draw the tourists in.

As with many of Morocco's poorer regions, the population of Figuig is predominantly made up of women and children as a large proportion of the male inhabitants have left the town in search of work elsewhere. In some cases, these migrants have returned to invest their money into building modern homes outside the crumbling old ksours giving the town of Figuig a modern look. While lack of tourist traffic means there is unlikely to be much income to be made from guesthouse/holiday let property in Figuig, it could be an interesting consideration to purchase a little house/street/neighbourhood inside a ksar, which would be incredibly cheap to buy, in the region of 48,000 dh (£3000) per home.

Estate Agents

Moroccan Properties Ltd, 50 Inwood Avenue, Hounslow, Middlesex, TW3 1XG;
☎ 0208 572 2422; e-mail info@moroccanpropertiesltd.com; www.moroccan propertiesltd.com.

Saffron Villas, Lumberg House, The Mount, Highclere, Berkshire, RG20 9QZ;
☎ 01635 253 121; e-mail info@saffronvillas.com; www.saffronvillas.com.

RABAT-SALE-ZEMMOUR-ZAER

Population: 2 million
Area: 9580sq km
Regional capital: Rabat
Main areas: Rabat, Salé

The region of Rabat-Salé lies in the north west of Morocco along the Atlantic coast, north of Casablanca and south of Tangier incorporating to its east agricultural fields and the 134,000 hectare forest of Mamora, with its cork oak, eucalyptus, pine groves and wild pear. 75% of the region's 2 million people live in the cities of Rabat and Salé, which lie on opposite banks of the Bou Regreg estuary, around half an hour's walk from one another. Rabat has an area of 9500 hectares, Salé, 15,000 hectares but a smaller population. Despite being the nation's capital, home to all the ministries, the permanent residence of the king and the 80 or so foreign embassies, Rabat has a small town feel to it, shops shut for a lunchtime siesta, nightlife ends around 10pm and the streets are calm and free from the traffic jams that asphyxiate most Moroccan cities.

There are no flights to Rabat-Salé from the UK or North America. To reach the region, one must fly to Casablanca and take either the 50 minute train journey or one of the two roads leading to the cities, (the coastal one being scenic, the highway being fast). There are three highways altogether heading out of the city, the Rabat-Casablanca, Rabat-Kenitra-Tangier and the Rabat-Khemmisset-Meknes-Fes. There are also two train stations in Rabat and one in Salé with connections to most stations in Morocco.

The climate of the Rabat-Salé region is generally temperate like most Atlantic coastal climates are. Spring and autumn are the most pleasant times to visit with temperatures around the 20-24°C mark. During the summer months, they rise to around 28°C and fall to 17°C or so during winter with most rain between December and February.

The history of Rabat-Salé is one of extremes where the two cities have yo-yoed from the grand to the backwaters and back again. Rivalry and alliances have been the hallmark of much of the last 800 years ever since the mid 11th century, when the Berber inhabitants of Sala Colonia, a port built by the Romans and now known as Chellah, moved across the estuary to Salé, to escape the orthodox Arabs who had set up a rabat (a community of warriors fighting for religion) to 'rid' them of their heresy. Sala Colonia, sank into obscurity, while Salé gradually became a prosperous port. Rabat was revived during the reign of the Almohad caliph, Yacoub el Mansour who following a series of successful campaigns against Spain, decided that it should become the Imperial City and built surviving landmarks such as the Oudaia gate, which was attached to the Oudaia Kasbah, 5 kilometres of pisé fortifications and the Hassan mosque. He died in 1199, before the mosque was completed and the capital was rapidly relocated to Fes leaving Rabat to fall into decline.

Meanwhile, Salé, was about to hit a peak with the arrival of the Merenids in the 13th century, who dug a channel from the Bou Regreg, through the gates of its city, to enable ships to safely enter. This led to the establishment of trading links with London, Genoa and Venice. Neighboring Rabat, however, spent the next 400 years as a small village with little more than a handful of houses.

It was during the 17th century that Rabat next came into its own when the Saadian sultan, Zaidan, offered the Muslim refugees, expelled from Andalucia, the empty city. Here, they built a medina in the style of their homeland, below the kasbah and entered into a period of piracy joining forces with Salé to become a self governed entity, the Republic of Bou Regreg and calling themselves, the Sallee Rovers. The piracy came to an end under the control of the fierce ruler Moulay Ismael, although it continued unofficially, for another hundred years before gradually fizzling out altogether sending both cities back into a period of relative obscurity.

It was the French in the 20th century who delivered Rabat to where it is today after transferring all political activity to the city and naming it the nation's capital. They built a ville nouvelle next to the medina, but left the old city and all its ancient monuments, intact. Little attention was paid to Salé by either the previous sultans or the French generals and it is now treated as more of a Rabat suburb than a city in its own right.

Cuisine

Rabat-Salé is the region of the sweet tooth. The vegetables in couscous are often replaced with caramelized onions and/or honey is added to the grains, shad is served with cinnamon and raisins or stuffed with dates, lamb is served with dried fruits and sesame seeds while peaches, apricots, melons, grapes, dried figs and prunes adorn the souks. Inside the palace compound, the Royal School of Cooking set up by the late King Hassan II and run by women, for women, produces some of Morocco's most skilled chefs. The ambition of most of the women training here is to work abroad in Moroccan embassies, to showcase their country's cuisine. Here, they are taught how to make the famous *warqa* pastry that is used for Morocco's speciality dish, *bastila*, a painstakingly laborious process that takes 3 months to learn.

There are 2 Marjane hypermarkets in Rabat, with a wide selection of imported and locally produced food available to suit the cities cosmopolitan inhabitants, while seafood and Moroccan fare tend to dominate the restaurant scene along with Mediterranean and French.

Rabat Today

Rabat, the nation's capital is not the place that springs to mind at the mention of Morocco, a number of non Moroccans have never even heard of it with most assuming the capital to be either Casablanca or Marrakech. Despite being steeped in history and having some of Morocco's most pleasant beaches, it is not a major tourist destination. Many consider it too squeaky clean and conservative, others think of it as filled only with briefcases and bureaucrats. This is, in many ways true but from an everyday living point of view, it is an incredibly easy and agreeable place to reside.

Getting around is generally free of some of the hassles that are present in Morocco's other cities such as endless streams of traffic, pollution and navigational issues ie; getting lost. Most roads lead off the central boulevard, Avenue Hassan II, which runs parallel to the medina walls and the ville nouvelle across the width of the city, east to the Bou Regreg and Salé and west, it points you in the right direction for the 70 kilometre highway to Casablanca. The ville nouvelle is full of tree-lined boulevards and luxurious residences, more in tune with a Parisian backstreet than a vibrant capital, while the old Andalucian-style Kasbah Oudaia has flat roofed, blue and white houses immaculately maintained with window boxes and views out to sea. The main street in the medina is Rue des Consuls, which used to be where all the foreign consulates were located prior to the building of the ville nouvelle. It is now one of the main shopping streets in Rabat for souvenirs, furnishings and traditional clothes.

Being the city of royalty, diplomats, politicians and intelligentsia means that Rabat has the best of everything in terms of healthcare with a number of specialized hospitals, leisure facilities, including the 45 hole, highly luxurious Royal Dar es Salaam Golf Club, one of the world's top 50 courses, 15 minutes drive out of the city centre and universities namely Mohammed V, the best in Morocco and the National Conservatory of Music, Dance and Dramatic Arts. It also has an American school located in the quartier of Agdal to the south of the city, gardens/parks including the picturesque Andalucian Gardens on the southern corner of the kasbah and les Jardins Exotiques, around 10 kilometres north of the city with a vast array of flora gathered from around the world. In terms of beaches, the most favoured are the Plage des Nations, 17 kilometres north of Rabat and Temara Plage 13 kilometres south of Rabat. It is also worth remembering that Rabat is the carpet/rug centre of Morocco (see *Buying or Renovating*) so an interesting place to shop for floor coverings for your home.

Rabat also benefits from having a well-established expat community as a result of the large number of diplomats living in the city, which can aid the process of settling in. These include societies such as the American International Women's Association, which holds monthly meetings for all English speakers (*contact American Embassy for details*).

Salé Today

Salé tends simply to be an extension of Rabat. The majority of the town's work-force make the journey each day over the Moulay Al Hassan Bridge into Rabat for administrative-style jobs. There is some industry in the town, mainly centering round Salé's port such as fish canning although ceramics and carpet weaving are also key activities. Just outside the town, on the banks of the Bou Regreg, there is the pottery hamlet of Oulja with around 20 kilns and a large exhibition/craft centre. There is only a small ville nouvelle surrounding the bus station with the main part of town being the small, whitewashed medina with a grand mosque, merdersa and Muslim cemetery.

While the government has great plans for increasing tourism to Salé and turning it into a vibrant metropolis, there is much simmering under the skin of the city's inhabitants. Salé was, until 2002 controlled almost entirely by Islamists funded, largely by Saudis. It was the headquarters of the highly dangerous, *Salafi Jihadi* (Salafist Combat), known locally as the 'Taliban', who have strong links to Al Qaeda and used (until it was raided by police and military helicopters) to work out of the city's Grand Mosque attracting followers from all over North Africa. It is believed to be from here that the Madrid bombers emerged.

PLANS FOR RABAT-SALE

The government is just a few steps away from finalizing their plans to redevelop the banks of the Bou Regreg estuary on both the Rabat and Salé sides with an 18-20km tramway being built to link the two cities. At Bab al Bahr, which lies at the mouth of the estuary, both the left bank (Rabat) and the right (Salé), will be developed with public spaces, roads and embankments. A marina will be constructed on the right bank and bordered by a city of arts and crafts, to boost tourism to the area. Residential sites will also be built around the marina as well as restaurants and guesthouses. Further down the estuary in Al Sahat Al Kabira, there will be leisure parks and shopping malls. On the Rabat side in the city centre and adjoined to a new palm lined artificial island, 15 hectares are being dedicated to up market residential buildings while a 5 star hotel and convention centre is planned for Salé on the opposite bank. These projects are expected to take five years to complete. Further plans are also underway to build a new city, Kasbat Abi Raqraq on the right bank close to the hotel and convention centre, which is expected to incorporate a university, research centre and office blocks as well as a vast number of residential buildings. It is expected the whole project will take about 20 years to complete.

Properties

Rabat has long been coveted by the French as the perfect place to buy property, particularly French retirees who are drawn to Rabat for its excellent healthcare fa-cilities, proximity to embassies, historical monuments, mild climate and road/rail networks. Admittedly, property prices here are more on a par with Casablanca than with Fes ie; on the pricier side, but this does not mean it is impossible to obtain good bargains especially with traditional homes in the medina, which are generally not as sought after here as in cities such as Marrakech. Around 60 foreigners (mainly French) currently own properties in Kasbah Oudaia where traditional homes sell for an average of 1.2 million dh (£75,000). Most retirees buy houses along the coast in places such as Harhoura, Sables d'Or and Skhirate where there is a vast array of properties from apartments and bungalows to large villas ranging in price from around 1.8 million dh (£110,000) to 4 million dh (£250,000). Land close to the beaches ranges in price from 500 dh/sq m (£31) to 3000 dh/ sq m (£187) depending on location and proximity to the sea. Other popular places to buy include the wealthy suburb of Souissi and Rue des Zaers, close to the famous Dar es Salam golf club. Prices here start from around 5 million dh (£310,000) up to and beyond 150 million dh (£940,000). Hay Riad is a new and increasingly popular suburb around 20 minutes drive from the city centre where many fonctionnaires choose to reside as it is close to government buildings. Apartments here cost around 840,000 dh (£52,000) for 2 bedrooms and large villas with private pools range in price from 2 million dh (£125,000) to 5 million dh (£310,000).

Agdal is a suburb to the south of the city close to the American School. This area houses many older properties, but a recent surge of new apartment building has decreased property prices with 3 bedroom apartments available from around 560,000 dh (£35,000).

Estate Agents

Ramses Consulting, 31 Avenue Tarik Ibn Ziad, Hassan, Rabat; ☎ 068 65 79 79/065 12 11 88; e-mail ramses_consulting@yahoo.fr. Specialises in property in Rabat, Kenitra and the surrounding coastline.

SOUSS MASSA DRAA

Population: 3 million
Area: 70,880sq km
Regional capital: Agadir,
Main areas: Agadir, Aglou, Mirleft, Sidi Ifni, Taroudannt, Ouarzazate

The region of Souss Massa Draa stretches from the south-west Atlantic coast east across the Anti Atlas range, which runs perpendicular to the High Atlas, through the Draa Valley to the desert town of Zagora, neighbouring Algeria. Southwards, it borders the camel town of Guelmim, incorporating 200 miles of exceptional beaches. Two rivers run through the west of the region, the Oued Massa and the

Oued Souss from the Anti and High Atlas mountains respectively. The Oued Draa and and Oued Dades, run through the east of the region. Souss Massa Draa boasts the best weather in Morocco. Warm and sunny throughout the year, temperate to hot on the Atlantic coast with the possibility to swim in the sea from February to November and hot and arid in the desert. Average temperatures in Agadir are 24°C, Taroudannt 28°C, Ourarzazate 30°C and Zagora 35°C. Zagora on the edge of the Sahara is known as consistently the hottest place in Morocco.

The Souss Massa Draa region is geographically isolated from the rest of Morocco by the High Atlas, which literally divides the country into the north and the south. As a result, it is almost like a different country, fiercely independent, highly protective of its Berber roots and until as late as the 1930's a dissident community, beyond the control of central government. The majority of the 3 million strong population stem from the Chleuh group of tribes and speak the Berber dialect, Tachelhite rather than Arabic, the official language. These Berber with their high cheekbones and lithe frames are the true people of the land, who have learnt to adjust to a harsh, bleak, unforgiving environment, industriously creating very much out of very little with a warmth and hospitality that is spontaneous and unguarded.

The history of the Souss Massa Draa region tends to perk up around the 15th century, when the Portuguese were first attracted to the coast surrounding Agadir as a place to trade with the Saharan caravans. Setting up a salt plant for fish, they began to do excellent business and transformed the port into a bustling fishing town. Outraged at the European intrusion, however, a tribe of Bedouin Arabs from the Draa Valley decided to take up arms and drive the Christians out. In 1540, they seized the port and conquered the Portuguese. For the next 120 years they reigned over Morocco, becoming the next dynasty, to be known later as the Saadians,

During Saadian rule, the port of Agadir, became the main outlet for produce of the Souss Valley; dates, sugar cane, gold and spices, which were traded in return for European cloth. The Saadians built the medina and kasbah in Taroudannt and made the city their capital. After 120 years of rule, they were succeeded by the Alawites, who shifted the trade routes to Essaouira further north and, fed up with a continuous series of regional revolts, forbade any more trading in Agadir. Saadians opposition to Alawite rule led the megalomaniac sultan, Moulay Ismael to flatten the city of Taroudannt showing no mercy to the buildings or their inhabitants, leaving only the rose red ramparts, which still exist today.

Agadir fell into decline only to be resurrected again at the start of the protectorate in 1912, by the French who saw its value as a useful port. It was also during the protectorate that the cities of Ouarzazate and Zagora officially started to exist, being set up as administrative towns.

On February 29th, 1960, Agadir suffered a major earthquake, which killed around 17,000 people leaving the city devastated and 50,000 people homeless.

The dire task of clearing up the bodies had to be abandoned due to an outbreak of cholera, so the decision was made to bury all the dead in a mass burial mound known as *Ancienne Talborjt*, north of the modern city.

Cuisine

Cuisine in the Souss region centres around the oil extracted from the argan tree (*argania spinosa*), a knobbly, slow growing plant, which grows only in the south west corner of Morocco within a 160km radius of the Souss Valley and, bizarrely, in a small part of Mexico. The tree thrives on very little rain, intense heat and prefers to grow on rough hill slopes. The fruit, which is green and fleshy, little larger than an olive, is loved by goats who climb into the branches of the 10 metre high trees, eat the fruit and excrete the nuts, which tend to hold 2 or 3 almond shaped kernels. These are then collected, roasted, ground and mixed with water. The nutty flavour of argan oil, not dissimilar to walnut oil, is drizzled over hot bread for breakfast, added to salads in place of olive oil or, most deliciously, added to honey and almonds to make the local specialty *amalou*. Argan oil is also used to make cosmetics and soaps, which are developing quite a market worldwide. In the coastal regions, there is an abundance of sardines in every souk or fish grill, along with *St Pierre* (John Dory), red snapper, lobster and prawns.

Cayenne pepper, known both for its taste and its theoretical ability to heal sore throats and toothache, is regularly added to tagines as is camel meat in desert areas, hedgehog, gazelle and foxes. In Zagora, tagines are accompanied by a bread called tagella, which is baked over the hot sands and eaten by the blue turbaned Sahara tribes known as the Tuaregs. Bananas, almonds and dates are cultivated widely as are a wide range of very delicious honeys.

AGADIR

After the earthquake, just four years post independence there was a strong desire to rebuild Agadir as a modern city that showed the country with its feet firmly entrenched in both the east and the west. As it was the start of the 1960's, utilitarianism was the trend and the general theme of much of the city centre is low, white, featureless buildings made out of cement and lacking in any of the ornate character, which gives Morocco its alluring appeal. Somehow, however, the city seems to get away with it. Its wide streets, 300 days a year of sun, 10kms of sandy beach, non-pretentious crowds and holiday atmosphere make up for the dull architecture. Admittedly, few go to Agadir to get a real taste of Morocco, it is a tourist resort full of large all-inclusive hotels, casinos, nightclubs, ice cream parlours, volley ball, bronzed bodies, gay men, the dreaded karaoke and an increasingly large number of Brits, scorned by Maroc-ophiles as being an unfortunate extension of the Spanish Costas. Charter airline and package tour companies tout it as a winter sun destination offering some of the cheapest flights to Morocco. Very recently, there has been a surge of British people buying retirement homes in Agadir to use either year round or as winter getaway homes.

The only historical relic of note is the kasbah sitting on top a hill 750 feet above the city, looking out over the Atlantic. It was built as a defence against attacks from the Portuguese. Following the earthquake, only a section of the original ramparts and the main gateway remain.

There are three golf clubs; two 9 hole courses in the city and a recently extended 18 hole course 12km out of Agadir en-route to Aït Melloul. Unsurprisingly tourism is the largest industry in Agadir, with its hotels able to accommodate over 25,000 visitors. It is also Morocco's main western fishing port, with its fishing boats, in combination with Safi further north, gathering over 170,000 tons of sardines a year. The mounds of silver fish at the huge fish market inside the gates of the port have become a top tourist attraction, as have the fresh fish cafés close by.

Construction has begun on a new 240km highway that will link Agadir with Marrakech. This is part of the 1000km national highway joining the north of Morocco to the south. Expected completion date is 2009. This will break the isolation of Agadir, which has always been relatively cut off from the rest of the country, accessible only via mountainous, winding roads.

Properties

Buildings in the city centre of Agadir are now anti-seismic following the earthquake in 1960. As they are modern, they are titled so the buying process is relatively straightforward and most are sold in a good condition. Three stories tend to be the norm for houses and apartment blocks in order to keep a uniformity about the city. Being hot year round means that the main focus is for properties to be cool and shady. Cement is the main building constituent, most properties are white with tiled stone or in smarter villas, polished wood floors, small, sometimes tinted or permanently draped windows and gardens/terraces shaded by high walls.

In line with the government's 'Vision 2010' for tripling tourism numbers to Morocco, Agadir and its surrounds are in the midst of a growth spurt. The new and exclusive area of Founty, close to the king's palace, south of Agadir has been developed with a string of 5 star hotels adding another 5000 beds. This has triggered the building of a number of large villas in the area, by primarily affluent Moroccans for equally affluent Moroccans to live in or rent out. Properties here tend to be two/three storey with basements and detached with small stretches of land on either side, kitchens, designed with a modern open plan layout are traditionally located in the basement where it is cooler, a large sitting room and sometimes a spare bedroom fill the first floor with two/three en-suite bedrooms on the second floor, balconies and a large roof terrace. Prices of such properties range between 2.5 million dh

(£155,000) to 3.5 million dh (£220,000). Though in a good location close to the beach, this area currently has a rather sterile, polished feel to it, almost too exclusive for its own good with villas closed off behind large gates. Being a couple of kilometres out of the city centre, there are for the time being, no shops in the vicinity, few passers by and a bleak landscape between houses that is crying out for grass and flowers. Much investment is being put into this area, however, so it is likely to be just a couple of years before it becomes more assimilated into the city centre.

The building of a new marina next to the port to the north of the beach is set to revive much of this bustling, industrial stretch. Here there will be shops, cafés, restaurants and a number of apartments for sale and rent with an expected completion date of June 2006 for phases 1 and II and June 2007, for phase III. The apartments with views over the sea, mountains and gardens, range in size from 60sq m for 2 bedrooms to 800sq m for an 8 bedroom penthouse and cost 13,000 dh per sq m (£800). To rent a berth in the marina costs an annual fee of around 15,000 dh (£950).

The centre of the city is around the boulevards of Avenue Prince Moulay Abdallah, Avenue du Prince Sidi Mohammed and Hassan II. Apartments are highly sought after in these areas and the adjoining avenues down to the beach and prices are on the rise. A new apartment block on Hassan II has 3 bedroom properties selling for between 900,000 dh (£57,000) and 1.3 million dh (£84,000).

Upcoming areas are Charaf and Les Amicales in the north of the city, 15 minutes drive from the beach, close to the affluent, primarily European area of Swiss Town. 3-4 bedroom properties in Charaf and Les Amicales sell for between 600,000 dh (£37,000) and 1 million dh (£63,000) and there is a real binge on to improve the areas with roads being paved and streets lit.

North of Agadir

North of Agadir is a prime area for investment. The minimum amount of land that people are allowed to buy along the coast is one hectare. Individuals are not permitted to buy land for building private properties. Being government land, it is reserved only for developers who can prove that their project will be of benefit to the wider community.

Such a rule does not apply, however to a particular Saudi royal who has bought up a kilometre of beach heading out of the city on the road to Essaouira and built a palace enclosed within high walls and guarded by heavy security. To make up for stealing the livelihood of many local fishermen, he has attempted to compensate by building a new hospital and several kilometres of highway. Agadir is popular with affluent Saudi's, many of whom own properties in the city, attracted to the relaxed, liberal atmosphere.

Idi Wadden. A newly built holiday village of small, basic apartments in Idi Wadden a few kilometres outside Agadir is selling 1-2 bedroom properties for 400,000 dh (£25,000). This area along with Tamaragt and Aourir, known for their banana plantations, is particularly popular with Germans and Italians many of whom own guesthouses or winter pads in the surrounding hills.

> **Taghazoute.** The surfing resort of Taghazoute, 17km north of Agadir and famous for its calamari, bananas and beach bums, is one of the six coastal resorts due to be developed as part of the government Plan Azur. At the time of writing, tenders were still out to international developers, but there are 685 hectares put aside for the development of hotels, villas, apartments, spa, a marina and a golf course with an expected completion date of 2010. This will alter the picturesque town of pink and white houses, cafés and campervans quite dramatically and property prices are already rising in the area. Note that old houses in Taghazoute are generally untitled.

> **Aghroud.** 10km on from Taghazoute is the pretty village of Aghroud, which like Taghazoute is one of the areas that the regional government are planning to spend money on to develop into a touristique region. It is perched high on a hill filled with argan and thuya trees and red painted houses, overlooking the Atlantic. This is becoming a popular area with foreigners as the beaches are sandy and uncrowded. A new apartment development of 1-2 bedroom properties with balconies, swimming pools and sea views costs in the region of 300,000 dh (£18,500).

South of Agadir

The area South of Agadir is changing dramatically, just a couple of years ago most of the beaches were deserted for much of the year, visited only by locals from Tiznit (80km south) looking to escape the city heat, and local fishermen. Now, though generally much more peaceful and undeveloped than those north of Agadir, the coastal towns are attracting a number of more pioneering foreigners and Moroccans, with an eye for future investments or those looking for some solace from the increasingly populated resort of Agadir.

While the beaches here tend to be ideal places to sunbathe, assuming the Atlantic winds do not bluster too heartily the sea does have strong currents, which for some of the year can make it unsafe for swimming. You would be wise to always check swimming conditions with local fishermen or in some cases, where they exist, military police coastguards, although they tend to only work during the summer months.

Tiznit. 80km from Agadir, past the flower filled meadows of Souss Massa National Park, with its red foxes, jackals, wild boar, gazelles, red-necked ostriches, flamingos and the very rare, bald ibis, is Tiznit a relatively new medina town of 80,000, built in 1881 by the Sultan Moulay Hassan, as a military base from which he could quell the uprisings of the rebellious Berber of the Souss. The medina is enclosed within 5 kilometres of ochre coloured pisé walls. Instead of building a new town from scratch, Moulay Hassan simply stuck the walls around a handful of already existing kasbahs. In 1912 it served as the base for the warlord El Hiba, the 'Blue Sultan' in his battle against French colonialism.

Located in a prime position, 10km from the beaches of the Atlantic coast, 70km from Tafraoute and the Anti Atlas, straddling the desert and the sea, Tiznit is a central point for much of southern Morocco. It is renowned throughout the country as the silver capital, stemming from the large number of Jewish silversmiths who settled in the medina when it was first established and passed their skills on to Berber craftsmen. The jewellery souk is filled with ornate silverware, jewellery and a vast selection of Berber daggers and sabres.

In addition to the jewellery trade and crafts such as tapestry and dress-making, Tiznit's main industry is agriculture; argan, date palms, almonds, mint and olives, with the majority of the surrounding population working as farmers. In terms of income, however, agriculture is a bit of a drain, only a small proportion of the area is cultivated, there is very little water and there are few markets for the produce besides Tiznit and its hinterlands. A plastics factory in the outskirts of the town has provided a small boost for local employment and as with much of Morocco, many hopes are being pinned on the tourism industry.

Tiznit is not a particularly popular place for foreign housebuyers. It is 10km from the sea and there is not much character in the town, unless you are particularly into jewellery, it is more of a place to drive through en-route to the south than stop off for extended periods of time.

AGLOU PLAGE

10km west of Tiznit is the idyllic beach and fishing village of Aglou, dotted with traditionally Moroccan, white, square, flat roofed houses belonging to both fishermen and an increasing number of Brits. At the far end of the beach, set into the soft soil cliffs, is a row of 50 troglodyte or prehistoric fishermen's homes. These are tiny, basic homes with bed and kitchen, which the fishermen live in all year round, but become filled during the summer months with the whole extended family.

Properties

The guesstimate for the nationality of homeowners living in Aglou, is 50% Moroccan, 50% foreigners with the new trend being to buy up simple, local properties, modernise them and sell them on as second homes. Such properties tend to be titled, costing in the region of 1 million dh (£60,000) to 2.8 million dh (£200,000) for 200sq m, 3/4 bedroom, 3 bathroom properties with 1000sq m of land on the beach. You will, however, get much better deals if you stay in the area for a while and get to know local people who will be able to inform you of unrenovated property for sale, which will be much cheaper to buy although, it is likely that these properties will be untitled.

Unsurprisingly, Aglou is also attracting a number of developers building luxurious villa complexes on the beach. Aglou Paradise consists of around 30 Moorish style properties, built by a Belgian/Moroccan couple selling to a largely British contingent as second/investment homes. Properties have three-bedrooms, sea views, private infinity pools and, in some cases, front doors virtually touching the sand on plots of land measuring between 724sq m and 1200sq m at a cost of around 2.5 million dh (£170,000). Phase II is underway with a completion date of 2007.

MIRLEFT

The exceptionally clean beaches around Mirleft, 10km south of Aglou with a population of just 6000, are totally undeveloped with the small, bustling town set back around half a mile, making way for great swathes of green shrub land, which gives the whole area a feeling of space. While the surrounding cliffs and mountains lure paragliders, the laid back, historical town, once the border between Morocco and Spanish Sidi Ifni, has for many years, attracted musicians, artists and a hippy crowd who spend their days floating between the cafés, which serve excellent seafood on the sandy main avenue and one of the six enticing beaches.

Properties

Property prices in Mirleft are higher than elsewhere along this stretch of the coast as it has always been a haven for affluent French. The French still dominate, buying up second homes or in one or two cases, whole districts, filling them with new modern properties and selling these on to other Europeans for high prices. The general trend is to buy up old properties, renovate them into luxury villas and sell them for around 2.5 million dh (£160,000) and upwards. Land near the coast is selling for around 1300dh sq m (£80). The price of older properties is also higher than in other areas, spurred on by the European interest.

SIDI IFNI

As Agadir gets more crowded and resort-like, many sun-loving expat Europeans are edging away from the city to more peaceful climes down south and Sidi Ifni, is one of the most popular spots. Sidi Ifni, 20km south of Mirleft, was given to the Spanish in 1860 by way of the Treaty of Tetouan, which granted Spain the right to have a fishing village on the coast, within easy reach of the Canary Islands. Spain did not heed the treaty until 1934, after the region had been pacified by French rule, at which time they moved in and built the town that still stands today. When

Morocco claimed back its independence in 1956, Spain refused to relinquish Sidi Ifni. Local wars were waged with the Moroccan Liberation Army and local tribes attempting to take over the town, but they failed due to the might of the Spanish Foreign Legion. In desperation, Morocco cut off all land communication to Sidi Ifni. In 1969, the Spanish eventually returned the town 13 years post-independence, much to the delight of the locals who still celebrate Independence Day from June 30th to 6th July, with a large festival. The town's architecture is a mix of light blue, white and very striking 1930's art deco and the more standard utilitarian square Moroccan style with courtyards and flat roofs. In the 1950's almost 60% of the population of the town was Spanish and there are still many remaining today owning guesthouses, which they rent out to tourists. Sidi Ifni has the reputation of being one of the friendliest places in Morocco.

Properties

While the prices of houses in Sidi Ifni, are on the up, it is still a very good place to buy for a highly reasonable price. It is important to note, however, that the property market here is still very unsettled. Prices for the same property can vary greatly depending on who the buyer/seller is. Popular with Europeans are the old single storey properties near to the sea in the affluent area of Gataa by the Suerte Loca hotel and the boathouse (in the shape of a boat). These are known as 'fishermen's' houses and are made out of argil and stone. They particularly appeal because there is not a huge amount of work that needs to be done on them and they have excellent sea views. In some cases they are bought, demolished and new houses built in their place, but on the whole they are kept intact and sometimes an extra floor added. These tend to sell for around 200-300,000 dh (£12,500-£18,000).

The most common trend, however, is to buy plots of land and build properties on them. Much of the town has been divided into saleable plots. Widadia is a district in the new town of Sidi Ifni. Plots of 102sq m are selling for around 200,000 dh (£12.500). This area is particularly popular with Moroccan expats living in Europe or north Morocco, but wanting a pad in the south. Buying property in Sidi Ifni is relatively straightforward. The municipality is efficient but wildly bureaucratic as with much of Morocco. There are quite strict regulations connected to the building of houses on to a plot of land with regard to number of floors, colour of the external paintwork etc. This varies from area to area and has to be heeded to in order for the property to be connected to electricity and other utilities.

TAROUDANNT

Located close to the High and Anti Atlas mountains and the stunning Tizi n Test pass, Taroudannt is known as little Marrakech for its dusty, red medina, African roots and bustling souks, Taroudannt sits in the Souss Valley in between the High

Atlas and the Anti Atlas mountains around 80km from Agadir. There are two routes to the city from Agadir, either the P32, which is a busy, lorry and bus-filled road or the slower, scenic P40, Agadir – Marrakech road, which winds around the mountains. Unlike Marrakech, the city is hassle-free, the people and lifestyle laid back and the traffic/pollution less overwhelming, with bicycles still a popular way of getting around. Taroudannt was at its most eminent during the 16th century as the capital of the Saadian dynasty. When Agadir's port was closed by Sultan Moulay Ismael, in favour of Essaouira's, it had a knock-on effect on Taroudannt, which also fell into decline only to be revived again at the start of the French protectorate when it became the stronghold for the rebellion against the French army.

It is the major market town of the Souss region with Thursday and Saturday being the busiest days of the week as the rural farmers from the surrounding mountains come down to the city to sell their produce. Taroudannt is an African city, one of the few cities in Morocco, which was not turned into a French administrative post. There is therefore, with the exception of French president, Jacques Chirac being born and owning a home in the city, very little French influence and no ville nouvelle. All aspects of the city are enclosed within the 5 kilometres of spectacular yellow, pink and orange pisé ramparts, which measure 7 metres in height and are one of the few remaining constructions of the Saadian period still existing in the medina.

In addition to the ramparts, which are at their most vivid as the sun is setting, Taroudannt is known for its vast array of foliage, which seems to burst from every crevice; bougainvillea, geraniums, date palms, banana leaves, roses, carnations, avenues of orange trees and surrounding eucalyptus, pomegranate and olive groves. Agriculture is the main industry, primarily the production of olives, citrus fruits, roses and argan oil.

Properties

Being 80km from the sea removes Taroudannt from the main tourist routes. Few package holidaymakers from Agadir make the short trip, unless they are with the excellent ecotourist operator Naturally Morocco. Independent tourists might pass by and stay the odd night but if they are simply looking for sights and monuments, they will have little reason to stay long in the town. Taroudannt has a subtle charm that comes from the general ambience of the place. It is Morocco at its most easy and uncluttered appealing most to Marocophiles who love Morocco for what it is as opposed to what it strives to be.

Like with many small Moroccan towns, there is no nightlife to speak of and restaurants are few and far between. The majority of land and many properties in Taroudannt are untitled and most need restoration work or modernising at the very least.

Prices in Taroudannt are generally lower than along the coast, with renovated riads costing an average of 750,000 dh (£45,000).

Tafraoute. Tafraoute is a small town of 5000 people located 100km east of Tiznit via a narrow, single carriage road that winds into the mountains offering some of the most spectacular landscape in Morocco, every shade of pink, yellow and mauve reflects off the craggy rock faces, which are scattered with mud brick Berber villages and small patches of cultivated land lush with almond trees and palms. Tafraoute itself lies in the heart of the Ameln Valley, surrounded by striking rock formations at an altitude of 1200 metres. In between the palms are cement houses, plastered in red with flat roofs, slit windows, courtyards and towers. Many of these properties are modern, recently built by money sent home from Tangier, Casablanca or Europe where most of the male inhabitants live and work. With the exception of almond cultivation, there is little in the way of industry in Tafraoute or its surrounds, the main inhabitants are women, children and the elderly.

There is not much demand for properties in Tafraoute, estate agents are likely to steer you away from it as it is largely agricultural and therefore difficult for foreigners to buy. It is unlikely it will ever appeal to the broad mass due to its remote location and lack of resources, but for the more hardy homeowner, who is prepared to go through the processes, it could hold charm as a place for a holiday home or a B&B being accessible by roads from both Tiznit and Agadir with good trekking opportunities and surrounded by some of Morocco's most beautiful gorges, valleys and oases.

OUARZAZATE

Ouarzazate is a modern city that sits in the middle of a dry plateau surrounded by the lush green vegetation of the High Atlas. It was built by the French during the colonial years to serve as an administrative post. There are roads connecting to Agadir in the west, Marrakech further north, Er Rachidia to the east and Zagora to the south. It is the main route to the Dades and the Draa Valleys. There is an international airport receiving package tours from the UK or scheduled flights via Casablanca, the 18 hole Ouarzazate Royal Golf Club with views over the Atlas Mountains, supermarkets and as with most cities in Morocco, a plethora of internet cafés. Most of Ouarzazate, including at the far end Kasbah Taourirt constructed in 1754, can be found on or just off Mohammed V, the main artery running through the city. In the 1980's it was decided that Ouarzazate should become a major tourist centre. A dedicated tourist zone was built north of Mohammed V, close to the airport, and filled with 4-5 star hotels and the city centre was spruced up with well-lit pavements and elegant piazzas. With the exception of those on package tours, however, most tourists who visit only stay for a short time whilst en route to the more scenic surrounds.

Ouarzazate's main claim to fame is its close connections to Hollywood. The area has long been popular with mainstream producers and directors with a biblical/historical lean, who love the ancient landscapes on offer around the city. Most sought after is the village of Aït Ben-Haddou, a UNESCO World Heritage site, 30 kilometres north west of Ouarzazate, which has one of the most memorable old towns in all of Morocco. A mixture of decoratively carved kasbahs, fortresses and towers, soaring ten metres high against the backdrop of a craggy red rock face have become the film set for such classics as Lawrence of Arabia, Jesus of Nazareth and Gladiator. Around 700 people live in the old town, but each year around 130,000 tourists visit. Most tend to stay either in the new town just across the shallow river, which has one or two small inns or in Ouarzazate.

To the east of Ouarzazate is the road to Er Rachidia, which runs parallel for some of the way with the Dades River and the famous Dades Valley, known as the land of the fig, in between the inhospitable volcanic terrain of Jbel Sarhro and the High Atlas. This stretch takes in some of the most beautiful kasbahs in Morocco particularly in the little oasis town of Skoura, surrounded by palm groves. Some of the kasbahs are semi inhabited or in one or two cases transformed into guesthouses but many have been deserted by locals in favour of modern breezeblocks and are gradually becoming ruins.

Just outside Ouarzazate is a large dam called the Barrage El Mansour Eddahbi, built in 1972, which is fed by tributaries from the High Atlas that join to form the Draa River, one of the longest rivers in Morocco. The dam irrigates the agricultural regions of southeast Morocco and provides electricity for the valleys. It also prevents the Draa from flooding. Life south east of Ouarzazate revolves around the Draa where palmeraies, kasbahs and Berber villages run in ribbon like strips along its banks, resembling a lush, green plantation that stretches out on either side for around 20metres, before a return to the brown, arid landscape of the desert.

At the bottom of the Draa Valley is the modern town of Zagora, built as another administrative post by the French during the protectorate. Prior to the French, the town was inhabited and it was from here that the Saadian's first began their occupation of Morocco. Zagora is best known for its intense heat and large number of dates, the town's main commodity.

Properties

It is ironic that in a country where family trades are passed through the generations, there are so few people capable of restoring kasbahs using traditional techniques. Such, however is the case. In this part of the Sous Massa Draa region, there are 2000 kasbahs, more than anywhere else in the country and many of them are almost ruins, crumbling back into the dense soil from where they originally emerged. For the majority of Moroccans living in the region, restoration, even using modern techniques, is unthinkable. It is far cheaper for most to simply desert the kasbah and build a new house, which is what many are doing. As a result, the region is a mix of the very old, elegant and ornate and the very new, simple and functional. A few of the kasbahs have been restored by affluent Moroccans and one or two Europeans. If you really hanker after owning a kasbah, moving into an already renovated one is by far the most hassle-free way of having your dream come true as you avoid the long, difficult buying process and the expense of restoration. For such properties, you can expect to pay between 4-6 million dh (£250,000-375,000) for authentic style properties, often built to be guesthouses, with eight-ten bedrooms, a swimming pool and land.

One of the trends for the region is to build 'modern' kasbahs, red plastered properties with towers and crenellated roofs, small windows, large doorways. These look authentic but have all the mod cons of a new property. The market for such buildings is still very new and only occasionally do they become available to buy. It is likely, however, that this region will become more popular over the next ten or so years especially with the renewed interest amongst film makers for the region's landscapes. Buying property, which can be rented out to film crews or tourists on the film trail is likely to be lucrative, especially at this current time when accommodation in the region is still quite sparse.

Tourism numbers to Ouarzazate and its surrounds are rising and the 200km Route d'Ouarzazate heading out of Marrakech is becoming an increasingly popular place to buy land, more so at the Marrakech end, but the gap between the two cities is gradually closing.

Most demand at this present time is for land around or close to the Barrage El Mansour Eddahbi, which costs in the region of 320,000 dh (£20,000) per hectare. Close to Aït Ben-Haddou, 1000sq m of land is likely to sell for around 200,000 dh (£12,000). Note that the majority of the land in this part of the Sous Massa Draa region will be agricultural land, which means that the VNA licence is necessary, prior to obtaining land (see *What Type of Property to Buy?*).

Estate Agents

Agence Immobilier d'Agadir, 18 Immeuble M2, Rue de l'Hotel de Ville, Agadir; ☎ 048 82 16 41/061 15 24 61; e-mail info@agadir-immobilier.com; www. agadir-immobilier.com.

Kantakari, 40 Rue des Banques, Kenneria, Marrakech Medina; ☎ 044 42 65 26/061 67 56 48; e-mail kantakari@menara.ma; www.kantakari.com. For information on property in Ouarzazate.

Mirleft Immobilier, ☎; 071.77.44.25; www.mirleft-immoblier.com. Properties in Agadir, Mirleft and Aglou.

Moroccan Homes, 43 Station Road, Thorpe on Hill, Lincoln LN6 9BS; ☎ 01522 535 052 or Calle Daire 46, Sedella Malaga, Spain; ☎ 95 25 08 961; e-mail info@Moroccan-homes.com; www.Moroccan-homes.com. English speaking agency with properties for sale in Agadir.

Moroccan Properties, Immueble El Khalil, Avenue Hassan II, Marrakech 40000; ☎ 44 43 04 65; fax 044 43 04 30; www.moroccanproperties.com. Has properties for sale in Aglou.

Mouloud Wadoud, Sidi Ifni, ☎ 067923280; e-mail wadoud88@hotmail.com. Property expert in Sidi Ifni.

TADLA-AZILAL

Population: 1.3 million
Area: 17,125sq km
Regional capital: Beni Mellal
Main areas: Beni Mellal

The mountainous region of Tadla-Azilal runs through the centre of Morocco between the Middle and the High Atlas mountains positioned in between the two Imperial cities of Fes and Marrakech in an area referred to by hikers as the Central High Atlas region, It takes in the richly agricultural Tadla Plain, which stretches for 360sq km, crossed by two great rivers, the Oum er Rbia from its east to its west and the Wadi el Abid from its south to its north. It incorporates Ighil Mgoun (4071m), to the south of the region, the second highest massif 100m lower than the peaks of Toubkal, near Marrakech, dramatic waterfalls, gorges and isolated valleys. It is trekking, caving and climbing territory earmarked by the Ministry of Tourism as an ecotourism destination with the majority of tourist accommodation being *gîtes* chez the locals.

While nearly 60% of the population work in agriculture, what really keeps the region's economy in a healthy state is the funds sent home by the Moroccan émigré community. Tadla-Azilal has an extraordinarily large number of Moroccans working in Europe with Italy the destination of choice.

Despite having a number of natural beauty sites, the region is highly unexploited in terms of tourism and foreign visitors in general. This is because it suffers from inaccessibility. The nearest international airport is Marrakech around 200km west of Beni Mellal, the nearest train station is either Khouribga (express train from Casablanca), around 90km west of Beni Mellal or Marrakech. The number of roads into and around the region are limited, although there is talk of a highway being built, which would link the region to the rest of Morocco. Most locals travel around by bus.

The main city in Tadla-Azilal is Beni Mellal located in the foothills of the High Atlas. Elsewhere the region is characterised by small towns and villages in the valleys and clinging on to the slopes. Azilal is the second biggest place, a small administrative town, which due to its status as provincial capital, has recently benefited from many new housing developments.

The key history of the region dates back well over 1000 years, prior to the arrival of Islam. Beni Mellal was inhabited by the Sanhaja, a nomadic Berber tribe and a large population of Jewish craftsmen. The first Muslim contingent appeared in the region in 789, headed up by Idriss I. Due to its position in between Fes and Marrakech, the Tadla Plain was considered of vital importance with each of the dynasties attempting to take control of the wild Tadla Berbers who ruled the territory. In the 17th century, Moulay Ismael established a line of fortresses along the plain in order to have control of the road to Marrakech and a new kasbah was built along the banks of the Oum er Rbia river. In 1700, he gave one of his sons the role of Pasha of the Tadla province and the new kasbah was enlarged into a provincial capital.

In the19th century, a coalition of Middle Atlas tribes defeated the government armies in the region and regained control. Attempts were made by Moulay Hassan to bring order to the plain, but he too was unsuccessful losing entire armies to the hostile terrain, Peace finally came to the region when the French took occupation of the Tadla Kasbah after a final campaign with the rebels, which lasted from 1915 to 1917.

The climate of the Tadla Plain is Mediterranean semi-arid with minimum winter temperatures of 0-5°C and average maximum summer temperatures of 38°C. There are around 55 rainy days a year with a humidity level of 63%. The higher you are in the Atlas Mountains, the chillier it gets. Winter snowfall can be heavy with the peaks often snow-covered well into the summer months and many high passes blocked for much of the year. In September 2005, three tourists froze to death in a snowstorm while trekking from Azilal to the 4068m peak of Makoun. This is not a common occurrence by any stretch, but is an indication of quite how cold it can get.

Cuisine

The region is irrigated by the 1500 million cubic metres of water in the Bin el Oui-dane reservoir, which was built in 1948 and has transformed the landscape from dry, barren and dusty to green and lush, filled with an abundance of oranges, olives, figs, peaches, walnuts, sesame and apricots. Freshwater fish such as pike, carp and salmon fill the rivers and reservoir. Berber cuisine is predominantly eaten in the mountains. Whole roasted lamb cooked on a spit *(mechoui)* is a mountain dish enjoyed on special occasions, as are liver brochettes, known as *tutlin* and Berber tagines *(reffisa)*, which consist of biscuits dipped in stock with onions and seasoning.

BENI MELLAL

Beni Mellal sits at 625m in the foothills of the High Atlas, surrounded by sun scorched orange and olive groves. With a population of 250,000, it is one of Morocco's fastest growing cities, thriving on the irrigation and electricity that the Bin el Ouidane reservoir provides. Rural migrants are the reason for the cities population growth and much work has gone into urban planning and development to accommodate the recent influx. Despite having a history that dates back to the early years AD, it is largely a modern city, the oldest feature being Kasbah Bel Kush located inside the medina, built by Moulay Ismael. There is little in either the old city or the ville nouvelle of architectural interest but there are good provisions in terms of banks, trekking tour agencies, a lively Tuesday souk and a huge bus station, which seems to dominate the city.

The main reason anyone might consider buying a property in Beni Mellal is because of the excellent surrounding trekking opportunities. Rising up behind the city are the foothills of Djebel Tassemit (2248m) and Djebel R'Nim (2411). To the south of the city past the reservoir are Laqroun (3117m), Mourik (3223m) and the Mellal Gorges.

Properties

Many minor local campaigns are underway to safeguard the architectural heritage of the region, particularly the old houses, which it is believed are of importance from a touristic point of view. Properties in the valleys are traditionally flat-roofed square or rectangular dwellings made of adobe, mortar and loam mortar. Houses are spaced apart from one another and often use brick walls to indicate their plots. Properties on the hills tend to be made of pisé and tightly packed in terrace style arrangements. The ground floor is reserved for livestock to roam around at will the first and second floors incorporate the family accommodation and kitchen. In the high mountains, houses are built on just one level with the outside walls reinforced with dry stone to withstand cold and strong winds. One of the main ways of safeguarding the old houses is through the organised gîte network, which has been very successful throughout the country. Most of the gîtes are owned by Moroccan farming families with the majority for the region, located in and around the village of Aït Bou Guemés, which is en route to the peak of Ighil Mgoun and is described in the Morocco Lonely Planet guidebook as a 'hidden Himalayan kingdom dropped into the Atlas'. While the property market for foreigners in the region is very small existing only really around the fabulous, non-commercialised *Cascades d'Ouzoud* (Ouzoud waterfalls), buying and restoring a dilapidated traditional house in the countryside (of which there are many) would be doing the landscape a service. There are the ecological issues to bear in mind regarding setting up holiday-lets as this could deter trekkers from the Moroccan owned gîtes robbing locals of a key income activity. Bear in mind that much of the land is agricultural, so there will be administrative issues involved with changing the status of the land (see *What Type of Property to Buy?*). Also be aware that much of the region is very isolated, while scenically picturesque, owning a property in a remote area comes with its own share of problems (see *What Type of Property to Buy?*).

TAZA-TAOUNATE-AL HOCEIMA

Population: 1.7 million
Area: 23,000sq km
Regional capital: Al Hoceima
Main areas: Al Hoceima and Taza

The region of Taza-Taounate-Al Hoceima incorporates the heart of the 300km long, ruggedly, bleak, orange/black Rif Mountains. It is crowned to the north by the calm, lapping beaches of the Mediterranean, to the south by the Taza Gap that divides the Rif from the Middle Atlas with the hill town of Chefchaouen marking its border to the west and the region of Oujda to the east. Of the 1.7 million people living in the region, only 21% are urban, the rest live rurally with around 60% of the active workforce involved in agriculture, primarily the cultivation of cannabis, cereals, almonds, olives and figs.

The region is cut in half horizontally by the Rif Mountains, which through the centuries have protected and isolated the interior of Morocco from Mediterranean civilisations. Despite their unspoilt, alluring appearance of interlocked valleys, gullies overflowing with gorse and landscapes flecked with marigolds and oleander, the Rif are the poorest, most troublesome and the most neglected parts of Morocco, having fiercely resisted both Spanish and French incursions and consistently rebelled against central control.

On February 24th 2004, at 2.30am a massive earthquake hit this region measuring 6.5 on the richter scale and killing 572 people. The worst affected were the poor living in the rural villages around the Mediterranean resort of Al Hoceima whose mud brick houses simply collapsed under the force. Despite being just a few kilometres from the Spanish coast, it took several hours for the relief effort to arrive due to the poor conditions (read lack) of roads in the region. While the tragedy in itself was horrific, some strides have been made, (predominantly verbal) following the disaster to integrate the neglected north into modern Morocco. One major difference will be the coastal road running from Tangier to Saidia, incorporating Al Hoceima en route.

A main issue facing the government in the region is what to do about the cultivation of cannabis (kif), which constitutes the main industry in the Rif. Over 135,000 hectares and 96,000 Riffian families (804,000 people - 2.5% of the active population) are involved in its cultivation with the Rif estimated to be responsible for 42% of the world's hashish production. If the government puts a halt to production they will lose a lot of money and a huge swathe of the Riffian population will lose their livelihood. If they do not put a halt to it, the unsavoury reputation of the Rif, not to mention the pressure from drug control organisations will continue.

The landscape of the Rif is one of the most inhospitable in Morocco. Steep slopes and poor soils in addition to irregular rainfall and a lack of irrigational infrastructure make most other crops unsustainable (cannabis cultivation brings 7-8 times more revenues than barley cultivation) and when you consider that the population density in the Rif is three times higher than anywhere else in Morocco, agricultural production needs to be economically viable especially when governmental investment has been virtually non-existent.

The kif growing capital is Ketama, 120km west of Al Hoceima. This area has the reputation of being dangerous, horror stories of aggressive drug dealers holding tourists at knifepoint and cars being nudged off mountainous roads abound. The most likely danger you will encounter, however, is over zealous guides keen to take you on the 'kif trail', and the risk of being thrown into jail by the police should you be found with any drugs in your possession.

The climate of Taza-Taounate-Al Hoceima is predominantly Mediterranean with hot dry summers (26-30°C), tempered by southwest trade winds and wet, mild winters (15-18°) with around 300mm of rainfall a year. Around Taza, however 175km inland, the climate is much drier as it is protected from the Atlantic air by the great barriers of the Rif and Middle Atlas Mountains. Winters here can get cold, sometimes as low as freezing, with very hot summers hosting temperatures in the mid-late 30's,

Cuisine

The cuisine is largely Mediterranean due both to the proximity of the region to Spain and the Hispanic influences of the past. Olives and olive oil, seafood and fish such as salted sardines (best enjoyed at the fishing port in Al Hoceima), vegetables, figs, and almonds find their way into a number of local dishes. Bread tends to be made from barley as opposed to wheat. Berber dishes predominate largely in the Rif. These tend to be vegetable and bean based with fewer ingredients than elsewhere in the country, pureed favas, for example, eaten with green onions, couscous made with sorgo, which is highly resistant to drought and turnip tagines, a speciality of Taza.

AL HOCEIMA

Al Hoceima is often referred to as a 'pocket of paradise' surrounded as it is by the bleak Rif Mountains and time consuming to get to via the dusty, mountainous roads. Royal Air Maroc fly direct from Brussels and the Netherlands arriving at Charif Idr airport 17km south east of the town and there are ferries from Almeria in Spain, which run during the summer months.

Al Hoceima, with a population of around 40,000, is a clean, well kempt, whitewashed city with a resort-style holiday feel to it. It sits on top of a bay at a point where the Rif Mountains drop away, making space for white sandy beaches that sink into a warm Mediterranean sea. Palm trees line the streets of wide, well ordered boulevards overlooked by wooded hills and spacious paved squares are fringed with cafés and restaurants. Al Hoceima is particularly appealing because everybody is left to mind their own business. Besides over-friendly children, there is very little in the way of pushy touts, forcing you into unwanted situations. This gives the town a relaxed and friendly air. During the summer, the town gets busy with predominantly Moroccan holidaymakers although it is also popular with Spanish tourists from both mainland Spain and Melilla, one of Morocco's Spanish enclaves and to a lesser extent, French and Germans. The best time to be in Al Hoceima both in terms of peace from the crowds and weather conditions is in the spring months, when the trees are in bloom, the weather warm but not intensely and the beaches empty.

Al Hoceima's history begins with a Spanish officer called General Sanjuro who founded the city in the 1920's after Spain had managed to suppress the Berber tribes in the mountains. They chose the location, as it was a prime site to keep an eye on Abd al- Krim el Khaddabi, the leading Berber rebel who had his base 10km away in Adjir.

When the Spanish left in the 1950's at the time of Morocco's independence, they did not leave much in terms of architecture, just a handful of white houses along the cliffs and most notably, their provincial HQ, which is a sandy yellow and brown building set behind high gates, close to the fishing port, which has now become a college and cultural centre. They did leave a large influence in terms of the culture of Al Hoceima, which is topped up by Spanish television, the preferred language to view in. Many inhabitants speak Spanish as a second language and foreigners are often assumed to be from Spain.

There are several beaches on either side of Al Hoceima. Plage Quemado is the town beach set against rocky, grey cliffs 75 metres high. It is the most crowded of all the local beaches and surprisingly, considering its location in the centre of town, remarkably clean. Deep sea diving, sailing, jet and water skiing are becoming increasingly popular as the predominantly calm sea provides the perfect environment for water sports. The beaches on either side of Al Hoceima are just that, beaches, with very little in the way of development besides campsites and fishing boats. Five km south of the town is Calabonita with a large campsite and some water sports. The prettiest, least crowded beaches however can be found 50km west. These are Cala Iris with strikingly white sand, a new quiet fishing port, restaurant and shop selling fresh food and not much else and the pebbly beach of Torres de Alcala, 4km west of Cala Iris, which is a small whitewashed fishing hamlet.

Immediately west of Al Hoceima is the Al Hoceima National Park, which stretches for 40km along the coast from Pointe Boussekour to Cala Iris interspersed with rocky cliffs and pebbled beaches. Protected species such as Audoin's Gull and Monk Seal have been spotted in the park, which is exceptionally wild and beautiful, though great sections of it are currently inaccessible. The local government is hoping to promote rural tourism in the national park through, for example, the opening of gîtes for trekkers as a way of diversifying away from kif production.

The 2004 earthquake did not do much damage to Al Hoceima itself as most of the properties had been built to withstand natural disasters. Most loss of life and damage occurred in the poorer surrounding villages of Aït Kamara, Izmorene and Ochenene where the mud packed houses had been built without anti-seismic foundations. Women and children were the main victims as a large proportion of the male inhabitants work away either in Europe, the Middle East or elsewhere in Morocco, sending money home to their families.

Properties

Much like in Saidia and around Tetouan, properties are gradually becoming more expensive in Al Hoceima, as the government starts paying attention to the Mediterranean coastline. The most popular property buyers are expatriate Moroccans living in Europe who invest their foreign earnings into smart new villas in the more modern part of town close to the principal square, Place Massira el Khadra and Avenue Mohammed V, the main boulevard.

For the best bargains, it is worth considering buying up land in the surrounding rural villages. Many of these, like Al Hoceima, also benefit from the beach. Land here can be bought for up to 200,000 dh (£12,500) per 100sq m. In Al Hoceima itself, villas in a frontline beach position start from around 800,000 dh (£50,000). While there are some hotels in Al Hoceima, there are not enough to accommodate the large tourist influx during the summer months. Buying a villa/apartment to let out to holidaymakers could offer both a good income and a sound investment as infrastructure primarily in the form of roads around Al Hoceima, improves.

TAZA

Taza is the largest province in Taza-Taounate-Al Hoceima with a surface area that incorporates around 60% of the region and a population of around 750,000. The town is 175km south of Al Hoceima, divided into a medina and a ville nouvelle around 3km apart from one another. The medina is one of Morocco's oldest, having been founded in the 10th century by Zenata Berber from the Meknassa tribe (same tribe that founded Meknes). Over the centuries it has been a city of vital strategic importance to every invading dynasty starting with the Romans and Arabs who entered the country via the Taza Gap, the only route from the east.

The Taza Gap is a naturally occurring corridor that divides the Rif mountain range from the Middle Atlas. Some theorists believe that the Gap is the original boundary between Europe and Africa claiming that the Rif used to be part of the Spanish Sierra Nevada and that the Mediterranean and Straits of Gibraltar came about when the land, by chance, became submerged.

Every dynasty has left its mark in Taza. The Almohads built the 3km of medina ramparts and began building the Grand Mosque in the twelfth century, the Merenids in the 13th century built a very attractive merdersa, finished building the Grand Mosque and restored the ramparts, the Saidians built the Bastion and restored the ramparts again and the Alawites made the town their military base in the 17th century restoring the ramparts yet again. Taza never really succeeded as a defensive base, however, mainly due to the Zenata Berber, who never ceased in their campaigns to rule the city. They succeeded in the 19th century only to lose control to the French in 1914. The French built the ville nouvelle and turned Taza into a garrison town from which they could control the Berber resistance.

The best feature of the old town is its position on the top of a hill, 150 metres high (350 steps up) with awesome views over the ville nouvelle and some of Morocco's most beautiful countryside.

The old town of Taza today is a peaceful place. Despite its past, not much really happens in the town anymore besides a Berber market which specializes in flat weave carpets woven by the Beni Ouarain tribe from the Middle Atlas.

Taza's main tourist attractions are its mosques, merdersa and souk, although none of these have been exploited for the tourist market. The religious monuments are either closed or out of bounds to non-Muslims and the *kissaria* (covered souk) caters to a local crowd although there is a wide selection of Berber jewellery and weapons, which could make interesting ornaments.

There is nothing exceptional about the ville nouvelle that sets it apart from other ville nouvelle except that it is overlooked by an attractive chain of mountains. Apartment blocks are typically around six stories high and white, avenues are wide and tree lined. As per the norm, Boulevard Mohamed V is the principal street running through the ville nouvelle with steps up to an attractive Place de l'Independence at its base.

There is a train station in Taza at the north end of the ville nouvelle with connections to Fes, Oujda, Tangier and Casablanca. The nearest international airport is in Fes 120km to the west.

Properties

While there is no current demand from foreigners to buy property in Taza, it is one of those places that will get more interesting as the eastern side of Morocco opens up, The medina itself with its yellow houses and deep Islamic green awnings, paved streets and magnificent views is not large (around one hour to explore), the houses are old and in need of restoration but prices will still be in the very low extremities 128-160,000 dh (£8-10,000). There are no listed estate agents, so property buying is likely to be done on a private basis, directly between you and the homeowner using a notaire, most probably, in Fes.

What makes Taza most attractive from a second home/investment point of view are the range of outdoor and sightseeing activities in its close vicinity. As well as the Rif and Middle Atlas mountains, which offer trekking opportunities, there is the Jbel Tazzeka National Park, 70km southwest of Taza, ideal for a day trip with its cork, evergreen oak and pine trees and Barbary deer. Around the park, it is possible to visit the *Gouffre du Friouato*, arguably Africa's deepest (180 metres) and most extensive caves with mouths stretching over 30m wide, accessed via a vast number of steps and the *Cascades de Ras el-Oued* (waterfalls). The village of Bab Bou Idir lying close to the summit of Jbel Tazzeka (1980 metres with views over Fes 100km away), was built by the French during the protectorate as a summer/ski hill station. It has a selection of alpine style chalets and a large campsite.

TANGIER-TETOUAN

Population: 2 million
Area: 11,570sq km
Regional capital: Tangier
Main areas: Tangier, Tetouan, Chefchaouen, Asilah and Larache

Tangier-Tetouan, encompasses the northern tip of Morocco including the pretty coastal towns of Asilah and Larache and the sleepy mountain town of Chefchaouen. Part of the region is in the Rif Moutains, historically known as the *land of the lawless tribes*, the other part, next to the sea, divided between the temperate breezes of the Atlantic and the warm winds of the Med. Since ancient days, this region, one of the oldest in Morocco has been of vital importance to its rulers due to its proximity to Europe and its location at the meeting point of the Atlantic and Mediterranean. Romans, Arabs, Spanish, French, Portuguese and British have had their turns at colonisation but it is the fiercely loyal, highly independent, Berber clans of the Rif who have had the longest period of rule, controlling the mountains from Neolithic times to the mid 1900's and conquered only by the strongest of sultans. During the protectorate, the region was colonised predominantly by the Spanish, with the exception of Tangier, which was turned into an international zone. Tetouan was the capital of the Spanish protectorate and Larache, the main port.

For the full thirty-eight years of his reign, King Hassan II pointedly ignored the Tangier-Tetouan region due to his dislike and mistrust of the Berber tribes in the Rif, whose final rebellion he quashed in 1958. Where the rest of the country got roads and industry, the region got nothing. 19th century sewers and drains in dire need of modernisation, overflowed into the streets, tour operators refused to send tourists, as hotels were unkempt and fundamentalist terrorist cells proliferated. It has only been with the ascension of the current king, Mohammed VI, who has no bone to pick with the north, that things have started improving.

The turning point was in 2002 when he decided to make Tangier the city from which to give his third annual speech where he vowed to make Tangier into 'one of the country's biggest ports' and the region and its surrounds, 'the most important resort on the Mediterranean'.

The climate of the north including the Rif Mountains is Mediterranean with wet, but warm winters from November to April and an average of 5-7 hours of sunshine a day. Summer begins in April/May and is reliably hot through to November with an average of 10-11 hours of sunshine a day. Despite having blue skies for most of the year, Asilah and Larache on the Atlantic coasts tend to have a more temperate climate than towns on the Mediterranean, with temperatures kept lower by the cool waters of the Canaries current and more cloud and fog during summer caused by the chillier, offshore waters. Due to the positioning of Tetouan sandwiched in between two large mountains, the climate in the town is very much dependent on the direction of the wind. If there is an easterly wind, the town will often be drizzly, foggy and grey, regardless of the time of year with mists coming up from the sea. Travel less than five minutes out of the town, however, and the sky will be blue.

Cuisine

Along with Fes and Marrakech, Tetouan is one of the three gastronomic capitals of Morocco with Tangier a close runner up. A history of colonisation, proximity to the Rif Mountains, the Mediterranean and the Atlantic and a wealth of indigenous wild herbs makes it the most diverse of the regional cuisines. In Tetouan, Spain's Moroccan capital during the protectorate years, the influence of Andalucia is most vividly experienced. Here, dishes are preferred sharp as opposed to sweet and the sauce is considered the central feature of any meal with tagines slow cooked and simmering for hours on end until the ingredients are, as the Tetouani saying goes, 'standing in their own sauce'.

Chicken is a key ingredient and local people boast that they know fifty ways of preparing chicken with no two ways the same. Paula Wolfert in her book 'Moroccan Cuisine' names all fifty including chicken stuffed with the wild herb bakoola, chicken with quince, honey, amber and aga wood, boned chicken wrapped in an omelette made with peas, couscous with chunks of chicken in a cinnamon-flavoured sauce. Spanish omelettes (*egga*) or in Spain known as *tortilla*, fish omelettes, fish tagines flavoured with the wild herb, sea kale, local to Tangier and fish stuffed with lemon and cinnamon flavoured egg are also specialities as is fried fish, which can be found throughout Tangier's medina. Food in the mountainous regions of the Rif tends to be centred on the more vegetable based Berber diet. One speciality is the savoury *brik*, which is traditional pastry (*warqa*) filled with egg and a dash of the chilli-based Moroccan sauce, *harissa*. Typically, tapas the Spanish style of eating many different little plates of food, is also enjoyed widely in the northern peak, with Tangier having a selection of tapas style restaurants.

TANGIER

'For the nine sightseers who are mildly amused by the chaos and absurdity of the place, frankly repelled by its ugliness and squalor, or simply indifferent to whatever it may have to offer, there is a tenth one who straight away falls in love with it'. Paul Bowles, novelist and composer's opinion of Tangier where he lived for 52 years.

Tangier or Tangiers (English spelling) is known as Tanja in Arabic, Tanger in French and Tánger in Spanish. That it has so many spellings is testament to its cosmopolitan roots, which are still as pronounced now as they were over the centuries. The city of Tangier is located at the peak of North Africa by the western entrance to the Straits of Gibraltar, 12km from where the Atlantic Ocean meets the Mediterranean at Cap Spartel. 350,000 people live in the city itself, a further 200,000 in the suburbs.

The city of Tangier dates back to the 5th century BC with the arrival of the Carthaginian colonists who named it, Tingis and established trading posts along the coasts to service and shelter their ships. Over the next 200 years, it came under Roman Rule, fell to the Vandals, became part of the Byzantine Empire and passed under Arab control before being parcelled between the Spanish, Portuguese and English for the next 300 years. In 1661, the Portuguese gave Tangier along with Bombay, to the British as part of Charles II dowry on his marriage to the Portuguese princess, Catherine of Braganza. The British, unfortunately did not do the city proud. Sick from malnutrition, lacking in funds and under constant attack from Morocco's sultan, Moulay Ismael, the British eventually retreated in 1684 but not until they had expelled all Jews and desecrated Muslim and Catholic holy sites.

Once in control of Tangier, Moulay Ismael tried to rebuild it but his attempts failed and the city gradually declined until by the mid 19th century, the population was little more than 5000.

Its prime location as the gateway linking Europe with North Africa meant that it was not down for long. In the late 19th, early 20th century, prior to the protectorate, it became a trading centre for European merchants and a focus for commercial and European diplomatic activities. During the protectorate, it was decided that Tangier should remain neutral. This became official in1923 when it was made an international zone administered by an assembly of 26 foreign representatives from France, Spain, Britain, Portugal, Netherlands, USA and Italy. During its time of belonging officially to everybody but at the same time, nobody, it became the perfect hang-out and hideaway for eccentrics, artists, gamblers, homosexuals, smugglers, spies and thieves. It was a place where anyone could exist without needing valid identification to identify them, where goods destined for other countries, could be loaded and reloaded without having to pass through a customs check and where banks and businesses flocked to take advantage of its relaxed tax laws. Italians, Swiss, British and American tourists passing through were enamoured by the city and never left. La Montagne, enroute to Cap Spartel, one of the most sought after neighbourhoods in the suburbs, became home for many Brits. Elsewhere, other parts of the city were becoming colonised by Europeans, such as the neighbourhood of Marshan for the Italians and the area around the port, for the Spanish. Much of this is still in evidence today. In 1956 with independence, the city was reunited with the rest of Morocco.

The Rolling Stones, Matisse and the playwright, Tennessee Williams have all made Tangier their home at one time or another, the American novelist and composer, Paul Bowles lived in the city for 52 years and as is very obvious when you walk around the city with its art deco buildings and colonial style opulence interspersed with mystery and poverty, it was the original setting upon which the Hollywood film, Casablanca, was based.

TANGIER TODAY

Unlike other parts of Morocco, a large number of urbanites living in Tangier speak Spanish as their second language and French as their third. Most tourists are initially addressed with an 'Ola' as opposed to a 'Bonjour', Spanish mobile phone sim cards are sold in shops and most city life revolves around the large port and the coming and going of ferries into and out of Spain. Though Tangier has been a part of Morocco for the last sixty years, it has a different vibe to the rest of the country. It does not feel Arab, Berber or African, nor does it feel Mediterranean or European. It feels quite simply, like a melting pot where you are as likely to come across an Iraqi exile sipping tea with a Palestinian poet or a German art dealer working in a second hand bookshop, than you are to find a Moroccan in a jellaba. This, in addition to its years of governmental neglect, gives it an air of 'anything goes' with some of the more restraining influences ever present in more conservative cities not apparent in Tangier. It is a city where the legacy of the recent past is still present today in the smoke-filled cafés, the cabarets, the gay bars and the literary, artistic communities. Faceless apartment blocks clogging up the views from the hillsides are interspersed with the grand facades of colonial houses water stained and tinged by exhaust fumes but still pleasing to the eye, that is, if you are able to draw your eye away long enough from the frenetic street side activity to look up. In Tangier everyone is 'doing business', wheeling and dealing their wares and out to make a quick buck ideally from a tourist fresh off the boat from Europe who before setting foot outside the port will have been offered a guide, a taxi, a hotel and a ticket back home again. Hustlers aside and they normally are aside once you get into the swing of the city, Tangier is a very lively, dynamic place, refreshingly unselfconscious in its subtle eccentricity.

With its whitewashed buildings, hills, sea and port, Tangier is an attractive city. Hours can be spent sitting on a balcony watching the ferries disappearing out to sea, or the endless stream of people strolling along the Grand Socco, one of the city's main squares straddling the old town with the new. As with the majority of large Moroccan cities, Tangier is made up of a medina positioned on a hill to the north east of the centre and a ville nouvelle, south, south-east and west of the medina with a rather grubby beach front running along Avenue d'Espagne and Avenue des Forces Armées Royales (F.A.R), shaded by tall trees.

The town beach has the potential to be beautiful, but like many public spaces in Morocco is covered in trash and too close to the port to make swimming a pleasurable option. This said many people, mainly Moroccans, who do not seem to be bothered by rubbish in the same way as Europeans, fill the yellow sands. The best beaches in terms of cleanliness, freedom from crowds and white sands are a short drive west of the city along the coastline of the Atlantic. The currently empty coastline around Tangier is on the road to change as great swathes of government land by the sea is being sold off to developers at very cheap prices around 100 dh per sq m (£6.25). This, in theory, only applies to developers who can prove that their project will be of benefit to the greater community in terms of employment etc, quite how strict these rules are, however, is debatable. The large Marjane supermarket is just out of town on the road to Asilah and there is also a Macro wholesale supermarket being built on the outskirts of the city. The airport is 8km out of town and the railway station serving all major cities in Morocco, 3km from the city.

Developing Tangier

Two major developments currently underway and set to open in 2007 are the Tangier City Centre project and Tangier Med. Tangier City Centre is a 630 million dirham (£42 million) tourist zone being created in Tangier Bay by the property developers Fadesa Maroc (also responsible for the new luxury property development in the eastern town of Saidia) and Anjoca. This will incorporate mall style shopping centres, three, four and five star hotels, residential properties, offices, cafés and restaurants. The Tangier Med development is Tangier's massive new port and free trade zone, which it is hoped will act both as a trade magnet, taking advantage of the region's strategic location near the Straits of Gibraltar and for the US, boost its free trading with Morocco following the signing of the Free Trade Agreement. The Tangier-Med development is being built in the town of Ksar es Sghir, 35km out of the city. It will cover an area of 500 square kilometres, employ around 145,000 people and is expected to attract investment of about 10 billion dh (£625 million). With the opening of the port, pressure will be removed from the existing port inside Tangier city, which currently gets heavily clogged up particularly during holiday seasons. The focus of this port will be on tourist traffic; tourist ferries, cruise ships etc into and out of Europe.

NEW INFRASTRUCTURE

Having been largely cut off from the rest of the country due to inaccessibility, the Casablanca-Tangier highway eventually opened in June 2005 increasing access to and from the north. In addition, the railway line is being improved between Tangier-Rabat-Casablanca with the aim of decreasing journey time, a high-speed rail link is being implemented between Tangier and the beach city of Al Hoceima and modernisation renovations are underway to Tangier railway station. An international airport is being built 10km south of the Tangier-Med, connected to Tangier by train.

The most important infrastructural project is the planned rail tunnel, which will link Spain with Morocco. After twenty years of discussions, building work is due to start in 2008 at a cost of 3-10 billion euro. Two adjacent tunnels will run from Punta Paloma (40km west of Gibraltar) to Punta Malabata close to Tangier. This particular route has been chosen as the Mediterranean is only 300 metres deep between the two points.

Properties

Medina. There are two main neighbourhoods or quarters (*quartiers*) in the medina, the medina itself and the kasbah. The kasbah sits at the top end of the old city, overlooking the medina's higgledy- piggledy rooftops, electricity wires, satellite dishes and the Straits of Gibraltar. This is where the large, grander properties can be found, those historically belonging to Moroccan sultans, occasionally interspersed with more modern properties built over the last century, in order to benefit from the views over the city. Much of the kasbah dates back 1000 years, although some of it was rebuilt in the 17th century after the British destroyed ancient relics such as the medieval fortress, prior to their retreat in 1684. In the kasbah, the alleyways are at their steepest and narrowest, although cars are, unusually, permitted to enter, somehow managing to squeeze themselves through the narrow gates. There are very few properties left in the kasbah that have not been renovated and modernised and only rarely do they come up for sale. The main gateway into the Medina quarter is via the Grand Socco (*socco* meaning souk or market in Spanish). Here you find narrow alleyways with worn out steps, the frenetic tourist bazaars of Rue des Siaghines (Silversmith's Street), mosques, some dating back to the 13th century, synagogues in the old mellah (Jewish Quarter) and tall, cream/peach coloured houses with elegant, rounded windows and decorative balconies.

As the medina is built on a hill, most properties are small, in the range of 45-90sq m. These tend to be priced between 700,000 dh (£43,000) and 1.3 million dh (£81,000).

Ville Nouvelle and Suburbs. Based on Moroccan's preference for new houses with all mod cons, as opposed to old medina style houses, it is in the ville nouvelle and its suburbs that most of the building and buying is going on. The heart of the ville nouvelle is around Café de France, which is on a bend a little way down from the Grand Socco close to the restaurant lined Boulevard Pasteur. Like the medina, much of the ville nouvelle is on a steep slope up from the sea, which means superb views and a respite from the choking traffic fumes.

The main buyers are affluent local Moroccans, expat Moroccans, who are residing in Europe but would like a place they can both invest in and stay for long weekends and Spanish people from Southern Spain, who are lured by the cheap property prices.

In central Tangier, most properties for sale are in apartment blocks, those high up, with views over the sea, tending to be cheaper than those on lower floors due to the Moroccan preference to be in close proximity to the ground floor A 95sq m two bedroom, two bathroom apartment on the ground floor, five minutes from the port costs 620,000 dh (£39,000), the same size apartment on the 6th floor 500,000 dh (£31,000). If you wish to buy an apartment with views over the sea, be sure to check that no new apartment block is going to be built in front of it, blocking your view. Relaxed planning regulations means that, compared to other cities, there are few aesthetic-style rules relating to the building of highrise blocks. As a result, they are being thrown up thick and fast with next to no regard for scenic views or privacy. You might note that there are a handful of empty apartment blocks hoarding prime locations in the centre of the city. These tend to belong to drug lords from the Rif Mountains, notorious for its cannabis (kif) trade, who have no desire or understanding of how to sell or rent out the apartments, but simply need a secure place to invest their money.

Around the city centre in quiet, residential neighbourhoods, three-five bedroom villas with balconies, mountain views and swimming pools cost around 1.8 million dh (£110,000). The most popular place to live, however, and one of the most exclusive is five minutes out of town in the suburbs of California close to the Royal Golf Club and cricket stadium (both of which have recently had $3million invested in them by a company from the UAE, bringing them up to championship level). Here, land costs in the region of 700-800 dh per sq m (£43-50) and large 5-8 bedroom villas, often modern but built in Andalucian/ Arabic style with archways, red tiled roofs, views over the golf course, swimming pool, balconies and lawns around 5 million dh (£315,000) to 8 million dh (£500,000). Equally sought after is La Montagne behind the Spanish Consulate on the inland road to Cap Spartel. This area is historically popular with garden-loving British expats. Villas tend to be very large averaging 10-13 bedrooms and sell for around 17 million dh (£1.1million). Cape Spartel, 14km from central Tangier, the point at which the Med meets the Atlantic is on the northwest corner of North Africa. Here, French cosmetic companies can be seen shooting glamour-style adverts against the backdrop of sandy bays and sheering cliffs. Properties cost around 5 million dh (£315,000) for 5 bedroom villas with views over the ocean and extensive land (commonly around 1200sq m). Alternatively,

2 bedroom/2 bathroom beach fronted apartments cost in the region of 720,000 dh (£45,000). Prime plots of land can also be found around Cap Spartel close to the beach costing around 1750 dh per sq m (£110 sq m). Note: At the time of writing, the rules that apply in other parts of Morocco, stating a limit on the amount of land foreigners are permitted to buy (see *What Type of Property to Buy?*), does not yet apply to Tangier.

The Marshan area, west of the medina and ten minutes from the city centre, previously a smart residential neighbourhood for Europeans, mainly Italians, but now a little more run down is less expensive but still benefits from fantastic cliff top sea views. You can expect to find three bedroom villas with swimming pool and large plots of land costing in the region of 3 million dh (£200,000). Nouinouch is a popular new area for villas on the hillside at the eastern end of the bay, 12km from the centre of Tangier, not far from the recently finished theme park and zoo on the road to Ksar es Sghir with 3-4 bedroom properties, balconies and sea views costing between 550-750,000 dh (£35,000-50,000). Unsurprisingly, land around the fishing town of Ksar es Sghir is becoming increasingly sought after (and expensive) in preparation for the new Tangier Med port. Land is currently between 400 dh per sq m (£25) to 1000 dh per sq m (£62).

TETOUAN

The whitey grey rooftops of Tetouan are located 55 kilometres south east of Tangier sandwiched on the steep Dersa hillside between two large mountains and surrounded by orange, almond, cypress and pomegranate trees. Andalucian in style, the medina is referred to locally as the 'daughter of Granada', having been 'born' following the surrendering of the Andalucian kingdom to the Spanish in 1492. Built in the 15th and 16th centuries, by Muslim and Jewish refugees led by the Granadan Sidi al-Mandri, the ramparts were constructed like a fortress with thick, tall walls to keep both tribal Rif warriors and, more crucially, the Spanish, out. During the late 16th and 17th century, the town saw an economic boom, ruled by the Naqsis family of Andalucian origin, becoming Morocco's main port for European commercial trade. In 1629, France followed by other countries, opened a consulate in the town, turning Tetouan into the diplomatic capital of Morocco in the 17th/18th century. During this time, the surface area of the town quadrupled to accommodate a population of 26,000 with new fortifications erected in the 18th century. In 1859, the Spanish took possession after a bloody battle in the hills, only to leave two years later in return for a very large payment, which sent the town's economy spirally into decline.

In 1912, the Spanish returned making the town the capital of the Spanish protectorate of Northern Morocco. They built the ville nouvelle next to the medina walls in a Hispanic style, with colonial buildings, squares and markets, all still very much in existence today.

Tetouan Today

Tetouan is an introverted town. It does not, by reputation, react warmly to strangers, especially camera snapping tourists. Until recently, the population was regarded as one of the most aggressive in the country in terms of hustlers, unwelcome guides that stuck to you like glue and petty theft, but a severe police crackdown has put an end to the worst of it, so much so, that locals are actually nervous to address tourists and will go out of their way to avoid being addressed. This is not the case, however, for the foreigners who reside in the medina. Once your face is known, which it soon will be as the town is not large, you will meet many warm, welcoming people just like in any other part of Morocco.

One of the greatest appeals of the medina is that it is largely unchanged since originally being constructed in the 1500's. It is characterised by squares, small gardens, low arches, covered passageways (sabat), fish souks, makeshift fruit and vegetable stalls stacked up on wooden boxes, craft shops selling leather from the tannery in the north of the medina, barbers shops and over 50 mosques. It is also the regional centre of culture housing a School of Traditional Arts and Crafts, which is reputed to be the best guarantor for the conservation and imparting of Arab-Andalucian heritage. In 1997, UNESCO granted the medina, World Heritage status.

Tetouan is built on limestone rock, so there is a network of underground cavities beneath the medina, stretching from east to west. During the 16th century, chambers were built inside the cavities to house Christian prisoners and slaves. They were closed down in the 18th century with the release of all prisoners and slaves and remain unused today.

The current population of Tetouan is 200,000. It is a market centre with the main souk day on Sunday, when farmers from the countryside and Berber women from the mountains, gather to sell their wares; honey, almonds, grain, livestock, citrus fruits, goat's cheese, herbs and butter. Tobacco, soap, matches and textiles are locally manufactured and printing and fish canning, the main industries.

Properties

Houses in the medina are tall, at least three stories, sometimes four, white, square and like most Moroccan houses, with flat roofs, used for hanging out laundry and housing satellite dishes. They are Andalucian in style with elegant wrought iron balconies, light blue shutters, solid, ornate, cedar wood front doors and, as is typical of Moorish architecture, non-elaborate in design. Despite being over 500 years old, there is much Andalucian nostalgia around, with many residents still inhabiting the homes their descendents lived in when the medina was first constructed. Along the main street, Rue Al Genoui, people display wrought iron symbols on their front doors, in the shape of the pomegranate, which is the heraldic motif for Granada, an indication of their Andalucian heritage. There is very little demand for properties in the medina as the market has not yet reached

Tetouan. Foreigners who do own property in the city, tend to live in the high rise (6 storey) apartments in the ville nouvelle on streets such as Boulevard Forces Armées Royales (F.A.R).

From Sebta (Spanish enclave also known as Ceuta) to Tetouan

It is the 40km of Mediterranean palm-filled coastline between the Spanish enclave of Sebta and Tetouan, which is currently attracting major attention amongst international property developers. Long favoured as a holiday destination for Moroccans who spend their summers camping along the beach to avoid the muggy heat of the cities, the golden sandy bays, cliffs, creeks and clear blue waters are now starting to lure a wider crowd, a large proportion of whom, are Brits. Touted in the UK press as the 'new Spain', but with prices equivalent to 20 years ago, holiday-style apartments and private residences are being built in prime locations, next to the sea. There is, in fact so much interest in this area, that there are rumours of a property boom with buyers putting deposits down on holiday apartments they have never even seen. One of the most notable 'new' areas is the resort of Restinga Smir with supermarkets, shops, tennis courts and Marina Smir. The marina, built in 1991was modelled on the exclusive Marbella resort of Puerto Banus. It has cafés, restaurants and a large number of interesting, mock-colonial style villas surrounding it. Close by is the 5 star Sofitel hotel with its spa and thalasso centre and the recently extended, 18 hole golf course. Across the road from the marina, is a new whitewashed development called Jawhara Smir, where 2 bedroom, 2 bathroom properties are selling for 590,000 dh (£37,000) to 640,000 dh (£40,000). A little further along the beach, 2 bedroom, 2 bathroom apartments with views over the sea, cost 1.1 million dh (£72,000) (see *compasspropertiesmorocco.com*).

Mdiq. Heading south there is the less developed little fishing village of Mdiq with its bustling market town feel and views over the resort of Cabo Negro 2 km away. Plans are underway to improve Mdiq's port and a 2 billion dh (£125 million) development plan is being implemented by the government, to make Mdiq more attractive to tourists.

Cabo Negro. Cabo Negro is one of the few places in the north that has, since the 1960's, been given a number of government subsidies to help develop it into a tourist resort. It has arguably, the best beach in this stretch for its white sand and clear, turquoise waters. Playa Vista, a new development of 400 apartments with swimming pools, ocean views and tennis courts is 15 minutes from Cabo Negro golf course with 2/3 bedroom properties selling for £45,000 (see compasspropertiesmorocco.com).

CHEFCHAOUEN

Chefchaouen (meaning; twin peaks), known also by its old name *Chaouen* (peaks) is a peaceful, laidback, pretty town of gardens, squares and pergolas twinned with Ronda in Spain. It has a sky blue and whitewashed medina positioned on a valley in the middle of the cedar-filled Rif Mountains of Jebel Maggou and Jebel Tissouka. Chefchaouen has long been a popular haunt with low budget travellers, lured by the abundance of hashish (*kif*) from the Rif, which is sold as readily as fruit and vegetables, so draws little attention to itself and causes no problems.

Built in the 15th century following the influx of Jewish and Christian refugees from Granada, the town, like Tetouan has a distinctive Andalucian feel with small balconies, citrus trees and window boxes. Despite, having a history of xenophobia, with only three Europeans having visited the town by 1920, the inhabitants are now used to tourists, who they tend to address in Spanish, relying on tourism along with the weaving of rugs and carpets, as a key income. Chefchaouen has always been a religious town, Islamicised from as far back as the arrival of the Arabs to Moroccan shores. It was a cultural centre during the 1500's, attracting religious scholars and students. Despite a population of less than 40,000, there are eight mosques, two per neighbourhood and nine mausoleums (*zawiyyas*).

One of the most appealing features of Chefchaouen is its fresh, mountain air and clean water. Tap/fountain water comes straight from source, 2km up and is guaranteed drinkable. Proximity to the source also means that the town benefits from being lush and green.

Steep hills and curvy stepped passageways characterise the medina with all main arteries extending to and from the cobbled area of Uta Hammam, the largest square in the medina, now filled with cafés and a central fountain and surrounded by trees. Every Monday and Thursday is market day.

Properties

Unlike most houses in Morocco, which are built with featureless, flat roofs, those in Chefchaouen are pitched with red tiles, an Andalucian feature stemming from the need to catch heavy downfalls of snow from the mountains. Underneath the sloping roofs are lofts, which were once used for drying fruit. A thin overhang fronted by ceramic tiles, protects the horseshoe shaped windows. Some properties are white, others blue, some white with the lower part painted blue (an Andalucian tradition believed to keep the houses cooler/insects out) or occasionally pebbledash beige. Unlike much of Morocco, where aesthetics are often forgotten in favour of functionality, much pride goes into the maintenance of houses. Few are run down with aid coming from the regional government of Spain's Andalucia for rehabilitation of the medina, most are freshly painted and many have window boxes filled with colourful flowers. The oldest and most beautiful properties are in the Suiqa Quarter in the south of the medina, with many of the most important residences clustered off into small cul de sacs behind tall, ornate gates. In some cases, the alleyways outside the houses are covered over, to enable extra floors to be built on top. It is possible to buy three storey, 4 bedroom properties in Chefchaouen's medina for around 580,500 dh (£37,000).

ASILAH

In the 1970's Asilah was a rat-infested heap of a town with a disastrous sewage system, no electricity, crumbling houses and piles of rubbish clogging up the streets. A group of local businessmen including the town's mayor who doubles up as the Moroccan ambassador to the USA, decided that things had to change so set to work restoring the town. Residents were encouraged to take part in the clean up by donating materials or labour for renovations, 10-15 properties were restored each year, out of a medina of 1200, school children collected all the litter from the beaches and, most notably, a Cultural Festival, featuring art and music, was organised in order to fund the works.

Thirty years on, Asilah is one of Morocco's most picturesque towns. Perfectly positioned with white, sandy beaches on both sides, a fishing harbour and the walls of the Portuguese built medina splashing against the Atlantic Ocean it is a highly attractive town for tourists. As it happens, however, it is never that busy. The short winter months can get chilly (18-21°C) being on the Atlantic Ocean while the annual Cultural Festival filling the months of July and August lures the biggest crowds as well as several artists and musicians who have made the town their home. While the beaches to the north of Asilah tend to get very crowded during summer, to the south, it is generally unpopulated and far more pleasant for sunbathing.

Part of the restoration plan was to not allow any hotel or B&B accommodation inside the medina because it draws funds away from the local residents who rely on the festival as a way of making an income by renting out their homes and also because too much commercial business was not in line with the desired image of the honeypot tourist town. As a result, all hotels are outside the medina in the Spanish built ville nouvelle and most of them, quite uninspiring. That said, many people, Moroccans and foreigners do rent out their medina homes year round, but few are marketed widely.

The town of Asilah, though smaller, is not dissimilar to Essaouira in layout and look, both having been built by the Portuguese and both being on the edge of the Atlantic. Colourful murals cover the whitewashed walls, houses are white with light blue shutters and the paved, narrow streets immaculately clean. The majority of little shops are full of souvenirs and popular furnishings (rugs, lanterns etc), specifically for the tourist trade.

Asilah is a sleepy town with a permanent population of 20,000. During the lunchtime siesta, it is hard to find a soul around and it rarely perks up much more during the wakeful hours. This means it is highly relaxing and on the whole, hassle-free.

Properties

It is highly unlikely you will find a completely unrenovated property in the medina of Asilah. The majority have been recently restored (within the last 25 years) and most have the appearance of being much cared for and loved with aesthetic extras, such as elegant outdoor lanterns and flowers bursting from window boxes and terraces. Some have even gone so far as to putting *Not* For Sale signs up, so keen are they to hang onto their houses. As with most Atlantic coastal towns, white is the predominant colour inside and out with a simple plaster the preferred internal finish. All houses benefit from a terrace, many with sea views, although you would be wise to check the impact of damp on the property and its contents should you choose a house very close to the sea. This can be done by seeing whether the fittings are rusty or through the general feel and smell of the house. Two-three bedrooms, two bathrooms traditional houses with high ceilings, terrace and salons and a surface area of between 70-200sq m will cost in the region of 600,000 dh (£38,000) – 2 million dh (£135,000).

Most attractive for property hunters is the land surrounding Asilah on the Tangier -Asilah road, which, while getting increasingly developed close to Tangier with hotels and golf courses, is pretty much beach for the last third of the journey, separated from the road by great swathes of flat farmland. Equally appealing are the beaches just south of Asilah where the Royal Asilah Beach Resort is being built with a range of ocean front apartments currently available to buy off plan with prices starting from £42,000 for 2 bedrooms. Land in the surrounds of Asilah is currently selling for around 200-300 dh (£16-22) per square metre and at the time of writing, there are no restrictions on the amount or location of land that can be bought.

Property prices in Asilah are likely to increase as the whole region gets more developed. The new highway linking Tangier with Asilah and the rest of the west coast will do much to increase visitors to the region, as will the coastal resort being built at Larache, 40km away. It is predicted that soon there will be a continuous line of development joining Tangier city to Asilah, so that Asilah is no longer a town on its own, but a suburb of Tangier.

LARACHE

Despite its location on the Atlantic coast, blend of Hispanic/Arab architecture and relaxed, liberal atmosphere, few tourists put Larache at the centre of their itineraries. It tends to be a town favoured by Moroccans, many who live abroad for most of the year (largely in the UK), but return home to holiday for the summer months taking up all of the otherwise empty, hotel rooms. Surrounded by cliffs to the west and colourful citrus groves to the south, it is a town that all but harks back to its 20th century heyday when it was the main port for the Spanish occupation. There is a bit of Spain on every corner; the buildings, tapas bars, restaurants owned by Spanish patrons, the Spanish Cathedral and cemetery and the plethora of Spanish spoken in second place to Arabic. The heart of the town is the Place de la Liberation, once the Plaza de Espana, which is the hub for the strolling crowds who emerge at dusk to drink tea or gather around the central fountain. Being mainly a resort for Moroccans, the medina is unsurprisingly the poorest part of town with the majority of affluent residents having moved out to the ville nouvelle, leaving the medina to the rural migrants.

Currently the main reason most foreign tourists visit Larache is for a visit to the Roman ruins of Lixus, 5km north on the road down from Tangier and Asilah. Lixus was the site of the first Phoenician settlement, although the visible ruins come from the Romans dating back to the fourth century BC.

> While few foreigners currently buy properties in the town, Larache has been chosen as one of the sites for a Plan Azur coastal resort, which will do much to put the town and surrounding area on to the tourist map. The development, spread over 490ha, will accommodate 15,000 tourists in 100 hotels, have 100 villas for sale, 2 golf courses, a riding school, marina, lakes, restaurants and cafés with a completion date of 2006/7.

Estate Agents

Compass Properties, Complexe Le Dawliz, 42 Rue de Hollande 90000 Tangier; ☎ 039 94 73 16; e-mail info@compasspropertiesmorocco.com; www.compasspropertiesmorocco.com. American/British run agency specialising in property along the Mediterranean coast.

International Property Link (IPL), Avda, Las Palmeras, Conjunto Los Nadales, Local 1, 29630 Benalmadena Costa, Malaga, Spain; ☎ 0800-955 5555/Intl. +34 952 577 793.fax 09 52 44 10 33; www.internationalpropertylink.com.

Moroccan Properties, Immueble El Khalil, Avenue Hassan II, Marrakech 40000; ☎ 44 43 04 65; fax 044 43 04 30; www.moroccanproperties.com. British run agency – Tangier specialists.

Moroccan Homes, 43 Station Road, Thorpe on Hill, Lincoln LN6 9BS; ☎ 01522 535 052 or Calle Daire 46, Sedella Malaga, Spain; ☎ 95 25 08 961; e-mail info@Moroccan-homes.com; www.Moroccan-homes.com.

Moroccan Properties Ltd, 50 Inwood Avenue, Hounslow, Middlesex, TW3 1XG;

☎ 0208 572 2422; e-mail info@moroccanpropertiesltd.com; www.moroccan propertiesltd.com.
Prestige Properties Overseas Ltd, 12-14 Hardman Street, Blackpool FY1 3QZ; ☎ freephone 0800-085 1601; fax 01253-753952; e-mail info@prestigeproperties overseas.com; www.prestigepropertiesoverseas.com.

WESTERN SAHARA

Two regions constitute Morocco's Western Sahara, Laâyoune-Boujdour-Sakia Al Hamra, with the regional capital Laâyoune and Oued Eddahab-Lagouira with the regional capital, Dakhla. As far as Morocco and Moroccans are concerned, these regions belong to them and are an integral and much loved part of the country. This is despite the fact that no official sovereignty has been by declared by the World Court and the territory is still very much in dispute.

Laâyoune, 700km south of Agadir and 30km from the Atlantic coast is the largest and most impressive town in the Western Sahara, boasting the highest per capita government spend in the country. Colonised by the Spanish in 1884, Morocco took control of the settlement in 1976, transforming it from a small village into a vibrant, prosperous town. It is inhabited, primarily by north Moroccans who have been lured to the region by the promise of double wages and tax free living and rural Saharawi (from the Sahara) migrants who have ended up in the city after several years of drought and gradually become esconced into Moroccan life. The town, heavily militarised is largely made up of the bureaucratic institutions needed to maintain the territory.

Stuck in the middle of the desert, it is hard to envisage quite what Laâyoune would run on if it were not for the millions of dirham constantly being injected into the region by the government. Besides the desert, there is very little of note surrounding the town, with the exception of a fishing port, 30km away on the coast, which is not reliant on Laâyoune for its survival. It is generally accepted that the reason Laâyoune exists at all is in order to have as many Moroccans occupying the Western Saharan territory as possible. The more of its countrymen in the region, the more chance Morocco has of winning the inevitable referendum and obtaining legal sovereignty over the land.

Dakhla, 550km south of Laâyoune constitutes the least populated part of Morocco (37,000 inhabitants). It was also colonised by the Spanish in the late 1800's as the striking white, Spanish cathedral will testify. Nowadays it is a military, administrative outpost, surrounded by deserted beaches and often described as 'seeming like the end of the earth'. As in Laâyoune, there has been heavy government expenditure on the town such as newly paved roads, subsidised apartment blocks and a massive new port, home to one of Morocco's largest fishing fleets specialising in octopus and calamari.

Both Regional Airlines and Royal Air Maroc fly to the two towns of Laâyoune and Dakhla several times a week from Casablanca and Agadir. Tourism is minimal made up primarily of Landrovers and mobile homes en route through Morocco to South Africa. Needless to say there are several mechanics in Dakhla and Landrover parts are easily obtainable.

Properties

If the idea of living in one of Morocco's least populated regions, several hundred kilometres from the rest of Morocco in disputed territory and surrounded by the military actually appeals, there is little in terms of government regulations, to stop you. In fact, the government are keen, as ever, for investment in the Western Sahara regions and land can be bought incredibly cheaply, particularly in the 500km stretch of land between Laâyoune and Dakhla, which is only really inhabited along the coast by fishermen in simple cabins. Bear in mind, it is incredibly windy along the coast, excellent for windsurfing but pretty antisocial otherwise. Apartments (2-3 storey) in the towns of Dakhla and Laayoune are relatively expensive considering the location but this stems from the fact that much of the population, particularly in Laâyoune is well off, thanks to the government.

There is next to no demand from foreigners for properties around the regions of Laâyoune-Boujdour-Sakia Al Hamra and Oued Eddahab-Lagouira. It is, however, quite well frequented by retired Europeans in campervans who prefer to spend six months of the year in the warm Sahara than pay heating bills in the cold climes of Europe.

Part III

THE PURCHASING PROCESS

FINANCE

FINDING PROPERTIES FOR SALE

WHAT TYPE OF PROPERTY TO BUY?

RENTING A HOME IN MOROCCO

FEES, CONTRACTS & CONVEYANCING

Foreign Exchange… How to get the most from your money

Although a dream for many, buying a property in Morocco can turn into a nightmare if vital parts of the buying process are neglected. Currencies Direct explain how one of the major causes of stress for overseas home buyers is overlooking the importance of the foreign exchange rate.

We would never dream of buying a house in the UK without knowing how much we were going to finally pay. So why when buying in Morocco is this exactly what many property buyers do? Whether buying a property outright or in instalments, the purchase will no doubt involve changing your hard earned cash into a foreign currency. Unfortunately, no one can predict the exchange rate as many economic and political factors constantly affect the strength of the pound. Exchange rates are constantly moving and there is no guarantee that they will be in your favour when you need your money, so it is vital that you protect yourself against these movements. A lack of proper forward planning could potentially cost you thousands of pounds and reduce your spending power abroad.

When buying property in Morocco you also need to take into account the fact that you are not allowed to import the local currency, the dirham, into Morocco. This means that if you need to pay for anything in dirhams you need to exchange your money within Morocco. Many property developers to get around this issue now price their properties in euros which mean that buyers can arrange the foreign exchange in the UK. Because of this in the example below we have looked at the euro rather than the dirham.

The affect the exchange rate can have on the cost of your property can be seen if you look at what happened to the euro during 2005. Sterling against the euro was as high as 1.5124 and as low as 1.4086. This means that if you were buying a property worth €200,000 it could have cost you as little as £132,240 or as much as £141,984, a difference of almost £10,000.

It is possible to avoid this pitfall by buying and fixing a rate for your currency ahead of time through a **forward transaction**. This is the *Buy now, Pay later* option and is ideal if you still have some time to wait before your money is due in Morocco or if you are waiting for the proceeds from the sale of your UK property. Usually a small deposit will secure you a rate for anywhere up to 2 years in advance and by doing so you will have the security of having the currency you need at a guaranteed cost and knowing exactly how much your new home will cost.

Another option available to you if you have time on your side is a **limit** order. This is used when you want to achieve a rate that is currently not available. You set the rate that you want and the market is then monitored. As soon as that rate is achieved

currencies direct

the currency is purchased for you. You can also set a 'lower' level or 'stop' to protect yourself should the rate drastically fall. This is ideal for when you don't have to make an immediate payment and you have a specific budget available.

If however you need to act swiftly and your capital is readily available then it is most likely that you will use a **spot transaction**. This is the *Buy now, Pay now* option where you get the most competitive rate on the day.

It is however fair to admit that many of us do not have the time or sufficient knowledge of these options to be in a position to confidently gauge when the foreign currency rates are at their most favourable, and this is where a foreign exchange specialist can help. As an alternative to your bank, foreign exchange specialists are able to offer you extremely competitive exchange rates, no commission charges and lower transfer fees. This can mean considerable savings on your transfer when compared to using a bank.

It is also very easy to use a foreign exchange specialist. The first thing you will need to do is register with them as a client. This is usually very straightforward and requires you to complete a registration form and provide two forms of identification, usually a copy of your passport and a recent utility bill. Once you are registered you are then able to trade. Your dealer will talk you through the different options that are available to you and help you to decide which one is right for you depending on your timing, circumstances and foreign currency needs. Once you have decided which option is best for you and agreed a rate you will then need to send your money. With clearance times at each end some companies can complete the transfer for you in as little as a week.

Even once you have bought your new home in Morocco you need to make sure that you don't forget about foreign exchange. It is highly likely that you will need to make **regular transfers** from the UK whether for mortgage payments, maintenance expenditure or transferring pensions or salaries, and using a reputable foreign exchange specialist can make sure that you get more of your money each time, even on small amounts. This is because unlike your bank they will offer you competitive exchange rates on smaller amounts, no commission charges and often free transfers.

Currencies Direct is a leading commercial foreign exchange company; offering superior rates of exchange and a personalised service they meet the needs of thousands of private and corporate clients every year.

With offices in the UK, Spain, Australia, South Africa and India Currencies Direct is always on hand to help you. For more information about their services, please contact one of their dealers who will be happy to discuss your currency requirements with you.

UK Head Office: 0845 389 3000
Email: info@currenciesdirect.com
Web: www.currenciesdirect.com

FINANCE

CHAPTER SUMMARY

○ **Banks**: There are no British banks in Morocco, but Moroccan bank accounts can be opened in the UK through the representative branches of Moroccan banks.

  ○ As the dirham is a restricted currency, foreigners must open a Convertible Bank Account so that their foreign currency can be moved freely in and out of Morocco.

○ **Mortgages**: The interest rates on Moroccan mortgages are around 7%. The banks will allow you to borrow up to 40% of your monthly net salary as your maximum monthly mortgage payment without any prior credit checks. You can borrow up to 70% of the value of the property.

  ○ It is better to borrow money in the UK and be a cash buyer in Morocco.

○ **Tax**: The Moroccan authorities will consider you a tax resident and tax you on your worldwide assets, if your principal income is generated in Morocco or if you are living in Morocco for more than 183 days (six months) of the year. This time period can run from and to any month of the year.

  ○ Morocco's taxation system is complicated and subject to change. You are advised to employ a recommended accountant to manage your accounts.

○ **Income Tax**: The highest rate of tax payable is 44%. This figure kicks in at 60,001 dh (around £4000).

○ **Real Estate Taxes**: In addition to legal fees, these amount to between 3 and 5.5% of the cost of your property.

○ **Local Taxes**: These are very low compared to the UK.

○ **Capital Gains**: If the property is your principal domicile or you make no income from it, there will be no capital gains tax after ten years.

○ **Inheritance Tax**: This does not exist in Morocco, but the UK will tax you on your worldwide assets.

BANKING

In Morocco, only 25% of the population has a bank account, which means that finance still means cash, good, solid and very grubby dirham notes or a constant supply of small coins for paying for taxis, porters, bread etc. as few small shops keep large quantities of change. Outside major tourist zones, you will find yourself paying cash for pretty much everything, with your credit card about as useful as a raincoat in the desert. This said, unless you are in the heart of the Atlas Mountains, you are unlikely to ever be more than a few miles from a multilingual ATM (guichet), so your credit or cashpoint card is likely to come in handy to withdraw money. Most currencies are easily exchanged at banks with rates varying little between them. Banque Marocaine pour le Commerce Exterieur (BMCE) and Crédit du Maroc are generally the most prevalent with many branches having a separate Bureau de Change, which is open at weekends.

All banking activity in Morocco is controlled by the central bank, Bank Al Maghrib, which has branches in 16 cities around Morocco. As well as working as a commercial bank, Bank Al Maghrib also regulates monetary policy and issues Moroccan currency. There are 17 onshore commercial banks in Morocco of which, following the recent merger of Banque Commerciale du Maroc and Wafa Bank, Attijariwafa Bank is now the largest, followed by the state owned (but soon to be privatised), Credit Populaire. With the exception of the non-Moroccan, Arab-British bank in which HSBC have around a 45% stake, there are currently no British banks in Morocco and only two representative Moroccan banks in the UK; BMCE and Banque Populaire (part of Credit Populaire). Both of these banks offer a house purchasing money transfer service from the UK to Morocco, free of charge or for a maximum fee of £25. It is also possible via Bank Populaire to transfer funds from the UK to Morocco on a regular basis up to £1000 per month. BMCE used to offer this service, but they tend now to deal mainly with large businesses as opposed to individuals.

In order to buy a property in Morocco, foreigners need to have a bank account with a bank in Morocco. All of the commercial banks generally offer the same range of consumer products with internet and telephone banking services (in French), credit cards and a plethora of ATM's, a common feature of each. This means that when it comes to choosing which bank best suits your needs there are three main considerations to take in to account. Firstly, is the bank within close proximity to the area where you plan to buy? There is no point travelling two hours simply to pay in a cheque. Secondly, is there anyone at the branch who speaks English? Most branches have one English speaking person but it is worth verifying this. If not, every employee will speak French. Thirdly, does the bank have a representative branch in the UK? This is only really of any benefit to you if, at least initially, you are spending more of your time in the UK than Morocco. A UK representative office can handle the opening of your account and the house purchasing bank transfers for you, free of charge without you having to pay high transfer charges, as would be the case if transferring funds to Morocco from a UK bank account. It will not, however, manage the day to day running of your account such as the ordering of new chequebooks, the transferring of small amounts or changes of address. These all need to be handled directly with your local branch in Morocco either face to face, which is more effective, or by fax. In both instances, follow up enquiries to confirm that the information has been received is recommended as in Morocco, out of sight tends to mean out of mind.

All banks in Morocco close for the siesta at lunchtime, but many are open on Saturday mornings. Standard opening times are generally, Monday to Friday 8.30am-12 noon, 2-5pm and Saturday 8.30am-12 noon.

Convertible Bank Accounts. The Moroccan dirham (MAD) is a restricted currency, which means that it cannot be obtained outside Morocco or leave the country. It is imperative, therefore, that the account you open is what is known as a convertible bank account, which will enable you to both deposit and repatriate any foreign currency you have paid in to the account plus any profits you have made from your property. Convertible bank accounts are given automatically to non-residents, as it is assumed that they will wish to be making all payments in foreign currency. All of the banks offer convertible accounts and will keep a record for you of what foreign currency deposits have been made, so that you can repatriate funds without having to go via the Office des Changes (Foreign Exchange Department), which used to be the case. It is not possible to pay dirham in to your convertible account so if you are self-employed in Morocco being paid in local currency, you will need to open a local currency non- convertible account.

Opening a convertible account is very straightforward. All you need to provide are:

- Passport or residence card
- Specimen of signatures
- Utility bill
- Money – as small or as large an amount as you wish

After the first deposit has been made in to the account, you will be given a chequebook and credit card. The credit card can be used internationally. These can be either collected from your branch in Morocco or if you are with a bank that has a UK representative office, picked up or issued from there. While it is wise to always keep a sum of money in the account to pay off bills and taxes, it is important to keep the account active. If no money is deposited or removed from the account for one year, the bank will automatically close it down and return the remaining balance to you. It will then be much harder to reopen your bank account through a UK representative office, as they tend only to deal with accounts opened specifically for the purchasing of property and other large investments.

Non-Convertible Local Currency Account. It is only really worth having a local currency account, if you are likely to be obtaining Moroccan dirham as a source of income, otherwise it is best just to stick to your convertible account, so as to avoid any possible problems with repatriating your funds. If you have a Moroccan residence permit, you will be able to open a standard local currency account in the same way as a Moroccan national. If you are a non-resident, you can still open a local currency account, despite what many people, including some banks will tell you, but it will be what is known as a 'Special' Account. This account will enable you to pay in any locally generated income or loans obtained in Morocco. You will not, however, freely be able to transfer such income out of the country without going via the *Office des Changes,* who will be able to transfer the money from dirham in to foreign currency for you. In order to do this, you must request your bank to contact the Office des Changes for you providing them with a detailed statement of expenses and receipts.

Banking Practices

Moroccan banks, ever cautious about lending money will not let accounts go overdrawn by putting an immediate halt on to any payments going out of your account. They will inform you of your misdemeanour by sending a bank statement but as there is an overlap between the sending and receiving, it can be sometime before you actually find out. If you are worried that you are likely to go overdrawn, then you can rectify it by speaking in advance to your local branch and proving to them that a transfer is underway. This will generally help, especially if you have already taken the time out to bond with your bank manager (easier for a man than a woman), which will do you no end of good and is a very common undertaking in Morocco.

Bank statements are sent out free of charge as often or as rarely as you request. The normal practice is monthly but if you choose to have them sent to your UK address, this can take longer, with arrival times, sporadic.

Cheques

There are no cheque guarantee cards in Morocco, but when writing cheques, you might be asked to show another form of identification. Morocco is a cash culture, where dirham notes or coins are the preferred method of payment, although large outlets such as hypermarkets and hotels all accept credit cards. People rarely write cheques in shops especially as illiteracy remains a fundamental problem, so you will find that the writing of cheques is mainly from individual to individual. It is important to note that Moroccan cheques are written in French using punctuation marks to separate numerals in the diametrically opposite way to the UK, 10,428.36 dirham for example, would be written 10.428,36 dirham.

If you write a cheque with insufficient funds in your account, the bank will simply not let it be cashed. You are most likely to find out that this has happened when the intended recipient of the cheque comes banging on your door at an inopportune moment and lets you know, in no uncertain terms. It is best simply to rectify the situation as rapidly as possible otherwise you will get blacklisted by the bank, your chequebook withdrawn and harassed by the would-be recipient until you pay up.

It is possible to cancel a cheque but this is a laborious task especially if your French is limited, as it requires you to tell the bank in writing, why you wish to make a cancellation. Moroccan cheques take over a week to clear, however, which means you have time to write, before the amount leaves your account.

Moroccan Banks

- Banque Centrale Populaire
- Attijariwafa Bank
- Banque Marocaine du Commerce Exterieur (BMCE)
- Banque Marocaine pour le Commerce et l'Industrie (BMCI)
- British Arab Commercial Bank
- Credit du Maroc
- Citibank Maghreb
- Credit Immobilier et Hotelier (CIH)

Money Transfers

Intra Bank Transfers. As said above, if you choose to open your bank account through a UK representative office, they will handle money transfers relating to the purchasing of your property or investments for you free of charge at reasonable rates of exchange. All you need to do is send a fax requesting the amount to be transferred and the representative bank will forward it on for you. As with most administrative tasks, it is prudent just to put in a telephone call ensuring the fax has been received and is being actioned, especially if you are keen for the transfer to be made quickly. While banks will insist that transfers take 2 days to clear, it is always necessary to allow extra time to allow for the many 'unexpected occurrences' that can crop up.

Bank to Bank Transfers. It is possible to send money from your UK bank account to either yours or some else's account in Morocco. To do this, you need to have the recipients account number, postal address of the bank and the SWIFT code. The maximum you can send tends to be around £5000 and costs start around £15. There are also payments to be made at both ends, so it is important to note who will be responsible for paying these prior to the money leaving the account. While to most places this service takes between 1-5 days, with Morocco it can be a lot longer up - to a couple of weeks, so it is not a recommended route if you wish for the money to be there fast.

Telegraphic Transfers. For a fast, reliable service one of the telegraphic transfer companies such as Western Union or its relatively cheaper compatriot, Money-Gram will be your best bet. Taking in to consideration the rapid sending time and efficiency of these telegraphic transfer companies, the cost is not incomparable to that of sending via your UK bank. These transfers take a matter of minutes with price dependent on how much money you are sending. All you need to do is provide the exact name of the person collecting the money (just a minor spelling mistake will prevent collection) and sometimes, a password known both to you and the recipient. The recipient will need to show either their identity card or passport and give the shared password in order to collect the money.

Currency Exchange Specialists. A specialised company such as *Currencies Direct* (51 Moorgate, London EC2R 6BH; ☎ 0845 389 3000; fax 020-7419 7753; www.currenciesdirect.com) can help in a number of ways, by offering better exchange rates than banks, without charging commission, and giving you the possibility of 'forward buying' – agreeing on the rate that you will pay at a fixed date in the future – or with a limit order – waiting until the rate you want is reached. For those who prefer to know exactly how much money they have available for their property purchase, forward buying is the best solution, since you no longer have to worry about the pound against the Dirham working to your detriment. Payments can be made in one lump sum or on a regular basis. It is usual when building new property to pay in instalments.

Useful Addresses

Banque Marocaine pour le Commerce Exterieur (BMCE); London Representative branch, 26 Upper Brook Street, London W1K 7QE; ☎ 020-7518 8250; www.bmcebank.ma.

Bank Populaire; 38 Star Street, Paddington, London, W2QB; ☎ 020-7258 0243; www.cpm.co.ma.

Crédit du Maroc; www.cdm.co.ma.

Attijariwafa Bank; www.attijariwafabank.com.

Office des Changes; B.P 71, Rabat, Morocco; ☎ 037 72 19 72; www.oc.gov.ma.

Western Union; www.westernunion.co.uk.

MoneyGram; www.moneygram.com.

MORTGAGES

It is currently not possible to obtain a UK mortgage secured on a Moroccan property although this is set to change very soon with international mortgage companies like Conti Financial Services planning to start working in Morocco very soon. For the time being, however, in order to raise the finance to purchase your property, you have the choice of either mortgaging or extending the mortgage on your existing UK home or borrowing from a lending bank in Morocco. It should be noted, that the former option is by far the most preferable.

Conti Financial Services Ltd, 204 Church Road, Hove, East Sussex, BN3 2DJ, ☎ 01273 772 811; fax 01273 321 269; email enquiries@mortgagesoverseas.com; www.mortgagesoverseas.com.

UK Mortgages

Taking out or extending a mortgage on UK property is becoming an increasingly popular way for UK homeowners to purchase second homes abroad. Low interest rates, a wide range of different repayment options and generally no extra fees to set up an additional loan makes this route arguably the most advantageous. Many foreigners buying houses in Morocco will use a combination of savings to, for example, purchase the property and equity from re-mortgaging an existing UK property, for the renovations, which in the case of traditional riads and farmhouses, tend to cost around the same as the purchase price.

Moroccan Mortgages

Preferring privacy on all matters financial combined with fear of job instability and being in debt to powerful institutions makes Moroccans generally sceptical about borrowing, with a report in 2001 showing that 81% of all properties purchased were self-financed. While recent economic reforms, positive feelings about the new king and a relative hike in property prices have caused this statistic to drop, the mortgage sector is not booming and interest rates remain relatively high at between 6-11%. For low interest rates, ease of capital repatriation, and avoidance of fluctuating exchange rates, your best option for financing your property is with a UK mortgage.

If you do decide to borrow from a lending bank in Morocco and note that not all banks will lend to foreigners, you must purchase a titled property, as banks will not lend money for the purchase of untitled properties (see *Fees, Contracts and Costs*). Moroccan mortgages are based on repayment only ie; the loan and the interest on it are repaid together through monthly instalments. There are no such things as interest-only, pension or endowment mortgages. You can have the choice of either a fixed rate or variable mortgage although all possible future renegotiations must be written up in the initial contract. The arrangement fee to set up a mortgage is around 1000 dirham (£65).

The normal loan period extends from 10 years to 15 and sometimes 20 years or until the borrower turns 65 although banks tend to recommend a fixed rate loan for 15 years and a variable for 20 years.

In order to secure their loan, banks will not offer any more than 70% of the value of the property to foreigners, although as an extra incentive to Moroccan expats who are a key source of revenue, it is possible to borrow between 80-100% of the value of the property. Banks will allow you to borrow up to 40% of your monthly net salary as your maximum monthly mortgage payment. For example, if you earn £2000 per month, you will be able to borrow up to £800 as your monthly mortgage repayment. At 7% this means you will be able to borrow approximately £113,000 to buy your house in Morocco. You will then need to source the final 30% elsewhere.

To obtain the mortgage, you need to provide proof of income through your last three-months pay slips or six months bank statements in combination, where applicable, with a letter from your employer. No prior credit checks are undertaken and no note is taken of any pre-existing obligations such as other outstanding loans.

The standard practice for obtaining a Moroccan mortgage is to visit the bank with the relevant documentation. Assuming that your Moroccan bank offers mortgages to foreigners and the rates are competitive, it makes most sense going via them as opposed to another bank completely, in order to save on money and time when it comes to making transfers. This needs to be done prior to your beginning the house purchasing process. After assessing your situation for around 1 month (faster if you pay a small fee), the bank will decide whether or not you are eligible. If they decide that you are, which is normally the case, they will provide you with a letter of pre-approval. You are then free to start the contractual process for purchasing a property. You must inform the notaire that you are planning to finance the property through a Moroccan mortgage and request he puts a clause in to the preliminary house purchasing contract stating it to be dependent on the obtaining of the mortgage (see Fees, Contracts and Costs). The notaire will also manage the mortgage paperwork on your behalf, liaising with the bank and surveyors.

Your Moroccan mortgage will be paid to you in dirham. You, therefore, need to either open a local currency non-convertible bank account if you are resident or a 'special' account (see above), if you are not, as you will not be able to pay the dirham in to your convertible bank account.

It is possible for you to repay the mortgage in foreign currency, by setting up a monthly direct debit from a UK bank account (with a charge at the UK end) but considering the time, cost and exchange rate fluctuations, this is not a reliable or economic route. The best repayment method is from your Moroccan convertible account (no charge if between accounts), in to your local Moroccan account. If you repay the Moroccan mortgage in foreign currency, ie via your Moroccan convertible account, you will be able to repatriate all the funds, but this will have to be done via the Office des Changes, so it is imperative that you keep all your bank statements and transaction information as proof of payment.

If a mortgage payment is missed you will be given six months to rectify the problem. If payments are still not being met after six months, you will be subject to legal proceedings, which could amount to the bank repossessing your property.

Insurance

It is not obligatory to obtain insurance prior to purchasing a property in Morocco, (although it is wise to do so not long after) unless you are taking out a Moroccan mortgage to pay for it, in which case, you need cover securing the property against physical damage such as fire, floods and earthquakes and life insurance covering you for death, accident or illness. You will need proof of having obtained this insurance prior to the signing of the final *Acte de Vente* document. The bank will recommend insurance companies to you, but the most widely used is AXA Insurance, found in virtually every town and city in Morocco.

PROS AND CONS OF MOROCCAN MORTGAGES:

Pros

- Charges involved with setting up a Moroccan mortgage are not high.
- Documentation required to set up the mortgage is minimal.
- You are allowed to borrow up to 40% of your monthly salary as your maximum monthly mortgage repayment.
- There are no prior credit checks.

Cons

- Interest rates are higher than in the UK.
- Moroccan banks will only offer up to 70% of the value of your property.
- If you are paying off the mortgage in foreign currency, you are subject to UK banking transfer costs and fluctuating exchange rates.
- In order to repatriate your loan repayments, you will have to get authority from the Office des Changes.

Baksheesh. Whatever your views are on underhand payments or tips, baksheesh is a way of life for many in Morocco, even though it is fundamentally illegal. Having said this, some Moroccans will take offence if you consider it as such, preferring it to be referred to as a tip instead of baksheesh, which has a seedy sounding edge. It is, however, a way to get jobs done quickly and efficiently. Salaries amongst public officials such as the police and government department workers are so low, that a few actually rely on the extra pay they receive and you can find that if you are not forthcoming with your dirham, your project might purposefully be shoved to the back of the queue until you pay up. If you find it hard to get your head around the concept, you might want to consider it like this. In Europe, we tend to have two main services, Standard and Express. If we want to get jobs done quickly or packages delivered fast, we pay for the Express service otherwise we go with the Standard and wait. In Morocco, there is no such official service as Express, so people create their own by paying extra to get jobs done fast. Admittedly, and note that the author is not necessarily condoning it, it can extend in to other environments; paying 50 dirham to the clerk at the Post Office to avoid ever having to queue or a small bung to the tax collector to turn a blind eye to your tardy tax return. Even if you choose not to go down the baksheesh route, it is worth at least getting to grips with the mindset and asking Moroccans how the system works, as it is just an extra way of ensuring you get something done on time.

MOROCCAN TAXES

Although the Moroccan proverb claiming tax evasion to be a national sport is less valid now than it was following a government clamp down ten years ago, quite how many Moroccans actually pay taxes today remains questionable especially when an underhand payment can get most people out of a fix. The general attitude of most Moroccans is that as long as you pay something, you are generally left alone. What taxes are meant to be paid, and by whom remains a murky area, whether you are a businessman, farmer or foreigner and no matter who you ask, you will be given several different answers to the same question. This is despite efforts by the government to bring transparency to the highly complicated state of affairs. Incentives and reductions add to the general mayhem and it is only when you realise that one particular tax is referred to in five different ways that you start to get a grip on how the system might be structured, for this year at least. While there is the temptation as a foreigner to bury your head and hope it all goes away, there is no guarantee that it will especially as the recent influx of foreigners are becoming a very necessary source of revenue for the Moroccan government. The best advice if you are going to be liable for a tax bill in Morocco is to employ a recommended accountant, which is not expensive, who will be responsible for managing your books, filling in your tax returns, paying your bills and hopefully, saving you a lot of money.

Taxation Status

The best first step for understanding the Moroccan taxation system is to assess your involvement in it. This means understanding exactly what your taxation status is. This generally boils down to the question, are you a tax resident or non-tax resident?

Tax Resident. The Moroccan authorities will consider you a tax resident if your main income is generated in Morocco or if you are living in Morocco for more than 183 days (six months) of the year. This time period can run from and to any month of the year. Being the carrier of a residence permit does not automatically make you a tax resident, although you are more likely to be a tax resident, if you have a residence permit. If you are a tax resident in Morocco, earning no money anywhere but in Morocco and spending all your time in Morocco, then all your taxation will be confined to within Morocco. If, however, you are still earning an income in the UK, perhaps through renting out a property or through pensions and shares or if you visit the UK for a minimum of 91 days per year, over four or more tax years, you are considered by the UK authorities to be 'ordinarily resident' in the UK. This means, that you will still be liable to pay some British taxes.

Non-tax Resident. If you have simply bought a second home in Morocco for investment purposes or winter sun but you spend the majority of the year in the UK and do not earn your principal income from your property, then your tax status in the UK will remain the same. Any income made from your Moroccan property will have to be declared both in Morocco and the UK although the UK authorities will deduct any taxes already paid in Morocco when calculating your UK tax liability. When it comes to selling the property, you will need to declare any profits you have made from the property to the UK Inland Revenue but again, the taxes you have paid in Morocco will be deducted.

Double Taxation Agreement. It is quite possible that you could be spending two-thirds of the year in Morocco and the rest in the UK. As a result, you may run the risk of being considered as tax resident in both countries and end up paying tax twice on the same income. In order to prevent this from happening, both Morocco and the UK, (plus many more countries) have signed up to a Double Taxation Agreement, which (if you choose to claim under it) includes a set of tests, which will tell you which country you are mostly resident of. The full text of the treaty is available at *www.opsi.gov.uk/si/si1991/Uksi_19912881_en_1.htm*

If after applying the tests, it turns out that you are mostly a Moroccan resident, you can ask for relief from paying UK tax on income such as private and state pensions, although not on Government Service pensions, which remain subject to UK tax regardless. Also if you get interest from a UK bank or building society account, it is possible to receive this without UK tax being deducted by filling in a declaration of non-residence on Form R105, although you will need to check with your bank or building society that they participate in the scheme.

The best way of obtaining information relating to your own specific taxation circumstances is via the *Centre for Non-Residents*, St John's House, Bootle, Merseyside, L69 9BB; ☎ 0151-472 6000; fax 0151-472 6067; www.hmrc.gov.uk/cnr/index. htm.

TAX

There are three main taxes you will need to pay if you buy or own a property and are generating an income from your property or other business activities in Morocco. These are income tax, real estate taxes and local taxes.

INCOME TAX IMPÔT GÉNÉRALE SUR LE REVENU (IGR)

Anyone generating an income in Morocco, whether they are tax resident or not, will have to fill in a tax return declaring their income. The Moroccan tax year runs from the 1st January to the 31st December but all tax returns relating to the year just passed, need to be submitted three months after the year end making March a very busy time in the life of an accountant. Most taxes are based on self-assessment relying on the individual to take responsibility for undertaking their own tax returns. As with all taxes, penalties for late payment stand at 15% for the first month and 0.5% for each subsequent month.

Depending on whether you are a tax resident or non-tax resident, employed or self employed will determine the way you pay taxes although the tax brackets remain the same. As with most administrative circumstances in Morocco, it really pays to hire a recommended accountant versed in Moroccan tax and bureaucracy to undertake the task of your tax return. While this is standard practice if you have a registered company, you might not consider it necessary to have someone on board all year round if you are a small, self-employed venture. In this case if you get in early enough before the last minute rush, you could ask one of the local hotels or guesthouses to borrow their accountant to do your tax return for you. Moroccans are always very happy to earn extra cash on the side. The most important thing you can do is to keep a record of all your receipts, income and spend. This way filling the form in should be relatively straightforward

Tax Residents

Employees. If you live in Morocco, working for a Moroccan company, then your tax will be deducted by the company on a PAYE basis much like in the UK. The highest rate of tax payable is 44%, a figure that depressingly kicks in at 60,001 dh (around £4000). It is compulsory for employees to pay around 2% of their earnings into the social security system, *Caisse Nationale de Sécurité Sociale (CNSS)*. The company will also contribute 2% on behalf of the employee. This payment covers retirement, sickness cover and, as part of a new initiative which began in July 2005, health insurance.

Self-Employed. If you are a self-employed tax resident, then you will need to declare your worldwide income to the Moroccan authorities. This includes your Moroccan income as well as statements of any income received elsewhere in the world such as savings, pensions or rent from properties. In these circumstances, you will also need to fill in a tax return in the UK. In most cases, the double taxation agreement will kick in and you will only be taxed once on any income you make away from Morocco, although this is not the case in all circumstances. If, for example, you live in Morocco but rent out your property in the UK, the double taxation agreement will not cover you and you might be charged twice. It is important you check both with the Centre for Non Residents; ☎ 0151-472 6000 in the UK who will be able to advise on double taxation in the UK and with a tax expert in Morocco who will be able to advise on your entitlements in Morocco. Tax declaration forms are obtained from your local tax office, the *Service des Impôts,* found in every town, and need to be submitted by the end of March. At the time of submitting your form, you will be provided with a tax identification number, which you will need to quote on all matters relating to tax. In June/July, you will receive an invoice stating what you need to pay. This is usually the same as the amount you declare, so there will be no unpleasant shocks. All tax bills are paid at the tax collection office, which every neighborhood has, known as the *Perception.*

Corporate Tax. An attractive route for many people wishing to make an income from their property is to form a limited company (see *Making Money from Your Property*). The current rate for corporate tax in Morocco is levied at 35% on all profits. In order to encourage foreign exchange, companies are not charged tax on foreign currency income for the first five years of business, although they will need to declare income paid to them in dirham. They will also, as is common for companies, be able to offset expenses such as start up costs. After five years, they will get a reduction of 50% on their foreign currency income. This is for an indefinite period of time. Annual income must be declared before the end of March but every quarter the company will be charged 25% of their future tax bill in advance, based on the previous year's declaration. Corporate tax bills are paid directly to the Impôts des Services, local tax office.

Non-Tax Residents

Self-Employed. Any income you earn in Morocco no matter how great or small needs to be declared. Even if it is between 1-20,000 dirham and therefore exempt from taxation, you are advised to declare it. As a non-tax resident, you will only be expected to pay tax on any income generated in Morocco, not elsewhere. You will then need to apply for tax relief when it comes to paying income tax on this back in the UK. You can obtain a tax return form from the local tax office, Service des Impôts. As with all non-corporate tax affairs, tax forms must submitted back to the Service des Impôts by the end of March at which time you will be given a tax identification number, which you will need to quote on all matters relating to tax. In June/July, you will receive an invoice through the post, stating what you need to pay. This tax bill must also be paid at your neighborhood tax collection office, the *Perception*.

INCOME TAX SLIDING SCALE	
1 to 20,000 dirham	Exempt
20,001 to 24000 dirham	13% with a reduction of 2600 dirham
24,001 to 36,000 dirham	21% with a reduction of 4520 dirham
36,001 to 60,000 dirham	35% with a reduction of 9560 dirham
60,001 dirham and above	44% with a reduction of 14,960 dirham

REAL ESTATE TAXES

There are two taxes you need to pay when purchasing a house in Morocco.

Registration Tax

While this is not officially a stamp duty, it is best, for purposes of clarity, to describe it as such. No house purchaser (with the exception of some new constructions being given government incentives), is exempt from paying it and how much you pay will depend on what you plan to do with the property or the type of property you buy. The standard rate is 2.5% of the purchase value of the house. If, however, you are planning on using the house to make an income such as turning it into a guesthouse or, if you buy land or a farmhouse in the countryside ie: out of the urban perimeter, this tax increases to 5% of the cost of the property.

Notary Tax

The other tax to pay, if you decide to use a notaire in place of a private lawyer, to undertake your conveyancing, is a Notary tax, this amounts to 0.5% of the purchasing price. Both these taxes are paid directly to the notaire responsible for your conveyancing along with the conveyancing fees, at the time of the signing of the final contract.

LOCAL TAXES

Taxe Urbaine (TU) and Taxe d'édilité (TE)

These two local taxes are like a council tax, covering the upkeep of your local surrounds; maintenance of roads, cleaning, dustbin emptying, streetlighting etc. 90% of the TU goes to the Urban Commune and 10% to the General State Budget, while all of the TE goes to the Urban Commune. Local taxes must be paid if your property is located in or within the peripheries of an

Urban Commune, which the majority of properties are. A tax bill covering both taxes will be sent to your property around April/May. You have 30 days in which to pay with late payment resulting in the standard 15% penalty for the first month and a 0.5% fine for each subsequent month you fail to pay. All payments are made at your neighbourhood Perception. It is best to pay off the taxes as soon as you get the bill to avoid the last minute, dirham-thrusting, scramble.

Local taxes are calculated upon the declared or estimated rental value of your property (estimated rental value being determined by the Census Committee and increased by 2% every 5 years).

LOCAL TAX EXEMPTIONS

If you live in a Rural Commune you are exempt from paying local taxes for public services as none are provided

You are exempt from paying local taxes for the first 5 years if you are:

- The first owner of a newly constructed property
- Using your property as a business activity

Taxe Urbaine. If you are declaring an income from your property, then the rate of TU is 13.5% of your declared annual rental income. If the property is your principal place of residence ie: your main home or second home and you make no income from it, you pay the following sliding scale based upon your estimated rental income but with a 75% discount on the final figure:

Sliding Scale for TU Payments	
Rental Value in Dirham	Rate
0-3000	Exempt
3001-6000	10%
6001-12000	16%
12001-24000	20%
24001-36000	24%
36001-60000	28%
Surplus taxed at	30%

Taxe d'édilité. Properties located inside the Urban Commune, must pay TE at a rate of 10% of declared or estimated rental value while the rate for properties in the suburbs of the Urban Commune is 6% of declared or estimated rental value.

VAT (T*VA*). As an incentive to boost tourism investment, VAT is charged at 10% for any registered company in the tourism industry from day one of business and 20% for all other industries. If company turnover is less than 1 million dirham, VAT is paid quarterly. If it is over 1 million, VAT is paid monthly. All company tax bills are paid directly to the Impôts des Services, local tax office. You can deduct any furnishings, machinery, equipments etc from your VAT declaration.

Wealth Tax. This does not exist in Morocco.

CAPITAL GAINS TAX (TAXE SUR LES PROFITS IMMOBILIERS)

A tax is levied on any capital gains made on property and land. This is calculated by deducting the purchase price including costs, building work, renovations etc from the selling price. Capital gains tax is set at 20% with a minimum of 3% of the selling price. There are no tax exemptions on properties sold within the first five years of ownership. If you have owned the property for more than five years and it is your principal residence, ie: it is your permanent place of abode or a private holiday home or if the property is valued at less than 1 million dirham, then you will receive a 50% reduction on capital gains. After ten years, if the property is your principal or private holiday home or if you sell it for less than 1 million dirham, you will be exempt from paying any capital gains tax in Morocco. If you are making an income from your property, then you will have to pay capital gains tax of 20% at any time you choose to sell. In order to minimize your liability for capital gains tax, it is imperative that you keep all receipts and invoices for any building or renovation works undertaken on your house. Homeowners are expected to declare their own capital gains within 60 days of selling their property. Declaration forms can be obtained from and submitted to the Impôts des Services and tax bills paid at the Perception.

INHERITANCE TAX

So long as you have made a Moroccan will stating whom you wish to pass your property on to in the event of your death and had it legally certified by a notaire in Morocco or the Moroccan Consulate in London or New York, you will be charged no inheritance tax in Morocco. The only cost you will incur, prior to death, is the fee to add the name of your successors on to the title deeds. This levies a charge of 1% of the property value, which goes to the Conservation Fonciere. If you are a British tax resident, however, inheritance tax will have to be paid based on your worldwide assets, which incorporates Morocco.

Wills

When you come to drawing up your Moroccan will, it would be wise to state what you wish to happen to you in the event of your death. If you plan to be repatriated back to the UK, you will need to ensure there are enough funds in your estate or family members prepared to pay for this, as neither the British Consulate nor the Moroccan authorities, will foot the bill. If there are not enough funds or any funds put aside at all, you will be buried in Morocco (cremation is not an option in Islamic culture), but do not expect any pomp or ceremony.

Useful Addresses

Financial Advice

American Chamber of Commerce, Hyatt Regency, Place des Nations Unies, Casablanca 20000; ☎ 022 29 30 28 ; www.amcham-morocco.com.

British Chamber of Commerce, 65 Avenue Hassan Seghir, Casablanca; ☎ 022 44 88 60/61; e-mail britcham@casanet.net.ma;www.bccm.co.ma

Cabinet Abdellatif El Quortobi – Financial Consultant, 57 bd Abdelmoumen, Immeuble El Hadi, B9, Casablanca; ☎ 022 26 36 70; www.audit-conseil.com.

Deloitte et Touche Maroc, 283, Boulevard Zerktouni – 4e etage, Casablanca; ☎ 022 36 99 10; www.deloitte.com.

Ernst and Young, 44, Rue Mohamed Smiha – 4 et 5 etage, Casablanca 20000; ☎ 022 54 58 00; www.eyi.com.

Investment Office, Direction des Investissements Extérieurs, Angle Avenue, Michelifin et Rue Hounain, 4th Floor, Agdal, Rabat; ☎ 037 67 33 75/67 34 20;www.invest-in-morocco.gov.ma.

Mohammed Ouarti_Accountant, Quartier Belair, Rue 16, no 2; ☎ 061 28 82 31; e-mail ouartima@yahoo.fr.

Price Waterhouse Coopers, 101 Blvd Al Massira, Al Khadra, Casablanca; ☎ 022 98 40 40; www.pwcglobal.com/cf/fra/main/home/index.html.

Legal Advice

The International Property Law Centre: Suffolk House, 21 Silver Street, Hull HU1 1JG; ☎ 0870 800 4565; e-mail internationalproperty@maxgold.com; fax 0870 800 4567; www.internationalpropertylaw.com. Specialists in the purchase and sale of property and businesses in Morocco, with in-house foreign lawyers. Fixed quote and no VAT payable. Contact Stefano Lucatello, Senior Partner, (☎ 0870 800 4565, e-mail stefanol@maxgold.com).

Embassies and Consulates

Moroccan Consulate UK, 97-99 Praed Street, London, W2 1NT; ☎ 020-7724 0719; www.morocco.embassyhomepage.com.

Moroccan Consulate USA, 10 East 40th Street, New York, NY, 10016, USA; ☎ 0212-758 2625; www.moroccanconsulate.com.

British Consulate-General, Casablanca, Commercial Section, Villa Les Salurges, 36 Rue de la Loire, Polo, Casablanca; ☎ 022 85 74 00.

British Embassy, Rabat; 17 Boulevard de la Tour Hassan Rabat; ☎ 037 23 86 00.

British Consulate Tangier; Trafalgar House, 9 Rue Amerique du Sud, Tanger 90000 BP 1203; ☎ 039 936939.

British Consulate, Marrakech; Residence Jaib 55 Boulevard Zerktouni Marrakech; ☎ 044 43 60 78.

British Consulate Agadir, Complet Tours, 1 Immeuble Beausouss, Angle Boulevard, Mohammed V Agadir; ☎ 048 82 34 01.

American Consulate General, 8 Boulevard Moulay Youssef, Casablanca 20000; acscasablanca@state.gov; www.usembassy.ma.

FINDING PROPERTY FOR SALE

CHAPTER SUMMARY

○ **The Seller Rules.** Property prices in Morocco are dependent on the price the seller wishes to obtain for a property as opposed to official valuations.

○ **Official Agents.** An official agent is more likely to give you accurate, researched information but they are more expensive.

○ **Unofficial Agents.** An unofficial agent is not accountable, so you take more of a risk but they are also less expensive.

○ **Working with Agents.** The best way of working with Moroccans is on the ground and face-to-face. Long distance relationships are not effective.

○ **Research.** Do extensive research on the type and location of property you wish to buy prior to beginning your house hunting as this will give you more control over the agent.

○ Estate agent websites are the best way of finding out about properties, but these are not regularly updated.

ESTATE AGENTS

UK Based Estate Agents

Unlike the well established property markets of France, Spain and Italy where there is an abundance of UK and international based estate agents, the number of British companies working with Moroccan properties number around nine, most of them very new to the country with the majority tending to focus on Marrakech and/or new build properties (mainly along the Mediterranean coast). While the good news is that an increase in demand is encouraging more international agents to add Morocco on to their books, the very good news is, that with or without a British agent, English-speaking people have enjoyed successfully purchasing properties in Morocco for the last ten years and more.

Many agents believe strongly in the potential of Morocco. Poonam Ball, director of Moroccan Properties states

When one thinks of Morocco you automatically thinks of cities like Marrakech or Casablanca, but what most of us don't realise it that it has it has some of the best coastlines the Mediterranean has to offer. Spain is just 9 miles away, by sea, yet you pay only a forth of the price in Morocco in comparison to the same property in the Costa del Sol.

Development in the Mediterranean side has just started and therefore capital appreciation will be far greater than in the well.-known cities. What's even better is that investors can benefit from exemption from rental tax for 5 years, no inheritance tax and no capital gains tax if the property is sold after 10 years."

While most UK based international agents will avoid the buying and selling of traditional properties in Morocco, some are now starting to take on the new build market. Such companies, working hand in hand with property developers, are selling Morocco as the 'new Spain', extolling its cheap property prices and low cost of living in comparison to Europe. For many people interested in buying in Morocco, but not quite sure if they can handle going through the 'foreign' system, this is ideal as they can do all their dealings with English speaking agents and buy uncomplicated properties in ideally suited locations at prices quoted in pounds sterling as opposed to dirham. Many agents will arrange inspection trips to the sites and put you in touch with English speaking lawyers or notaires in Morocco, who will help you through the conveyancing process.

Estate Agents in Morocco

There is no shortage of estate agents (*agence immobilière or simsaar*) in Morocco, whether these are officially registered agents, with the government stamped licence (*Roksha*), an office and website, the 'unofficial' agents with an 'Agence Immobilière' sign written in black marker pen and selotaped to their shop counter or the 'flash in a pan agent' who is the brother, uncle or cousin of a seller, out to make a quick buck by seeking a potential buyer. While the official agent will charge a standard 2.5% plus VAT commission to the buyer and the seller based on the value of the property or the selling price, for the other two agents, the commission rate can be negotiable.

The Seller. In Morocco, the seller holds the reins. Unlike in the UK, where property price is based on an official valuation, which tends to be related to the location, size, number of rooms and features, in Morocco it is dependent on the price the seller wants or feels he/she can obtain for it. This is especially the case for old riads in the medina, where no two properties are the same therefore there is no standard price for people to rely on. Most sellers will base the property value on what they heard their neighbour got for theirs, on gossip in the local café, or by looking on the internet to find out how much properties are generally going for and pick a figure within a similar ballpark. The price will then go up and (very occasionally) down, based on the amount of interest being shown by potential buyers.

There is no such thing as loyalty to any one agent. Once the seller decides he wants to sell his property, he contacts as many people as he can, from official agents, who are more likely to have high paying foreigners on their books, to unofficial agents, relatives and friends. Whoever comes up with the best price first (or last if it beats the previous price), gets the property. Many official agents attempt to pin sellers down once they have accepted an offer by asking them to sign a contract stating that they have agreed a final price, but this does not count for anything if a better offer with a different agent, comes in. As a result, the estate agent game in Morocco, lucrative as it can be, is cut throat and will remain so until it is effectively regulated.

Working with an Official Agent
To become an official agent in Morocco, all you need to do is pay some money and obtain a licence. This means that anyone can become an official agent. Having said this, in order to stay ahead of the competition, agents must know their stuff. For official agents, the buying and selling of property is their main profession. They should be able to tell you which properties are titled/untitled, clean/unclean (ie: with/without loans attached) and upcoming plans for the area. Some speak English, deal with recommended notaires and are used to working with foreigners so will have a clearer idea of your demands. Many will have a wide range of properties on their books and/or a good number of contacts 'in the field' who they can rely on to keep them in touch with properties matching your preferred style/taste and budget. Some will stick by you through the purchasing process, ensuring you have the right documentation, answering your questions, signing documents on your behalf if you grant them power of attorney, explaining costs and fees and keeping you informed of what is happening if you have to leave the country.

Note that just because an agent or an agency is 'official' it does not make them reliable or trustworthy. Try to work with an agent who has been personally recommended ideally by a homeowner who has recently bought a property.

Bear in mind that as official agents work on a set commission, it is in their interest to get the highest price for the property and many will mark it up even higher than the seller's original asking price. In some cases, if you are working with more than one agent, you might see the same property twice but with a totally different value. Drop the agent with the highest asking price as they are quite simply ripping you off. The only way you will know if you are being charged well above the odds is through your own research. See as many properties as possible with a broad range of agents, ask homeowners how much they paid for their properties and research property websites.

Do try to work with a non-pushy agent who gives you the space and time to decide what you want to do. Trust those who tell you to go away and think about it. Do not trust those who tell you that there is great demand for the property or that the owner has already dropped his price as low as he can go. Both circumstances are unlikely.

Working with an Unofficial Agent

Unlike official agents who tend to have an office, a website, a marketing budget and sometimes a receptionist, the unofficial agent is likely to have just a mobile phone, a handwritten sign and perhaps a small space inside a shop. While the Arabic word for estate agent is *simsaar*, this phrase tends to be related more nowadays to the unofficial estate agent than the official as simsaars rarely speak English and sometimes not French, yet most are very much in touch with the property scene in the local areas where they work. Many official estate agents work with simsaars to help them find properties (in return for a commission of course) and the number of properties that simsaars have on their books is likely to be a lot higher than official agents as they tend to be working on behalf of friends and relatives who have no burning desire to sell their properties, but will if the price is right. If you can find a simsaar who speaks English, then it would be as worthwhile working with him as an official agent, especially as you should be able to negotiate a better rate of commission (based on the fact they are unofficial) or even a set fee, which will remove any onus on their behalf, to push up the price. Some simsaars will ask for payment of around 10-20 dirham per property they show you (separate from the overall fee) to cover their 'expenses'. Occasionally, if you go ahead with the purchase, you will get this back, but there is no guarantee of this.

Be aware that being unofficial means that these agents are not under threat of having their licence revoked and therefore are accountable to no one. Always double check the information they give you about the status of the property (although the notaire will also do this on your behalf, but sometimes not until after you have paid your deposit). Also unofficial agents are less accustomed to the tastes and style enjoyed by foreigners, therefore much time could be wasted just traipsing around while they show you their full repertoire of properties, regardless of your budget or wishes.

It is unlikely that these agents will carry you through the house buying process like an official agent or stay in touch with you while you are out of the country. If you choose to work with an unofficial agent, then you will probably have to be a lot more hands on in the buying process.

Working with a Flash in the Pan Agent

While many people do purchase property via this route, be aware that you are not working with a professional in any form. The only reason this person is working with you at all is because he wants your money and will tell you all kinds of yarns in order to get it. Do not just launch straight in without first doing research on the property, primarily on the price, location (is it as prime as he says?) and status in terms of ownership.

Buying Property Privately

Everybody would prefer to cut out the middleman and save on commission, but the tricky thing is finding the owners who want to sell or the buyers who want to buy. There is always the possibility of just knocking on a few doors and asking people if they might consider it and the results can be quite promising especially when they see a foreigner (read $$$) on their doorstep. The downside of this approach is that if/when they sense you are keen it gives them total freedom to crank up the price to whatever silly amount they feel like. The other option is simply by word of mouth, which is the most effective route for the imparting of information in Morocco. The most ideal situation would be a friend coming to you directly and asking you if you want to buy his/her house as this cuts out any risk of a middleman, but for this to happen, you need to have been in Morocco long enough to find such a friend you can trust to give you a fair price and not involve a middleman (read cousin/brother) who will attempt to extract a commission for any services rendered.

> **While most foreigners new to Morocco prefer to buy through an agent, some such as Claire Randall in Agadir, chose not to.**
>
> *I chose not to use an estate agent when deciding to buy my house in Agadir as I did not want to pay the marked up prices agents ask for or the 2.5% commission. Instead, I asked a Moroccan friend to look around for me and see if he could find any suitable properties close to the beach. When I was next back in Agadir a couple of months later, my friend showed me a three-storey house, sold fully furnished with a separate apartment in a quiet residential area. It was in very good condition, titled and only 500,000 dirham (£30,000). I paid my friend a flat fee of 6000 dirham (£400) for his help in finding it. This did not go via the notaire, but straight to him in cash. I know that buying my house this way got me a much better deal and I have recommended my friend to other people, so even though, he is a carpenter by trade, he has got himself a bit of estate agency work on the side.*

It is easier to buy a house privately in a place like Agadir where properties are modern and mostly titled. It is less recommended in ancient cities such as Marrakech and Fes where the history and ownership of homes is much more complicated.

PROPERTY VIEWING

It is very difficult to do any type of business with Moroccans unless you are on the spot and face-to-face. The only response you will get to any communication you undertake by remote ie; e-mail, fax or telephone (if you get any response at all) is being told to 'get in contact when you are in Morocco'. This does not stop you, however, from doing your own property research from the armchair of your sitting room.

If you are serious about buying and investing in a place like Morocco, where there is no regulated system yet in place for finding and negotiating properties, the value of information cannot be underestimated. Keep a copy of any articles, property or non property-related you find on Morocco, which might spread light on upcoming regions, browse the internet to find out what type of properties are available, how much and what you get for your money, put out feelers on to internet forums such as *buyingmoroccanproperty*.com to find other people who have or are considering purchasing property in Morocco. This way, when you arrive in the country, ready to start house hunting, you already have a foundation of knowledge on which to build and, more importantly, on which to prove to whoever is showing you properties, that you are not a green shrub fresh off the plane, but a hardnosed, intelligent investor who does not want to waste any time or money.

From the UK

Going via an estate agent's website is likely to be your first port of call when arranging property viewings from the UK. Be warned, however, that the property photos on the majority of these are not kept updated. They are a good place to look for an indication of style and price but in many cases, properties you are looking at will most likely have been sold over a year ago and are now fully renovated and occupied. Most websites have a 'contact us' page giving you the opportunity to send an e-mail stating what you are interested in viewing on your upcoming trip. You should get a speedy response to your requests for information but, again, the most likely answer will be telling you to 'come to Morocco and look around'. If you have only a limited amount of time in Morocco, you would be wisest to try and arrange all estate agent meetings (and you should definitely see more than one) in advance. This way you will be able to make an itinerary and not waste any time when you are there, waiting for agents to become available. It is also a good idea to print up the photos of some of the properties you particularly like from the websites and show them to agents, so that they can have an idea of what exactly you are looking for otherwise you are at risk of being shown a vast number of totally inappropriate properties which do not come close to matching your budget, which wastes your time.

It is very likely that out of the, for example, six agents you choose to meet, three will be totally unsuitable so have a 'get out quick' plan ready. The problem is that until you meet the agents, it is hard to know how they are going to be. Sometimes the quality of information and design of the website is a good indicator.

On the Spot

This is by far the easiest way to find properties and agents. To get recommended agents, you could try knocking on the doors of guesthouses or renovated properties and asking the owners to recommend you to an agent. People love talking about their experiences and everyone has a 'someone' they can put you in touch with. Alternatively, you could telephone some agents and arrange to visit their offices (if they have them) or ask them to meet you at your hotel. Some estate agents in the more popular tourist regions, now have street-side offices complete with glass-fronted facades displaying photographs of properties for sale, as in the UK, which enables you to browse the most up-to-date information prior to meeting the agents.

It is impossible to know from the outside, which properties are for sale, as only some land and occasionally office space in Morocco tend to have a For Sale (A Vendre) sign. This means that you do need someone to show you.

It is very unlikely that estate agents will ever just give you the keys and tell you to show yourself around firstly because it is unlikely you will ever be able to locate the house you wish to look at and, more importantly, because you might find the owner there and negotiate a private deal. You are therefore always accompanied, sometimes by just the official agent, but normally by a simsaar as well who will be the one with the keys but not the English/French to communicate. Do not expect to be given any literature on the property. Floor plans and photo handouts are rarely, if ever, provided

You will find that some estate agents (more likely to be unofficial) have the infuriating habit of not telling you how much properties are selling for until you have seen all around them. This is because they are hoping either to gauge your level of interest, which will help them set the price, or because you are more likely to feel the price is good, once you have seen all over. It is not easy judging a property without knowing its price as it may be well out of your price range, therefore a waste of time even looking, or so cheap that you figure there must be something wrong with it. Insist that you are told the price, prior to entering the property. If the agent refuses then tell them that you are not interested in a viewing.

After a couple of hours of viewings, all properties tend to roll into one, so it is well worth taking a digital camera with you and photographing each place as you go around and also, if you remember, the name of the street the property is on. This is especially useful if you are in the medina where it is very easy to get lost. Once you have the name of the street, you can do your own research to assess whether or not it is a central/peaceful/upmarket/ locale to be in.

Tim Wellspring's story; do your research and be patient

Before coming on our house-hunting trip to Morocco, we spent ages browsing the internet in the UK deciding where exactly we wanted to buy and what type of property we could get for our £65,000 budget. From the UK, by e-mail, and telephone, we contacted around four estate agents who we found on the internet and arranged to meet them during our five day trip to Essaouira. We turned up with a file packed with information, which I think surprised the agent, but was quite a good technique for showing we meant business. We had to run the gauntlet of hearing phrases like, 'you will get nothing for less than 1 million dirham (£70,000)' and 'high competition buy now' and as this was the time of the property boom in the UK, we actually believed it and started panicking, especially as we quickly learnt that five days was not enough time to house hunt in Morocco. Luckily the comments were totally unfounded and our final meeting was with a very laid back, helpful agent, who told us to relax, go home and think about everything in the cool light of day. 1 month later, I flew back to Morocco and put an offer in on one of the properties we had liked. As I was much calmer, I was able to negotiate with the owner more effectively especially when he tried shoving the price up by 30,000 dirham (£2000). As I had to spend large chunks of my time in the UK, I found the agent really useful for keeping me in the loop as to what was happening on the house buying front. He called regularly and liaised with the notaire on my behalf. During the actual signing of the final contract, it was a comfort having him there and on my side.

ADVERTS AND THE PRESS

Morocco is gradually starting to seep into the pages of overseas property magazines such as *Homes Overseas* and *Homes Worldwide*, generally under the title of 'emerging markets' with articles talking about upcoming areas, the buying process and what you can get for your money, but it is not featured regularly and Marrakech still seems to be the main point of focus. Few international property exhibitions feature Morocco and those that do tend to focus specifically on the new build market along the Mediterranean coast and Marrakech. Once in a while the Sunday Times will feature a riad for sale amongst a whole range of villas in Spain and sometimes, international property agents will release 'news' about new developments which tend to be found in the property sections of the tabloids or the Your Money/Money/Bricks and Mortar pages of the broadsheets.

Websites

Generally, the best way of finding out about properties for sale in Morocco, bar actually visiting is via the specific websites of estate agents on the internet, a large number of which are either written with an English section or translated. The websites are a good guide to see what types of properties are available and some give information on the buying/money lending process. Each of the estate agents named below will have websites. A general browse on a search engine such as

Google is unlikely to throw up much more than a range of Moroccan properties for rent or a few random international property websites displaying one or two Moroccan properties, but these are unlikely to give you very specific information or introduce you to many more agents than those shown below.

Useful Websites

www.buyingmoroccanproperty.com
www.compasspropertiesmorocco.com
www.fesmedina.com
www.houseinfez.com
www.immobilier-maroc.com
www.moroccan-homes.com
www.marrakech-immobilier.net
www.marocannonces.com
www.propertyborders.com

ESTATE AGENT SPEAK	
1er étage	first floor
Ascenseur	lift
Aménagér	converted
Arroseur	sprinkler
Avec gout	with taste
Balcon	balcony
Bejmat	glazed mosaic floor tiles
Béton	concrete
Bois	wood
Bon état	good condition
Bord de mer	by the sea
Cagibi	box room
Campagne	country
Cave	cellar
Chambre	bedroom
Chaudière	water heater
Chauffage	heating
Chauffe eau	hot water tank
Cheminée	chimney
Climatisation	air conditioning
Clôture	fence
Clôturé en murs	walled enclosure
Couloir	corridor
Cuisine	kitchen

Darbouz	balcony
Débarras	junk room
De surface au sol	ground surface area
Douiriya	a small house, usually an annexe of the main house
Entièrement paysager ment paysager	fully landscaped
Entretien	maintenance
Escalier	stairs
Ferme	farm
Ferraillage	ironwork
Fosse septique	septic tank
Foyer	fireplace
Gardien	caretaker
Goudronné	tarmac
Hammam	bath
Isolation	insulation
Maison de campagne	country house
Maison mitoyenne	semi detached or terraced house
Meubles	furniture
Menzeh	large pavilion on the terrace of an upmarket riad
Meublé	furnished
Mur	wall
Non-meublé	non-furnished
Pièce	room
Pilier	pillar
Piscine	swimming pool
Plain pied	single storey
Prise	electric socket
Rez de chausée	ground floor
Raffiné	refined
Refait	restoration
Réservoir	cistern
Restauré	restored
Saqaiya	fountain
SdB	salle de bain
Salon	sitting room
Séjour	living room
Sol	ground
Superficie	surface area
Tadelakt	marble like wall covering
Tapis	carpet
Terrasse aménagée	converted terrace

Toit terrasse	Roof terrace
Transats	deckchairs
Vallonné	hilly
Vue impregnable	unrestricted view
Wust-i-dar	salons around the central courtyard of a riad
Zelliges	hand cut geometrically patterned tiles.

English Speaking Estate Agents
Casablanca and Mohammedia
TB Immobilier, 22 Résidence Nakhil, Avenue des F.A.R, 20800 Mohammedia; ☎ 023 32 27 34/061 13 44 65; fax 023 32 27 35; e-mail tbimmobilier@yahoo.fr.
Vernet Immobilier, 158 Blvd d'Anfa, Casablanca; ☎ 022 36 88 66; fax 022 36 90 89; www.vernetis.com.

El Jadida and Oualidia
Jadida Locations, no 9, Rue 8 Cité Portugaise 24000, El Jadida; ☎ (in France) 04 94 87 43 35; www.jadidalocations.com/sommaire.htm.
Moroccan Properties, Immeuble El Khalil, Avenue Hassan II, Marrakech 40000; ☎ 44 43 04 65; fax 044 43 04 30; www.moroccanproperties.com.

Fes
Carre d'Azur, 16 Avenue Lalla Aicha, Champ de Courses, Fes, ☎ 055 93 02 92; www.carredazur.com.
fesproperties.com.

A view to another world...

Easy travel from Europe takes you to the evocative cities and coasts .

Easy travel through our website takes you to the best information and selection of property for sale.

We have a wide range of properties in Morocco. And can help with everything from viewings , architects, building through to completion.

email info@moroccan-homes.com
www.moroccan-homes.com

Moroccan Homes, 43 Station Road, Thorpe on Hill, Lincoln LN6 9BS; ☎ 01522 535 052 or Calle Daire 46, Sedella Malaga, Spain; ☎ 95 25 08 961; e-mail info@Moroccan-homes.com; www.Moroccan-homes.com.

Rabat
Ramses Consulting, 31 Avenue Tarik Ibn Ziad, Hassan, Rabat; ☎ 068 65 79 79/065 12 11 88; e-mail ramses_consulting@yahoo.fr.

Marrakech and Essaouira

Most Agents based in Marrakech will also work in Essaouira and Ouarzazate

Agence Immobiliere Mogador (Mohammed Rkhaoui), 12 Rue Skala-Sous, B.P. 616 Essaouira 44000; ☎ 0061 33 88 54; e-mail fouad.soleil3@cara-mail.com.

Atlas Immobilier, 245 Ave Mohammed V, Imm Watanya Gueliz, Marrakech; ☎ 044 42 26 72; e-mail contact@atlasimmobilier.com; www.atlasimmobilier.com.

Cabinet Charles El Fassy, Residence Excelsior, Rue Tarik Ibn Ziad, Marrakech; ☎ 044 44 63 23/061 13 45 04; e-mail charles.elfassy@iam.net.ma; www.celfassy.com.

Le Comptoir de l'Immobilier, 94 Rue de Tensift, Quartier Semlalia, 40000 Marrakech; ☎ 044 43 32 17; e-mail contact@Marrakech-immobilier.net; www.marrakech-immobilier.net.

Francophiles, Barker Chambers, Barker Road, Maidstone, Kent, ME16 8SF; ☎ 01622 688 165; fax 01622 671 840; e-mail sales@francophiles.co.uk; www.francophiles.co.uk.

Jemaa el Fna Immobilier, Rd point du Jet d'eau, Ave Mohammed V, Appt no 2, Imm Berdai, 40000 Marrakech; ☎ 044 44 63 89; e-mail cr@villafrance.com; www.immobilier-pro-maroc.com.

Kantakari, 40 Rue des Banques, Kenneria, Marrakech Medina; ☎ 044 44 60 29/061 67 56 48; e-mail kantakari@menara.ma; www.kantakari.com.

Karimo (Marrakech), 171 Blvd Mohammed V, Gueliz, Marrakech; ☎ 044 42 01 03; e-mail info@karimo.net; www.karimo.net.

Karimo (Essaouira), Place Moulay Hassan, 44100 Essaouira; ☎ 044 47 45 00; e-mail info@karimo.net; www.karimo.net.

Marrakech Riads, 8 Derb Cherfa Lakbir, Mouassine, 40000 Marrakech; ☎ 044 39 16 09/044 42 64 63/061 16 36 30; e-mail immobilier@marrakech-riads. net; www.marrakech-riads.net.

Mauresque Immobilier, 5 Derb Kettara; Zaouia, Marrakech Medina, 40000; ☎ 060 00 66 66/060 00 55 55; e-mail contact@mauresque-immobilier.com; www.mauresque-immobilier.com.

Moroccan Homes, 43 Station Road, Thorpe on Hill, Lincoln LN6 9BS; ☎ 01522 535 052 or Calle Daire 46, Sedella Malaga, Spain; ☎ 95 25 08 961; e-mail info@Moroccan-homes.com; www.moroccan-homes.com.

Moroccan Properties, Immueble El Khalil, Avenue Hassan II, Marrakech 40000; ☎ 44 43 04 65; fax 044 43 04 30; www.moroccanproperties.com.

One Source Home Search, 3 at 1 Munroe Terrace, London, SW10 ODL; ☎/fax 0207 376 7689; e-mail enquiries@onesourcehomesearch.com.

Vernet Immobilier, 28 Rue Tarik Ibn Ziad, Gueliz, Marrakech; ☎ 044 42 14 23; e-mail info@vernetis.com; www.vernetis.com.

Saidia

Moroccan Properties Ltd, 50 Inwood Avenue, Hounslow, Middlesex, TW3 1XG; ☎ 0208 572 2422; e-mail info@moroccanpropertiesltd.com; www.moroccanpropertiesltd.com.

Saffron Villas, Lumberg House, The Mount, Highclere, Berkshire, RG20 9QZ; ☎ 01635 253 121; e-mail info@saffronvillas.com; www.saffronvillas.com.

Agadir, Sidi Ifni, Aglou, Mirleft and Ouarzazate

Agence Immobilier d'Agadir, 18 Immeuble M2, Rue de l'Hotel de Ville, Agadir; ☎ 048 82 16 41/061 15 24 61; e-mail info@agadir-immobilier.com; www. agadir-immobilier.com.

Kantakari, 40 Rue des Banques, Kenneria, Marrakech Medina; ☎ 044 42 65 26/061 67 56 48; e-mail kantakari@menara.ma; www.kantakari.com.

Mirleft Immobilier, ☎; 071.77.44.25; www.mirleft-immoblier.com. Properties in Agadir, Mirleft and Aglou.

Moroccan Homes, 43 Station Road, Thorpe on Hill, Lincoln LN6 9BS; ☎ 01522 535 052 or Calle Daire 46, Sedella Malaga, Spain; ☎ 95 25 08 961; e-mail info@Moroccan-homes.com; www.Moroccan-homes.com.

Moroccan Properties, Immeuble El Khalil, Avenue Hassan II, Marrakech 40000; ☎ 44 43 04 65; fax 044 43 04 30; www.moroccanproperties.com.

Mouloud Wadoud, Sidi Ifni, ☎ 067923280; e-mail wadoud88@hotmail.com.

Tangier and Tetouan

Compass Properties, Complexe Le Dawliz, 42 Rue de Hollande 90000 Tangier; ☎ 039 94 73 16; e-mail info@compasspropertiesmorocco.com; www.compasspropertiesmorocco.com.

International Property Link (IPL), Avda, Las Palmeras, Conjunto Los Nadales, Local 1, 29630 Benalmadena Costa, Malaga, Spain; ☎ 0800-955 5555/intl. +34-952577 793; fax 09 52 44 10 33; www.internationalpropertylink.com.

Moroccan Properties, Immueble El Khalil, Avenue Hassan II, Marrakech 40000; ☎ 44 43 04 65; fax 044 43 04 30; www.moroccanproperties.com.

Moroccan Homes, 43 Station Road, Thorpe on Hill, Lincoln LN6 9BS; ☎ 01522
535 052 or Calle Daire 46, Sedella Malaga, Spain; ☎ 95 25 08 961; e-mail
info@Moroccan-homes.com; www.Moroccan-homes.com.

Moroccan Properties Ltd, 50 Inwood Avenue, Hounslow, Middlesex, TW3 1XG;
☎ 0208 572 2422; e-mail info@moroccanpropertiesltd.com; www.moroccan
propertiesltd.com.

Prestige Properties Overseas Ltd, 12-14 Hardman Street, Blackpool FY1 3QZ;
☎ freephone 0800-085 1601; fax 01253-753952; e-mail info@prestigeproperties
overseas.com; www.prestigepropertiesoverseas.com.

Property Websites

Marocannonces.com
Maroc.green-acres.com

WHAT TYPE OF PROPERTY TO BUY?

CHAPTER SUMMARY

O **Buyer's Market**. Morocco is a buyer's market catering to all budgets.
O **Traditional Properties**. Riads and dars are traditional properties found in the medinas.
O **Renovations**. You have to decide whether you want to buy a renovated or unrenovated property. There are pros and cons to each.
O **Processes involved in buying land**. Buying land and building on to it is becoming increasingly popular, but it does not come without its obstacles. There are many processes involved in the buying process and you would be wise to hire a recommended notaire to help you.
O **Off Plan**. The introduction of the VEFA contract means that more people are buying unbuilt or semi-completed properties on the basis of their plans.
O **Apartments**. These are the residences of choice for city dwellers and there is no shortage of available properties.
O **Villas**. Many Europeans prefer villas to traditional riads as they have gardens, space and views.

BUYER'S MARKET

Over the last ten years, Morocco has come to value its property market very highly. Developers are moving into every square metre of urban land and building apartment blocks, foreigners are buying up and renovating ancient properties in the medina, the bourgeois are building villas in high walled neighbourhoods, the government are commissioning the erection of thousands of social housing establishments, great swathes of once derelict coastlines are being transformed into upmarket condominiums. For the foreigner considering purchasing a property

in Morocco, the opportunities are endless whether your budget is £30,000 or a
£ million, your preference; sea, mountain, or cityscape, it is a buyer's paradise or
at least will be when the cranes and scaffolding have moved out. This means that
your greatest challenge is deciding from the vast range of options, what type of
property will best suit you and your tastes.

How Moroccans Live

While Morocco is world renowned for its intricate mosaics and woodwork, its
delicate minarets and elaborate arches, its imposing doorways and tranquil courtyards, the reality is that these features do not really appeal to the majority of
Moroccans. If given a choice, most would prefer to live in a modern villa or apartment block with all mod cons, a garage, proximity to neighbours and, if possible,
a guard dog. Unlike Europeans who cherish open plan spaces, big windows and
daylight seeping into every crevice and will make knocking down internal walls
a renovation priority, Moroccans value privacy; reception areas where unknown
visitors can be met without entering into the family domain, doors they can shut
to block out the sun and small windows which they can see out of but none can
see in. Functionality generally beats aesthetics; ground floor apartments sell for
more than those with sea views, car parking takes priority over a garden and a
fridge or gas fire is often the main feature of a room. When it comes to building,
concrete is the material of choice and is without doubt one of the most lucrative
industries to be in.

What Property Will Best Suit You?

Hyped by international property developers dazzling you with the low prices for
a spot by the sea or interior design magazines throwing pictures of Moroccan
palaces under your nose, you might already have decided exactly what type of
property you want to buy and be in hot pursuit of your dream. There are several
considerations to take into account, however, when making the choice, which are
not always immediately apparent. How much work are you prepared to put into
your property so that it resembles the interior design magazines? Have you got
the budget to do this? Cheap though it might be, is your spot by the sea actually
as well built as £40,000 might indicate? Will the gentle lapping of the sea actually be as soothing as you think when it is obscured by the sound effects of sixty
neighbouring apartments? The following section will show the full range of places
you can live in Morocco and the types of properties available.

MEDINA

If you are planning on renting out your property or turning it into a guesthouse
for tourists, the medina, based on novelty, history and architectural interest, is a
good option.

Medinas are the old towns enclosed in fortified walls and imposing gates (*bab*), built to protect citizens from invaders. Here, a number of Moroccans live, work, attend school, play, eat, pray and shop. Most medinas date back a minimum of 100 years, while in the case of Marrakech and Fes, the first stones were laid, 1000 and 1200 years ago respectively and simply evolved from there. Medinas are built in maze-like labyrinths of winding alleyways, arches and dead ends, interspersed with artisanal craft shops, fruit carts and market places (souks). Their narrow streets, sometimes no more than a metre wide, make them the ideal place to be in the searing heat of summer. Behind the higgledy-piggledy walls are thousands of uniquely shaped and styled properties, distinguishable only by solid, studded front doors and small, unreachable windows. If you are used to space, open air and tranquillity, having a house in the medina will come as a shock to the system. Outside the tranquillity of the home, it is noisy, busy and crowded. Children play ball, dogs bark, roosters crow, chimneys smoke, wedding processions chant and if you are unfortunate or indeed fortunate, enough to choose a house next to a mosque, the muezzin will disturb your dreams at the crack of dawn every day of the week.

Having said this, such immersion into Moroccan life is what many consider living in Morocco is all about. It gets you close to society, embroiled in a new culture, involved in local activities and a network of local friends. It also greatly appeals to tourists on a few days trip to Morocco, which it is important to bear in mind if you plan to make an income from your property.

Most medinas are divided into neighbourhoods or quartiers. In the medina of Fes, for example, the are 187 quartiers, each one comprising, by law, a mosque, communal oven, Koranic school, a water fountain and a hammam (public bath). Navigation around the more sprawling medinas is very difficult for newcomers (and many lifelong inhabitants), so most people get to know their local neighbourhood (quartier) first and expand their world from there.

Cars are generally not permitted inside the medina, which means that for once in Morocco, pedestrians rule, that is, after mopeds, pushbikes, donkeys and fruit barrows. The benefit of no cars is that it is safe for children to play and, bar the smoke from the chimneys and meat grills, pollution free. A downside, however, is that transporting shopping, suitcases or young children from outside the walls does become more of a chore especially if your property is a long way inside the medina. It is for this reason that property prices are higher the closer you are to the medina gateways. Also bear in mind that despite a recent drive to replace old cobblestones with flat paving, this is not the case in all medinas making walking a precarious activity for the more vulnerable.

While many people want to live in the medina because of its age and history, the fact that they are old means they are more susceptible to infrastructural problems such as blocked or overflowing drains, water shortages and damp. Also living in close proximity to many people raises issues of hygiene, especially as some Moroccans think nothing about throwing bags of rubbish or bones for stray cats out of top floor windows or filling already overflowing bins. Having said this, rubbish build up never becomes a major occurrence as the streets are usually cleared up and swept, on a daily basis.

Life in the medina starts early in the day with children off to school, women off to buy food for lunch and men off to work. It closes down at lunchtime for the 2-3 hour siesta ands sparks up again in the late afternoons. Evenings are the busiest times when families go shopping en-masse, or stroll along the narrow streets taking in the sun-free evening air, nibbling bags of steaming chickpeas. By 11pm, unless it is the month of Ramadan, which generally constitutes an all night party, the streets are empty. This can be disconcerting for night owls who only start revving up as the sun goes down. While the ville nouvelle offers more to do, post-dark, bear in mind that walking back late at night into the deserted medina, though unlikely to be dangerous, can feel unnerving as there are very few people about.

RIADS

These are the picture book properties of Morocco, enclosed within the ramparts of the medina, the traditional homes of the old cities. No two riads are the same size or shape, no two doorways matching. It is with great plans to restore and renovate the old riads that many foreigners have made their debut on to the Moroccan housing market. In return, many Moroccans lacking the finances or inclination to restore the properties have been only too pleased to rid themselves of the often decrepit old houses and buy, in return, the all mod con villa.

Riads can best be described as inside out houses where from the outside, with the plain walls, small windows and solid wood front doors, it is impossible to fathom what lies within while on the inside a rectangle or square garden fills the centre and the rooms, often long and narrow, with high ceilings and windows on to the corridors, surround it. Most are two stories high, some three, with balconies overlooking the garden and terraces with views across the rooftops. You might also hear riads referred to as dars. These are similar to riads, but smaller and often less grand in terms of features, with light wells in the centre as opposed to gardens.

The most popular area for purchasing riads is in the chic touristy regions of Marrakech and Essaouira, where many people have transformed them into guesthouses while in places like Fes, the riad trend is starting to take off. The process involved in buying a riad is now well established with many estate agents specialised in such properties. This does not mean that they are always easy to buy. Only those recently bought tend to have titles, so the long process plus the extra fee involved in obtaining a title is par of the course and many people can be let down at the last hurdle when a family member cannot be traced or refuses to sell.

Unless you are buying a second generation riad, ie: one which has been bought within the last 6 years, titled and renovated, then chances are, it will be in a very sorry state when you obtain it, in need of modernisation-plumbing, electricity at best, a complete rebuild at worst, depending on how run down its previous recipients have let it get. Often you will find semi-renovated riads where the owners have attempted to restore it themselves, but run out of money half way through. Do not progress with the buying of the property until you have a clear indication of how much it is going to cost to renovate. Rule of thumb is that you will generally pay the same to renovate as you did to buy, so basically, double whatever you paid for it and you will have the finishing price. Note: keep receipts for all works done on the house as you can offset these against capital gains tax.

Prices of riads tends to be based on size and location as opposed to architectural features, so you could buy a riad rich in original features for a very modest sum. Rules and regulations regarding issues such as height limits on properties (max 14 metres) have been implemented over the last couple of years and much like building laws in the UK, these need to be strictly adhered to. Additionally, when buying ancient properties, you will come up against odd laws, for example; if you buy in the kasbah quarter of the Marrakech medina, you are not permitted to own the ground floor of your property. You can live in it, but it must remain the property of the state. Also many houses are strange shapes, for example, you might find that your neighbour's entrance way is underneath your bathroom or your salon on top of theirs. This is because many of the houses used to be for one family but were later divided up. The notaire, well versed in medina law will inform you of any such quirks prior to your purchasing the property and will ensure that it is correctly documented on the title deeds.

While some people will adamantly only consider unrenovated riads, others like the idea of buying an already finished property. There are advantages and disadvantages to both.

Buying a Renovated Riad
Advantages

- The work is already done so you do not need to do it.
- Chances are, it will already be titled so you do not have to undertake the proceedings.
- There are no budgeting issues. What you pay is what you get.
- You can move in or start renting it out immediately.

Disadvantages

- ○ It will be someone else's vision and design – not yours.
- ○ How can you be sure that the works, (structural, plumbing, electrics) have been done to a good and safe standard?
- ○ You might pay above the odds for the property as your negotiating position is lessened by the fact the house is finished and ready for occupancy.

Buying an Unrenovated Riad

Advantages

- ○ You can make the property anything you wish it to be – it is your vision.
- ○ You can expect to pay less for the property as it is in need of work (although, if your offer is too low, the seller will have no qualms about selling it to someone else).
- ○ You can be sure that the works (structural, plumbing, electrics) are done to the best standard.
- ○ You can have a lot of fun shopping around for tiles, wood, fittings and furnishings.

Disadvantages

- ○ Chances are it will not be titled, which means you will have to go through what can be a long-winded and expensive process, getting it titled.
- ○ Undertaking a build, even from a distance is very hard work and time consuming – you have to be more than sure about what you are taking on.
- ○ Hiring and managing Moroccan builders is a tricky process due to language barriers, different work ethics and dissimilar standards of finish.
- ○ Unless you have a very good knowledge of Moroccan labour, building materials and furnishings, staying within budget is likely to be hard.

THE ADVANTAGES OF BUYING A RIAD

- ○ It is architecturally unusual – nothing like you can have back home.
- ○ No one else will own a property quite like yours.
- ○ You are more likely to be able to make an income from the property, as it will have novelty value.
- ○ You can fill the house with features, such as arches and fireplaces, which work best in an old traditional property.
- ○ There will always be a market for riads as they are unique.
- ○ The walls are so thick (up to a metre) that you have tranquillity from the noisy streets outside.
- ○ They are designed to be cool inside, so you can escape the summer heat.

VILLE NOUVELLE

Outside the medina are the ville nouvelle or new towns, the majority of which were built by the French protectorate during the building boom of the 1930's, as a way of injecting a piece of home into North Africa. There is still a French feel as you walk down the tree-lined boulevards past the art deco buildings, cafes and boutiques and many shops and restaurants bear French names. It is in the villes nouvelles that the majority of building works are underway with apartment blocks, and villas sprawling several miles out of town and new neighbourhoods springing up where a couple of years ago, there was just scrub.

The ville nouvelle tends to appeal mostly to foreigners who have already lived in the medina and are looking for more space and a garden, urbanites who are not looking for exotic, 'real' Morocco but for good eating out and shopping opportunities and for families with young children. Villas here offer space, gardens, garages and often, swimming pools. Hospitals, international schools and French-style hypermarkets are located in the ville nouvelle as are golf courses, sports clubs, boutiques, restaurants and offices. To live in the ville nouvelle, it helps to have a car or access to private transport (local taxis are cheap), as to reach most places, will warrant a drive. If you are in the heart of downtown, the roads are busy with cars and pollution and traffic jams are an inescapable fact of life.

APARTMENTS

Morocco's wise policy of keeping apartment blocks low rise, around 5-7 stories is the standard, means that you never feel totally swamped by the extraordinarily huge number, which now inhabit the downtowns of most cities. So popular is the apartment building trend that anyone owning a house on land popular for development, can create a fantastical selling figure even if it is a decrepit run-down heap, quadruple it and pretty much guarantee a sale from a developer keen to build upwards.

Moroccan apartment blocks range from uninspiring concrete squares with small windows and plain balconies where the emphasis is on the functional not the fanciful to large, open plan retreats with big windows, split level rooms and swimming pools. Casablanca, for example, has a store of funky, European style duplexes along the chic avenues of Racine and many art deco delights left over from the days of the French and many of the new resort style apartment such as those recently built by Spanish property developers, Fadesa (*www.fadesa.es*) in Saidia on the north coast of Morocco are catering much more to the European market, so put an emphasis on light, features and outdoor/recreational space. It is common practice to divide large riads into three or so apartments. Due to their age and higgledy-piggledy layouts, these tend to be interesting or unusual shapes and sizes.

The majority of city dwelling Moroccans will choose to live in apartments, as they are cheaper to buy and maintain. They are also residences of choice for single or coupled foreigners working in the cities and for pied-a-terre clientele from, for example, Casablanca who keep an apartment in Marrakech for weekend shopping or from southern Spain who buy in Tangier, just across the sea, for weekend breaks. Many Europeans prefer apartment blocks with lifts, swimming pools, outdoor spaces and a concierge, for extra security, especially if they will be leaving the apartment empty for parts of the year.

When it comes to considering budget, bear in mind that Moroccans do not place huge value on views, figuring that if you want to look at the sea, you go down to the beach, so you tend to pay less the higher up you are although you will find that little planning goes into ensuring pleasant views. Also don't be fooled by first impressions. Developers will often put a lot of effort into the entrance hall; marble staircases, walls and floors, wide doorways and gold plated door handles. This is simply a ruse to make you think the whole block will be luxurious. Once on to the first floor, however, the marble ends and the concrete begins.

When you buy an apartment in Morocco, you also buy into a share of the responsibility for the upkeep of the block. If the block is newly constructed, then it is likely the developer or developing company will take control of the management in return for an annual fee. This is the most ideal situation as the developer knows the make up of the build intimately and will have a handful of skilled workers at his fingertips to call on as and when the need arises. In other words, the job will get done. In top end apartment blocks in uptown areas, most are well maintained by communally elected managers, who will take on the responsibility of managing the upkeep of the property. This is in return for a very modest monthly fee, which everyone pays.

The problems arise when you are living in low/medium priced apartment blocks, where similar undertakings for electing a manager take place, but are much less effective. This is because, even though, apartment blocks are, by law, expected to elect a manager in charge of maintenance, the contractual framework is rarely enforced. Moroccans generally take the view that unless it is beyond the point of no return, there is very little need to fix it; if it is still possible to climb the steps, why replace the missing ones? If buckets can collect the dripping water, why pay for a new roof? As a result, few will actually pay the manager, so there will never be any funds to maintain the block. As a foreigner, you might find this attitude very trying and seek ways of being proactive. This is unlikely to achieve any great changes and you will most likely end up having to pay for the works yourself. The best advice is to be sure you know the effectiveness of the system in place before you purchase, which can best be done by speaking to your potential neighbours.

When it comes to the buying of apartments, the process is generally the standard, although note that only notaires are allowed to undertake the conveyancing for apartments not lawyers. Quite why this is the case is unclear although the most unanimous view is that it is because there are too many notaires and not enough work to go round. It is highly likely the apartment will be titled. If it is not, it is best to steer clear of it as it could mean that the developer never obtained titles for it so it will not officially belong to you. If you are buying a semi-completed apartment, you will have to wait until the apartment block is fully built before the developer splits the title deeds from one for the whole block, into individual units. You must make sure this is written as a clause in the preliminary contract, so that you are not at risk of losing your apartment.

VILLAS

One of the first things a Moroccan will do when they have some money is to buy a property. If they are feeling flush, they will buy a villa or, even better, build their own. To live in a villa is a sign that you are successful, affluent and a little elite. Those who live in villas will also have a maid, perhaps a gardener and almost certainly a watchman or guard dog. Villas are generally located just on the outer edge of the city centre, where the air is cleaner, the bougainvillea and palm trees livelier and the neighbourhoods devoid of any street life.

Typical Moroccan-style Villas

These tend to be detached properties hidden behind six-foot, painted brick walls, accessed through a metal gate with steps up to the front door. Many have basements housing the modern kitchen or spare bedrooms, with sliding doors on to a little patch of grass or compact swimming pool. Garages, accessed through an automatic gate are off to one side or alternatively, cars will park outside the villa in private parking spaces. Most villas tend to be three-storey including the basement with a large sitting room on the ground floor, normally, if inhabited by Moroccans, filled from wall to wall with lavishly embroidered cushioned benches, a sizeable TV, dark furnishings and invariably a gold framed photo of the king. Bedrooms, usually with en-suite bathrooms and walk in dressing areas are on the top floor along, sometimes with a small, concreted terrace or a balcony. All have flat roofs enabling another terrace on the top floor, but this is generally used for the maid to either live in a small outhouse and/or to dry laundry.

The benefits of living in Moroccan style villas is that they tend to be in close proximity to the city centre without any of the pollution and noise, which normally accompanies downtown living. It does also mean, however, that the plots of land are generally small and, in typical Moroccan style, most houses have been built to the maximum lot space, leaving just a small area for a garden.

While for Moroccans, there is a novelty factor connected to buying a villa, prices tend to be reasonable as values are based on square metreage, this means that there is the potential for money left over to renovate the style of the property more to your personal taste.

European-style Villas

The less typical, more European style villas largely built by international developers, which are gradually starting to appear on the property scene, tend to put more emphasis on garden space and outdoor recreation such as BBQ areas and swimming pools. Inside tends to be tiled rather than carpeted, open plan and split-level with a kitchen incorporated into the living area rather than hidden away and latticed wood (*mashrabiyya*) or wrought iron fittings in place of concrete. It is not uncommon for developers to build modern villas in the shape of the typical riad with the garden in the centre and the rooms around. Many incorporate the old and the new, blending traditional mosaics, *tadelakt*, a polished sand and quick lime wall covering and wood clad ceilings with spotlights and modern fittings.

Gated villa residences are now becoming popular in places such as the Route d'Ourika outside Marrakech, taking the concept of quiet neighbourhood one step further. There are tennis courts and private/communal swimming pools all for the exclusive use of residents. The advantage of such properties is that they are ideal holiday homes for either renting out or for personal enjoyment and based on Morocco's warm climate, have the added bonus of being pretty accessible all year round. Most developers will also manage the properties on your behalf, keeping them clean and watered and renting them out to clients in return for a fee, which means all you really need to do is buy the villa and then leave the running of it and collecting the income from it to someone else.

There are also a number of unusual style villas, built by Europeans, primarily the French and Spanish over the last ten to twenty years. These tend to be in prime locations such as along the beachfront of Essaouira, on the coast road, leading north out of Agadir or east out of Tangier. These can be any shapes or sizes, depending on the whim and quirks of the initial owner and can be fun places to buy as they are likely to be rich in features and character, more so than typical Moroccan villas.

Typically, villa neighbourhoods tend to be very quiet and, after the hustle of the busy city, sometimes too quiet. There are no honking horns, growling engines or raised voices. In fact, very often, there is no one at all. This can be either very appealing or quite unnerving, depending on your disposition. Villas are becoming more and more popular with foreigners who feel they have 'done their spell' in the real Morocco having spent a couple of years living in a riad in the medina and now crave the space and tranquillity of a villa. Many will rent out their riads and buy either the land to build a villa of their choice or a ready built villa complete with swimming pool, garage and a view.

It is not likely you will come across any complications when buying a villa. It will almost certainly come with a title and the buying process, if done through a reliable notaire, should go without any unforeseen problems.

MOUNTAINS & COUNTRYSIDE

Morocco's countryside ranges from the scenically stunning; meadows of irises, orchids, marigolds and crocuses, dramatic waterfalls, walnut, chestnut and cedar forests, lakes, palms and the Atlas peaks to the mundane; kilometre after kilometre of flat, barren scrub with little more than a dehydrated tree or scruffy village. People used to the built-up, overcrowded countryside of the UK will be astounded at quite how much countryside there is in Morocco and quite how little of it appears to be in use. It is no surprise, therefore, that buying land and building is becoming a popular undertaking for Europeans, Moroccans and international developers.

Morocco's countryside generally constitutes anywhere beyond the peripheries of the towns and the cities, while the mountains are the Rif in the north, running parallel to the Mediterranean, the Anti Atlas in the south and the High and Middle Atlas, which wind vertically through the country. Tempting as it is to choose a remote plot or mountain retreat as your dream location, it is worth considering the realities of living in the countryside and mountains, many of which will be issues that do not so commonly crop up when considering a similar-style purchase in Europe.

While the climate in the mountains is sunny and hot in the summer months, especially in the High Atlas where temperature can soar to 40 degrees, the winters, starting around October, can be harsh and bitterly cold segueing into a merciless monsoon-like rainy season in April/May. This means that in some mountain regions, you can spend the majority of the year very hot, very cold or very wet. How remote you wish to be (and the majority of people prefer to stay in the outskirts of towns and cities) will depend on your access to roads. Less than half of Morocco's rural population have 365 days a year access to roads. Many are impassable for between 30-60 days due to the extreme weather conditions. Improvements are underway in the form of a $37 million loan from the World Bank but completion is not until 2015. This means that you can be very cut off not only from a social life, but also from anything beyond the most basic of necessities. Although there is a plethora of pharmacies in some villages, there is usually little else, besides scatterings of fruit and vegetables, bread, one or two butchers, a cafe and tinned food (especially tuna) with perhaps a market day once a week. While this can be sufficient for short periods of time, if you are planning on spending large portions of the year in the countryside, it can become quite tedious very quickly. It is also worth considering that the majority of Morocco's villages are still without running water, which does raise the issue of hygiene. It would be good to be within driving distance of either a small supermarket, found in larger towns, or a hypermarket, which means being close to a city.

If you are planning on making an income from your property, such as renting it out to holidaymakers or running a business, you will need to consider factors such as accessibility of your property for tourists or colleagues. How will people travel to you from the airport? What is there to do when they arrive? Are you close to tourist attractions such as waterfalls and lakes? A new and popular option is to build and run gîtes or inns (*auberge*) for trekkers, climbers and skiers as the popularity of these activities is on the rise. This provides valuable jobs for local people and the generation of regional income. Large fireplaces, comfortable but simple brick style accommodations are the norm in the Middle Atlas around Azrou or the skiing town of Ifrane and the High Atlas, most popularly in the foothills of Toubkal, the highest peak in North Africa. As there are no restaurants nearby, however, tourists will have to be totally dependent on you for their food and drink. Are you prepared to run/manage a catering service?

As 45% of Morocco's population live in the countryside, it is likely that you will have neighbours in the not too distant vicinity. With the majority of the rural population residing on around 50 dirham (£3) a day, it means that no matter how simply you choose to live, you will appear very rich. Are you prepared for this? Chances are your neighbours will definitely not speak English, it is unlikely they will speak French and they might not even speak Arabic. A large majority of rural Moroccans are Berber and have very little to do with the urban lingo. There is also a much deeper-rooted sense of tradition amongst rural people in terms of dress sense, medicine, male and female relations and religion. Country people tend to be very superstitious, many are uneducated and a large number, illiterate. They are likely to have chickens, donkeys or dogs that roam free. Are you prepared to share your idyllic space with your neighbour's farm animals or the sound of braying cattle? This is not to mention highly curious children, who will do little to hide their fascination for everything to do with you. The cultural gulf combined with being unable to communicate and feeling like you are constantly on show can become tiring after a while, however positive your intentions are in the first place.

Water and electricity are also in short supply in the mountains and countryside. The government is on a binge to get electricity throughout the country with 70% now covered, but conditions can be pretty bleak in the more remote regions. Solar power is becoming a popular option for those who can afford it, but this does not take into account the extreme weather conditions and a back up system would be needed. Unless you are very ill advised, it is highly unlikely you will purchase land without access to water. Many people have romantic notions of obtaining their water supply from the garden well. Lovely as this might seem in the heat of summer, it can be a very depressing state of affairs when the winds are howling and all you want is a hot bath.

You will have to have the quality of the water checked prior to purchasing the property and implement your own plumbing and sanitation systems.

LAND

Buying land and building on to it is fast becoming a popular trend in Morocco. Land is still comparatively cheap (very cheap in some areas) and there is a tremendous amount crying out to be filled with something other than barren scrub. Be warned, however, that the buying of land can in some situations, be complicated especially for foreigners, with obstacles to climb, leap and roll over. It is not simply a case of choosing the landscape and saying, 'I'll take the land from this tree to that.' Sadly (or luckily) those days have passed and there have been many regulations implemented over the last few years.

In Morocco, the majority of the land is divided into zones; touristique, constructible, agricultural, industrial, habous (religious), government, military, or as of yet, unzoned. Depending on what zone the land you wish to purchase is in, will depend on whether you are allowed to a) buy it and b) build on to it. For those who are prepared to bowl their way through the obstacles, the benefits are outstanding; views over the snow capped Atlas, swathes of flowering meadows and cliff top retreats.

It is important to note, that the laws for the buying of land are not yet universal. What might apply in one region might be non-applicable elsewhere. In this section, the author has attempted to give an overview of the general rules and regulations but if this is the route you wish to go down, you will have to undertake personal research of the land you want to buy specific to your circumstances and the location.

Buying Land within the Urban Perimeter

The urban perimeter refers to land within the city and suburbs, as opposed to rural land. In Marrakech, one of the most popular regions to buy, most of the land within the urban perimeter will have been zoned as constructible or touristique and much of it will have already been titled and assigned into saleable lots by the Urban Agency. This means that it is much easier and quick for people to buy, as they will know exactly the area of land they are buying and from whom they are purchasing. Land within the urban perimeter is also likely to be close to both water and electricity. Such land, however, does not come without urban zoning regulations relating to the size of property you wish to build in relation to the size of the land and the type of property (number of floors etc) you are allowed to build.

When it comes to urban zoning, the best advice is to obtain the title number of the land you wish to purchase from the Conservation Fonciere and to go to the Urban Agency, who will be able to inform you as to which zone it is in (your notaire will do this on your behalf). The general rule is that one hectare (10,000 square metres) is enough land on which to build a private home. If you wish to buy more than 1 hectare, you will have to prove that the building project you have in mind will be touristique eg: a guesthouse or small hotel (minimum 5 bedrooms) in order to obtain the necessary building permission.

The administrative processes involved in building your own house are covered in *Building or Renovating.*

Buying Land Outside the Urban Perimeter

All land outside the urban perimeter is generally considered agricultural, even if it is rocky with just one tree. This means that foreigners are not permitted to buy it unless they undertake the task of transferring the land from an agricultural zone to a constructible zone. Until January 2005, such an activity was nigh on impossible as it involved obtaining the Vocation Non-Agricole (VNA) licence from the Ministry of Agriculture in Rabat, which took a very long time causing most people to give up and look elsewhere. The system for obtaining permission has now been localised to the wilaya (regional) level, which means it is speededd up (weeks instead of months) with the process having generally got easier although it is not without its hiccups.

While Moroccan nationals do not need to obtain a VNA and are permitted to purchase as much or as little agricultural land as they wish and then sell off individual plots, a foreigner, if they manage to obtain a VNA is not allowed to buy less than 1 hectare of land. (This is the general rule although you will find it varies from region to region). There are no legal limits on the amount of land they are allowed to buy, but they are not permitted to buy and then sell off individual plots.

The buying of non urban land is further complicated by the fact that much of the land is melkia land meaning that it does not have a title, but, instead a contract written up by the adoul (see *Fees, Contracts and Conveyancing*). Most landowners will have purchased their land through the adoul and chances are, this was a very long time ago before the lifetime of the current owners. This means that all information relating to the land will be written in Arabic, the boundaries indicating the size of the land will have been drawn through the use of landmarks (from this tree to that) as opposed to more scientific methods of measuring and, there are likely to be a vast number of family members scattered around the world, each with an entitlement to the land and an opinion as to what to do with it.

The Processes Involved in Buying Agricultural Land

It is important to note that a good, recommended notaire will undertake all the processes involved in the purchasing of agricultural land on your behalf with you having to do very little except pay him/her. The following is just an indication of what is involved in the procedure, to ensure you are kept in the complicated loop.

Land Registry (*Conservation Foncière*). The first activity after deciding on the land you wish to purchase is to visit the Conservation Foncière to check the history of the land. If you are planning on doing this without the help of a notaire, you are advised to take an Arabic translator, as much of the documentation is likely to be in Arabic. The Conservation Foncière will hold information regarding the title status of the land, to whom it belongs and how many family members have an entitlement to it. If the land is untitled, which it is likely to be then the notaire will have to start the proceedings for obtaining titles including sending out a surveyor to accurately measure the exact boundaries of land (see *Fees, Contracts and Conveyancing*).

You will also be able to ascertain whether or not the land is clean ie: does it have any outstanding loans. If it does this could be one of the first hurdles jeopardising your ability to buy, unless, that is, you are prepared to pay the loans off. To be sure you are obtaining the correct information from the Conservation Foncière, you are recommended either to tip them on arrival or to request a Declaration of Ownership (*Shahadat al Melkia*), which is an officially stamped document from the Conservation Foncière. This only costs 60-100 dh and is your guarantee that the person giving you the information is doing the job effectively. Based on this information, you should request to see the identity card of the landowner selling you the land as cases do arise where the seller is not actually the owner but an opportunist out to make a buck.

Urban Agency. In order to obtain information regarding the future plans for the area in and around your land such as new infrastructure, buildings and zoning issues, your next port of call should be the Urban Agency to request a *Plan de Management*. This takes 48 hours to obtain and costs around 200 dh.

Accord de Principe. Assuming all is well and good to this stage, you can start undertaking the relevant proceedings for obtaining the VNA. As well as working with a notaire, you might want to consider talking to a recommended architect at this stage, who will have a good idea of what will or will not work best on the land. The process involves drawing up a plan called the *Accord de Principe*, stating your overall aims, ideas and vision for the land you wish to buy. This is not the same as building permission, which requires detailed plans.

The Accord de Principe, is submitted to the Urban/Rural Commune who will submit it to the regional committee responsible for issuing the VNA via the Centre for Regional Investment (CRI) (*see below*). The decision-making process takes 1-2 months. If the answer is positive, you will be issued with a VNA. You are generally recommended not to proceed with the purchasing process until the VNA has been issued but if you are keen to get the ball rolling, it is imperative that you have a clause (*condition suspensive*) put into the preliminary contract stating it to be dependent upon the obtaining of the VNA and subsequent building permission.

The VNA is issued only for the project stated on the Accord de Principe. It is non-transferable between individuals ie: you cannot sell your land with the VNA. If you sell your land, the VNA goes too. It is easier to obtain a VNA if the project you have in mind is touristique ie: involves the employment of local people and the generation of local revenue. If your Accord de Principe is rejected, you can log an appeal with your Urban or Rural Commune or the Centre of Regional Investment who will instigate a reassessment of the project on your behalf.

Once the land has been transferred from an agricultural to a constructible zone and you have tracked down all the owners of the property, you are free to progress with the purchasing process and building plans.

STEPS TO BUYING AGRICULTURAL LAND

1. Choose the land you are interested in.
2. If it is inside the urban perimeter, find out which zone it is in from the Urban Agency.
3. Visit the Conservation Foncière to assess whether the land you wish to purchase is a) titled and b) clean ie: does not have any outstanding loans.
4. Obtain a Plan de Management from the Urban Agency to find out what developments and infrastructures are planned for your surrounding area.
5. If you are buying agricultural land, hire an architect to help you with the drawing up of the Accord de Principe.
6. Submit the Accord de Principe to your Urban/Rural Commune.
7. If you are issued with a VNA, find a recommended notaire (if you have not already) who will commence with the obtaining of titles/buying process for you.

Centres of Regional Investment (CRI)

CRI's were introduced in January 2002 as a government initiative to boost each of the 16 regions by making them responsible for their own development and investment. Housed in modern, often state of the art buildings, the CRI refer to themselves as a 'one stop shop' for the investor offering all the advice, help and documentation they need in order to put their money into the region.

Where the CRI really come into their own is with people wishing to spend up to 200 million dirham (£13 million) buying land and transforming it into money-making ventures of benefit to the local region. In these situations, they will arrange meetings between the landowner and each of the relevant administrative departments, offer assistance with the permission processes and help with putting people in touch with recommended builders, engineers and architects. They tend to be less involved with individuals wishing to purchase single properties. Having said this, if you have purchased a house and are running into problems obtaining building permission or overcoming zoning issues, it is possible to visit the CRI who also have a role as problem solvers and should be able to help you launch appeals or advise on alternative solutions.

Centres of Regional Investment (CRI)

CRI Agadir, Avenue Mohammed V, Agadir; ☎ 048 82 69 77; e-mail klahlou@ cri-agadir.ma; www.cri-agadir.ma.

CRI Al Hoceima, 48-50 Rue El Alaouyine, Al Hoceima; ☎ 039 98 39 83; e-mail badich@alhoceimainvest.ma; www.alhoceimainvest.ma.

CRI Beni Mellal, Avenue Bayroutl; ☎ 023 48 20 95/48 23 13.

CRI Casablanca, Avenue Hassan II, Casablanca; ☎ 022 48 18 88; e-mail nja-mai@casainvest.ma; www.casainvest.ma.

CRI Dakhla, Siege de la Chambre des Peches Marimitime de l'Atlantique Sud, Route de Nouveau Port, Hay Errahma, Dakhla; ☎ 048 89 85 35; www.da-khlainvest.ma.

CRI Fes, Place de la Resistance angle Bd, Moulay Youssef et Allal Al Fassi, Fes; ☎ 055 65 20 57; www.crifes.ma.

CRI Guelmim, Bd Mohammed VI, Guelmim; ☎ 048 77 17 77.

CRI Kenitra, 19 Avenue des F.A.R; ☎ 037 37 46 27; e-mail inform@kenitrain-vesti.ma; www.kenitrainvesti.ma.

CRI Laayoune, Bd Mekka, laayuoune; ☎ 048 89 11 89.

CRI Marrakech, Jnane El Harti, Avenue John Kennedy, Gueliz, Marrakech 40000; ☎ 044 42 04 93; e-mail moumni@crimarrakech.ma; www.crima-rrakech.ma.

CRI Meknes, Avenue Okba Bnou Nafii VN, Meknes; ☎ 055 52 44 69.

CRI Oujda, 2 Bd Nations Unies; ☎ 056 68 28 27.

CRI Rabat, Siege de la Wilaya, Prefecture de Rabat, 3e etage, Rabat; ☎ 037 73 13 07; e-mail info@rabatinvest.ma; www.rabatinvest.ma.

CRI Safi, Avenue Liberte, Safi; ☎ 044 61 21 39.

CRI Settat, Siege de la Wilaya de Settat; ☎ 023 72 37 61.

CRI Tangier, ☎ 039 94 01 16/039 94 68 24; www.tanger-tetouaninvest.ma.

FARMHOUSES

The benefit of buying land with a farmhouse attached is that you already have a basic structure on which to build. In addition, you are likely to be close to water and depending quite how basic the property is and how much you enjoy camping, a place to stay prior to the building works and in some cases, during them. Having said this, most farmhouses are pretty basic, often deserted by families who have left the fields and mountains, in search of more lucrative work in the cities. While some will come with a communal or if you are fortunate, a private well, none will have running water. As of recently, electricity is likely to be accessible but not installed and most will have a standard squat-style loo but no kitchen, or certainly nothing resembling a kitchen. As an extra treat, you will most probably find that much of the house has been shared with farm animals. Typical Moroccan farmhouses are square, concrete blocks with small windows, metal shutters and metal front doors often Berber in design. They are built in the riad-style, usually two stories, with a courtyard in the middle, rooms surrounding and half a metre thick walls.

As you are buying a property on agricultural land, you are firstly not permitted to buy less than 1 hectare (again, this rule will vary from region to region) and secondly, you will need to go through the process of obtaining a VNA, which involves the same procedure as for the purchasing of land without an existing property. It is highly unlikely that the farmhouse will be titled, so the notaire will also need to undertake the task of tracking down all family members with a stake in the house, which might be a lengthy procedure and, as it involves the selling of a family house, emotionally fraught.

Your local community are likely to be very poor, most just scraping a living through meagre agricultural activities. This does not stop them from being very hospitable especially to new, foreign neighbours. Once they have got over their initial shyness, you will be warmly greeted and treated. Stories abound of a welcoming bowl of couscous being left on stranger's doorsteps. Be aware, though, that you will be very (very) rich in their eyes, no matter how hard up you feel yourself to be. As is the Moroccan way if you find yourself having your back scratched by your neighbour, you will no doubt soon be requested to scratch their back in a much more satisfying way perhaps to the tune of paying for a relative's heart operation or driving the family on a country-wide expedition to visit a dying cousin. Such demands can become tiresome after a while and if they do not appeal, you are best advised to set up your 'friendship boundary' from day one and stick to it.

COASTAL PROPERTIES

Buying properties or land along the coast is perhaps where the biggest trend currently lies. Morocco has over 3500km of coastline much of it still undeveloped, but with government plans underway to transform great stretches of beachfront into upmarket or ecological tourist zones. Many developers are seizing on the low cost of land and building apartment or villa developments overlooking the sea. Focus is on the Mediterranean coast, which had been previously neglected in favour of government investment in the interior regions. The major consideration to take into account when buying along the coast is damp. This is particularly an issue on the Atlantic coast where the winds are higher. Next to the coast in Essaouira, for example, the combination of salt, wind and humidity is so extreme that iron kitchen utensils left out in the morning can be rusty by sunset. Climate on the coast is generally much more temperate than inland. It can be 40 degrees in Marrakech and just 25 degrees in Agadir, 3 hours drive to the southwest. As a result, coastal regions tend to be very busy during weekends as people leave the interior desert heat and head for the cool.

If buying by the sea, you need to research future developments in the region. Just because you have a sea view now, can you guarantee that next year, no new hotel or apartment block is going to be constructed in front of your window? You will also need to make sure that the beach you are buying on or near is clean. When it comes to litter and waste, Moroccans tend to have little respect for public places and will drop their litter with no concern for their surrounds. Many of the beaches immediately next door to Tangier, for example, are dirty, but a little way up the coast, you will find them pristine and idyllic. You will also need to find out whether the beach is public or private property. Many large hotels are currently, and more soon will be, buying up great chunks of beach specifically for the private use of their guests or for paying visitors from outside. As these beaches are well maintained, it might be worth paying a 'residents' fee to the hotel for access to these private beaches and deck chairs. If you are planning on spending your summers on the more popularised beach, you will need to prepare for crowded sands, wolf whistles and stares from hordes of male youths. While this is annoying if you want to be left alone, it is harmless and the culprits soon tire of showing interest, especially if you avoid eye contact. The worst thing you can do is show amusement as Moroccans love a sense of humour and will go out of their way to get you laughing. That said, harassment is no more extreme in Morocco than any other male-dominated society.

Income opportunities are excellent for properties along the coast as there is always a market for sun, sea and sand. If you are renting out your property, you will have to make it hardy to withstand sandy feet, salty swimming costumes and a number of surfboards. Bear in mind that not all the coast is conducive to swimming many areas along the Atlantic around for example Casablanca suffer from strong currents, which make swimming and general waters sports unsafe. It will be well worth checking the general status of the sea before you buy.

BUYING OFF PLAN OR SEMI-COMPLETED PROPERTY

Morocco is a developer's paradise. Land can be bought very cheaply, sometimes for next to nothing if the developers can prove they will transform it for the greater good, government incentives abound and there is still so much of the country largely unexplored that the government are keen to transform into hip, happening cities. This means that villas and apartment blocks are shooting up faster than you can say, 'mortgage' and there seems to be no end of takers snapping them up or putting down deposits before even visiting the site or surrounding region.

The most popular places for developers are:

○ Around Marrakech, where exclusive gated residencies with guards, private gardens, swimming pools, garages and views over the Atlas are selling to top end clientele.
○ Next to the Atlantic coast north and south of Agadir
○ In the north of the country along the Mediterranean coast from Tangier, through to the Spanish enclave of Sebta.
○ Saidia on the northeast edge close to the Algerian border.

In Morocco it is becoming increasingly popular to buy properties either off plan or semi-completed based on their plans. This is a trend that has only really started to take off over the last couple of years as the system for doing so has become more organised. This is largely due to the introduction of two new systems. Firstly, every developer needs to prove to a bank or guarantor, prior to starting a build that they have in their possession, 50% of the capital needed. Secondly, every developer must work with a lawyer to draw up a contract called a *Vente en l'etat futur d'achévement (VEFA)*. This contract was introduced as law in 2002 and works as a two-way security enabling people to purchase uncompleted properties. For the buyer, it ensures that what the developer says he will do, he will actually do, right through to the completed build and for the developer, it ensures commitment from the buyer by way of deposits and graduated payments in advance of completion.

The VEFA

The VEFA is drawn up by a notaire or property lawyer after the foundations and ground floor, have been built and prior to the promotion of the project to potential buyers. The VEFA contract must contain the following information:

○ The building permission documents
○ Selling price
○ Delivery schedule
○ Stages of payment
○ Methods of payment
○ Guarantee from bank that capital is secured
○ Certified copies of architect plans
○ Attestation from engineers that the foundations and ground floor are completed

Stages of payment are generally stipulated as:

Payment 1 – Following completion of the foundations and ground floor
Payment 2 – Following structural completion
Payment 3 – Following the completion of the property

Once you are happy with the contents of the VEFA, you and the developer will sign it, in front of the notaire and a deposit will be paid. At the same time as signing the VEFA, you should receive what is known as a *Cahier de Charge*. This is a notebook detailing exactly what building materials, furnishings, fittings, white goods and finishings you will have in the property from foundations to roof. This is drawn up by the developer and is a further guarantee that what you pay for, you will receive. At the end of the build, if the developer has stuck to the time scale and fulfilled his contract, the Urban/Rural Commune will issue him with a *Permis d'Habitation,* stating the development to be suitable for habitation. At this stage, the water and electricity can be switched on. The final contract, the *Acte de Vente* is drawn up by the notaire and signed by the buyer and the seller and the title deeds transferred from the developers name to yours at which time the property becomes your own.

Despite great pains to enforce the implementation of a VEFA, there are still circumstances where developers will not work with a VEFA. It is very important that you try to avoid such developers no matter how cheap or attractive they say their project to be. You cannot prove they have the authority to build, which means the properties might have to be pulled down at any time, you have no way of securing your payments and, chances are, the building or the promised infrastructure will not be completed and you will be left high and dry (or low and wet if it happens to be the rainy season).

LEASEBACK

The leaseback concept is like a formalised, buy-to-let scheme, which originated in France as a way of increasing the number of quality holiday accommodations in tourist regions. In Morocco, the scheme is starting to catch on and is being offered as a failsafe incentive to foreign investors.

As the owner, you are usually given use of the property for around 6 weeks of the year. The rest of the time it is in the hands of a management company who will manage it and rent it out on your behalf guaranteeing a rental income of usually between 2.5-6% per annum, which goes towards paying off any mortgage you have taken out to finance the property. The scheme normally lasts for a period of nine to eleven years, although you can sell at any time. At the end of the agreed leaseback period, the property returns fully to you to do with it as you please.

For somebody wishing to simply purchase a property for investment purposes, this is an excellent scheme. You have the advantage of a guaranteed monthly rental income, no maintenance costs on your property and the chance to live there for a little chunk of the year. You pay no VAT and benefit from the capital gains at the time of selling.

Useful Address

IMOINVEST, Grove House, Suite 8, 320 Kensal Road, London W10 5BZ; ☎ 020-8960 5888; e-mail london@imoinvest.com; www.imoinvest.com.

DESERT

Morocco's desert begins south of the High Atlas and stretches down to the threshold of the Sahara interspersed with green, lush oasis valleys, palmeraies and reservoir lakes. While the dramatic soaring sand dunes lie to the south east of the country, much of Morocco's desert is made up of never ending flat, stony terrain, known as *hammada*. Temperatures are intense during the day, sometimes as high as 50°C, but plummet at night to 0°C. Annual rainfall amounts to around 3 days a year, providing a mere 68mm. Most life in the desert revolves around the oasis valleys where vegetation flourishes in thin strips along riverbeds that drain from the Atlas. Life, however, is tough and unpredictable, fully reliant on nature. People exist on very little but are incredibly enterprising in survival techniques many of which are largely unchanged since ancient days.

There is very little in the way of infrastructure. Great distances have to be travelled in order to get to the nearest hospital or clinic, away from the oasis valleys, generators are needed for electricity and water is often obtained via artesian wells.

The main appeal is the stunning scenery, palm and olive groves, rugged rocks, roaming camels and glistening sand dunes. If you have set your heart on living in the desert, you will need to prepare for sandstorms, dust and isolation. It will be virtually impossible to exist without transport, ideally a 4X4 and you will always need to keep a supply of spare petrol as petrol stations are few and far between. Markets tend to run on a weekly basis, when farmers and traders tout their wares, although ideally, you do not want to be too far from one of the larger towns such as Er Rachidia, Guelmim or Ouarzazate.

KASBAHS AND KSOURS (SINGULAR KSAR))

Exotic and fairytale like as they may seem, most property-minded folk will warn you off all attempts to purchase a kasbah. That is, unless you are as entrepreneurial as Richard Branson (who recently bought and renovated Kasbah Tamadot in the Atlas Mountains) with money to match. Kasbahs and Ksours are Berber concepts found throughout the southern deserts of Morocco, a kasbah is not so much a house as a castle with crenellated towers and vivid geometric designs, belonging to a family or a tribal chief with rooms for a harem, retainers and dependents while a Ksar is a town housing hundreds of families, mosques, bread ovens and shops, all enclosed within heavily fortified walls. Unlike the traditional riads and dars, which are plain on the outside, the façade of the kasbah is ornate and embellished, while dark and simple on the inside. In many cases, kasbahs and ksars run into each other making it difficult to tell where one ends and the other begins. The walls of both are made of *pisé* (mud and straw) with foundations of mud and stones. A drive through the Draa Valley in the deep south of the country reveals an almost continuous line of one hundred year old buildings, many now just ruins washed away by the annual rains, but those that are still used are mainly inhabited by Berbers.

Inside, the ceilings are palm branches set over wooden beams, the walls are two feet thick and the floors, simple earth. The buying and renovation process needed in order to obtain and restore a kasbah makes the buying of land seem like a stroll on the beach. While you are not likely to come up against any obstacles regarding permission to actually purchase the property, which in the case of a kasbah is likely to be privately owned, you will be amazed, if not staggered at the number of family members/dependents and retainers with a stake in the house who will have to be sought prior to the purchasing process going ahead. This could take years without any guarantees that the vote to sell the kasbah will be unanimous. It is highly unlikely you will find a kasbah for sale with just one or two named family members.

The other major obstacle is related to the build. Very few kasbahs in use today will be using the original pisé, most will have been done up using modern building materials and often rebuilt within the original walls. In order to make your kasbah inhabitable for the present day, you will have to throw vast sums of money into undertaking a complete rebuild, also considering that there are very few architects skilled in such works.

The final obstacle, although it need not be viewed as such, is planning what you want your kasbah to be after it has been bought and renovated. Most are too large to maintain as a private residence and it is highly likely you will wish to recoup some of the outgoings you spent on getting it to an inhabitable state. Most kasbahs are transformed into hotels or large guesthouses but if this is the route you plan to take, it will require extensive research, most ideally with those who have been brave, rich and patient enough to undertake the activity before you.

Useful Addresses

Kasbah du Toubkal Discover Ltd, Timbers, Oxted Road, Godstone, Surrey UK, RH9 8AD; ☎ 01883-744392; fax 01883-744913; www.kasbahdutoubkal.com.

Kasbah Agafay, Sarl Kenitra limited, BP226- 4000, Marrakech Medina, Morocco; ☎ 044 36 86 00/044 42 09 60; fax: 044 42 09 70; www.kasbahagafay.com.

Kasbah Tamadot, Limited Edition by Virgin, Voyager House, 5 The Lanchesters, 162-164 Fulham Palace Road, London W6 9ER; ☎ 020-8600 0430; fax 020-8600 0431; www.virginlimitededition.co.uk.

RENTING A HOME IN MOROCCO

CHAPTER SUMMARY

○ **Benefits of Renting**. Renting a property in Morocco prior to buying enables you to choose the right location and the best type of property to suit your needs.

○ **Short Term Rents.** The most likely short term property you will be able to rent is a fully furnished holiday let but you should be able to negotiate a good price for a longer stay.

○ **Finding accommodation through estate agents**. Most estate agents also deal with rental properties, although these tend to be for long term rents, 6 months to 1 year minimum.

○ **Agency Fees.** If you use an estate agency, expect to pay 1 month's rent in fees.

○ **Homestays.** Moroccans are incredibly hospitable and you might find yourself being offered a room in their house. If you accept the offer always pay your way even if they refuse payment, otherwise things could get complicated in the future.

○ **Rental Deposit**. This is usually 1 months rent.

○ **Holiday Booking Agents**. Most holiday booking agents ask for 30-50% deposit when making the rental booking.

○ **Condition of the property**. Make sure that there is a general agreement on the state of the property and its contents (*état des lieux*) prior to moving in.

○ **Renting Privately.** If you are renting a property directly from the owner, ensure there is a written agreement on all aspects of the rent.

○ **Receipts.** Always request receipts for any payments made including the deposit.

The decision to buy a house abroad should not be rushed into, especially when it is in a place like Morocco, which is so culturally different from home in pretty much every aspect. The best way of ensuring that you make the right decision on whether, where and what to buy is by renting a house in Morocco and spending time really getting to know the country.

There is no shortage of rentable property in Morocco, whether it is an apartment in a city, a holiday let, a room in a guesthouse, a house share with Moroccans or a furnished villa. Most estate agents deal with renting as well as buying and selling, in addition there are a number of websites offering properties to rent and most useful of all, plenty of people on the ground, offering word of mouth recommendations.

Benefits of Renting Prior to Buying

- If you have set your heart on buying a house in Morocco but do not know which region/area/neighbourhood will best suit you, you can rent properties around the country and decide.
- It enables you to familiarise yourself with the characteristics of the area in which you want to buy. What is it actually like to live there as opposed to being a tourist? Will the lack of shops/bars/nightlife bother you in the long term?
- It can help you decide what type of property to buy. Perhaps you had set your heart on a riad in a medina but after renting one for a month, you might decide you prefer the idea of a villa near the sea.
- It is an excellent way of getting to know people and of people getting to know you and the more people you know in Morocco, the better your experience of the country and its systems.
- It is a good way of getting to grips with the buying process, perhaps finding individuals who want to sell their property privately, saving you agency fees.
- If you are in rented accommodation, it will be much easier for you to choose and buy your property in an unhurried way. There is nothing more stressful to a buyer or pleasing to a seller than a rushed, 'that'll do, I've got a plane to catch' type of house purchase.
- Staying in rented property in Morocco, ideally negotiated at a good rate will be a lot cheaper than going back and forth to the UK to view houses and sign contracts.

SHORT-TERM LETS

If your sole reason for renting a house in Morocco is to have somewhere to stay while house hunting, then you will most probably want a furnished (*meublé*) short-term let, short term in Morocco, being three months or under. Searching for 'properties to rent in Morocco' via the internet on a search engine such as *Google*, will throw up a predominance of holiday-let style properties for tourists visiting Morocco on short breaks. While these can be wonderful places to stay, usually with all mod cons and interesting architectural features, they are likely to be at the pricier end of the market out to attract tourists looking for something a little bit special. Many but not all, come with additional perks such as maid service and breakfast. It is quite probable that you will be able to negotiate a cheaper rate for a longer term let, as many homeowners would be happy to have the guarantee of occupancy. To get in touch with owners you can either click directly on to properties presented on search engines or via websites such as holiday-rentals.com or internationalrentals.com, which have a selection of properties and put you in touch directly with owners via their e-mail addresses/ telephone numbers. It is also possible to book up such properties through booking agents such as riadomaroc.com, villasofmorocco.com or marocselection. com, who have a wide number of properties on their books, normally but not exclusively, at the more luxurious end and will organise contractual paperwork and reduced rates on your behalf.

Most estate agents in Morocco also deal with rentals (*location*). It is in fact the main source of business for a number of them, with a large selection of standard, ie non-holiday style, properties to choose from. The benefits of finding rental property through estate agents is that they will deal with all the paperwork for you, liaising with landlords and collecting deposits. As in most parts of the world, there is a charge for engaging an agent. In Morocco, the fee is normally one months rent. Note, however, that most estate agents only really deal in long-term rentals, so you might find it difficult to find a place for less than 6 months to a year.

Another way of finding property to rent is simply by asking people on the ground in Morocco, everyone knows someone who invariably knows someone. Moroccans being as hospitable as they are might offer you a place to stay in their house, especially if you are alone. While this is an excellent way of getting to know Morocco and Moroccans you will have less freedom to do your own thing, very little personal space and be expected to fit into someone else's way of life. Be prepared for your 'host family' to refuse payment from you as part of their hospitality and 'future favour' type attitude. Try not to end up owing anything otherwise, you might find yourself being requested a much bigger favour further down the line.

Another option for finding property is to go to a website forum. The best of these is *buyingmoroccanproperty.com* which is the first English speaking website dedicated to buying property in Morocco. Here you can post questions up on to the site, regarding looking for rental property and you should be offered a few options in return. Another place to look is the French language website *marocannonces.com* and clicking on the Immobilier-Location down the left hand side. The site is filled with properties for rent placed by the owners, who you can respond to directly. You can also place ads on to the site (if your

French is up to it) stating what you are looking for and an e-mail address and you will more than probably be contacted by someone with accommodation along those lines.

Furnishings. If you rent a furnished property from a Moroccan landlord, be prepared for the furnishings to be different to those you might be used to. Moroccans, for example, tend to sleep on banquettes. These are narrow, long, foam filled cushions on wooden bases pushed up against the wall with no back for support. The concept of a bedroom is sometimes unfamiliar in Morocco. Family members, simply sleep wherever there is a banquette, and it could be a different banquette each night. The same banquettes are also used for sitting on to eat, assuming, the table is high enough to accommodate this. Otherwise, people sit on the floor or on cushions to eat from low, round tables. Kitchens are likely to be quite basic. Moroccans tend to cook on three ring cookers that sit on the surface, attached via a rubber hose, to a gas bottle. There is also likely to be a fridge, a sink and perhaps cupboards but do not expect a warm, glowing hearth. Moroccan kitchens and bathrooms can tend to be quite utilitarian. You will most probably want to bring your own bed linen with you as it is hard to find good quality sheets etc in Morocco unless they are imported, which generally means expensive.

GLOSSARY OF RENTAL TERMS

Ascenseur	lift
Bail	rental contract
Cave	cellar
Chambre	bedroom
Chauffage Central	central heating
Charge Comprise CC	rent including utility and community expenses
Cheminée	chimney
Climatisation	air conditioning
Concierge	man who takes care of the building
Cuisine Americaine	breakfast counter
Cuisine Equipée	fitted kitchen
Depôt de Garantie	deposit
Durée de contrat	rental period
Etat des Lieux	inventory
Immeuble	building
Locateur	tenant
Location	renting
Loyer	rent
Meublé	furnished
Niveux	levels

Placard	cupboard
Propriétaire	landlord
Rez de chaussée (RdC)	ground floor
Salle a manger	dining room
Salle de bains (SdB or sdb)	bathroom
Salle de douche (SdD or sdd)	shower room
Salon	sitting room
Studette	little studio or utility room
Vide	empty or unfurnished

FORMALITIES OF RENTING

Through an Estate Agent. Common practice when renting a property in Morocco is to pay the landlord a deposit, which is usually 1 month's rent. Some landlord's demand three months rent for a deposit if they feel there are furnishings and objects in the properties, which are worth a lot. This can, however, be negotiated. Much like in the UK, the estate agent will handle all the paperwork such as the rental contract for you to sign and the deposit payment, which you pay to them and they normally keep on behalf of the landlord. Make sure you get a receipt for everything you pay for. Monthly rent is also paid to the agent, who in turn pays it to the landlord. Be sure to ask your estate agent to draw up an *etat des lieux* (inventory) for you. This is normally done at a minimal extra cost, but is a very worthwhile document to have as it highlights the exact state of the property prior to your moving in. This prevents the landlord from charging you for any damage you did not do and also protects the landlord enabling him to charge you if there is any damage you have done.

See *Where to Find Your Ideal Home* for a list of estate agents for the regions

Through a Holiday Letting Agent. The most common way of booking rental accommodation with a holiday letting agency is via the internet or telephone, less so in person. If websites are in French, click on the Union Jack usually in the top right hand corner, to translate into English. You, as the potential tenant will not need to pay the bookings agency as they receive their payment from the landlord, but it is likely that landlords raise their rental prices a little in order to cover the agency fees. In most instances, you select a property you like the look of on the internet, reserve it and send over your details via an online booking form along with a credit card deposit of between 30-50% of the booking price. The balance generally needs to be paid two weeks before the date of arrival although this will vary between companies. You need to make sure that the agency you are booking with has a licence or *patente* number. This is normally located in the small print under the 'contract' or 'rental terms and conditions'.

Naturally Morocco.com, an eco-friendly villa company with properties to rent in Marrakech, Essaouira and Taroudannt.

Riads au Maroc, properties to rent in Rabat, Fes, Ouarzazate, Marrakech and Beni Mellal; www.riadomaroc.com.

Drimlo Agency, properties to rent in Marrakech; www.dreamsimmolocation. com.

Terre Maroc, properties to rent throughout Morocco; www.terremaroc.com.

Demeures du Maroc, properties to rent throughout Morocco; wwwdemeuresdu-maroc.com.

Fez Medina, properties to rent in Fes; fesmedina.com.

Through the Owner. The benefit of renting a property directly from the owner is that you are more likely to negotiate a good rental price, as there is no middle-man involved. It is, however, important that you do as much as possible to cover yourself from the outset no matter how friendly or accommodating the landlord seems. Get a written agreement on start date and length of stay, rental price per month, method of payment, contract termination terms and any extra charges such as utilities and service charges to, for example concierges. Ask for a receipt for the deposit and for every monthly payment. Make sure there is an inventory for the property and go through this with the landlord on your arrival to confirm that everything stated to be in the house is there.

Jack's Apartments, a wide range of serviced apartments to rent in Essaouira; www.jackapartment.com.

Holiday Rentals, mainly covers properties in Marrakech and the Atlantic coast; www.holiday-rentals.com.

International Rentals, properties in Marrakech, Essaouira and Tangier www.in-ternationalrentals.com.

Abritel, properties throughout Morocco; www.abritel.fr.

Marocannonces, list of rental properties available throughout Morocco; www.marocannonces.com.

Special Places to Stay, properties throughout Morocco; www.specialplacestostay.com.

Other useful websites for posting requests for rental accommodation:
www.buyingmoroccanproperty.com
www.africaguide.com

FEES, CONTRACTS AND COSTS

CHAPTER SUMMARY

O **Buying Process.** The buying process in Morocco is not complicated so long as you work with a recommended notaire.

O **Conveyancing costs**. Including real estate taxes, these costs will be between 5% and 12.5% depending on whether or not;

   O The property is titled.

   O You choose to work with an estate agent.

   O You are planning to use the property for commercial use or buying land or property in the countryside.

O **Haggling.** Few people successfully haggle over the price of a property. The maximum you can expect to negotiate the price down is 10%.

O **The notaire**. A good notaire is at the heart of a successful house purchase, although some people nowadays are choosing to work with a lawyer instead. There are pros and cons to each.

O **Preliminary contract**. After the price has been agreed, the notaire will draw up the preliminary contract and a 10% deposit is paid.

O **Titled properties.** Notaires will only work with titled properties. It is not wise to purchase an untitled property.

O **Draft contract.** Prior to signing the final contract, you will receive a draft. It is worth getting this document legally translated.

O **Final signing**. Prior to the final signing, check your property one last time to ensure that nothing has been removed or damaged.

FEES

The process of purchasing a property in Morocco can seem bewildering as reams of paperwork written in French and covered in endless stamps keep appearing along with demands for fees that need to be paid. This need not be bewildering so long as you have the basic facts at your fingertips, the most important of which is the various costs that you will incur when purchasing a property in Morocco.

If you are buying a property for your own personal use, the total conveyancing costs work out at 5% of the property price. If you are using an estate agent, which is advised, add an extra 2.5% (plus 20%VAT) and if you are purchasing an untitled property, add a further 1.5-2.5%, dependent on the size of the property and the amount of administrative work involved in tracking down all stated owners. This means that you have a low of 5% and a high of 10% to pay in addition to the cost of your property.

BREAKDOWN OF FEES AND TAXES:

2.5% registration tax

0.5% notary tax

1% to the Conservation Foncière to transfer the title deeds

1% notary fees (plus 7% VAT)

2.5% estate agent fees (plus 20% VAT)

1.5 - 2.5% to obtain titles if not already titled

You will also pay 150 dirham (around £9) for your certificate of propriety, 75dirham for stamps and 3520dirham (around £220) for administrative expenses.

If you are purchasing a property for commercial use eg: a guesthouse or if you are purchasing land or a farmhouse in the countryside, the registration fee increases from 2.5% to 5%. This means that you have a low to pay of 7.5% and a high to pay of 12.5%. All these fees are paid directly to the notaire at the time of signing the final contract and handing over the payment for the property.

Example of Costs on a Titled 1 million dirham (£62,500) property

25,000 dirham	registration tax
5000 dirham	notary tax
10,000 dirham	notary fees (exclusive 7% VAT)
10,000 dirham	to register the title deeds
25,000 dirham	estate agent fees (exclusive 20% VAT)
150 dirham	to obtain the certificate of property
75 dirham	for stamps
3520 dirham	for administrative costs

Total 78,745 dirham (around £5000)

NEGOTIATING THE PRICE

After finding a property that you like, the first step is to put in a verbal offer. This can be either through the estate agent or, if you are doing a private purchase, directly to the seller or the non-official mediator. The only reason most Moroccans are actually selling their homes is for money. This means that they will be prepared to wait for the absolutely best offer. Do not expect souk style negotiations to win you a good bargain. Unlike haggling over a rug, where you can expect to knock up to 50% off the initial price, with a property, you will be lucky to knock it down 10%. In fact, you might even find the original property price rising before your very eyes as the seller attempts to assess quite how high your level of interest might be. Don't forget, Moroccans are well versed at negotiation and know all the tricks of the trade. Never act too keen, never appear in a hurry to buy and, most importantly, be prepared to walk away. Only by appearing disinterested, will you be able to obtain any sort of control. Gazumping is a typical part of the house buying process. The seller will most likely have many estate agents working on his behalf not to mention cousins, brothers and uncles and will think nothing of dropping you if a better offer comes in. This does not mean you need to panic. Morocco is still a buyer's market and despite what your estate agent or the seller tells you, houses do not get swooped up in a day, most sit on the market for a couple of weeks at least. It is better you feel you are making the right decision, than charge in blind, throwing all caution to the wind.

Once the offer has been accepted, the estate agent, if you decide to work with one (see *Finding Properties for Sale*) will swing into action. Do not feel obliged to them. It is as much in their interest that the sale goes through, as yours. Also, tempting as it is, do not put yourself completely in their hands. This is your purchase and your money. If you want to delay in order to get a document properly translated, then do it. If you are not happy with the notaire that they recommend, then most certainly seek recommendations for another. You must stay in control of the situation. Moroccans will respect you for it. It is better if you have the notaire you wish to work with already lined up prior to placing the offer, so that the process can kick off soon after.

WORKING WITH A NOTAIRE

The notaire is a public official appointed by the government, whose main role when it comes to property conveyancing is to make sure that all processes have been undertaken correctly and all fees and taxes paid. The big task in Morocco is finding a notaire you can feel comfortable working with who you believe will do everything they can to ensure you are not missing vital information regarding the property you are purchasing. It is not difficult finding a notaire, although in smaller towns like Essaouira, you currently have just one, who everyone uses, which eases the process of choosing. All estate agents will have a notaire they can recommend and every house-owning European will have another they can put you in touch with. It is best to look for a notaire who speaks English, so that you can communicate with him/her directly. It is important to note, that unlike a solicitor in the UK, the notaire is not working to your best advantage. Their role is, quite simply, to undertake the conveyancing process. They are not paid to offer impartial advice and few will give it if you ask.

Mainly, the notaire will:

- O Draw up and witness the signing of the house purchasing contracts.
- O Work with the Conservation Foncière (land registry) in obtaining title deeds and undertaking searches on third parties with entitlement to the property or land.
- O Make sure that the property or land you are buying is 'clean' ie: clear of any outstanding loans.
- O Hold and transfer funds from you to the seller via their blocked bank accounts.
- O Ensure all fees and taxes are paid.
- O Engage a translator to work with you for the signing of the final contract.

Notaire or Lawyer (Avocat)?

In 2002, much to the general dismay of notaires, avocats were given the authority to also start undertaking the conveyancing process. While the notaire remains the 'legal' of choice, some people, particularly in larger cities such as Casablanca are choosing to go with a lawyer. There is no right or wrong choice but there are benefits and downsides to each:

Advantages of the Notaire

- O Conveyancing is the notaire's main undertaking, which means he is best placed to know all the loopholes and ramifications involved.
- O The notaire has a escrow bank account meaning that he is able to hold all monies relating to the property safely in his possession until the final contract has been signed.

Disadvantages of the Notaire

- O Will not offer impartial advice.
- O Will draw up more generic-style contracts.
- O Is immersed in government bureaucracy.

Advantages of the Avocat

- O Offers impartial advice.
- O There is no 0.5% notarial tax to pay.
- O More likely to speak English.
- O Will write up tailor-made contracts to suit the individual.

Disadvantages of the Avocat

○ Conveyancing is not their main activity and many will still be quite new to it, which means there is the potential to miss out vital information.

○ Does not have an escrow bank account, which means that all monies will have to be transferred directly from the buyer to the seller or via the avocat, but this is not secure.

○ Less accountable as they work for themselves and are not appointed by the state.

THE PRELIMINARY CONTRACT (COMPROMIS DE VENTE)

Following the verbal offer (written offers are not common in Morocco) and agreement on the price between you and the seller, the first step is for the no-taire to draw up the preliminary contract called the *Compromis de Vente*. This contract is binding both on you and the seller. After receiving the Compromis de Vente you have a 2 week cooling off period to decide whether you wish to proceed with the purchase (the cooling off period is either heeded as a particu-lar timeframe or not, you would be advised to check). If you do, you will sign the contract and return it to the notaire. Even if your French is adequate, you would be wise to get the document legally translated, to ensure that you fully understand its content and then, if possible to check it through with a solicitor in the UK. At the time of signing the contract, which for the Compromis de Vente, does not need to be done in front of a notaire, you will also be expected to provide a deposit of 10% of the sale price. You pay this directly into the notaire's escrow bank account. He will give you all his banking details. Do not pay it to the estate agent. If you do not proceed with the transaction and as-suming all the get out clauses have been met, you will lose the deposit. If the seller does not complete the transaction, the deposit will be returned to you. In both cases, the Compromis de Vente will be null and void. When you are entirely happy with the contract, you should initial the first two pages, date it on the last page and add your full signature(s) preceded by the words '*bon pour achat*'.

The Content of the Compromis de Vente, though not conclusive, should include the following information:

○ Name, date of birth, nationality and identification card number of the Seller(s).
○ Name, date of birth, nationality, passport number of the Buyer(s).
○ Address of the property.
○ Total surface area or habitable area of the property.
○ Description of the property.
○ Proof that the seller is the rightful owner through identification and ownership documents.

O A breakdown of the condition you must accept the property in.

O Your responsibility for all taxes and charges relating to the property from the date of possession.

O Responsibility by the buyer for all purchasing costs.

O Agreed selling price.

O Receipt of deposit.

O Get out Clauses (*Conditions Suspensives*) and a set date for when they must be met.

O Penalties if one of the parties withdraws from the transaction.

O Statement claiming the seller to be prohibited from selling the property to anyone else.

O Statement requiring the seller to provide proof that any mortgage on the property is cleared by the date of the signing of the final contract – *Acte de Vente.*

O You will also be given a photocopied land registry map and asked to verify the exact location of your property.

The Get Out Clauses

The get out clauses (conditions suspensives) are very important and are an area where legal advice can be very helpful. If, for example, you are awaiting approval from a mortgage lender either in the UK or Morocco, this should be added as a clause stating that the final contract is dependent on obtaining the necessary finance. You are also wise, especially if buying land but also with houses as well, to state that the signing of the final contract is dependent on the obtaining of building permission and, where applicable, the VNA licence (see *What Type of Property to Buy?*).

Tenants

Many properties in Morocco are rented out to extended families of tenants who, unless you have specifically agreed their date of departure in a contract, will not leave your property despite the fact that you are the official owner. Dreadful stories abound of excited new homeowners turning up at their new house to find it filled with people who will not leave. Many sellers will claim to not being able to remove the tenants until they have received the money from selling the property, as they need it to buy somewhere new. In this instance, what you must do is ask the notaire to add a clause into the contract stating a departure date for the tenants, stipulating that any day past the agreed departure date will incur a rental fee of a set amount. You could also ask the notaire to withhold paying the full amount to the seller until he has proved all the tenants are gone. This tends to procure a speedy response.

Under Declaring the Sales Price

While under declaring the sales price in order to save on fees and taxes is illegal with the government in the throes of a crackdown to start controlling it, you will find that many people still accept it as the 'done' thing. Very occasionally you can adamantly refuse and the seller might just agree, but it is the accepted route and generally unavoidable. It tends to happen at the Compromis de Vente stage. Into the contract, the notaire will under declare the sales price claiming it to be a couple of hundred-thousand dirham less than it is. On a separate legally certified document, he will then state that you must pay the difference to the seller. Into the final document, the Acte de Vente, the notaire, will write the actual sales price. Doing it this way, both the buyer and seller benefit from lower property purchasing taxes, while the buyer does not actually have higher capital gains tax to pay as the real sales figure is stipulated on the Acte de Vente, which is the only document that stays on record,

Before the Signing of the Final Contract

Between the signing of the Compromis de Vente and the signing of the final contract, the Acte de Vente, anything from a couple of weeks to a couple of years can elapse, depending on how straightforward your purchase is. During this time, the notaire will visit the Conservation Foncière to check on the status of the property ie; does it have any outstanding loans, and is it titled? He will also put in a request for the cadastral department of the Conservation Foncière to visit the property or land to measure out the exact boundaries.

TITLE DEEDS

Regardless of what anyone tells you, it is very unwise to purchase a property or land without obtaining the title deeds, even if this extends the purchasing process by a couple of years. If you do not have title deeds, you can never be sure that the property or land that you have paid for actually belongs to you. Stories arise of people privately buying land and building luxurious villas only to be informed that the previous owners would like the land back as it is still officially theirs, villa and all. If you build on to land without title deeds, it is unlikely the Urban/Rural Commune will issue you with a Permis d'Habitation, which means you are unable to obtain water, phone lines or electricity.

Most modern properties ie: those built within the last 20-30 years within urban perimeters, should already be titled. This means that when you buy a property, there is just the simple process of transferring the title deeds to your names, which amounts to 1% of the property purchase price. Most renovated riads in the medina, especially those being sold by Europeans, will have title deeds, whereas most unrenovated ones, will not. When you buy new properties, the developers will transfer the title deeds from the land, which is under their name into your name for your individual plot. In most other circumstances, it is likely that the property or land you buy will be untitled.

The Adoul. In place of the title deeds, which are legally certified by the notaire, many untitled properties and land you come across will have a contract known as *melkia*, written up in the form of a scripture by an *adoul* who is an official scribe used in the days before the notaire. Many such documents can date back hundreds of years, handwritten in old-fashioned Arabic. The adoul will have documented the names of the landowners, the boundaries of the land or property and how much they paid to purchase it. The number of owners a property/land has will dictate how many pages are in the scripture. Deciphering it is a long, arduous task but not as arduous a task as tracking down all the names it holds.

Obtaining Title Deeds. There are two stages to the obtaining of the title deeds. The first is undertaken by the notaire, whose job it is to track down all the named owners of the property, wherever they may be. Once tracked down, each family member needs to consent to the sale going ahead. This can be an emotional time especially if the price is not agreed and family arguments and break ups are a common feature of such proceedings. Agreement to sell must be signed by each of the family members and witnessed by the notaire. As many people, especially in rural regions are illiterate, a thumbprint is approved in place of a signature. If you are fortunate, the titling process can be relatively straightforward ie; there are only a couple of family members to track down and all consent quite happily. Worse case scenario is that it can take up to two years if the family is very extended, although this is rare.

The signing of the final contract, the *Acte de Vente* takes place when the title deeds are transferred from seller to buyer. The Acte de Vente is recorded with the Conservation Foncière and your name registered as the new owner. At this stage, however, you do not have the official title deeds instead you have what is known as a requisite title. This is almost as good as a title ie; you can sell the house with just a requisite title, but it is worthwhile, more for peace of mind, to obtain the real titles deeds as soon as you can.

The procedure for obtaining the real deeds can take up to a year, as certain activities have to be undertaken. These include, the Cadastre sending out a surveyor to measure the ground surface area of the property and also a notice, advertising the transfer of ownership being displayed both in the Cadastre and Urban/Rural Commune for 4 months, giving people the opportunity to contest the title ie; if there is an outstanding loan on the property, for example. This is known as a periode d'opposition– it is highly unlikely, especially if the notaire has done his homework properly, that anyone will ever contest.

Draft of Final Contract (Projet de l'acte)

Around one month prior to the signing of the Acte de Vente, you will be sent a document called the *projet de l'acte*. This is a draft of the final contract, which must be checked by you. Even though its content is unlikely to differ widely from the Compromis de Vente, it is again, worth shelling out the cash to get it officially translated. It is, after all, the draft of a very important document. It is also at this stage that you should set in motion the transfer of funds for the purchase of your property from your UK bank account into your convertible Moroccan account to ensure that everything is in place for the day. Do not forget that on top of the actual purchase price there will be the cost of the fees and taxes, so be sure to transfer enough.

Power of Attorney

If, for any reason, you or your partner is unable to attend the actual signing of the Acte de Vente, it is important you find someone you can trust with the Power of Attorney to sign on your behalf. The notaire will write up the Power of Attorney document for you. It must contain the following information:

- The name, nationality and passport number of the person who is giving the Power of Attorney.
- The name, nationality and identity card or passport number of the person who is receiving the Power of Attorney.
- Address and brief description of the property in question.
- Price of the property in question.

The document must be signed by the person giving the Power of Attorney. If they are in Morocco, the signing needs to be witnessed by a notaire. If they are in the UK, the signing will have to be witnessed by the Moroccan Consulate in London, who will take a photocopy of the passport and verify it with a 50 dirham (£3) stamp.

THE FINAL CONTRACT (ACTE DE VENTE)

En-route to the notaire's office for the signing of the final acte, you are advised to make a brief detour via the property or land you are about to purchase just to make sure it is still standing, no walls have been knocked down, everything agreed to be in the house is in the house and the boundaries look the same as they did the day before. This might sound paranoid, but check, check and check again is the best motto for undertaking any kind of business transaction in Morocco.

Most people will admit to being more than a little tense on the day of the signing especially as it is likely the seller will have brought half his extended family with him who will be eyeing you up suspiciously or at least, it will feel that way. In addition to the seller, there will be the notaire, sitting behind his desk, the notaire's clerk invariably running around getting all the last minute paperwork in place, the estate agent and a translator in the room. Everyone will be chatting away in Arabic, like old friends and you can be forgiven for feeling a little outnumbered.

The notaire will present you with the Acte de Vente and the translator will go through it with you word for word explaining anything, which might appear unclear. Prior to signing the contract, the notaire will request the payment for the property and the additional payment of all fees and taxes. This includes estate agent's commission. The best payment method and the one most notaires are happiest with, is a banker's draft or certified cheque drawn up by your local branch in the name of the notaire. This takes seconds to do, is free of charge and is proof for the notaire of cleared funds in your account. It is likely you will be asked to write a separate cheque to pay the fees and taxes. All the funds go into the notaire's escrow account and he will make the individual payments from there. There will also be a payment to the translator, which you pay directly. The Acte de Vente is signed by the seller and the buyer and stamped and verified by the notaire at which time you become the owner of the property.

UK Based Lawyers

The International Property Law Centre: Suffolk House, 21 Silver Street, Hull HU1 1JG; ☎ 0870 800 4565; e-mail internationalproperty@maxgold.com; fax 0870 800 4567; www.internationalpropertylaw.com. Specialists in the purchase and sale of property and businesses in Morocco, with in-house foreign lawyers. Fixed quote and no VAT payable. Contact Stefano Lucatello, Senior Partner, (☎ 0870 800 4565, e-mail stefanol@maxgold.com).

Recommended Notaires and Lawyers in Morocco

Maitre Wahid El Khiry, 16, rue El Houcine Ben Ali, ex Murdoch, Casablanca; ☎ 022 22 07 83/ 22 27 55 36; fax 022 20 12 57.

Maitre Said Serrah, 26, rue de Constantinople, Casablanca; ☎: 022 80 15 77; fax 022 80 07 57.

Leila Najieddine, apt 1, 281 Boulevard Al Massira, Casablanca; ☎ 02 22 25 68 02.

Maitre Ali Ait Lahcen, Villa no 17 Bis, Avenue Aqaba, Quartier des Dunes, Essaouira; ☎ 044 47 51 00; fax 044 47 51 01.

Maitre Adil Berrada, Boulevard Youssef Ibn Tachefine, Residence El Afif 6,Tangier. 90000; ☎ 039 32 25 21; fax 039 32 25 22.

Maitre Fouad Bensouda, Ave des FAR, Immeuble Ettajmouti, Fes; ☎ 055 64 33 75.

Maitre Mohamed Benjelloun Benkacem, 38 bis, Avenue Mohamed Slaoui, Fes; ☎ 055 94 21 69/055 94 21 70; fax 055 94 21 71; e-mail etude-ben@menara. ma.

Leila Lakhdar, 36 Agl, rue Ibn Aicha et Allal Ben Ahmed, Gueliz, Marrakech; ☎ 044 43 35 42; fax 044 43 37 15.

Boualam Mohamed Azzeddine, 6 Rue des Vieux Marrakchis Apt No 6, 2ème Etage, Gueliz, Marrakech; ☎ 044 43 53 78; fax 044 43 98 15.

Maitre Malika Sedki, 7 Avenue Ferhat Hachad, Mohammedia; ☎ 023 32 18 76; fax 023 32 19 34; email mesedki@hotmail.com

Part IV

WHAT HAPPENS NEXT

SERVICES

MAKING THE MOVE

BUILDING OR RENOVATING

MAKING MONEY FROM YOUR PROPERTY

SERVICES

CHAPTER SUMMARY

- **Drinking water**. The *Office National de l'Eau Potable*(ONEP), is responsible for the production of Morocco's drinking water.
- Drinking water is distributed by the public Régies the private Concessionaires and ONEP.
- Water bills are sent out by post every 3 months.
- **Wells**. Water diviners are most commonly used for locating groundwater prior to digging a well.
- **Electricity**. Despite a long process of liberalisation, Morocco's electricity is still a monopoly of the Office of National Electricity (ONE)
  - The main bodies responsible for the distribution of electricity are the public Régies the private Concessionaires and ONE.
- **Solar power**. By 2007, it is expected 1 million Moroccans will have solar power.
- **Gas**. There is no mains gas in Morocco. Everyone uses bottled propane or butane.
- **Telephones**. There are around 1 million fixed line telephone users in Morocco versus 8 million mobile phone users.
- **Staff**. The majority of foreigners in Morocco employ a cleaner or housekeeper.

WATER

In Morocco's urban areas, water is almost universally safe to drink (98%). It is, however, still considered 'dodgy' by the majority of foreigners who avoid it out of principle as opposed to necessity, in favour of bottled mineral water. In the countryside and for Morocco's urban poor, potable or drinkable water is supplied to just 58% of households, a figure the government aims to increase to 92% by 2008 through its National Programme for Rural Water Supply and Sanitation (PAGER). Currently, however, around 38% are reliant on the self-provision of water through ground or surface sources. Many of the very poor living in urban slums or run down medina homes who are unable to afford a connection to the national water supply, still use communal wells or informal water vendors who often charge 10 times the price of public suppliers simply by selling containers of utility supplied water.

The main body responsible for the production of drinking water is ONEP (*Office national de l'eau potable*), which also distributes it to around 300 small to medium sized towns (28% of the urban population). In the majority of cities, however, water is distributed by municipally owned (and generally under funded) Régies (31% of the urban population). This is with the exception of the coastal cities of Casablanca, Rabat, Tangier and Tetouan, where it is supplied by privately owned consortiums called Concessionaires (38% of the urban population). Tariffs for the Régies are currently controlled by the Prime Minister although this is set to change in the near future when the individual bodies will be permitted to regulate their own costs in addition to the charges relating to water connections. Private Concessionaires control their own rates. Water is metered with a bill sent out by post every 3 months. This is paid directly to the Régies, Concessionaires or local ONEP buildings either by going to the desk (*guichet*), which generally requires a bit of a wait or in some cases, by depositing payment in a box at the front door, which will be acknowledged with a receipt a few days later. It is also possible to pay via direct debit at the bank. At the time of writing water tariffs ranged between 2.64dh/m3 (16p) in the region of Meknes and 7.16dh/ cu meters (44p) in Greater Casablanca. Both Régies and Concessionaires also provide electricity and sanitation services.

In order to get your water supply turned on, you will need to provide your Permis d'Habitation or Acte de Vente (see *What Type of Property to Buy?*) and your residence card (*carte de sejour*) or passport to the relevant public utilities supplier (*Régies, Concessionaires or ONEP*). The Régies and Concessionaire are known by different names depending on the city you are in:

City	Water Supplier	Known as the..
Tangier and Tetouan	Concessionnaire consortium for Tangier and Tetouan	AMENDIS
Greater Casablanca	Concessionaire consortium for Greater Casablanca	LYDEC
Settat	Régie Autonome de Distribution de Settat	RADEEC
Fes	Régie Autonome de Distribution d'Eau et d'Electicité de Fes	RADEEF
El Jadida	Régie Autonome de Distribution d'El Jadida	RADEEJ
Larache	Régie Autonome de Distribution de Larache	RADEEL

Meknes	Régie Autonome de Distribution de Meknès	RADEEM
Marrakech	Régie Autonome de Distribution de Marrakech	RADEEMA
Nador	Régie Autonome de Distribution de Nador	RADEEN
Oujda	Régie Autonome de Distribution d'Oujda	RADEEO
Safi	Régie Autonome de Distribution de Safi	RADEES
Beni Mellal	Régie Autonome de Distribution de Beni Mellal	RADEET
Taza	Régie Autonome de Distribution de Taza	RADEETA
Kenitra	Régie Autonome de Distribution de Kenitra	RAK
Agadir	Régie Autonome de Distribution d'Agadir	RAMSA
Rabat	Concessionaire consortium for Greater Rabat	REDAL

Morocco's private water companies, the Concessionaires are owned by international water suppliers. LYDEC, the Concessionaire for greater Casablanca has been owned since 1997, by the Franco-Spanish consortium, Suez-Lyonnaise des Eaux, REDAL, the Concessionaire for Greater Rabat has since 2002, been a wholly-owned subsidiary of French group Veolia Environnement. AMENDIS, the Concessionaire for Tangiers and Tetouan since January 2002, is the first consortium to involve Moroccan private parties. Its ownership includes Veolia Environnement of France (51 percent), Hydro-Québec of Canada (18 percent), and the Moroccan companies ONA (16 percent) and SOMED (15 percent). By contract, Moroccan ownership cannot drop below 31 percent.

Buying Land with Water

The very first thing you must do before falling in love with a piece of land is make sure it has access to water. If there is no visible water on the land you might be told that everyone in the surrounding area has water so you do too. This, however, is not always the case. Not all land has water. The most obvious way of looking for water is to see if there are any surface sources such as streams, rivers, springs or entry points to wells. Bear in mind, though that just because there is, for example, a stream running through your land at the time of your visit, this does not guarantee it will be flowing all year round. Streams, particularly in hot, arid countries like Morocco, run the risk of drying up during the summer months (or at the other extreme, flooding during the rainy season). Your best bet is to check the water levels at different times throughout the year or, if this is not possible, ask local people.

A spring occurs when the water seeps to the surface through, for example, a crack in a rock. If you are interested in purchasing land with a spring on it, do not be put off if the spring water looks like it is little more than a trickle. A constant trickle over the course of a minute can turn into a lot of water over the course of a day when you have a holding tank to gather the water. It might be worth calculating the flow of the spring, ideally during the hottest months, simply by measuring how much seeps out during a minute and multiplying this by 60 to calculate the flow per hour and then by 24 to calculate the flow per day.

While surface water sources are excellent for irrigation etc, they are not reliable for providing clean drinking water. The only way this can be sought is by digging underground. You might be highly fortunate and buy land that already comes with a well. This is usually the case if your land has a farmhouse attached. More often than not, however, you will have to provide your own water source. Groundwater can be found in permeable materials such as clay, sand or gravel or limestone and sandstone, which are common ground materials in Morocco.

The bureau responsible for water resources is the *Administration de l'Hydraulique* with offices in most towns and cities throughout Morocco. They usually have a map indicating depth and location of groundwater for individual regions. Most commonly used, however, are water diviners, particularly where groundwater levels are known to be shallow such as around Marrakech where you rarely need to dig deeper than 20-30meters. In these instances, the whole process of digging a well costs in the region of 80,000-100,000 dh (£5000-6250).

In other parts of Morocco, groundwater is much deeper underground, requiring wells to be drilled with heavy machinery. The cost of drilling a well is dependent on the depth of the groundwater, the accessibility of the surrounds and the toughness of the earth. Price tends to be charged per meter and costs in the region of 500-2000 dh (£31-£125).

You will need to get any water found, fully tested before attempting to drink it. This can be arranged by the Administration de l'Hydraulique.

In order to draw water from the well, you will most probably need to install a pump, this is unless your water source is for example up a hill or slope, where it can flow downwards, in which case you can rely on a gravity flow system. If your well is very shallow (around 6 meters deep), you can most probably get away with having a gasoline powered centrifugal pump, which sucks water up and forces it out. Your best bet, however, would be an electric pump such as the electric submersible well pump, which is placed at the bottom of the well and can force water up (around 10 gallons per minute from 60 metres down). The electric pump does require electricity, which will be a consideration if you are buying land away from the national grid.

ELECTRICITY

Despite the decade-long process of liberalisation for the electricity sector, Morocco's domestic supply of electricity remains a monopoly of the public utility *Office of National Electricity* (ONE), which was created in 1963 and holds 4th position among the 500 biggest Moroccan enterprises. ONE's role is to generate/transmit power and to distribute electricity to a number of provinces around Morocco, particularly in rural regions. Be warned, however, despite a price drop of 28% over the last 6 years, it does not come cheap. In fact, you are unlikely to find much difference between the rates charged for your UK electricity supply and your Moroccan, which can come as quite a shock when so many other prices in Morocco are much lower.

The Ministry of the Interior oversees the domestic electricity consumption, which is distributed in most large cities via the municipally owned Régies (who also distribute water, see above), in smaller towns/villages directly from ONE or, in the case of Rabat, Casablanca, Tangier and Tetouan, through the private Concessionaires, LYDEC, REDAL and AMENDIS. With the exception of the individual rates set by private Concessionaires, electricity tariffs are, for the time being, set by the Prime Minister. Bills are sent on the 15th of every month and like water bills, can be paid directly to the Régies, the Concessionaires or ONE's local office, or via a direct debit system set up with your bank.

ELECTRICITY TARIFFS

Monthly Consumption	*Price per kWh inc all taxes in dirham*
0 to 100kWh/month	0.8420dh
101 to 200kWh/month	0.9055dh
201 to 500kWh/month	0.9851dh
More than 500kWh/month	1.3464dh

Price between 5-8 pence per kWh

If, for example, you use 357kWh of electricity per month, the price is calculated as follows:

For the first 100kWh, you are charged 0.8420 dh per kWh. For the next 100kWh, you are charged 0.9055 dh per kWh and for the final 157kWh, you are charged 0.9851 per kWh. The total of your bill will therefore be 339.76 dh (£21). In addition to this, you will also have a monthly charge of around 13 dh (80p) for the meter and a maintenance fee of around 10 dh (62p), which also appear on the bill.

Getting Connected. When you move into your new home, you will have to contact your local electricity supplier (see above) to switch names from the previous owner to your own. Sometimes when sellers move out they ask for the power to be turned off, as they are worried that they will keep being charged. In these instances, you will need to request for the electricity to be turned back on, which, although promised to take 24 hours can in some places, take up to a week. Also be warned that sometimes sellers move out without paying their electricity bills, which means that unless you inform the electricity supplier quickly that you have moved in, the debt will fall to you.

In order to get connected, you will need to present the electricity supplier with your Permis d'Habitation or Acte de Vente (see *What Type of Property to Buy?*), an application form, which can be downloaded from www.one.org.ma and your residence permit (carte de sejour) or passport. An appointment then needs to be arranged with the electricity supplier to arrange the connection. An individual connection of 6kWh or less, costs 186 dh (£11).

Renewable Energy. Around 60% of national power comes from the Jorf Lasfar power plant owned by a Swiss and American consortium. The Moroccan government is on a binge to electrify the whole country by 2007 via its Global Rural Electricity Programme (PERG). Much of this will be through the use of solar power, particularly in the more remote villages, where it would cost too much for connection to the national grid. By 2007, it is expected that around 1 million Moroccans will use solar power. Quite how effective the panels on offer are, however, is questionable. At the subsidised price of around 65dh/month (£4) 12 volt panels offer 50 watts, enough to power 4-8 light bulbs and a television, but not enough for a fridge, which requires bigger panels at a higher cost (too high a cost for around 20% of solar customers).

Wind power is also a fast growing area. A 50.4 MW wind park with 84 turbines in Tetouan covers 2% of Morocco's energy consumption and 2 more large parks are being built in Tangier and Essaouira, financed by ONE and expected to become operational in 2007.

Voltage. Morocco, on the whole uses the same electricity voltage as Europe, 220 volts 50 cycles, although some properties, mainly older ones tend to use 110 volts. Two pin, European style round plugs are the norm so adaptors will be needed for goods with British style plugs.

SANITATION

While Morocco's urban water supply is of a satisfactory quality, its sanitation operations are less so with around 30-50% of capacity lost due to clogging and frequent (highly unpleasant) sewer overflows. As with the water, the main sanitation providers are the 13 municipally owned Régies for most cities, the private Concessionaires (for the large coastal cities) and ONEP for smaller towns and rural regions. As is so often the case in Morocco, it is the rural regions, which suffer most from lack of developed sewage facilities (42% versus 80.4% of urban dwellers) with 28% of rural inhabitants providing their own sewage facilities through for example, septic tanks.

There are no regulations regarding the use of septic tanks in Morocco, except, obviously that they should be positioned a fair distance from a clean water pump to avoid the risk of contamination. A septic tank is a large, underground watertight container of around 9 feet long, 4 feet wide and 5 feet tall that is connected to the sewer line running from the house. Raw wastewater flows into the tank where the heavier solids separate from the liquid and sink to the bottom of the tank to be broken down by bacteria. Light waste such as soap suds float to the top to form a layer of scum, which needs to be pumped out, while the liquid flows into a network of underground perforated pipes, connected to the tank.

GAS

There is no mains gas (*gaz de ville*) in Morocco. Everyone uses bottled propane or butane, which is known as *Butagaz* for heating up ovens, hobs and hot water heaters (better to use gas for water heaters than electricity as it means you can enjoy unlimited hot water). If your kitchen appliances are located close together, you can most probably get away with having one gas bottle and a branching hose otherwise you will need one bottle per appliance. You will originally need to buy a full bottle of gas for a deposit of around 150 dh (£9). When finished, you return the empty bottle and get a full one for simply the price of the gas. Although, remember to keep a receipt for the original bottle or you could be charged again.

Many foreigners are not used to using bottled gas and it is important to note that if used incorrectly, it can be deadly. Always make sure there is some ventilation, an open door or window to the outside, when using a bottled gas appliance. If you smell gas and are unable to ascertain where the odour is coming from, open the windows, turn off the bottle via the knob at the top and replace it. Do not turn on an electric light or spark up a match until you are absolutely sure the gas is switched off and the odour has passed.

When working with bottled gas, it is important that you buy a high quality automatic regulator. These can be obtained at any decent appliance shop such as the *Comptoir* or *Marjane* hypermarket. Cheaper regulators if adjusted wrongly can give a much higher gas pressure to appliances, which can be dangerous. The role of the regulator is to adjust the gas pressure to the appliance, so that it is constantly maintained at an industry standard pressure. Also if you are renting out your house, you might consider buying a gas alarm. These work in a similar way to smoke alarms sounding a deafeningly loud noise, if there is a gas leak.

TELEPHONE

Fixed Line. There are currently only a little over one million fixed line subscribers in Morocco versus 8 million mobile phone users. This is because fixed line tariffs are comparatively expensive and phone lines limited to around 5.2 per 100 people, which does little to satisfy Moroccans unquenchable desire to chat. As a foreigner living in Morocco, you might prefer to have a fixed line, however, so that you can speak more cheaply to family and friends overseas and have access to the internet.

The main fixed line telecom provider is Maroc Telecom, although two new fixed line licences have recently been awarded to Meditel and Maroc Connect, who are planning big investments into the sector. Provided there are phone lines in the general vicinity of your house, the installation of a line is relatively straightforward involving a visit to the Post Office or local Maroc Telecom office, to fill in an application form. You will need to show your Permis d'Habitation or Acte de Vente (see *What Type of Property to Buy?*) as well as your residence permit or passport. If you do not have telephone lines close by or are in an area where there is a high demand for lines, installation can take a long time (up to 4 months) and requires endless trips to the Post Office or Maroc Telecom to spur them into action. Installation cost is around 500 dh (£31) plus 20% VAT with a minimum monthly charge of 70 dh (£4). Local and national calls are charged between 0.16-1.2dh/minute with a 50% overnight and weekend reduction. International calls to Europe cost around 4dh/minute (25p) and to the US, around 6dh/minute (37p). Phone bills are sent out monthly and can be paid either automatically through the bank via direct debit or by cheque to the bank.

Mobile Phones

Mobile phones are known as p*ortables* (pronounced *port-ar-ble).*

Pay-As-You-Go. If you are not planning on living in Morocco all year round and simply want a Moroccan mobile phone for making local calls, then you would benefit the most from using a pay-as-you-go system crediting your phone from units on a phone card available from téléboutiques (in abundance in every town, city and village). The main advantage of this system is that there are no monthly charges or bills. Once the phone has been bought you can use it as little or as much as you like for simply the price of a phone card. There are often good deals on phone cards, for example, 400 dirham worth of service for 200 dh. The downside is, however, that even the most expensive phone card barely covers an overseas connection let alone a chat and most phone cards expire after 3 months, which means that if you are out of Morocco for an extended period of time, you will have to get a new phone card regardless of how many units had been used on the old.

Subscription. If you are living in Morocco for most of the year, then you could consider a mobile phone subscription. These come with a 12 or 24 month contract, a one off set up fee of 100 dh (£6.25), which is added to your first bill and a monthly charge of 125 dh (£7). There are also a number of tariffs to choose from which best suit your needs such as cheap evening and weekend calls. Normal rate national calls tend to cost around 2dh/minute (12p), calls to Europe around 8dh/minute (50p) and to the US around 9dh/minute (56p). Phone bills are sent out monthly and can be paid either automatically through the bank via direct debit or by cheque to the bank.

The main mobile phone providers are Maroc Telecom and Meditel. Maroc Telecom tends to have wider coverage particularly in rural areas.

DOMESTIC STAFF

Most foreigners and a large number of Moroccans hire domestic staff to help with cleaning, cooking, laundry, security and odd jobs. This is so much the norm that you are actually considered strange (and a little bit mean) if you do not. Usually the people you employ to work for you are divorced, single or widowed women or those with husbands too lazy (or drunk) to work. It is highly probable that the wages you pay will be the only income the extended family receives (not that you should feel this a pressure). The most sought after employers for these women are foreigners, ideally Europeans or North Americans who not only pay better but also tend to treat staff well and the most coveted job is the full time role of *femme de ménage* or housekeeper.

Femme de Ménage. The femme de ménage traditionally runs the domestic side of the house, from laundry and cleaning to, if desired, cooking and shopping. As Morocco is so culturally different to Europe you will need to be very prescriptive about how you want jobs done. The most ideal femmes de ménage are those who have already worked for foreigners so have an idea of their standards and attitudes. If you employ someone with no experience, you will have to spend much time training them so that they understand what you like and how you like it.

Many people prefer a part time helper who comes in every day for a couple of hours or just a couple of days a week to clean. How much help you require completely depends on the size of your house, the number in your household, whether or not you are renting out your house/rooms to holidaymakers and how much work you are prepared to do yourself. It is worth noting that in

Morocco, the lack of technology means that just doing the most simple activity can take a very long time; buying gas, paying an electricity bill, waiting while the shopkeeper looks for change for your 100 dh note, returns from prayers at the mosque or opens up his shop after the siesta. Trying to get a lot done in one day is invariably impossible, so at least having a maid means that someone else can take responsibility for keeping the house in order. They also can be a great source of information, help and support when you are new to a country and only speak a little French, taking you under their wing and introducing you to society, local norms and customs that make you feel much more at home.

Security and Handyman. It is also worth considering having a man about the house especially if you plan to be away for long periods of time. There are many young men desperate for a foot into European society even if it is by way of fixing light bulbs and carrying wood. The man around the house can guard the house for you in your absence, keep the fires lit and swept, carry your bags, buy gas, sweep the leaves, get taxis and run errands. Do not expect them to do 'women's work as they won't and nor will many women step into the man's domain. Roles tend to be strictly segregated in Moroccan society.

Hiring Staff
Paying Cash. Most hiring of domestic staff is done on a cash in hand, unde-clared basis. This arrangement is better for the staff as they do not need to declare their wages, and for you as you do not need to pay them more to cover the high taxation. You would be advised, however, to draw up some sort of employment contract, which both you and they sign so that you have something to fall back on should the relationship sour. The contract should ideally cover a 3-6 month employment period. If everything is still working out well after this time period, you can draw up another contract for a further 3-6 months and so on. Even if everything seems to be working well, you would be wise to have a contract. With-out one it will be much harder to terminate the working relationship should you need/want to.

Rate of pay again depends on how much work you want done. If you ask your staff how much he/she wants to get paid, they will throw the ball uncomfortably back into your court and say, 'how much do you want to pay me?' Be prepared for this. Prior to talking money with a Moroccan be sure to have some figures in your head that you are happy to pay. Moroccans are incredibly shrewd when it comes to money. They know the going rate for everything, how much all of their friends get paid and which Europeans are the least/most generous. Ask fellow Europeans what they are paying their staff and base your figures on this. While payments vary, based on location, the amount of work done and experience of the femme de ménage, you could work on the following guidelines bearing in mind that the minimum wage is 1,841.84 dh per month (£115) for full time workers:

1000dh/month (£62) for a part time femme de ménage (3 days a week)
2000dh/month (£125) for a full time femme de ménage (5 days a week).

Official Employment. There might be circumstances when you wish you to employ staff on an official basis. This is likely to be the case if you are running your property as a guesthouse/hotel and it has company status. In these circumstances an official contract is drawn up between you (the company) and the employee. This can be either a fixed term or a permanent contract. If it is a permanent contract, the employee will be eligible for compensation should they be made redundant. This is equivalent to:

- 48 days pay for 5 years of service
- 72 days pay 6-10 years of service
- 96 days pay for 11- 15 years of service
- 120 days pay for 15 years of service and above

In addition to their salaries, the employer must pay social service contribution amounting to 17% of the gross monthly salary. All employees are entitled to a paid leave of absence after 6 months of continuous work. One and a half working days for each month of service, 2 days for employees under 18.

Your Relationship with Staff. Foreigners, particularly Europeans and North Americans have the reputation in Morocco of being excellent to work for. This is not only because they pay better and tend to add bonuses and tips to work extra well done, but also because they treat staff very well. In some cases too well, so much so that the domestic staff start considering themselves on an equal footing with their employer, stop working and start spending their salaried hours sitting drinking cups of tea/chatting to friends outside the front door/bossing you around in your own house and generally taking advantage of your kind nature. This often happens when the employer is new to a foreign speaking country and keen to find anyone who can help them get to grips with comprehending day-to-day life. Your domestic staff will appear so knowledgeable (much like you would to a non English speaking Moroccan if they came to the UK) and you will rely on them more and more to handle issues relating to your life. Before you know it, they are not so much domestic staff as bosom buddies. This is when things go wrong. How do you then reverse the relationship into one of boss and employer especially after they have helped you out so much, invited you to meet their family, scrubbed your back in the hammam and know all the ins and outs of your life in Morocco? The answer is: with great difficulty. No matter how much you are in need of someone to show you the ropes, make it ideally an unpaid individual who can become a friend. For your domestic staff set the ground rules for the relationship on day one and stick to them. They will respect you more if you are professional with them as this is what they would expect from a Moroccan employer.

MAKING THE MOVE

CHAPTER SUMMARY

O **Local furnishings**. Half the fun of owning a house in Morocco is to fill it with furnishings made by local artisans as opposed to shipping all your furniture from home.
O **Customs**. Clearance in Morocco can take from 2-14 days.
O **Foreign registered cars**. Bringing foreign registered cars into Morocco on a permanent basis incurs very high taxes and duties.
   O A temporary admissions document enables you to bring your car into Morocco for a maximum period of six months.
   O As soon as you enter Morocco with a vehicle, you must get it insured.
O **Pets**. In order to take your pet with you to Morocco, you need to have an Animal Health Certificate, which can be obtained from local DEFRA offices.
   O Pets travelling from Morocco into the UK do not qualify for the PETS Travel Scheme. When returning to the UK, they must enter quarantine for six months.

REMOVALS

The first thing to bear in mind when considering removals to Morocco is whether or not the furnishings that so well suit your northern European home will look good in an ancient riad, city apartment or coastal villa in your African home. Very often foreigners moving to Morocco assume they will yearn for all their home comforts so immensely that they bring them over often at great expense only to find them totally out of place and less comforting than they originally thought. Half the fun of owning a house in Morocco is to fill it with handmade furnishings made by skilled local artisans; tables, chairs, curtains and sofas, ornaments and wall hangings are sold in the souks and galleries, while white and electrical goods such as fridges and freezers, televisions and DVD players are available widely to buy or can be rented for very low prices. An increasing number of international removal companies are now including Morocco in their destinations, but some will only travel so far as customs and leave you to do the customs clearance and transporting. If you wish for a door-to-door delivery, you will need to verify at the start of your research with removals companies that this is one of the services they offer.

Your most likely shipping options will be for a 1000 cubic foot container (full 20ft container), a 500 cu ft container (half container) or a 250 cu ft case/crate, which would be sent as a Less than Container shipment (LCL). Although you are sending a smaller shipment of effects, the LCL option can actually work out comparatively more expensive than the container option as it requires the building of a purpose built crate specifically for your household goods. Prices for shipments tend to range between £2000-4000, exclusive of customs duties, taxes and insurance.

If you send your household goods to Morocco with a removals company, you will not need to be present at customs. Your shipment needs to be accompanied by an inventory of household goods (the removals company will do this) and will be physically inspected although household goods and personal effects in reasonable quantities can be imported into Morocco duty free so long as they have been owned for more than 6 months. You will also need to provide the removals company with a letter for customs giving permission for the destination agent to clear your shipment.

Customs clearance in Morocco can take anything from 2-14 days depending on how far in advance they receive your customs paperwork and how efficiently the paperwork has been filled in. In order to obtain clearance, you will need to provide customs with the following:

- A colour photocopy of your passport
- Residence Permit (carte de sejour)
- Inventory of shipment (this can be sent in English and will be translated into French by the destination agents in Morocco)
- Work contract (this is only necessary if you are going to Morocco for employment)
- Proof of property purchase (if you have bought property)
- Tenancy agreement (if you are renting property)

Timescale for Removals. The timescale for removals tends to be 2-3 days for packing up household goods and transporting them to the port. 9-10 days travel to Casablanca (the main port for shipments), 2-14 days for customs clearance and 3-5 days for delivery to your home.

Man with a Van

Hiring a van or a large car and driving it down to Morocco is currently the more popular option for bringing smaller furnishings and possessions into the country. Bear in mind that in order for you to take the van into the country duty-free, it needs to be strictly a utility vehicle with no side windows or seats (see *Temporary Admission* below). Be prepared for customs officials to search through every item of your baggage. If you have bought anything new to take to Morocco, you would be advised to remove it from its packaging and make it look as 'lived in' as possible in order to avoid drawing untoward attention to it and being charged duty.

ITEMS THAT ARE DUTIABLE, RESTRICTED OR PROHIBITED

Dutiable
- New items less than 6 months old. You will need to provide receipts for these.
- Electronic and electrical items.
- Antiques – detailed and valued inventory needed.

Restricted
- Medicine (a permit from the Ministry of Health required).
- Hunting arms – Firearm acquisition certificate and hunting permit needed.
- Food and alcohol – small quantities permitted.

Prohibited Items
- Moroccan currency.
- Pornographic and politically sensitive materials.
- Narcotics and drugs.
- Walkie Talkies.
- Explosives.

Useful Addresses
Federation of International Furniture Removers (FIDI); www.fidi.com
Fox Moving and Storage, 10 Somerset Road, Cwmbran, Gwent, NP44 1QX; ☎ 01633 866 923; fax 01633 873 026; www.fox-moving.com.
Bishops Move Overseas, Overseas House, 102-104 Stewart's Road, London SW8 4UG; ☎ 0207 501 4930; fax 0207 622 1794; www.bishopsmove.com.
Allied Pickfords, Heritage House, 345 Southbury Road, Enfield, Middlesex, EN1 1UP; ☎ 0208 219 8000; fax 0208 219 8001; www.allied-pickfords.co.uk, *Moroccan Customs*, www.douane.gov.ma.

IMPORTING A CAR

Temporary Admission. Due to the very high taxes and duties incurred on vehicles imported to Morocco, bringing foreign registered cars into the country is not a popular option. People that do, tend to do so only for short periods to, for example, transport household objects from their old homes to their new, taking advantage of the Temporary Admission scheme, which enables private vehicles to be imported into the country free of charge for 6 staggered or continuous months within a single calendar year (3 months for light utility vehicles such as minivans and pick up trucks).

The Temporary Admission document, known as the D16I, is issued to vehicles on arrival in the country, or can be downloaded off the Moroccan customs website (French/Arabic) at *www.douane.gov.ma*. Bear in mind that the Customs department does not take kindly to any vehicle that overstays its 6 month deadline without being either re-exported or officially cleared by customs with high penalties as well as standard duties and taxes to pay for any unregistered vehicle. Note that motorcycles over 50cc's are considered vehicles by the Moroccan Government.

Permanent Admission. If you wish to keep your car with you for a prolonged period (more than 6 months), you will need to be in possession of a residence permit (*carte de sejour*) prior to permanent registration.

Duties and taxes are currently set at 59.25% (including VAT) of the vehicles new, pre-tax value depending also on the cheval valeur (CV) of the car. This is a fiscal power rating introduced by the French, which relates to the size of the car's engine, a Renault 4 for example is 4 CV, a Land Rover Diesel is 10 CV, a Mercedes C220 petrol is 13 CV. Older cars are eligible for the following discounts:

- Less than 1 year old   0%
- Less than 2 years old   10%
- Less than 3 years old   20%
- 3 years old or more   25%

In order to register your car, you will need the following documentation:

- An international driver's licence or one from a European Union state.
- The vehicle registration document, known in Morocco as the *carte grise* or grey card. This was most likely issued to you when you originally bought the vehicle.
- Your residence permit (carte de sejour) or passport.
- The original receipt of purchase of vehicles 3 years old and under.
- A proxy issued by the owner and legally authorised in the country from which you are departing if the car does not belong to you but you are importing it for someone else.
- The Temporary Admission declaration relating to the vehicle, so that this can be ceased.

Until you have officially registered your car, it is illegal to sell it or use it for commercial purposes. Once it has been registered and duties paid, you will be issued with black on white number plates. If you are moving to Morocco for work in an embassy, an international organisation with its HQ in Morocco or a government office, you have the possibility of importing a car duty and tax-free. This will be issued with yellow number plates (*plaque jaune*). In order to obtain these plates, you will need to provide proof of work contracts and *attestation de travail* (work certificate).

As well as having high duties to pay, there are other disadvantages to importing a car to Morocco the main one being related to the fact that if you are coming from the UK, you will be manoeuvring a right hand drive vehicle in a country where cars drive on the right hand side. When roads in Morocco are already notoriously dangerous and the overtaking of cumbersome trucks on single carriageways a major pastime, do you want to up your risk by being unable to clearly see the road ahead? If you have really set your mind on bringing a car into Morocco, you might want to consider buying a car in France or Spain where prices are considerably lower than in the UK with the added benefit of being left hand drive.

Insurance and Road Tax. It is necessary to insure your car as soon as you drive into Morocco. The insurance document is known as the *carte verte* (green card). This can be initially obtained at ports of entry and costs in the region of 1800-3400 dh a year (£110-210) depending on the size of the vehicle, the CV and the intended usage. At the time of writing there are no known insurance companies outside Morocco, that offer primary liability insurance valid in Morocco. Road Tax (*vignette*) is obtained from the *Recette Fiscale*, which is in every neighbourhood and again the higher the CV the more you will pay. Cars with small engines are charged in the region of 600 dh (£37), large engines such as Land Rover 3000 dh (£185).

Buying Cars in Morocco. Instead of importing cars into Morocco, many people choose to buy second hand cars when there (Korean and Japanese are most highly recommended as they are cheaper with easily accessible spare parts and service departments with trained staff). Moroccans are not well known for looking after their vehicles. Few put the time into waxing and polishing their car bonnets on a Saturday morning. Regular servicing is a rarity, any servicing at all pretty unlikely and this is despite Morocco having some of the best and most innovative car mechanics in the world. Unless it is smoking, hobbling or stuck fast and blocking 4 lanes, few Moroccans will actually get their cars fixed. This means that a large number of second hand cars are in a pretty sorry state. The benefit of this is that, they are generally cheap to buy the downside is that most will probably not last very long. Your best bets are to buy an old banger very cheap and wear it out, buy from a foreigner who is likely to have put a bit more time into car maintenance or buy from a recommended second hand dealer where you will generally have to pay a little more but the car will come with a full warranty. Alternatively, it is possible to pick up a new car such as a small Kia, for around 100,000 dh (£6000). In order to buy a car in Morocco, you will need to be a resident and have a carte de sejour.

EXPORTING PETS TO MOROCCO

As Morocco is still afflicted by rabies, animals returning to the UK from Morocco do not qualify for the PETS Travel Scheme. This means that if you decide you want your furry friend to accompany you to your new house, it is likely to be on either a one-way ticket or with the grim prospect of 6 months in quarantine should you decide to move permanently back to the UK. It is also worth considering what you will do with your pets while in Morocco should you need to travel to and from the UK. Morocco is not a pet-crazed country. With great swathes of the population hitting their knuckles on the poverty line, animals kept 'for fun' are few and far between and tend to be more of the French coiffeured rat variety than the loveable Labrador. Unless you find a fellow animal loving expat to pamper your pets while you are away, you could find you are quite tied to them in the absence of anything resembling a cosy kennel or cattery.

That said, on an official level, making the move with an animal in tow is not a complicated procedure. You will need to obtain the application form for an Animal Health Certificate from your local Department of Food, Environment and Rural Affairs (DEFRA) office (see *www.defra.gov.uk/corporate/contacts/ahdo.htm* for regional locations). After filling this in, this gets returned to DEFRA who process it and send the export certificate on to your vet who will confirm that the following has been undertaken:

- Rabies vaccination (this needs to be given at least 30 days prior to departure)
- A declaration from you that the animal has been in the UK from birth or for the last 6 months
- A final check of the animal, which needs to be undertaken within 48 hours of your departure.

You will then travel to Morocco with the certificate and the pet.

Returning to the UK

If you choose to bring your pet back with you from Morocco, the six-month spell in quarantine is unavoidable. The best you can do is find a premises, which you think will best suit you and your pet. DEFRA has a list of all the authorised

quarantine establishments in the country, see http://www.defra.gov.uk/animalh/
quarantine/quarantine/qindex.htm info/map.htm.

In order to secure a place at the quarantine of your choice, you will need to
book it up well in advance of your arrival back to the UK especially if you are
returning during the holiday season. There is no need for any health certificates
or vaccinations when brining animals into the UK but be aware that not all ports
and airport accept animals for quarantine. These are the approved UK entry
points you can travel to with a pet from Morocco:

Ports

- Dover Eastern Docks
- Harwich, Parkeston Quay
- Hull
- Portsmouth
- Southampton

Airports

- Leeds
- Edinburgh
- Manchester
- London Gatwick
- London Heathrow
- Prestwick
- Glasgow
- Belfast

BUILDING OR RENOVATING

CHAPTER SUMMARY

O **Managing the works**. If you are simply giving your property a cosmetic facelift, it is likely you will be able to manage the works yourself.
  O Ensure prices agreed for works are inclusive of everything.
  O Never pay the builders the full sum in advance.
O **Building contractor**. If you are working with a building contractor, you are advised to obtain a certified contract especially if you are likely to be absent for much of the build.
  O Be sure to put clauses into the contract such as penalties for over running and bonuses for works completed on time and budget.
O **Building permission**. Works that require building permission must legally have plans drawn up by an architect.
  O It takes an average of two to three months to receive building permission. It comes in the form of a stamp on the plans.
O **Foreign architects**. It is not possible to hire a non-Moroccan architect to work on your property unless they work in conjunction with a Moroccan architect.
O **Architect fees**. To oversee a build from start to finish, architects will charge around 5% of the build price.
O **Signing off**. At the end of the build if the architect is content with the quality of the work, he/she will sign the property off with a *Certificat de Comformité*.
O **Receipts.** Keep all receipts and invoices relating to the build for tax purposes.
O **Restoring property**. It is highly unlikely that you will be able to simply buy your unrenovated *riad* and move in. The majority of properties need extensive renovations, which you will need to budget for.

> **O Artisans**. Morocco has some of the best artisans in the world.
> Take advantage of handmade furnishings.

As a short tour through any medina will verify, building and craftsmanship is in the blood of Moroccans. It stems as far back as the original Berber settlers, who expressed their primitive beliefs through geometric patterns and symbols, then to be reinforced by Islam, which calls for creative and artistic expression as a way of life for all Muslims. Embellishment is a sign of wealth, the more decorated the home and the more intricate the design, the richer the owner. This is why in the medina of Fes, once the city of the rich and elite, there is hardly an inch of bare wall from the roof to the floor in many of the homes. It is this architecture and craftsmanship, which lures foreigners to buy Moroccan properties. Windows, archways, ceilings, woodwork and plastering, which would cost thousands to rec-reate in Europe, are standard fare for Morocco's builders and craftsmen, many of whom have had 'the trade' passed down to them through scores of generations.

LOCAL BUILDERS

While there maybe a hotchpotch of foreigners living in Morocco drawn from all circles and walks of life, the things most have in common, especially those buying traditional houses, are building works, building materials and builders. Everyone has a story to tell about their experiences (not to mention a few extra crow's feet or, at worst, a nervous twitch). Builders, the world over have a reputation for be-ing unreliable, hard to get a hold of and when you do get a hold of them, hard to keep a hold of, and in Morocco, this is no exception.

Unlike in Europe where building is a multi-ethnic trade; Polish plasterers working alongside Brazilian plumbers, in Morocco, all builders are Moroccan and the thought of hiring someone from the UK or elsewhere, to work on your Moroccan property is very unlikely, not to mention, very expensive. The concept of DIY is also unheard of in Morocco, where the view is that only poor people will do their own work, as the cost of labour is so cheap. As with all builders, be very strict with money. Do not assume that a good relationship/ friendship means that your builder will not be charging you double behind your back. The best way to cope with doing building works in Morocco is to forget everything you have learnt about doing similar style works in Europe and to adopt the Moroccan mentality. Do not believe the timescale you are given for a build to be accurate. Moroccans, with their lives dictated by fate, do not work to timescales. The job will get done when fate dictates and most are of the belief that this is out of their hands. For Moroccans, family life is paramount so do not be surprised if your contractor disappears for a few days at a critical moment, with the excuse of a wedding, funeral or arrival home of a long lost family member. If you are getting work done during Ramadan, be prepared for tired, hungry, clock watching workers who will leave on the dot of the sunset siren.

Having said this, Moroccan builders love working for foreigners, or actually, love the amount of money they can charge foreigners for working for them and so will have no qualms about dropping a local job if a higher paying European appears on the scene. While it is quite easy to feel disgruntled that you are paying above the standard Moroccan rate, it is best to look at it like this; Firstly, the amounts that you will be paying are still very low in comparison to Europe. Secondly, if you haggle builders down to rock bottom prices, you will simply be charged more ie; the amount prior to haggling, indirectly on things like building materials, which you have less ability to control. Thirdly, the less you pay, the slower and more drawn out the build will be and the more time you will spend having to track down your builders (pay peanuts get monkeys). If you are renovating a property to rent out for an income, surely it is better to get the job done as quickly as possible and reap the high rental income than haggle the builder down to bottom rung prices and wait two years to complete.

It is not uncommon for Moroccan builders to 'move in' to your property when they are building, especially if it is a large project (and assuming you are not living there yourself). This is because many hail from the countryside, so have no urban abode. It can be a little surprising to arrive at your home and find a makeshift mattress (or four), discarded clothes, shoes and invariably, a stove and metal teapot. Unlike British builders who exist on sweet, weak tea and biscuits, the way to a Moroccan builder's heart is to buy them bread, mint and if you are feeling especially fond of them, butter and honey.

Who Will Manage your Build?

There are two ways of undertaking building works in Morocco; the official way and the unofficial way. The official way involves the drawing up of plans by an architect, the rubber stamp from the engineers, contracts and building permissions. This route takes time and is more expensive. The unofficial way involves employing a builder to do the works for you without proper plans, contracts or permissions. The price quoted for such works is likely to be considerably lower than the 'official route' but it both unwise and dangerous and can lead to you having to rebuild the property once it is finished or pay out vast sums of money at a later date to obtain the necessary documentation. The Moroccan government is cracking down on so called illegal builds and however tempting it is to cut corners, it is not advised.

Whether you wish to manage all the works yourself, hire a building contractor to oversee the works and/or an architect to manage all the works, will depend on the amount of work you are doing.

Facelifts. If you are simply giving your property a modernising facelift, painting, tiling and woodwork for example, then you can most probably get away with hiring each individual worker and overseeing the works yourself. Do not underestimate the importance of a property facelift, however. Often the finishing touches are the most stressful part of a build as they are the bits that show. Wonky railings, drippy paintwork and cracked tiles are very noticeable and make a big impact on the finished look. If you are overseeing such works yourself, bear in mind that it will be a full time job. Stories abound of owners returning after a day away to find that the tiles they requested to be laid straight have been laid in artistic, but totally incorrect, zigzags, perfectly painted walls have been damaged by overzealous ironworkers attempting to fit a balustrade, or doors have been squeezed into ill fitting frames, so fail to close. On the whole, Moroccan builders do not have the same level of respect for aesthetics as European homeowners, Many are of the belief that if you are not there to make a decision, they will make it for you, which can have dire consequences. Never leave anything to chance, always add contingency time and budget into such works to accommodate mistakes and be prepared for the fact that they will inevitably happen.

Do not undertake any work without first agreeing a written price signed both by you and the builder. This estimate, known as the devis, should include everything otherwise, you will be constantly harassed by the builder to give him 10 dirham (70p) here or 15 dirham (£1.10) there, as he needs little extras he had not thought of in the first place. It is not uncommon for example, for a simple build to have in excess of 700 cartloads of rubble, which needs to be removed from the medina, usually by donkey and disposed of some distance out of town. Each cart costs up to 50 dirham (£3), so petty cash style payments quickly build up.

You will find that you get a broad ranging style of devis, from the typed up and logo'd A4 sheet, giving an in depth description of all works to be done, to the grubby, back of an envelope, handwritten scrawl, giving a few words, ie; 'plumbing the house'. However in depth the devis ends up being, you must make it clear that the agreed price is fully inclusive. *Kul-shee* means 'everything' and is a very useful word to have at times like this.

You will need to give an upfront payment for the buying of building materials ie; a third. If it is a big job, you could agree to pay another third after a particular milestone has been reached but always keep an outstanding payment for when the job is completed and you are happy. Though you will be constantly hassled to do so, never pay all the money in advance or you will lose your builder and the job will never get done. Also, remember to obtain signed receipts for all payments.

Building Contractor. It is possible to either hire a building contractor who will oversee all the works including the hiring of builders, plumbers, electricians, painters, or to hire a building contractor simply to oversee the masonry work, from demolition (if relevant) to laying the bricks and mortar and then to hire your own people individually from then on. Both approaches have their benefits and downsides. The benefits of hiring a building contractor to manage all the works from start to finish is that the job will (should) be properly co-ordinated. In such situations, it is less likely you will have the plumber turning up to make holes in walls two days after the plasterer has finished his plastering or the tiler laying the wall tiles, two days after the painter has given you a spotless finish. The downside is that once you are in with a contractor, you are in a sense, totally reliant on him and the whole job will depend on how good/committed/reliable he is.

You will probably need to be very involved in the build yourself, visiting the site regularly and checking on progress/craftsmanship especially, when it comes to the 'behind the scenes' works such as the quality of the bricks and the laying of pipes. You need to be sure that these are of an excellent quality, made to last, rather than crumble or leak after a few years in action. If you are not able to make it to the site regularly, it might be worth asking a friend living close by to visit it for you and take photographs, just to be sure that the quality of the build and building materials are the same as those originally agreed upon.

Do not work with a building contractor without having first sought references (verbal from fellow home owners are the most likely) or better, visited properties built by him to check the quality of his work. If you are having trouble finding a building contractor, you could contact one of the British/American Consulate offices, which have a list of unofficial British/American representatives for each region. These representatives tend to be a mine of information on all things relating to their local town or city and will be able to put you in touch with residents who have recently had work done. Alternatively, you could e-mail or visit the Centre of Regional Investment (CRI) for your region (see *What Type of Property to Buy?*), who should have a list of contractors and engineers.

You are advised not to enter into any sort of relationship with a building contractor without having a contract legally certified by a notaire. This is most important if you are likely to be absent for much of the build. You can either write this up yourself or ask a notaire to write it up. This is not always ideal for contractors who like to keep work 'under the table' so as to avoid paying tax, but from your point of view, it needs to be legally certified otherwise you have no cover or proof of payments. The contract needs to layout the payment structure for the build ie; at what stage of the build different payments will be made. This will be based on the devis given by the contractor. The norm is to pay the contractor a salary based on the square meterage of the property. A ballpark is between 2000 dh (£125) and 3000 dh (£187) per square metre, although, this will depend on the previous experience of the contractor, the region you are in and how badly you want him to work for you. The contract must also include get out clauses for you if you are not happy with the quality/speed of his work. You should also add clauses such as a bonus if work is completed within time and budget and is well done and money deducted if it overruns by a certain amount of time or money. A figure such as 500 dh deducted from a 1 million dirham build for every day it runs over, tends to get the job done, although some builders will be reluctant to sign for such clauses.

It is important you keep up the pressure. Be firm with the contractor. If you are not happy with something, tell him, do not just grin and bear it. If the contractor feels he can get away with things, he might cut corners at your expense.

It is possible to break your contract with the building contractor if you are not happy with his work, especially if a get out clause is written into the contract. This can get complicated, however, in terms of payment ie; when to pay them up to especially if they have already purchased the building materials and also tricky for you if you do not have an armful of reliable people you can call on to finish the job. It is best to be totally sure prior to starting the build that you have chosen the right person to work with, even if it means delaying the works in order to broaden your research.

Architect. It is not possible to hire an architect from Europe to work for you in Morocco unless they work in conjunction with a Moroccan architect, who will sign off the plans. Until recently, with the opening of a couple of private schools, the majority of Moroccan architects practising in Morocco, will have undertaken the six year architectural diploma at the *Ecole Nationale d'Architecture (ENA)*, a publicly funded university in Rabat. Once they have their diploma they are registered with the Society of Architects, which is a good place to find an architect, if you have not been recommended any on the ground.

There are two types of architects; private architects, who draw up the plans and public architects, who check them. Public architects work in the Urban Agencies and Communes, ensuring that the plans drawn up by the private architects are accurate prior to the issuing of building permissions.

Whether or not you choose to work with an architect will depend on the type of build. Renovations that require building permission ie: those that involve altering the external appearance of the property (extra floors, extensions, outhouses, driveways) or structural alterations to internal walls will legally require an architect to draw up the plans.

It is possible to hire an architect simply to draw up your plans and then, if you prefer, to hire a building contractor to handle the actual build. Alternatively, you can hire an architect to oversee the whole build from plans to finish. While this is more expensive, it is a preferred route if your build is complicated or if you are likely to be absent for much of the works and want extra security that the job being done is to a high standard.

To oversee the build from start to finish, most architects will charge around 5% of the build price. This figure will increase to around 8% if they need to hire civil engineers to undertake, for example, land and soil studies.

Included in the 5% is the drawing up of plans for building permission and the *Cahier des Prescriptions Speciale*, which is a booklet indicating all the works that need doing and the exact building materials that need to be bought. This booklet, which needs to be signed by both the contractor and/or any extra individual workers in front of a local government official, is a guarantee that the works and materials specified by the architect, will be adhered to. The architect will oversee each individual stage of the build and be responsible for making the stage payments to the contractor when he is satisfied with the works done. At the end of the build if he is happy with the final product, the architect will sign a document called the *Certificat de Conformité*, which is a confirmation that the work was done as specified in the Cahier des Prescriptions Speciale.

As the architect's fee is calculated on a percentage of the build price, it is very easy for them to boost up the prices. It is important, therefore, that you get a clear written statement at the start of the job of exactly how much the build is going to cost. If this sounds far too high, then look around for other architects and obtain other quotes. Do not assume that just because the quote is high or the company logo dazzling, that the work is going to be of a superior quality. Get a full range of quotes, interview the architect, ask for recommendations and make your decision based on that, not only the bottom line.

As with the contractor, it is necessary that you draw up a contract with the architect, which very clearly specifies the total price for the works on the property and the stages of payment to the architect. Again, you need to include a get out clause if you feel the architect is charging too much or not effectively doing his/her job and also to offer an incentive for the architect to keep the build to within the specified time and budget.

If you are going to be absent for long periods, you might need to draw up a document giving the architect the power of attorney to manage your build and collect official documents such as the building permission. Ensure you make the document very specific to the works related, so that the architect does not receive too much autonomy.

Structural Engineer. Structural engineers are hired privately, sometimes on the recommendation of the architect, although it is better if you seek your own independently. This can be done by speaking to other people who have renovated/built properties, estate agents, who tend to be a mine of knowledge on the building profession or to your regional CRI who will be able to put you in touch with the relevant bodies.

When the architect has completed his plans, they need to be submitted to the structural engineer, who will check them and make the relevant calculations relating to thickness of walls, diameter of pillars, pressure points etc. Without the rubber stamp from the structural engineer it is not possible (and not wise) to obtain building permission. You can expect to pay the structural engineer around 10 dh, (70p), per square metre, although this depends on the size and complexity of the build.

Europeans. You might find yourself approached by Europeans offering to manage your build for you. While this can be a good thing, based on the fact that being Europeans, they are likely to be more attuned to your tastes and to work with you on a European level ie; with effective money management and timescales, do not assume that just because they are European, they are going to give you a fair or good service. Rumours do emerge of European-style mafias severely ripping other Europeans off and making their lives misery. If you do decide to work with a European, treat them in the same way as if they were Moroccan by undertaking the contractual process and obtaining prior recommendations.

BUILDING PERMISSION (ROKHSAT AL BINAA)

Permission is needed if you are building a property from scratch, changing the external appearance of an existing building or the internal walls if you are undertaking structural conversions. Even if you are having relatively minor works such as the construction of a new fence or garden path, permission will need to be sought.

In order to obtain building permission, you must legally employ an architect to draw up the plans. Plans are submitted to the *Jema'a* (Urban or Rural Commune), who in conjunction with a team of technical advisers will check their validity. If the build is complicated or if you wish to change the local zoning laws ie; build three stories in a two storey zone, it is likely your building plans will be passed up to the Urban Agency at the next level, who will decide whether or not you can proceed. If the plans are agreed and your property falls within an Urban Commune, you will be requested to pay a building tax of 20 dh (£1.60) per square metre of property, prior to the issuing of the building permission. This covers the electricity, drainage and water that you will need to connect to, during the course of the build.

It takes an average of two to three months to receive building permission, which comes in the form of a stamp on the plans highlighting approval by the Urban/ Rural Commune. It can sometimes take longer, up to a year. Occasionally with the arrival of a new governor to a province, all building permissions are halted while stock is taken of local developments. Building permission remains valid for 1 year during which time you must commence your build.

After the completion of the build and the architect has issued the homeowner with the Certificat de Conformité, the Urban/Rural Commune will need to be notified. It is up to the homeowner to notify the Commune by handing in the Certificat de Conformité, proving that the work has been done to plan. A representative from the Commune will then visit the property to ensure from their point of view that the property is lawfully and safely habitable at which stage they will issue the homeowner with a Permis d'Habitation.

If you have built your property from scratch and its total surface area is over 240square metres, you can expect a visit from the taxman not long after you have moved in. He will want you to prove that you have paid VAT for building materials and professional services. It is imperative that you keep all invoices and receipts relating to the build, ideally on company paper. If you have no proof of payments, the taxman will assume that you have not paid VAT and will charge you what he thinks you should have paid, which can be astronomical; 14% VAT for building materials, 20% for professional services. It will also cause you problems when it comes to capital repatriation. The best way to stay organised, especially as Moroccans love their paperwork, is to have a 'Building' file with a section dedicated to the collation of invoices and receipts.

English Speaking Architects

Though based in one particular region, most architects will work in all parts of Morocco.

AM Studio Architects (Adnane Draoui), 9 Rue Khalid Ibn El Oualid no 6, Tangier; ☎ 039 94 94 28; e-mail amstudio@menara.ma.

Fatima El Bouyahyaoui, 182 Ave A Khattabi apt 12, 3éme étage, Gueliz, Marrakech 40000; ☎ 044 42 13 11/069 21 51 71; e-mail faatje2000@hotmail.com.

Hicham Ech Chefaa, 182 Ave A Khattabi apt 12, 3éme étage, Gueliz, Marrakech 40000; ☎ 044 42 13 11/063 48 43 20.

Rachid Haloui, Fes; ☎ 055 62 00 25/061 13 56 70.

Alaa Said, 14 Derb Sbaa Louyate, Seffarine, 30200, Fes Medina, Fes; ☎ 071 11 35 28; e-mail kate.kvalvik@c2i.net.

English Speaking Building Managers

Carre d' Azur Fes: ☎ 055 93 02 92; www.carredazur.com

Michel Welter, Marrakech: ☎ 044 44 60 29, www.kantakari.com

Nourredine Marzagui, Essaouira; ☎ 044 78 37 53/062 20 41 74

Working with Artisans

No matter how basic their training there is an element of snobbery in the Moroccan building trade, where each builder sees himself as a bit of an artisan (craftsman). Whether it is their ability to mould arches and doorways, hone *tadelakt*, the smoothed, polished sand and quicklime wall covering or lay pipes. The reality is that the majority of builders you come across will be just that, builders/plumbers/electricians and not traditional craftsman however precious they might appear. Artisans are the doyen of the building trade, responsible for transforming a house from bare walls to opulent, plain to embellished. They are the costume designers and make up artists, giving the look to the house and the 'wow' to the walls. Artisans do not so much become artisans as evolve into the trade, many becoming apprentices at a very young age, closely supervised by the master craftsman, known as the *ma'alem*, who is responsible for ensuring that there is no break from tradition when it comes to tools and techniques. In most cases, an artisan today will be working with the same materials and in the same environment as his forefathers, 500 years ago. It is this traditional lineage, which makes Moroccan artisans so unique, not to mention, heavily in demand by the foreign community. Artisans are best found through recommendation, there is as ever in Morocco, minimal self-marketing. Some will have their workshops in the medina but many will live in the countryside and come into the cities simply on demand from clients or to sell their wares. It takes time for artisans to do their work and there is no point attempting to speed them along, as they will not risk rushing through the job and giving a shoddy finish as they have their reputations to uphold. It is important, when commissioning artisans, that you are very involved in the 'creative' process. Photographs of works you would like them to duplicate help, especially when language is a problem. You, with the help of the artisan, are responsible for choosing the colours and patterns you want. Be specific - do not assume that just because they are masters of their trade, they have good taste. Designs and colours are very personal. Ensure that the pictures drawn by the artisan and agreed by you are the same as the final product. Also do not accept any substitutions. Sometimes, if a particular material or colour is out of stock the artisan will simply buy what he assumes to be the closest to your original choice. This can be worlds apart and could ruin a whole finish. If you feel very strongly about it, it is important that you tell the artisan that nothing but the material of choice will do.

It is possible to buy artisan wares 'off the shelf' simply by browsing the many little craft shops that fill the streets and alleyways of the medina. In such places you will be paying 'tourist' prices. Another alternative is to seek out the artisan's atelier or workshop. Some medinas have a neighbourhoods specifically dedicated to artisans. Here by buying direct from the artisan ie; missing out the middleman you can get much better prices sometimes as much as three times cheaper. If you have something very particular in mind, then you could commission the artisan to create it for you. Artisans love commissioned work. As so much of their work is churning out the same 'sort of stuff' for the tourist market, which is invariably the same 'sort of stuff' as the neighbouring workshop, a commission enables them to really show off their expertise plus it is excellent marketing for them as you will, assuming you are impressed, spread the good word (and address) of their work to all your European cronies. Do not be surprised, however, if you see your design duplicated in a number of shops only a few days after signing it off.

Unrestored Traditional Homes. In order to see the potential of many of the traditional properties you look around, you will need to have vision. Many will be in
such a run down state that you have to trip over rubble or a muddy puddle of water
just to get through the front door, walls will be chipped, floors filled with potholes,
kitchens small and dank, the loo a hole in the ground, the roof above the courtyard corrugated plastic (and heavily visited by birds) and the roof terrace a storage
space for mutton hides, rusty satellite dish and laundry. Being able to see beyond
the façade and envisioning the property as it might be, is half the skill and all the
attraction when purchasing traditional houses. Based on the age and thickness of
the walls in the medina, it is unlikely that the 'run down' effect will be structural
although this is something your architect can check for you, prior to purchase.

How much work will be needed completely depends on the age and state of the
property and your budget, tastes and needs. Older properties generally need more
work, although age can be deceiving. In the Fes medina, a date from the Islamic
calendar is usually carved on to the plasterwork above one of the salon doorways,
but this indicates only when the plasterwork was done and not the actual age of the
property, so you could have 200-year old plasterwork on a 700-year old house.

It is highly unlikely you will simply be able to just move into your property
and hopefully you will have budgeted for this. Nearly all unrenovated traditional
homes will be in need of modernisation, primarily plumbing and electricity and
many will be crying out for TLC in the aesthetics department. Cheap labour and
a plethora of craftsmen means that you can have a lot of fun deciding on ways of
making your property traditionally or uniquely special (see *Interior Design* below).
As price of property is dependent on size and location as opposed to the array of
original features, you could find yourself blessed with a property rich in archways,
stained glass, sculpted plasterwork and zelliges dating back to when it was first
built, costing no more than a similar sized but seemingly featureless property. Do
not assume that just because you cannot see the features, however, that they do
not exist. In some cases, plaster might hide wonderful archways or paint might be
covering original brick and woodwork.

Most traditional homes are restored within keeping to local styles and building
materials. Red predominates in Marrakech, white and blue in coastal towns and
light blue in the mountain town of Chefchaouen. In many regions, it is against
regulations to paint the outside of your property a colour which is not within
keeping to the local surrounds, even variations on a particular colour such as cream
instead of white, is heavily frowned upon.

INTERIOR DESIGN

In a country swaddled in deep colours, soft tones and intricate shapes, where the
earth is moulded into cities and artisans devote their lives to perfecting a single
skill, it can be quite tricky deciding how best to decorate and furnish your own

home, taking advantage of the abundance of local materials and expertise. It is highly likely that where you choose to buy will to some degree, dictate the style you choose. Every region has its own distinct but to a certain extent, formulaic look, which provides a style upon which you can, if you wish, elaborate. In Marrakech, houses are ochre reds, pinks and amber. Simple, unfussy shapes built into the masonry design; rounded arches, dome ceilings and floors that seamlessly run into walls. It is a style that could not differ more from the intricately sculpted plasterwork and complex mosaics of Fes, the whitewashed Andalucian curves of Tetouan with its jutted horseshoe arches or the black marble interiors of Erfoud.

By visiting artisan's workshops, browsing the souks for furnishings and inviting yourself to as many houses as seems fit, you should quickly develop an idea of the local style and how you can incorporate it into your own home.

Walls

Tadelakt. Tadelakt is a waterproof, shiny limestone plaster, that can be mixed with whatever coloured pigment you choose, and used to cover walls, fireplaces (a non traditional Moroccan feature), columns, shower, basins etc. Due to the large natural deposits of limestone around Marrakech, it is the building material of choice in the city and few restored houses are without it. The reason tadelakt so appeals, is because it gives a wonderful, smooth, moulded marble style finish (tadelakt means to knead), rounding the edges of hard corners and giving a warm earthiness to the room. It is also heat and steam proof making it ideal for bathrooms and hammams where it is most commonly used.

Tadelakt is applied to flat walls and left to set. It is then polished with stones that bring out the marble-like effect and glazed with egg whites. The final polish is given using black tadelakt soap, which is based on olive oil and gives it its waterproof quality.

Wall Tiles (Zelliges). Morocco's tiles are among the most vividly coloured in the world. They are one of Morocco's main specialities used throughout the country, with the main tile production centre being based in Fes (where it is much cheaper to buy tiles, particularly if you buy them direct from the artisan). Zelliges are normally used to cover the lower half of the wall, while the middle section is generally painted white and kept plain. Along the top of the wall, complementing the zellige lining, there is sometimes a frieze of chiselled plaster (see below). Zellige are also used to adorn columns, staircases and archways. Very little has changed in their method of production over the last few centuries. Local clay is mixed with water, which then gets kneaded by an *ajjan,* who removes all the stones. The clay is then moulded into rectangular shapes and coated in layers of different coloured glaze. It is fired in an oven, heated by grasses, wood and olive stones. The designer works on the patterns with a bamboo stick, dipped in ink. The patterns are always geometric with shapes like triangles, stars, flowers, squares and crescents. The tile cutter (*taksir*) cuts the tiles with a hammer sharpened on both side against marble. The main skill when it comes to zelliges is not so much their individual design, as the colour combinations bought about when they are laid out, which is the job of the ma'alem. Zelliges need to be laid very close together so that there is as small as gap as possible between each tile. A good way of depicting the age of a property is to see whether the colours on the zelliges have worn or faded. The more faded the colours, the older the property.

Chiselled Plaster (Gebs). Fes is best known for its chiselled plasterwork, which hangs lace-like in friezes along the walls just below the ceilings, above doors, around archways, pillars and windows, each carving made on site, by the hand of a skilled ma'alem, known as the *ghabbar*, who will sometimes spend hours perched on a precariously built scaffolding in order to perfect his craft. Like zelliges, shapes must follow the Islamic geometric grid, but can range in shape, the most popular being floral, honeycomb, diamond and stars. Gebs are made using a small amount of plaster, which the ghabba spreads onto the wall using a trowel. The shapes are carved into the plaster, using a knife and compass. The chisel is then used to tap away at the remaining plaster, 2-3cm deep.

Gebs can be left their natural eggshell colour or, painted either white or vivid colours. The general view is to leave them natural. Painting them white tends to make them too bright so they stand out above everything else and it is an incredibly laborious job attempting to remove and clean paintwork, if you decide you no longer want it.

Floors

Bejmat. Bejmat are glazed or unglazed half bricks, rectangular in shape (usually 15x5cm). They can be coloured, generally, blue, green, white or a natural terracotta and sometimes interspersed with zellige motifs. Natural terracotta is the most commonly used colour for floors used in combination with a scattering of bright colours. Though, on the whole a very solid, resistant surface, bejmat, if attached to a moveable structure such as wood, can move out of position, dislodging the joins. If this is the case, be prepared to re-do certain areas on a yearly or so, basis.

Marble. Marble is abundant in Morocco. In Erfoud, it is black and fossilised, in Sefrou near Fes, it is beige and pink and in Marrakech it is white and veined. For the most affluent Moroccans, however, nothing but Italian marble will do. Marble is used on pillars, capitals, walls and fountains. On floors, it is normally used in combination with zelliges, which prevents it expanding or contracting with Morocco's extreme weather changes.

Carpets. Carpets are an excellent addition to rooms, adding colour to white-washed houses along the Atlantic coast and warmth to bejmat floors, which can get nippy underfoot during the cool winter months. Moroccan carpets are renowned for being long, up to 15 feet. They can be pile weave (knotted) or flat weave, wool or sometimes silk. They are always geometric in design and generally use soft shades of red, mauve, blue, yellow, white and green. There are two main classifications of Moroccan carpets: the urban and the tribal. Urban pile weave carpets are produced in Rabat and Mediouna (close to Casablanca). Predominantly pinkish red, older carpets (pre World War I) tend to have several bands of border (the greater the number of borders, the greater the price) and brightly coloured motifs usually double-ended octagonal medallions, diamonds or triangles. Newer ones are less bold often carrying floral motifs with a predominance of tulips. Older carpets are made with vegetable dyes, which produce a much better quality than the newer chemically dyed carpets. The best place to look for Rabati carpets is along the Rue des Consuls in Rabat's medina. Urban rugs are often priced per square metre according to the quality of the wool and the amount of time it took to make.

Tribal carpets often flat weave, known in Morocco as hanbel or more commonly as the Turkish killim, are produced by Berber tribeswomen in the Middle Atlas. Hanbel are lighter and more supple than pile weave carpets and so are often used as wall hangings and throws in addition to floor coverings where they are less durable than urban rugs. Designs are often borderless with horizontal lines running up to the edges, lozenges and lattice-shaped diamonds and squares. Common motifs include the evil eye, snakes and camels.

Non-carpet connoisseurs prefer flat weave carpets for their free-style originality (no two carpets are ever alike) and diversity of colours. They are cheaper to buy as they take less time to weave than pile carpets (days as opposed to months), although as their popularity grows, so too do their prices. If you have the time, it is best to buy your carpets directly from the producers in the regions where they are made, both to ensure a good price for you and so that the women get fair prices for their work, cutting out of the well-versed middle salesman and his copious glasses of mint tea. The main tribal weaving areas are around Khemmiset and Khenifra and between Azrou and Midelt. Alternatively for a rapid education into the wide choice of carpets, you could pay a visit to one of the majestic carpet bazaars in the medinas of Fes, Marrakech, Rabat, Meknes or Tetouan.

Ceilings

Cedar. Along with tadelakt, one of the most popular ceiling coverings in Morocco is cedar wood (*ilerz*) beams, sometimes carved, sometimes plain, sometimes painted (see below). Cedar is a dry and rot proof wood, which does not need varnishing or treating, managing to withstand even the most harsh weather conditions. It is naturally protected from insects by the oil in the wood and has a wonderful fragrance.

Due to its durability, cedar wood is one of the most popular woods used in Morocco for, in addition to ceilings, furnishings such as doors, lintels, cabinets and shutters. Most of the cedar wood comes from the cedar forests of the Middle Atlas where it grows to around 120 feet. Its sustainability is under threat from a combination of drought, logging, the overgrazing of goat and sheep and the large community of Barbary macaque living in the forests who are responsible for damaging the cedar trees by stripping the bark in order to get water. Attempts are being made to overcome the latter problem by increasing the water supply in the forests.

Furnishings

Painted Wood (Zouag). 'A wooden work of art is only complete when it has been painted' or so many Moroccans believe hence the roaring trade in painted wood. Internal doors, shutters, lintels, balustrades, mashrabiyya (see below), tables, chests and ceilings are all subject to intricate, colourfully painted decoration that when glanced at look like embroidered fabric, the most common patterns being plants, flowers and to a lesser extent, geometric shapes. Painters on wood, known as *zawwaqas,* make their own paintbrushes out of hairs from donkey's tails. Paintwork is protected by a linseed oil based varnish. In Fes, zouags tend to be more intricately patterned than in Marrakech using many more lines and the predominance of blues, yellows and whites. In Marrakech, patterns are less complicated and the main colour used, yellow.

Mashrabiyya or Mouchrabieh. Mashrabiyya refers to the carved latticed wooden screens traditionally used to cover up windows but more recently as an addition to doorways, balconies, balustrades and walkways in parts of the home frequented by women. It offers privacy from prying male eyes by being designed in such a way that it can be seen out of but not into. The narrow gaps in the lattice also control the flow of light and air into the house. The word mashrabiyya is actually derived from the Arabic word 'drink' dating back to the time when small water jars were placed next to a lattice opening by the window to be cooled down by the passing air. Mashrabiyya is a wonderful aesthetic feature to have in the home adding much interest to wood and creating wonderful shadows on plain walls.

Wood Furnishings. Carved wooden chests, engraved front doors, polished tables inlaid with mother-of-pearl and sculpted bookshelves are sold in abundance throughout Morocco each one made meticulously by the hand of an artisan specialised only in his individual discipline. The most popular woods for furnishings are the hard, durable cedar (see above) and thuya. Thuya is a coniferous tree, related to the cedar that grows only in the south west of Morocco around Essaouira and Agadir. In Essaouira, there are around 6000 artisans employed in thuya production. It is the root and the trunk of the thuya, which produces the much sought after hard, gnarled wood that is inlaid with ebony, mother-of-pearl, copper and walnut. Go to Essaouira and you will be inundated with shops selling the highly polished wood with its fantastically vivid grain and sweet, lingering fragrance.

Over 80% of the tourists visiting Essaouira buy thuya handicrafts, usually souvenirs such as small boxes, bracelets and picture frames. Many such small products are manufactured in bulk on electric lathes as opposed to by hand. Such mass production is depleting reserves of the rare thuya tree requiring the implementation of re-growth projects and threatening the livelihood of skilled thuya artisans who are having to pay much more for raw thuya wood. When buying thuya products, try to purchase them directly from the artisans in their workshops or from shops solely dedicated to thuya furnishings as opposed to from touristy souvenir shops in the medina.

Berber doors are sold throughout the medina and are fantastic decoration for the home. They come in all shapes and sizes, some no higher than a couple of feet and normally with geometric design engravings such as stars and circles. Most salesmen will tell you that their doors are very old coming from remote regions in the High Atlas. This can be the case, but sometimes the doors are in fact very new, straight out of the carpenter's workshop but made to look old. If you have set your mind on a real Berber door, try going shopping with someone who knows a lot about wood and who can instruct you on the age and authenticity of the door, otherwise, delight in the fact that you have a solid wood door for a very reasonable price – new or old. You could consider making a coffee table out of the door, hanging it from a wall for decoration with or without hooks for coats, turning it into a bedstead or perhaps, simply use it as a door.

Ironwork. Ironwork is commonly found throughout Morocco but particularly in towns influenced by Andalucia such as Fes, Tetouan and Chefchouaen where it gained in popularity during the 19th and 20th century as a cheaper and more sturdy alternative to mashrabiyya. It is normally sighted on window bars, balustrades and balconies but you can ask the artisans (many have workshops in the medina) to create anything you desire out of ironwork from four-poster beds to fire grates. Just give them the measurements and a rough drawing of what you like and they will make it for you, normally for a highly reasonable price, embellished with patterns perfected through the centuries. Be prepared for the iron to rust if you live close to the coast. Nothing, not even a good dose of Hammerite will prevent this from happening, the upside is that it gives the house an aged look, which can be a good thing.

Pottery and Ceramics. Moroccan ceramics come in the form of plates, mugs, jars, tea services, soap dishes, fruit bowls, urns, oil lamps, soup tureens and tagines.

Most of the ceramics you see for sale in the medina will have been produced in either Fes or Safi the main pottery centres. The local clay in Fes is quarried 12km east of the city and either left unglazed or set to dry in the sun before being fired in kilns, which turns the clay white. Fes pottery is distinctive for having blue on white decorations drawn on by the highly skilled ma'alem, which mirror the elegant zelliges of the city.

Safi pottery, derived from yellow clay is bigger and bolder using bright greens, blues and yellows and large motifs such as fish, moons and suns. The clay is mixed by being trampled on with bare feet, and the kilns are still powered by dried hardwood.

It is also possible to buy utilitarian-style Berber pottery; earthenware pots such as tagines and water cups from High Atlas regions such as the Ourika Valley. Pottery is seen as sacred in many Berber communities as it wards off evil spirits.

When buying pottery, make sure that it is not chipped or too bubbled and that it balances evenly when perched on a flat surface. You also need to check that the pottery has actually been fired in a kiln as opposed to simply dried in the sun, otherwise it will collapse when/if filled with water.

Contemporary Furnishing. Moroccans like to compare their own home grown *Kitea* with the Scandinavian giant Ikea (yet to come to Morocco). With the exception of the name, which sounds mildly similar and the range of utilitarian style furnishings, the similarities are few and far between. Kitea can be found in most of Morocco's big towns and cities. Like Ikea it has a range of modern furnishings for all rooms in the house including beds, desks, kitchen fittings and sofas. Unlike Ikea, it tends to close for a lunchtime siesta.

Another place to look for contemporary furnishings is in the hypermarket, *Marjane*, again, located in most cities, which as well as selling imported food also sells pretty much everything in the contemporary household goods line including fridges, freezers, microwaves, cookers, deckchairs, baby high chairs and travel cots.

Le Comptoir is Morocco's equivalent to the UK's 'Currys' and 'Comet' selling all household electrical items. The benefit of buying such products from an established retailer is that most items are returnable and come with guarantees.

Research Books on Moroccan Design

Living in Morocco, Design from Casablanca to Marrakech; Lisl and Landt Dennis; Thames and Hudson; (£19.95).

Villas and Courtyard Houses of Morocco, Corrine Verner; Thames and Hudson; (£24.95)

Moroccan Interiors, Lisa Lovatt-Smith; Taschen; (£9.99)

Morocco, Sabine Bouvet and Philippe Saharoff; Flammarion (£30)

INTERIOR DESIGN GLOSSARY

Bab	gate or door
Bab-i-dar	Front door
Bejmat	terracotta half bricks for floors
Fakhkhar	Ceramist
Farrash	tile setter who sets zelliges on to walls
Gebs	plaster
Ghabber	artisan plasterer
Izar	Frieze made from wood, zelliges or plaster
Jeer	lime
Kilim	woven carpet
Ma'alem	master craftsman
Mashrabiyya	lattice wood that can be seen out of but not into
Medluk	similar to the wall covering tadelakt, but coarser and not quite as shiny
Menzeh	large salon on the terrace for entertaining guests
Nejjar	Joiner
Pisé	bricks made from sun-dried earth, water and lime
Quermoud	tile
Raml	sand
Riad	inside courtyard or garden (also refers to the actual properties)
Rkham	marble
Rqaimi	cabinet-maker
Saqaiya	fountain
Squef	ceiling
Tadelakt	wall and sometimes floor covering, like Italian stucco. Made from sand and quicklime, smoothed on by tablets of stone and black soap
Tataoui	thin strips of painted laurel arranged in patterns – decorative features
Thuya	wood used by artisans of Essaouira
Woust ed dar	atrium.
Zelliges	mosaic of tiles – geometrical and abstract
Zawwayiq	wood painting artisans
Zouak	painted patterns on wood.

MAKING MONEY FROM YOUR PROPERTY

CHAPTER SUMMARY

O **Property for holiday lets**. In order to maximise your income opportunities, the decision to rent out your property to holiday makers needs to be made prior to purchasing the property, so that you can consider the wider needs of the market.

O **Staff**. If you are renting out your property when you are not in Morocco, you will need to have a good, trustworthy house manager/cleaner to run the house for you and keep it spotlessly clean.

O **Agencies**. Letting agencies and villa companies charge around a 20% commission for renting out your home, but they also ensure a steady stream of tenants.

O **Guesthouse regulations**. The government has recently tightened up its laws relating to guesthouses, giving them graded classifications and in depth guidelines to follow.

O **Selling privately**. Selling the property privately saves you from having to pay the agent 2.5% commission

O **Selling through several agents**. If you employ a number of agents to sell your property, you run the risk of them dropping the price in order to 'win' the commission.

O **Selling through one agent**. Employing a sole agent from a reputable company to sell your property is likely to get you a better price as there is no competition and the agent is officially employed by you to do a good job.

HOLIDAY LETS

A number of British people who have bought property in Morocco are second homeowners with a house in the UK, which they live in for much of the year, coming to Morocco for regular holidays. When they are not staying in their Moroccan home, most try to rent it out on a short-term-let basis to holidaymakers. At least 4 million tourists visit Morocco each year and an increasing number are independent holidaymakers preferring to experience 'living' in Morocco as opposed to relying on hotels to cater to their needs. Renting out your property on either a self catering or, more commonly breakfast-included type basis is an excellent way of making money from the property, paying off its mortgage and/or affording enough for regular maintenance.

If this is a route you intend to take, much time and thought will need to go into ensuring you get the right property in the right location and equip it in the best way to maximise your rental opportunities.

Your Home is My Home and Their Home. The decision to make money from letting your property, needs, ideally, to be made prior to starting the house hunting as the prerequisites of where you live and the type of home you choose to buy changes once you have to start thinking beyond your own personal wishes. As well as the emotional issues involved in opening your house to the public, renting out your property requires a solid understanding of the market you will be working with and its level of expectation. People on holiday are very different from people at home. A holiday is a luxury, something people work hard to afford and then excitedly anticipate. On holiday, people like to forget about work and home and focus solely on themselves and those around them. Once you decide to provide a service to holidaymakers, you have to adopt the service provider mindset. You, with the cleanliness of your house, the quality of your breakfast (if you choose to offer it) and the staff you hire, have the capacity to make or break a person's holiday experience.

The best way to obtain an understanding of the needs of tourists is to hire a property/couple of properties for a few weeks in your chosen area in Morocco, as a holidaymaker and decide for yourself what you liked or disliked and then use this research when planning the letting of your own home.

Location

As with all tourist destinations, location is paramount and requires extensive market research on what is now or has the potential to be a significant tourist region. Proximity to the airport, a beach, cultural/historical attractions, souks/boutiques, restaurants, new tourist developments, a swimming pool, mountains for skiing and golf courses can make the success of a property just as isolated, inaccessible locations need something very spectacular to attract a market or are, quite simply, no goers from the start. Having said this, Gite Ras el Ma is a large stone house catering to ecotourists just outside the Middle Atlas towns of Azrou and Ifrane. It is seemingly in the midst of nowhere, in a non-touristy location, difficult to get to without a car and with none of the normal attractions such as swimming pools, shops, restaurants or beach. It is, however, doing very well. Its main attraction being that it *is* seemingly in the midst of nowhere. Tourists can just relax and really feel they are getting away from it all. A bit of a risk involved in deciding to rely on an income from such as place, but it has paid off. On the whole, however, especially if you do not know Morocco that well, it is most probably wise to stick to the more guaranteed tourists attractions.

According to the Moroccan tourist board, the Moroccan cities most visited by tourists in 2005 were:

1.	Marrakech	5 million
2.	Agadir	4.2 million
3.	Casablanca	1 million
4.	Tangier	665,000
5.	Fes	630,000
6.	Rabat	510,000
7.	Ouarzazate	500,000
8.	Tetouan	338,000
9.	Meknes	184,000
10.	Essaouira	153,000

Each of these places offers fantastic rental opportunities as they have high tourist footfall. They all have special features, which appeal to tourists; culture, architecture and shopping in Marrakech, climate and beaches in Agadir, windsurfing, picturesque medina and beaches in Essaouira. They are, therefore ideal places for tourists to visit. The downside of such destinations, however, is competition from other holiday lets, guesthouses and hotels. You will need to think hard about what you can offer that is different from any of the other places (views, proximity to the sea, walking distance to the boutiques, stylish furnishings, sauna/hammam). You will also have to keep your rates more competitive and stay ahead of the game in terms of services provided and marketing (see *Marketing the Property* below).

If the whole purpose of your buying property in Morocco is simply income based, then, getting to really know the country prior to buying will make you privy to other places, that are starting to attract tourists but not yet fully fledged destinations. Here, you have the opportunity to buy a property for a cheaper price and turn it into the one good place to stay in the area, which, if marketed properly, catches the eye of tourists looking for somewhere a little bit different. You will find this has happened in the desert around Merzouga close to the sand dunes of Erg Chebbi where some of the more pioneering property purchasers have bought up and built on land or renovated kasbahs, which are becoming increasingly popular places to stay as more and more tourists visit these remote parts of Morocco. If this sounds like too much of a challenge, you could consider buying property in a place which has a large annual festival like Asilah, on the Atlantic coast close to Tangier, which attracts a regular flow of tourists, year round but really comes to life during the summer months when its art and music festival kicks in, offering a virtually guaranteed rental occupancy for two months of the year.

Location	Airport	Architecture	Beach	Culture	Festival	Gastronomy	Golf	Nature	Shopping	Skiing	Trekking	Windsurfing
Al Hoceima	√		√									√
Agadir	√		√				√					√
Asilah		√	√	√	√							√
Azrou			√					√			√	
Casablanca	√		√	√	√		√		√			√
Chefchaouen		√		√				√			√	
Er Rachidia	√							√			√	
Essaouira	√	√	√	√	√	√						√
El Jadida		√	√				√					√
Fes	√	√		√	√	√	√		√		√	
Ifrane								√		√	√	
Marrakech	√	√		√	√	√	√	√	√	√	√	
Meknes		√		√		√	√					
Merzouga								√			√	
Mirleft			√									√
Mohammedia			√				√					
Oualidia			√				√	√				
Ouarzazate	√							√			√	
Oujda	√	√						√			√	
Rabat	√	√	√	√			√		√			√
Sefrou		√			√			√				√
Sidi Ifni		√	√	√				√				
Tangier	√	√	√	√			√		√			√
Taza		√						√			√	
Tetouan	√	√		√		√	√				√	

Location in terms of accessibility is also vital to consider when choosing your property. Tourism industry research indicates that around a quarter of all package tourists like to be within one hour of an airport when visiting an overseas destination. While it is safe to say that people prepared to rent self-catering holiday accommodation will be a tad more adventurous, such a statistic should be borne in mind. Tourists visiting Morocco for a week's holiday do not want to spend two days of their precious trip getting there and back. There are a number of airports around Morocco, but only a few are currently international. While this could change within the course of a couple of years, for the time being you will have to go via the hub Casablanca in order to get to most remote airports. This is generally not a problem as flights are, on the whole relatively frequent but do, sometimes, include an overnight stay in Casablanca, if for example flights to the airport near your property, only leave early in the morning. In such instances, it would be wise to have a place you can recommend your clients to stay in Casablanca to prevent them having to do too much research themselves.

You will also need to consider how easy it is for tourists to navigate themselves to your property. Road names in Morocco are sporadic the further out of the city you are and in the medinas it is virtually impossible to find properties hidden down unmarked alleyways unless they are next door to landmarks or advertise themselves with big signs. Medina maps rarely show all the alleyways and those that do tend not to name every street. While such mystery is half the charm of these houses, it is vital that you have someone on hand to meet your clients at well-known locations who can lead them to the house. There are few things more likely to quell the holiday spark than arriving in a new country tired after a long journey, speaking very little of the local language and having no idea which of the same looking, narrow, dark alleyways lead to your home.

The Right Property

When it comes to choosing a holiday let property, potential tourists tend to have four main priorities:

1. Location
2. Price
3. Number of beds
4. Looks.

If making money from your Moroccan property is your main priority, then much thought will need to go into making sure you buy a property, which will appeal to a market larger than you and your mates. You might be happy being on the fourth floor of an apartment block with no lift and views over a factory or in a farmhouse miles from anywhere with generators for electricity and a well for water but is this really going to appeal to the wider tourist market?

Riads. For many tourists coming to Morocco, a riad or traditional house is where they have set their hearts on staying. Riads *are* Morocco, well as far as any interior design magazine is concerned, they are. You cannot get a riad at home, they are part of the Moroccan experience, much like the thatched roof cottage is part of the quaint British village experience. Therefore, when you come to Morocco, you stay in a riad, simple as that. Riads greatly lend themselves to being holiday lets as they have many rooms, which give privacy and a large courtyard for communality. Being out of the sun and protected from the elements, they do not need a huge amount of maintenance, unless you decide to add a small pool or luscious garden. They are also very secure, hard both to access or to be viewed from the outside, which is a great comfort to holidaymakers. If you are renovating your riad, you will need to think about keeping/building features such as fireplaces, archways and stained glass windows (even if these do not appeal to you) as these are generally what tourists want in order to feel they are getting the real experience.

You also need to consider child proofing your riad (if indeed you allow children at all) or at least supplying furnishings such as stair gates. Riads tend to have many steep staircases and stone floors, not a good combination for an adventurous toddler.

Villas. Why stay in a riad behind thick walls shaded from the glorious African sun when you could be in a villa with a garden, swimming pool and views? Villas are becoming increasingly popular holiday lets in Morocco. Many new developments are being built purely for the property investor to stay in for one or two weeks of the year and rented out to tourists, generally by a management company, for the rest. If you want to buy a villa to rent out, it needs almost certainly to have a swimming pool and views (ideally not over the neighbouring villa). It is also good if it is away from a road. Moroccan features such as a tadelakt bathroom, fountain and/or zelliges (see *Building or Renovating*) are a bonus as they at least differentiate your villa in Morocco from most other villas worldwide.

Some new villas are being built within the grounds of 4-5 star hotels. The benefit of these is that tourists can enjoy all the hotel facilities (usually free of charge) but have their own personal space – an excellent selling point.

As villas are generally newly built, they tend not to need too much updating or modernising. Make sure you can offer all mod cons (see *Equipping Your Property* below) as this is what tourists will expect. Swimming pools are the main bugbear as they are expensive to build and require regular maintenance. If you are considering buying a property, which is part of a development, it is more than likely there will be a swimming pool person on site who will tend your pool for you, otherwise you will need to hire someone to come to maintain it on a regular basis.

Apartments. The most important priority to think about when it comes to buying an apartment to rent out is noise. Even if thin walls and noisy neighbours do not affect you, they can ruin someone else's experience of your property. You also need to consider access to the apartment. Having a lift is essential if you are more than a couple of stories up and views are a real bonus. It is also important that your apartment block has a welcoming communal hallway as first impressions count. If your first impression of the apartment hallway is not a good one, then you can be pretty darn sure it will be even worse for a tourist who has paid to spend a week in the surrounds.

Apartments are convenient properties to own for letting out as they are generally easy to locate from a navigational point of view. Arrangements can be made with neighbours/concierge to hand out keys/stock the fridge/clean the property. Some apartments come with communal swimming pools and gardens. These are great selling points, but it is also good if you can consider buying an apartment with at least some sort of private outdoor space such as a balcony or veranda. When visiting a hot country, people want to eat their breakfast in the sun or dinner under the stars. Being cooped up indoors peering out through windows is something they can do at home every day of the year. If you do have some outdoor space, then invest in a barbecue (and all the bits). Barbecues spell summer time, they smell fantastic and are great ways of varying the self-catering.

In some cases, grocery shops and cafes are built next to or inside new apartment/duplex developments. These can be a real perk as they remove the pressure from the self-caterer to be too forward planning with meals (something they most probably do not want to have to be when on holiday) and prevent them from having to carry heavy bags of groceries long distances either on foot or in taxis.

Equipping Your Property

Household furnishings are important to people. Even those who have paid what you might consider, a low price for their holiday let will be expecting a particular standard. Bear in mind that while it is relatively easy to get tenants to stay in your property, getting them to come back on a repeat visit or to recommend you to family and friends requires you to give them that little bit more than their money has paid for. If, for example, families constitute your main market then adding extra touches that appeal to children will earn you great praise from parents as will surf boards or tennis rackets and balls appeal to a leisure oriented market.

As well as the basics such as cutlery, crockery, glasses, kettle, cooker, fridge, a tagine, sofas, table and chairs and beds, you will also be expected to provide all bedding (duvets better than sheets), good quality mattresses (very important) and mattress/pillow protectors, towels (including beach towels), electric fires, cot/highchair, loo roll, soap, coat hangers, sun loungers and stereo. Extra perks, which really show you have put thought into the let include TV with satellite channels, DVD player and DVD's, bathrobe and Moroccan style babouche slippers, a welcome bottle of wine/mineral water/flowers (don't forget champagne if you are aware of it being a special event), candles, BBQ area and cookbooks for local-style cuisine. Having, for example ADSL (for connecting to the internet) and a *WiFi* router is likely to be loved by some tenants and hated by others depending on their level of respect and tolerance for computers.

Equipping a property is not cheap costing anything from £3000 upwards and it needs to be budgeted for. It is very easy to get so wrapped up in the building/modernising costs that you forget to put any money aside to actually fill the property up. Tempting as it is to buy cheap fittings and utensils under the assumption that they will get ruined by tenants, this is actually a false economy as you end up having to replace them more often as they look tatty quickly and are more likely to get damaged. Buying hardy, quality items, which can withstand being overheated, dropped, left outside in the sun is much more economical in the long run as well as being more pleasant to use.

You should also put together a book/pack on the house, which you can send/e-mail to clients either prior to their arrival or have waiting in the house for them when they arrive. This should give details such as how to work the cooker, TV, DVD player etc. It can also, where relevant, introduce the staff with photographs and recommend restaurants and attractions.

Employing Staff

The best scenario with holiday lets is to let them run themselves without you around. This is especially the case if you are out of the country for much of the year. In order for this to happen, you need to employ a good and reliable *femme de ménage* or cleaner and, ideally someone to manage the house for you. Unless the property is busy all the time, this employment can be on a part time basis. Some estate agents/property developers offer a holiday let management service in return for around 15-20% of the rental price. While this suits some people especially those buying new build properties for investment purposes only, hiring someone privately through friendships and recommendations provides more of a personal touch.

The main role of the house manager will be to:

- Take booking details for tenants from either you or an agency.
- Book taxis to meet tenants (optional).
- Make sure the house is spotlessly clean prior to the arrival of new tenants and during their stay. Cleanliness is absolutely essential to running a successful holiday let business.
- Meet and greet clients and show them around the house and hand over keys.
- Keep the house stocked with all the necessary cleaning products/food etc.
- Help tenants out with any questions/advice they might have/need.
- Run an inventory on tenants arrival and departure.
- Keep accounts of the house spend.
- Pay electricity/water bills and local taxes.
- Contact maintenance workers for minor repairs.
- Pay the salary to the femme de ménage/cleaner.

The main role of the femme de ménage/cleaner will be to:

- ○ To keep the house spotlessly clean.
- ○ Shop for and prepare breakfasts.
- ○ Manage the laundry, during and after each tenant.

For details on the logistics of employing staff and wages, see *Services.*

Marketing the Property

The ideal (and cheapest) way of marketing property is through word of mouth. Excellent routes for this include your own personal network and any other network you can dip into; work colleagues, parents from school, neighbours. This can work well to a certain extent but if you are seriously hoping to make a good income from your property, it is unlikely this route will offer enough clients to bring an adequate return on investment. Another option is to use the internet to rent out your home via holiday property sites, such as holiday-rentals.com or internationalrentals.com who for an annual fee of around £180, enable you to advertise details and photographs (the best photographs you can take) of your property on their site. This can provide a good response rate and allows you to have complete control of bookings. It does demand organisation and professionalism from you in terms of following up leads, obtaining payments and deposits, imparting information and ensuring individual needs are met.

Another option for marketing the property is through a riad/villa agency or small tour operator who will promote it to an already established network of clients in return for a 20-30% fee. The fee covers all booking handling and administration. What generally happens is that you have a shared availability chart, which enables both you and the agency to check when the property is/is not booked up. While working with an agency/tour operator usually increases occupancy, it does mean you lose an element of control of your property and find that you are often talked in to changing decor or offering special deals, in order to maximise the villa company/tour operators ability to place bookings.

- ○ *Riad/Villa Agencies and Tour Operators*
- ○ *Riadomaroc.com*
- ○ *Cvtravel.net*
- ○ *Rusticblue.com*
- ○ *VillasofMorocco.com*
- ○ *i-escape.com*

BUYING A GUESTHOUSE (MAISON D'HÔTES)

If you are planning on spending the majority of your time in Morocco and would like to make money from your property, you could consider the option of either offering a casual bed and breakfast service, which need not be official or turning your home in to a guesthouse. As with holiday lets, if you choose to run a guesthouse, you will need to decide that this is the route you wish to take prior to buying the property as space, number of rooms, style of house and new, strict regulations, need to be taken into account.

If you have already had experience of owning a guesthouse, you will be aware of the amount of work involved in the day-to-day running of the property and know what you are getting yourself into. If, however, you are struck with the idea while sipping morning coffee and listening to the birds tweet, it is worth putting a great deal of time and energy into ensuring this is really the route you wish to take.

Running a guesthouse is incredibly hard work. It is more a way of life than a job and some say, more a labour of love than a money-spinner. The most important pre-requisite is for you to really like people and enjoy their company. It is a very sociable job and an excellent way of meeting people from all over the world and every walk of life. It is also an all-encompassing job, often hard to leave or hand over to someone else to take the reigns should you want to take a break.

The last few years have seen a number of guesthouses opening in Morocco, the majority being riad-style properties, which lend themselves to accommodating several people as they normally have many rooms/salons and the communal courtyard, which is an ideal place for serving breakfast and other meals. In line with the government plan to increase tourism to Morocco, strict new regulations were enforced in 2003, regarding the running of maison d'hôtes including their classification into grades 1 and 2. These regulations include there being:

- A minimum of 5 bedrooms.
- A ground surface area of no less than 150sq metres.
- A minimum of 0.9 employees per bedroom for grade 1 properties and 0.7 employees per bedroom for grade 2 properties.
- A guesthouses manager who has a diploma in tourism and/or hotel training and/or proof of experience in the management of tourist accommodation.
- Reception staff who apart from Arabic are able to speak two foreign languages.
- Basic health and safety training for all staff.
- Safety lighting in all guest areas and corridors.
- Clear and visible evacuation plans.
- Fire exits.
- Grade 1 and 2 properties must be in a select location, have an attractive entrance area, be well lit at night and have a sign stating the name and classification of the property clearly marked from the outside.

○   A distance of 100 metres or less to the nearest fire hydrant.

○   No mosque within the close vicinity.

Prior to purchasing a guesthouse, permission needs to be sought from the Urban Agency (see *What Type of Property To Buy?)* who will want to check your paperwork and plans.

Setting Up A Company

An attractive route for guesthouse owners is to set up as a limited company. Not only does this mean they can run their guesthouses tax free on all foreign currency for the first 5 years (and then with a 50% reduction on tax for an indefinite period of time after this), it also means that they can own shares in the company as opposed to actually owning the property. This means that when it comes to selling the property, you simply sell your shares as opposed to the property, which means there are no costs for transferring titles.

SARL. There are two main types of company in Morocco, the limited liability company, known as the *Societé a Résponsabité Limiteé* (SARL) and the stock company, *Societé Anonyme* (SA). The company most suited to small business ventures such as guesthouses is the SARL. In order to set up a SARL, you need to have paid-in capital of at least 100,000 dh (£6250) and between 1-50 shareholders. It takes around 3 weeks to set up. The Societé Anonyme (SA) is for larger ventures requiring paid-in capital of 300,000 dh (£18,750) and at least 5 shareholders. The fee for setting up a company is 0.5% of the capital. In order to open a company, you must have a residence permit (*carte de sejour*) and inform the Ministry of Employment.

RUNNING A BUSINESS FROM YOUR PROPERTY

The wonderful thing about Morocco is that it is an entrepreneur's playground. There is so much that can/is being done and so many people keen to share the dream. Good and bad, being a foreigner means that you are blessed with the added benefit of supposedly having money/contacts in high places. This means that your project ideas/plans will get a much better airing than similar ideas/ plans coming from a Moroccan. You should be able to secure meetings with important officials and government departments much more easily than you would in the UK or indeed, than a Moroccan could. Do remember, though, that Morocco is a place where talk is the main pastime. Do not get too fired up by offers of support and eye shining enthusiasm from influential people. All the legwork/research/market statistics will need to be done/obtained by you and you alone although having contacts should help move things forward at a speedier pace.

There is no end of ideas to consider when deciding what type of business to run from your property. Obvious ones include:

○ Teaching English (many Moroccans are desperate to learn)
○ Translator
○ Gardener (managing absent foreigners flowers/lawns)
○ House manager for house lets (meeting and greeting guests etc)
○ Tour guide
○ Jewellery maker (for selling abroad)
○ Website designer
○ IT support
○ Writer
○ Artist

Less obvious ideas include:

○ **Estate agent**. With the increased interest from the British market and the dearth of English speaking agents, this could be a lucrative venture.
○ **Project manager**. If you obtain adequate experience of the building and restoration process in Morocco, you would be highly sought after to manage the builds of English people keen to buy an old, unrestored property.
○ **Location scout/fixer for TV/film makers**. Get to know a part of Morocco particularly well and sell yourself as a location scout or fixer to one of the many film crews working in Morocco.
○ **Maid agency**. Good femme de ménage (cleaners/housekeepers) are greatly sought after in Morocco. A maid agency could put foreigners in touch with recommended maids.

As well as contacts, contacts and more contacts, you could try contacting the British/American consulates in Morocco who should have detailed, practical information on setting up businesses. Alternatively the British or American Chamber of Commerce should be able to put you in touch with professional accountants etc who will help you get established (see *Finance* for a list of addresses/ telephone numbers). You should also contact the Centre of Regional Investment for your area (see *What Type of Property to Buy?*). For most businesses, you or a business partner will almost certainly need to speak French or Arabic in order to be taken seriously by your Moroccan counterparts. You will certainly need to have a good knowledge of Morocco and Moroccan culture and some background knowledge/experience of the business you are about to undertake.

SELLING YOUR PROPERTY

One of the main priorities you need to consider when buying your property is selling it at a later date especially if you are buying it as an investment. Assuming nothing dire hits Morocco, one thing you can be gingerly sure of, especially if you buy sooner rather than later is that property prices will appreciate (between 15% and 20% a year in some areas, even higher in others). Obviously prices in more popular places such as Marrakech, where competition is higher, will rise less than in upcoming areas around, for example, Tetouan and Fes, but you could argue that Marrakech is more of a tried and tested sure thing when it comes to the popularity stakes therefore in some ways a safer place to buy.

Estate agents will claim that the most popular time to sell properties is between November and February with much potential house hunting done during the summer months. This makes sense if you consider that the reason many people choose to buy property in Morocco is because of the year-round warm/sunny climate. This is most accentuated during the wintertime, when Britain is cold and miserable and Morocco, warm and inviting.

The selling process in Morocco is relatively straightforward. You have the option of selling your property privately through websites, word of mouth etc, employing a number of different estate agents to sell the property on your behalf (*mandat non exclusif*), paying commission to the first who finds you a buyer or employing a single agent to sell your property (*mandat exclusif*) for you via a written mandate. The mandat exclusif is signed for a period of 3-6 months.

Selling Privately. The benefit of the private route is no commission fee for the agent from either you or the buyer (agents usually charge 2.5% from both the buyer and the seller). It is up to you to value the property, which you should base on its location, its number of rooms, its features and similar style properties in your neighbourhood. You will need to be available to show people around, which can be tricky if you are out of the country for much of the time. If this is the case, you could ask a friend or member of house staff to show people around for you.

It is up to you to market the property widely. This can be done free of charge on websites like buyingmoroccanproperty.com or marocannonces.com (although the downside of marocannonces.com is that there is no space for vitally, important, photographs), or in *Clefs en Main*, which is a French speaking monthly property magazine available from most magazine shops, with a vast range of properties throughout Morocco's main cities.

Selling Through a Number of Agents. Most people who choose to employ a number of agents do so because they believe that more agents mean more potential buyers. The reality is, however, that there are only a finite number of buyers looking for a particular type of property at any one time, particularly in a relatively new market like Morocco. What tends to happen is that the buyers simply end up seeing the same property over again each time with a different agent. There is the risk that agents competing with one another to sell the property will reduce its price in order to 'win' the commission. This is obviously excellent for the buyer, but not so good for the seller. The seller could also find themselves in the uncomfortable position of being charged double commission by two agents both claiming to have found the buyers themselves.

Selling Through a Sole Agent. Working with one agent, particularly a reputable company which publicises itself well is likely to be much more beneficial to you, than employing a number of agents. A sole agent is likely to dedicate much more time to selling your property and should be able to secure a better price due to having no competition. Through the written mandate, the agent is more committed to you than to the buyer and will therefore do a better selling job on your behalf, marketing the property widely and keeping you up to date with what is happening.

CASE HISTORIES

JANE BAYLEY

Jane Bayley, owner of the ecological tour operator, Naturally Morocco, bought a nine- bedroom house in Taroudannt ten years ago, which she uses as a guest house from which her staff run the 'real Morocco' experience. She has recently bought a piece of land to build a new house, again, in Taroudannt.

Why do you particularly like Taroudannt?
Geographically it is in an excellent location, closer to the Anti and High Atlas than Marrakech, just one hour from the sea and near to the famous Tizi-n- Test pass. It is also the warmest place to be in Morocco between October and April. The town is typically Moroccan and the people are incredibly friendly and welcoming.

Are there many other foreigners living in Taroudannt?
When we first started coming here ten years ago, there were very few and I am almost certain that I was the only Brit owning property in the town. Recently, when we bought our plot of land, the lady at the municipality was throwing her arms in the air at the number of foreigners now buying here. Taroudannt seems to attract people who want a project in a real Moroccan environment in stark contrast to the Spanish costa type environment of Agadir just an hour away which is convenient for services including airport, modern hospital etc.

Did you run into any problems when recently buying the land?
There were a couple of complications. The first was that we were shown the land by two individual estate agents, this lead to problems when it came to buying the land as both of them tried charging us commission. In the end, after quite a bit of wrangling, we only ended up paying the first agent who we had spent most of our time with. We also ran into the same problems most people run into in Taroudannt, that being that most of the houses and land, are untitled. Because of this, we had to obtain a title to verify the ownership of the property, which involves considerable paperwork and patience.

How do you find working with Moroccans?
Moroccans are blessed with the most wonderful sense of humour. They bear no grudges when things go wrong and have an amazing ability to turn every situation into a joke, which is very refreshing. Despite living in a laboriously bureaucratic environment, they tend to lead simple, uncluttered lives. The owner of the house we bought turned up with all the paperwork folded up in the hood of his jellaba, while the estate agent barely carried any paperwork at all and managed to keep all our complicated purchasing details stored in his head.

CAROLE AND DENNIS STEDMAN

Carole and Dennis retired to Morocco in 2003, buying a dar in Essaouira's medina. After a couple of years, they also bought a farmhouse in Ounara, 25km from Essaouira, which they go to for a break from town life.

Why did you choose to retire in Morocco?
We knew we wanted to spend our retirement outside the UK, but we were not sure where so we decided to do a road trip around Europe looking for the perfect place to live. We thought we would most probably end up in Spain, but when we got there, it didn't really feel like us. We carried on driving south until we arrived in Morocco, which we just loved. It seemed to have everything we were looking for; fantastic weather, excellent food, relaxed laws, great people and lovely houses.

What is a typical day in your life in Morocco?
Depends on the weather really. Normally after a leisurely breakfast we will read books and potter about the house. Take the dogs out for a walk along the beach. Maybe stop off to eat fresh fish in the fish market. Go shopping for the day's food in the souks, which always takes ages as we keep bumping into people we know, having a chat and maybe mint tea or four. In the evenings, we normally have people around for dinner. Essaouira is a really sociable place where everyone knows everyone, which is good and bad – there are very little secrets and people love to gossip.

How do you find the bureaucracy in Morocco?
Really tricky – there is so much of it and it is particularly hard to get your head around if you don't speak fluent French or Arabic. Generally, if you don't ask the right questions, you never find out what is happening. Then if you ask why you are never told what is happening, the answer is, because you never asked. We received a fine the other day for being out when a government surveyor came round to the house. We had no idea that he was coming, he had made no appointment and no one had told us to expect him, but still we received a fine. Unfortunately,

the bureaucracy being what it is combined with the language barrier meant that we could do nothing but just pay up.

Do you ever worry about your health as Essaouira is a long way from any good hospitals?
Yes, we do worry when we think about it, so we try not to think about it. Agadir, 2.5 hours away, has some good clinics. There is also talk of a hospital being built in the ville nouvelle sometime in the near future. So let's hope nothing happens between now and then.

What do you particularly miss about 'home'?
Besides our children, a trip out to the theatre and going to an English-speaking cinema, very little really, unless you include bacon, strong cheddar cheese, loose leaf tea (we are fed up with Liptons) and Branston pickle.

CAROLINE AND ADAM HOLLIS

Caroline and Adam are a British couple with two young children. A couple of years ago they bought a riad in Marrakech medina, which was in such a bad state of repair they had to knock it down completely and rebuild. Recently, they sold the riad and bought a large plot of land on Route de Fes, where they are building four villas to sell (see www.villas-laarousse.com).

Why did you decide to buy property in Morocco?
We were on holiday there, a romantic holiday, before the kids and just fell in love with Marrakech. Normally we conflict on the choice of holiday destinations but we were in total agreement on Morocco. We were having dinner at a beautiful riad restaurant in the medina and just started dreaming about what it would be like to own a property in Morocco. Quite by chance, we met a Moroccan woman, Rachida, who has just stopped working for an estate agency and she convinced us that it was an excellent thing to do (not that we needed much convincing). We stayed in touch with Rachida after returning home and she kept telling us about properties that were coming up for sale. In the end we bought a riad near to Bad Doukkala.

You did a big restoration job on your riad. How did you find working with Moroccans?
Great – we had no problems at all. Rachida introduced us to a contractor. We viewed his work and thought it was beautiful so employed him to restore our house. We gave Rachida power of attorney to manage the works in our absence, which was the best way as being Moroccan there was no cultural/language divide between her and the workers. We went over once every three months to check the

build and write cheques. I think the contractor really appreciated the fact that we were not too interfering in his work. We believed he had good taste, so gave him pretty much free reign with the finishes. He even gave us little extras such as an additional top terrace with great views over the medina.

How do you find the slow, laid back pace of life in Morocco?
It really suits us. Just going for a short drive with a Moroccan tends to turn into a day trip including lunch with his family, a play with his children, and a few detours via interesting sights. There is no point rushing Morocco, as it is never going to speed up for you. It can be frustrating when you are waiting for some paperwork, which is stuck in a bureaucratic loop, but on the whole, it is a great pace, which puts spending time with people above all else.

Have you found Morocco an easy place for children?
Moroccans love children. They are welcome everywhere and given great attention. Whenever Moroccans see a baby they click their fingers at them to attract their attention. Little children rush up and kiss babies and young children on the lips. This can be a little bit unnerving, but Moroccans believe that kissing babies will bring their families good luck, so you don't really want to deny them that.

What advice would you offer to people thinking about buying property in Morocco?
The main thing to consider is, do you really like the place? The Brits that we've met all love the place so they will come back and enjoy some of the quirks that you can expect in your day-to-day dealings. It is all very personable and everyone can help you in Marrakech. Our main advice with building and renovation is to find someone that you trust and don't commit much money at first. Don't give them everything up front, but realise that everyone has a limit and you shouldn't be disrespectful. If you give a bit, you'll get a lot back. Once you have the trust that person will treat you like family. Don't try to understand everything. Tips are part of life out there and let the locals work with each other. We have dealt with people face to face, visited their homes, built up trust and had a really good time in the process!

GLOSSARY

1er étage	first floor
Acte de Vente	final property sales contract
Adoul	An official scribe with the authority to document the ownership of property
Ascenseur	lift
Amazigh	Berber dialect
Aménagér	converted
Arroseur	sprinkler
Atelier	workshop
Avec gout	with taste
Bab	gate or door
Bab-i-dar	front door
Balcon	balcony
Bail	rental contract
Bejmat	terracotta half bricks for floors
Béton	concrete
Berber	indigenous people of Morocco
Bois	wood
Bon état	good condition
Bord de mer	by the sea
Cagibi	box room
Campagne	country
Carte de sejour	residence permit
Cave	cellar
Chambre	bedroom
Chaudière	water heater
Chauffage	heating
Chauffage central	central heating
Chauffe eau	hot water tank
Charge comprise (CC)	rent including utility and community expenses
Cheminée	chimney
Climatisation	air conditioning

Clôture	fence
Clôturé en murs	walled enclosure
Compromis de vente	preliminary property sales contract
Concierge	person who takes care of the building
Couloir	corridor
Cuisine	kitchen
Cuisine Americaine	breakfast counter
Cuisine equipée	fitted kitchen
D-darija	Moroccan colloquial Arabic
Dahir	decree law
Dar	traditional Moroccan house
De surface au sol	ground surface area
Débarras	junk room
Depôt de Garantie	deposit
Derb	alleyway
Devis	bill estimate
Douiriya	a small house, usually an annexe of the main house
Durée de contrat	rental period
Entretien	maintenance
Escalier	stairs
Etat des Lieux	inventory
Fakhkhar	ceramist
Farrash	tile setter who sets zelliges on to walls
Fassi	inhabitants of Fes
Ferme	farm
Ferraillage	ironwork
Fosse septique	septic tank
Foyer	fireplace
Gardien	caretaker
Gebs	plaster
Ghabber	artisan plasterer
Goudronné	tarmac
Habous	religious property
Hammam	bath
Immeuble	building
Isolation	insulation

Izar	Frieze made from wood, zelliges or plaster
Jama	mosque
Jeer	lime
Kasbah	a fortified city
Kif	cannabis
Kilim	woven carpet
Lavabo	wash basin
Locateur	tenant
Location	renting
Lotissement	housing estate
Loyer	rent
Maison de campagne	country house
Maison mitoyenne	semi detached or terraced house
majlis al-mustasharin	upper chamber of counsellors
majlis al-nuwab	lower chamber of representatives
Makhzen	elite
Mashrabiyya	lattice wood that can be seen out of but not into
Medluk	similar to the wall covering tadelakt, but coarser and not quite as shiny
Melk(melkia)	old fashioned land title
Mellah	salt (also refers to a Jewish neighbourhood)
Menzeh	large salon on the terrace for entertaining guests
Meublé	furnished
Meubles	furniture
Menuisier	carpenter
Moudawana	family law
Moulure	moulding
Moussem	annual pilgrimage to visit the tombs of saints
Mur	wall
Notaire	notary public
Nejjar	joiner
Niveux	levels
Non-meublé	non-furnished
Pièce	room
Pilier	pillar
Piscine	swimming pool

Pisé	bricks made from sun-dried earth, water and lime
Pipe a sortir	evacuation pipe
Placard	cupboard
Plain pied	single storey
Plomberie	plumbing
Plombier	plumber
Polisario Front	military group representing the indigenous people of Western Sahara
Poussiere	dust
Prise	electric socket
Peinture	paint
Prix du m	total cost of the property divided by its area
Programmes Neufs	new developments
Propriétaire	landlord/owner
Quartier	neighbourhood
Quermoud	tile
Raffiné	refined
Raml	sand
Refait	restoration
Restauré	restored
Rez de chaussée (RdC)	ground floor
Riad	inside courtyard or garden (also refers to the actual properties)
Rkham	marble
Robinet	tap
Rqaimi	cabinet-maker
Salle a manger	dining room
salle de bain	bathroom
Salle de douche	shower room
Salon	sitting room
Saqaiya	fountain
Séjour	living room
Simsaar	estate agent
Sol	ground
Squef	ceiling
Studette	little studio or utility room
Superficie	surface area
Tadelakt	wall and sometimes floor covering, Made from sand

	and limestone, smoothed on by tablets of stone and black soap
Tapis	carpet
Tataoui	thin strips of painted laurel arranged in patterns – decorative features
Terrasse aménagée	converted terrace
Thuya	wood used by artisans of Essaouira
Toit terrasse	Roof terrace
Transats	deckchairs
Vallonné	hilly
Vide	empty or unfurnished
Vue	view
Vue impregnable	unrestricted view
Wilaya	region
Wali	regional governor
Wust-i-dar	salons around the central courtyard of a riad
Zawwayiq	wood painting artisans
Zelliges	mosaic of tiles – geometrical and abstract
Zouak	painted patterns on wood

Index

Complete guides to life abroad from Vacation Work

Live & Work Abroad

Live & Work in Australia & New Zealand	£12.95
Live & Work in Belgium, The Netherlands & Luxembourg	£10.99
Live & Work in China	£11.95
Live & Work in France	£11.95
Live & Work in Germany	£10.99
Live & Work in Ireland	£10.99
Live & Work in Italy	£11.95
Live & Work in Japan	£10.99
Live & Work in Portugal	£11.95
Live & Work in Saudi & the Gulf	£10.99
Live & Work in Scandinavia	£10.99
Live & Work in Scotland	£11.95
Live & Work in Spain	£12.95
Live & Work in Spain & Portugal	£10.99
Live & Work in the USA & Canada	£12.95

Buying a House Abroad

Buying a House in France	£11.95
Buying a House in Italy	£11.95
Buying a House in Morocco	£12.95
Buying a House in New Zealand	£12.95
Buying a House in Portugal	£11.95
Buying a House in Scotland	£11.95
Buying a House in Spain	£11.95
Buying a House on the Mediterranean	£13.95

Property Investment

Where to Buy Property Abroad - An Investors Guide	£12.95

Retiring Abroad

Retiring to Australia & New Zealand	£10.99
Retiring to Cyprus	£10.99
Retiring to France	£10.99
Retiring to Italy	£10.99
Retiring to Spain	£10.99

Starting a Business Abroad

Starting a Business in Australia	£12.95
Starting a Business in France	£12.95
Starting a Business in Spain	£12.95

**Available from good bookshops or direct from the publishers
Vacation Work, 9 Park End Street, Oxford OX1 1HJ
☎ 01865-241978 * Fax 01865-790885 * www.vacationwork.co.uk
In the US: available at bookstores everywhere
or from The Globe Pequot Press (www.GlobePequot.com)**